ABOUT THE AUTHORS

Carl Endorf, CISSP, CISM, is a senior technical security analyst for one of the largest insurance and banking companies in the United States. He has practical experience in intrusion detection, forensics, corporate investigations, and Internet security. Carl has written many security articles for industry publications as well as three security-related books. He has a masters certificate in information security management and is currently finishing his master of science degree at the University of Illinois in management information systems.

Eugene Schultz, Ph.D., CISM, CISSP, is a principal engineer at Lawrence Berkeley National Laboratory of the University of California. He is the author/co-author of four previous books: one on Unix security, another on Internet security, a third on Windows NT/2000 security, and a fourth on incident response. He has written over 100 published papers. Gene is the editor-in-chief of *Computers and Security* and is an associate editor of *Network Security* and *Information Security Bulletin*. He is a member of the editorial board for the SANS NewsBites, a weekly information security-related news update and is on the technical advisory board of three companies. He was adjunct professor of computer science at Purdue University, where he taught courses and participated in research in the CERIAS (Center for Education and Research in Information Assurance and Security) program. He has received the NASA Technical Excellence Award, the Information Systems Security Association (ISSA) Professional Achievement and Honor Roll Awards, the ISACA John Kuyers Best Speaker/Best Conference Contributor Award, the National Information Systems Security Conference (NISSC) Best Paper Award, and has been elected to the ISSA Hall of Fame. While at Lawrence Livermore National Laboratory, he founded and managed the U.S. Department of Energy's Computer Incident Advisory Capability (CIAC). He is also a co-founder of FIRST, the Forum of Incident Response and Security Teams. Dr. Schultz has provided expert testimony before committees within the U.S. Senate and House of Representatives on various security-related issues and has served as an expert witness in legal cases.

Jim Mellander is a principal engineer at Lawrence Berkeley National Laboratory of the University of California and holds the position of incident response manager. Jim and his team detect, investigate, and respond to cyber security incidents, using many of the techniques in this book. Jim has written several notable security software programs, including Update, a Unix-based sniffer detector, and Kazaa Obliterator, which disrupts many types of unauthorized peer-to-peer traffic in an enterprise. Jim is the author of a number of articles and was the recipient of the 2001 Best Paper Award in *Information Security Bulletin*. He lives in the San Francisco Bay Area with his wife, three dogs, and a cat.

ABOUT THE CONTRIBUTING AUTHORS

Chad Schieken is a senior network systems consultant for International Network Services. He is responsible for the delivery of security engagements including risk assessments and infrastructure design. He has worked in the security field for eight years, with experience in some of the largest and most complex networks and organizations in the world. His background includes several years of Unix systems administration as well as studies at the University of Pittsburgh and Rutgers University. Chad speaks at seminars and conferences; most recently at the Philadelphia chapters of the Infragard and ISSA.

Patrick "Swissman" Ramseier, CCNA, CISSP, is a CSA systems engineer at Cisco. Patrick started out as a Unix systems administrator. Over the past 14 years, he has been involved with corporate-level security design, architecture reviews, vulnerability assessments, VPN support, physical, network and operating system security (Unix-Solaris, Linux, BSD, and Windows NT/2000), training, research, post- and pre-sales. He has a B.A. in business and is working concurrently on his masters and doctorate in psychology.

Frank Simorjay, CISSP, MCSE+I, is a senior system engineer working with NFR Security. He has been responsible for designing and securing executive level networks in banking, telecommunication, and other major verticals for over 10 years. Frank is the Founder and Chapter President for the Puget Sound ISSA, and has been providing education and training to the community for over four years. Frank is also the creator of the Northwest's first true security conference, Secure World Expo, for the second consecutive year.

James C. Foster, CISSP, CCSE, is the director of research and development for Foundstone, Inc., and is responsible for all aspects of product, consulting, and corporate R&D initiatives. Prior to joining Foundstone, James was a senior advisor and research scientist with Guardent, Inc., and an adjunct author at *Information Security Magazine*, subsequent to working as an information security and research specialist at Computer Sciences Corporation. With his core competencies residing in programming, web-based applications, cryptography, protocol analysis, and search algorithm technology, he has conducted numerous code reviews for commercial OS components, Win32 application assessments, and reviews on commercial-grade cryptography implementations.

James is a seasoned speaker and has presented throughout North America at conferences, technology forums, security summits, and research symposiums, with highlights at the Microsoft Security Summit, MIT Wireless Research Forum, SANS, MilCon, TechGov, InfoSec World 2001, and the Thomson Security Conference. He is frequently asked to comment on pertinent security issues and has been cited in *USA TODAY*, *Information Security* magazine, *Baseline*, *Computerworld*, *Secure Computing*, and the *MIT Technologist*. He holds degrees and certifications in business, software engineering, management of information systems, and numerous computer-related or programming-related concentrations and has

attended or conducted research at the Yale School of Business, Harvard University, Capitol College, and the University of Maryland.

James is a published author of many commercial and educational papers and computer books. He is a contributing author of *Hacking Exposed: Fourth Edition* (McGraw-Hill/Osborne, 2003), and a technical reviewer for *Anti-Hacker Toolkit Second Edition* (McGraw-Hill/Osborne, 2003), and *Anti-Spam Tool Kit* (McGraw-Hill/Osborne, 2003).

ABOUT THE TECHNICAL REVIEWER

Scott Campbell is a network security analyst at the National Energy Research Scientific Computing Center at Lawrence Berkeley National Laboratory. He is responsible for both day-to-day computer security incidents and response as well as research and development of new intrusion detection technologies. Scott has also contributed to several open source intrusion detection projects. His background includes 10 years of large-scale security, networking, and system design projects both in and out of the business world.

INTRUSION DETECTION
& PREVENTION

CARL **ENDORF**
DR. EUGENE **SCHULTZ**
JIM **MELLANDER**

McGraw-Hill/Osborne
New York   Chicago   San Francisco
Lisbon   London   Madrid   Mexico City   Milan
New Delhi   San Juan   Seoul   Singapore   Sydney   Toronto

The McGraw·Hill Companies

McGraw-Hill/Osborne
2100 Powell Street, 10th Floor
Emeryville, California 94608
U.S.A.

To arrange bulk purchase discounts for sales promotions, premiums, or fund-raisers, please contact **McGraw-Hill**/Osborne at the above address. For information on translations or book distributors outside the U.S.A., please see the International Contact Information page immediately following the index of this book.

Intrusion Detection & Prevention

1234567890 CUS CUS 019876543

ISBN 0-07-222954-3

Publisher
  Brandon A. Nordin
Vice President & Associate Publisher
  Scott Rogers
Executive Editor
  Jane K. Brownlow
Project Editors
  Jenn Tust, Jody McKenzie,
  Elizabeth Seymour
Acquisitions Coordinator
  Jessica Wilson
Technical Editors
  Scott Campbell
  Daniel Peterson
Copy Editors
  Andy Carroll, Marcia Baker,
  Lisa Theobald

Proofreader
  Paul Medoff
Indexer
  Valerie Perry
Composition
  Dick Schwartz, Lucie Ericksen
Illustrators
  Kathleen Edwards, Melinda Lytle,
  Michael Mueller
Series Design
  Dick Schwartz, Peter F. Hancik
Cover Design
  Theresa Havener

This book was composed with Corel VENTURA™ Publisher.

I would like to dedicate this book to my beautiful wife, Stashi, and to
my two children.
—*Carl Endorf*

The portion of this book that I wrote is dedicated to my three daughters, Sarah
Schultz, Rachel Schultz, and Leah Schultz, all of whom I could not be prouder.
—*Gene Schultz*

To my wife, Marilynne, who patiently kept the home fires burning during the
completion of this project.
—*Jim Mellander*

AT A GLANCE

CONTENTS

Part I

Intrusion Detection: Primer

Part II
Architecture

Contents

xvii

FOREWORD

My introduction to intrusion detection was abrupt. A small group of us was soaking in a hot tub at Sonoma Mission Inn when Tsutomu Shimomura leapt into the room with evidence of the first successful TCP sequence-guessing attack. Until then, I had felt confident that firewalls were all we needed, but the incident convinced me that we were going to need better network monitors that were carefully tuned to detect unusual security-relevant traffic. It's been nearly 10 years since then, and today there are dozens of systems designed to detect network intrusions or hostile activity, at all layers of the protocol stack. Intrusion detection has become a substantive field in its own right; so much so that there is now a flood of innovations and improvements.

It seemed inevitable to many of us that intrusion detection would go mainstream and we were right; the number of new startups in the intrusion detection space is daunting. It's also exciting. To add to that, recent entrants to the intrusion detection market have blurred the boundaries between firewalls and intrusion detection systems with products that purport to be "intrusion prevention" systems. It's hard to sort the marketing from the substance but, as with all new approaches to existing technologies, there will be some good

ideas, some bad ideas, some winners, and some losers. No matter what happens, it'll be interesting.

So, who are you, dear reader? Are you interested in intrusion detection because you're tasked with implementing one for your corporate network? Are you a security practitioner who wants to broaden your knowledge? Are you an engineer who is studying the history and existing approaches to intrusion detection because you are trying to come up with a better idea? Or are you a manager, trying to understand the reality behind the slick marketing you see at trade shows?

No matter which of these you are, you're holding a valuable resource in your hands. The authors of this book are folks who have "been there and done that" when it comes to intrusion detection. They've crammed this book with as much up-to-date knowledge as they could fit in, and as much detail as they could pin down about this rapidly changing topic.

Regardless of the tools you already have in your arsenal of security capabilities, this book contains the most important: knowledge. Learn from it and, most of all, enjoy it!

Marcus J. Ranum
Bellwether Farm
Morrisdale, PA

ACKNOWLEDGMENTS

Many people contributed to the writing of this book. Thanks to Scott Campbell for his excellent technical editing. Special thanks to Chad Schieken for his contribution of Chapter 9, "Cisco Secure IDS," and Patrick Ramseier for helping with the Okena/Cisco portion of that chapter. Thanks to James Foster for his contribution of Chapter 8 on RealSecure; and to Frank Simorjay for his chapter on NFR Security. The direction, cooperation, and helpfulness of the entire McGraw-Hill staff with whom we worked, including Jane Brownlow (executive editor), Jody McKenzie (senior project editor), Jenn Tust (project editor), Elizabeth Seymour (project editor), Jessica Wilson (acquisitions coordinator), copy editors Andy Carroll, Marcia Baker, and Lisa Theobald, and DTP composition specialist Kelly Stanton-Scott, are very gratefully acknowledged. These dedicated professionals made all the difference in the world in how our writing and revision efforts went, and in the way this book turned out. Finally, the book would not have been a success without the support of our families!

INTRODUCTION

WHAT IS THE PURPOSE OF THIS BOOK?

This book has been written to give the security professional a complete picture of the intrusion detection and prevention capabilities that are currently available and where the field needs to move in the future. The goal is to go beyond learning how a product works, while focusing on how to use the information it gives you. Four of the most popular intrusion detection systems will be covered. The reader will learn to implement the product, understand essential administration and maintenance tasks, fine tune, and use the data appropriately. In addition, this book will cover what needs to be known when dealing with intrusion detection on a day-to-day basis, how to respond to new and relevant issues, business issues, and the future direction of IDS.

WHO IS THE AUDIENCE FOR THIS BOOK?

This book is appropriate for any security professional, system administrator, and auditor who will be dealing with intrusion detection and prevention.

WHAT THIS BOOK IS NOT

What this book is not is a rehash of the information that is available in other books. The focus is on relevant and fresh issues that a real-world security professional will need to understand and deal with. While this book does touch on crucial theory, it is not focused on theory alone. This book is

designed to give the security professional useful information that can be used on a daily basis. Finally, this book is not a "cookbook" that you can read and just follow to detect and prevent intrusions. It will help to equip professionals with the knowledge and skills that can help them do their jobs correctly.

THE ORGANIZATION OF THE BOOK

The book is organized into four sections: Intrusion Detection: Primer, Architecture, Implementation and Deployment, and Security and IDS Management. Sections and chapters will cover the following:

Part I, "Intrusion Detection: Primer" consists of Chapters 1–5. Chapter 1, "Understanding Intrusion Detection," written by Carl Endorf, is an introduction to intrusion detection. An overview of IDS, this chapter defines the terms and sets the basis for the rest of the book.

Chapter 2, "Crash Course in the Internet Protocol Suite," written by Jim Mellander, focuses on understanding the TCP/IP and IP protocols that are crucial to knowing intrusions and how they work.

Chapter 3, "Unauthorized Activity I," written by Jim Mellander, focuses on IP layer abuses, IP protocol abuses, and application layer abuses.

Chapter 4, "Unauthorized Activity II," written by Jim Mellander, focuses on denial-of-service abuses, system-level abuses, IDS evasion, and other abusive activities.

Chapter 5, "Tcpdump," written by Jim Mellander, covers deploying tcpdump, its command line options, and making sense of the output.

Part II, "Architecture," consists of Chapters 6–7. Chapter 6, "IDS and IPS Architecture," written by Gene Schultz, covers architecture issues such as tiered intrusion detection models, sensors, agents and servers.

Chapter 7, "IDS and IPS Internals," written by Gene Schultz, covers data acquisition, protocol handling, signature matching, and anomaly detection and traffic normalization.

Part III, "Implementation and Deployment" consists of Chapters 8-11. Chapter 8, "Internet Security System's RealSecure," written by James Foster, provides an overview of the product and covers the implementation, fine tuning, and upgrading of the product.

Chapter 9, "Cisco Secure IDS," written by Chad Schieken and Patrick Ramseier, offers an overview of the product and covers the implementation, fine tuning, and upgrading of the product.

Chapter 10, "Snort," written by Gene Schultz, gives an overview of the product and covers the implementation, fine tuning, and upgrading of this product.

Chapter 11, "NFR Security," written by Frank Simorjay, provides an overview of the product and covers the implementation, fine tuning, and upgrading of the product.

Part IV, "Security and IDS Management," finishes the book with Chapters 12–17. Chapter 12, "Data Correlation," written by Gene Schultz, covers the basics of rule-based and statistical correlation, and both real-time and after-the-fact correlation.

Chapter 13, "Incident Response," written by Carl Endorf, explores the incident response team, tools needed, and forensics.

Chapter 14, "Policy and Procedures," written by Carl Endorf, examines the basics needed within the security policy covering IDS, and the procedures that should be included.

Chapter 15, "Laws, Standards, and Organizations," written by Carl Endorf, addresses the rules of evidence, laws, and case studies.

Chapter 16, "Security Business Issues," written by Carl Endorf, covers defining threats, risk management, determining ROI, and architecture and technology decisions.

Chapter 17, "The Future of Intrusion Detection and Prevention," written by Gene Schultz, looks at emerging trends and probable developments as well as topics that need to be researched further.

PART I

Intrusion Detection: Primer

CHAPTER 1

Understanding Intrusion Detection

On June 11, 2003 the Gartner Group, a research and advisory firm, reported that intrusion-detection systems are a market failure, have failed to provide value relative to their costs, and will be obsolete by 2005. While this brought Gartner a lot of attention, the fact is that intrusion detection and prevention is here to stay, not as a silver bullet, but as part of a strong defense strategy. Many industry research groups and the thousands of companies that have deployed or are planning to deploy intrusion-detection and intrusion-prevention systems are a testament to the usefulness of this technology.

Intrusion detection has had its problems, such as false positives, operational issues in high-speed environments, and the difficulty of detecting unknown threats. In addition, intrusion prevention is still in its infancy. Most of the problems with intrusion detection are caused by improper implementation and misunderstanding of what the technology can and cannot do.

This book focuses on what intrusion detection and prevention can and cannot do. We will examine ways to get the most from this technology, and look at how it can be managed to benefit your organization.

This chapter will introduce intrusion-detection system (IDS) and intrusion-prevention system (IPS) technologies, explaining what they are, as well as pointing out their differences. We will examine why these systems may be important to your organization, and look at the general types of analysis processes used by both IDSs and IPSs. Finally, we will review the pros and cons of both IDS and IPS technologies and clear up some of the myths about them.

INTRUSION-DETECTION AND INTRUSION-PREVENTION BASICS

Any dictionary will provide a definition of *intrusion*, but its meaning in the computer security context has been debated. Many people consider intrusions to include unsuccessful attacks, while others see a distinct difference between attacks and intrusions. We'll work with the definition that an *intrusion* is an *active sequence of related events that deliberately try to cause harm*, such as rendering a system unusable, accessing unauthorized information, or manipulating such information. This definition refers to both successful and unsuccessful attempts.

Security professionals may want to have IDS systems record information about both successful and unsuccessful attempts so that security professionals will have a more comprehensive understanding of the events on their networks. One way this can be done is by placing devices that examine network traffic, called *sensors*, both in front of the firewall (the unprotected area) and behind the firewall (the protected area) and comparing the information recorded by the two.

What Is an Intrusion-Detection System (IDS)?

An intrusion-detection system (IDS) can be defined as the tools, methods, and resources to help identify, assess, and report unauthorized or unapproved network activity. The *intrusion detection* part of the name is a bit of a misnomer, as an IDS does not actually detect intrusions—it detects activity in traffic that may or may not be an intrusion. Intrusion de-

tection is typically one part of an overall protection system that is installed around a system or device—it is not a stand-alone protection measure.

You can loosely compare firewalls to locked doors, intrusion detection to alarm systems, and intrusion prevention to guard dogs. Let's say that you have a warehouse full of secret documents that you want to protect with a fence around the perimeter, an alarm system, locked doors, and security cameras. The locked doors will stop unauthorized individuals from entering the warehouse. By themselves, they do nothing to alert you of an intrusion, but they deter unauthorized access. The alarm system will warn you in case an intruder tries to get into the warehouse. By itself, it does nothing to prevent an intrusion, but it alerts you to the *potential* of an intrusion. The guard dog, in some instances, is able to prevent an intrusion by taking measures to thwart the attack from happening by biting intruders before they can enter the protected perimeter, thereby stopping the intrusion.

As you can see, the door locks, alarm system, and guard dog play separate but complementary roles in the protection of this warehouse. This is also true of firewalls and IDSs and IPSs. All of these are different technologies that can work together to alert you and can prevent intrusions into a network. In addition, how these technologies are implemented determines whether or not they increase security. For instance, in the warehouse example, the most effective strategy may be to place alarms and locks on all the windows and doors, as well as motion detectors inside the warehouse. You may also want several dogs deployed within the perimeter to watch for possible intruders. Implementing IDSs and IPSs is no different—the placement of the technology makes all the difference between a secure network and an unsecured one.

It is also important to note that IDSs and IPSs are just two of many methods that should be employed in a strong security program. Using a layered approach, or defense in depth, based on careful risk analysis is critical in any information protection program because a network is only as secure as its weakest link. This means that a network should have multiple layers of security, each with its own function, to complement the overall security strategy of the organization. Figure 1-1 illustrates a defense-in-depth approach that will protect a network on many levels.

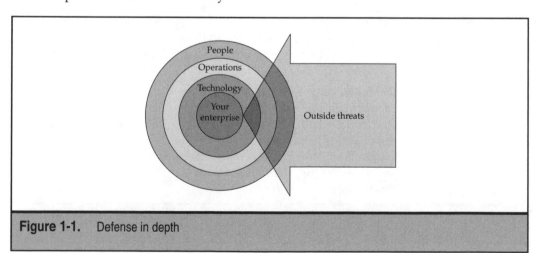

Figure 1-1.   Defense in depth

IDSs work at the network layer of the OSI model (see Table 1-1), and passive network sensors are typically positioned at choke points on the network. They analyze packets to find specific patterns in network traffic—if they find such a pattern in the traffic, an alert is logged, and a response can be based on the data recorded. IDSs are similar to antivirus software in that they use known signatures to recognize traffic patterns that may be malicious in intent.

Layer	Function	Protocols
Application (user interface)	This layer is used for applications, such as HTTP, specifically written to run over the network and allows accesses to network services. It handles issues like network transparency, resource allocation, and problem partitioning. The application layer is concerned with the user's view of the network, like formatting. In addition, this layer allows access to services that support applications and handle network access, flow, and recovery.	DNS, FTP, TFTP, BOOTP, SNMP, RLOGIN, SMTP, MIME, NFS, FINGER, TELNET, APPC, AFP,
Presentation (translation)	The presentation layer helps to translate between the application and the network formats. This is also where protocol conversion takes place.	Named Pipes, Mail Slots, RPC, NCP, SMB
Session	The session layer helps to establish, maintain, and end sessions across the network.	NetBios
Transport (packets; flow control and error-handling)	The transport layer manages the flow control of data between parties across the network.	TCP, ARP, RARP, SPX, NWLink, ATP, NetBEUI
Network (addressing; routing)	The network layer translates logical network addresses and names to their physical addresses and is responsible for addressing and managing network problems such as packet switching, data congestion, and routing.	IP, ARP, RARP, ICMP, RIP, OSFP, IGMP, IPX, NWLink, OSI, DDP, DECnet

Table 1-1.   Layers in the OSI Reference Model

Layer	Function	Protocols
Data link (data frames to bits)	The data-link layer turns packets into raw bits on the sending end, and at the receiving end turns bits into packets. It handles data frames between the network and physical layers.	
Physical (hardware; raw bit stream)	The physical layer transmits the raw bit stream over the physical cable or airwaves (when dealing with wireless). It defines cables, cards, and other physical aspects.	IEEE 802, IEEE 802.2, ISO 2110, ISDN

Table 1-1.   Layers in the OSI Reference Model *(continued)*

Types of IDS Systems

IDSs fall into one of three categories: host-based intrusion-detection system (HIDS), network-based intrusion-detection system (NIDS), and hybrids of the two.

A HIDS system will require some software that resides on the system and can scan all host resources for activity; some just scan syslog and event logs for activity. It will log any activities it discovers to a secure database and check to see whether the events match any malicious event record listed in the knowledge base.

A NIDS system is usually inline on the network, and it analyzes network packets looking for attacks. A NIDS receives all packets on a particular network segment, including switched networks (where this is not the default behavior) via one of several methods, such as taps or port mirroring. It carefully reconstructs the streams of traffic to analyze them for patterns of malicious behavior. Most NIDSs are equipped with facilities to log their activities and report or alarm on questionable events. In addition, many high-performance routers offer NID capabilities.

A hybrid IDS combines a HIDS, which monitors events occurring on the host system, with a NIDS, which monitors network traffic. Table 1-2 shows some of the differences between a HIDS and a NIDS.

The basic process for an IDS is that a NIDS or HIDS passively collects data and preprocesses and classifies them. Statistical analysis can be done to determine whether the information falls outside normal activity, and if so, it is then matched against a knowledge base. If a match is found, an alert is sent. Figure 1-2 outlines this activity.

What Is an Intrusion-Prevention System (IPS)?

It is still early in the development of intrusion-prevention systems (IPSs), but generally an IPS sits inline on the network and monitors it, and when an event occurs, it takes action

Collecting Data

There are two primary ways to collect data on a switched network: port mirroring and network taps. *Port mirroring*, also referred to as *spanning*, is when copies of incoming and outgoing packets are forwarded from one port of a network switch to another port where the packets can be analyzed. *Network taps* are put directly in-line of the network traffic, and they copy the incoming and outgoing packets and retransmit them back out on the network. Both methods have advantages and disadvantages that should be explored when making implementation decisions.

based on prescribed rules. This is unlike IDSs, which do not sit inline and are passive. Some people see IPSs as next-generation IDS systems, because they take detection a step further, but others think in broader terms and consider the IPSs to be yet another tool in the security infrastructure that could help prevent intrusions. IPS has developed out of IDS, but they are really different security products that have different functionality and strengths.

IPS systems are similar in setup to IDS systems—an IPS can be a host-based IPS (HIPS), which work best at protecting applications, or a network-based IPS (NIPS). User

NIDS	HIDS
Broad in scope (watches all network activities)	Narrow in scope (watches only specific host activities)
Easier setup	More complex setup
Better for detecting attacks from the outside	Better for detecting attacks from the inside
Less expensive to implement	More expensive to implement
Detection is based on what can be recorded on the entire network	Detection is based on what any single host can record
Examines packet headers	Does not see packet headers
Near real-time response	Usually only responds after a suspicious log entry has been made
OS-independent	OS-specific
Detects network attacks as payload is analyzed	Detects local attacks before they hit the network
Detects unsuccessful attack attempts	Verifies success or failure of attacks

Table 1-2.   Network-Based vs. Host-Based Intrusion-Detection Systems

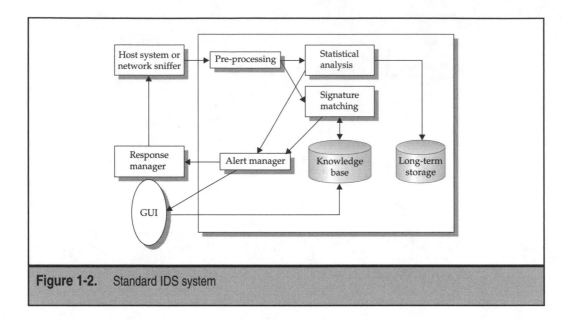

Figure 1-2.   Standard IDS system

actions should correspond to actions in a predefined knowledge base; if an action isn't on the accepted list, the IPS will prevent the action. Unlike an IDS, the logic in an IPS is typically applied before the action is executed in memory. Other IPS methods compare file checksums to a list of known good checksums before allowing a file to execute, and to work by intercepting system calls.

An IPS will typically consist of four main components:

▼ Traffic normalizer

■ Service scanner

■ Detection engine

▲ Traffic shaper

The traffic normalizer will interpret the network traffic and do packet analysis and packet reassembly, as well as performing basic blocking functions. The traffic is then fed into the detection engine and the service scanner. The service scanner builds a reference table that classifies the information and helps the traffic shaper manage the flow of the information. The detection engine does pattern matching against the reference table, and the appropriate response is determined. Figure 1-3 outlines this process.

IDS vs. IPS

IDS and IPS technology each have their own place in a security program because they perform separate functions. Table 1-3 clarifies some of the differences between them.

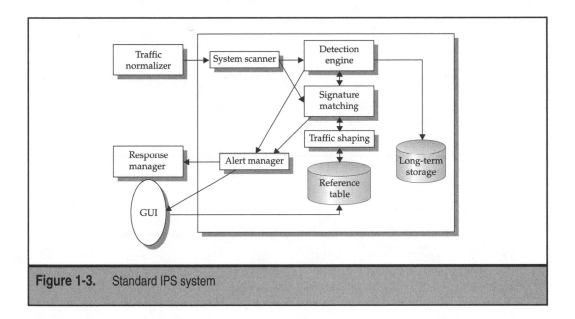

Figure 1-3.   Standard IPS system

THE HISTORY OF INTRUSION DETECTION AND PREVENTION

Intrusion-prevention technology is fairly new and is still evolving, whereas intrusion detection has a bit more history behind it. However, both IDS and IPS have their roots in auditing. In 1980, James Anderson wrote a technical report called *Computer Security Threat Monitoring and Surveillance* for the U.S. Air Force. The paper showed that audit records

IDS	IPS
Installed on network segments (NIDS) and on hosts (HIDS)	Installed on network segments (NIPS) and on hosts (HIPS)
Sits on network passively	Sits inline (not passive)
Cannot parse encrypted traffic	Better at protecting applications
Central management control	Central management control
Better at detecting hacking attacks	Ideal for blocking web defacement
Alerting product (reactive)	Blocking product (proactive)

Table 1-3.   Intrusion-Detection Systems vs. Intrusion-Prevention Systems

could be used to help identify computer misuse and identify threat classifications, and it offered suggestions to improve auditing of systems to identify misuse.

In 1985, SRI International was funded by the U.S. Navy to develop intrusion-detection research. Dr. Dorothy Denning helped lead this team to develop a prototype that would analyze audit trails from government systems and track user activity. Her team named this system the Intrusion Detection Expert System (IDES), and it was the foundational research into IDS technology. One year later, in 1987, Dr. Denning published a paper called *An Intrusion Detection Model* for the 1986 IEEE Symposium on Security and Privacy that helped describe the basic workings of behavioral analysis. *Behavioral analysis* looks for deviations from the type of behavior that has been statistically baselined, such as relationships in packets and in what is being sent over a network.

While SRI was working on IDES for the Navy in 1987, Los Alamos National Laboratory was working on the Haystack project, which produced an IDS system that could analyze audit data against defined patterns. Several people from the Haystack project worked with designers and developers from University of California-Davis and Lawrence Livermore National Laboratory (and later Trident Data Systems) to develop an IDS called the Distributed Intrusion Detection System (DIDS) for the U.S. Air Force. DIDS became the basis for a commercial IDS (Net Stalker), with similar functionality, by Haystack Labs.

In 1989, Todd Heberlein, a student at the University of California, Davis, built an IDS system called Network System Monitor (NSM). NSM was different from IDES and DIDS in that it would analyze network traffic rather than system logs. NSM, along with the now commercially available Stalker IDS, helped to create new awareness and interest in IDS research for the commercial and public sectors.

The 1990s saw a great deal of improvement of and interest in IDS technology. The U.S. Air Force commissioned Science Applications International Corporation (SAIC) to develop the Computer Misuse Detection System (CMDS). Marcus J. Ranum created a commercial IDS called Network Flight Recorder (NFR). Christopher Klaus and Thomas E. Noonan founded Internet Security Systems (ISS) and released a network-based intrusion-detection system called RealSecure. In addition, the U.S. Air Force Cryptologic Support Center created an IDS system called Automated Security Incident Measurement (ASIM), which was the first IDS to incorporate both software- and hardware-based solutions. Some of the developers of ASIM formed the Wheel Group and commercialized the product. Cisco Systems acquired the Wheel Group in 1998, which ultimately led to Cisco Systems developing IDS to be included in their routers functionality. During this time, Haystack Labs and the former development team for SAIC merged to form the Centrax Corporation, and it released host-based intrusion detection for Windows NT called eNTrax.

Starting in the late 1990s, intrusion prevention emerged. In the beginning, just detecting attacks was a huge undertaking, but as that discipline matured, it was clear that we needed to go beyond detection and prevent attacks in real time. The ISS RealSecure product had some features such as the rs-kill feature that would "kill" or stop traffic based on specific patterns. In 1998, SNORT, an open source libpcap-based packet sniffer and logger, which can be used as a lightweight NIDS and was developed by Marty Roesch, was made available and allowed many people to use and become familiar with intrusion

detection. In 1999, Okena Systems created one of the first IPSs called StormWatch based on their INCORE architecture (Intercept Correlate Rules Engine), which intercepts file and network actions and correlates rules and application states to make real-time decisions based on application behavior. Okena was acquired by Cisco Systems in 2003. The development of intrusion prevention has just begun.

 NOTE   Libpcap is a system-independent interface for user-level packet capture, and it provides a portable framework for low-level network monitoring. Applications for libpcap include network statistics collection, security monitoring, network debugging, and so on.

WHY IDSs AND IPSs ARE IMPORTANT

IDSs and IPSs are important for many organizations, from small offices to large multinational corporations. IDSs and IPSs offer many benefits:

▼ Greater proficiency in detecting intrusions than by doing it manually

■ In-depth knowledge bases to draw from

■ Ability to deal with large volumes of data

■ Near real-time alerting capabilities that help reduce potential damages

■ Automated responses, such as logging off a user, disabling a user account, or launching automated scripts

■ Strong deterrent value

■ Built-in forensic capabilities

▲ Built-in reporting capabilities

These are all very good reasons to implement these technologies, but there are three main reasons that justify the need more than the others:

▼ **Legal and regulatory issues**   In 1998, the U.S. Presidential Decision Directive 63 (PDD 63) established steps to increase the use of intrusion detection and prevention to protect the national infrastructure. British Standard 7799 was first published in February 1995 and identified a comprehensive set of controls defining "best practices" for information security. Regulations such as the Health Insurance Portability and Accountability Act of 1996 (HIPAA) and Gramm-Leach-Bliley Act of 1999 (GLBA) require audit controls to record and examine suspicious data-access activities. The preceding regulations may or may not be necessary, depending on the nature and location of your organization. In addition, implementation of an IDS/IPS program is not a requirement for complying with any of these, but will help to meet the requirements.

- ■ **Quantification of attacks**   IDS and IPS allow a systems administrator the opportunity to quantify attacks against the organization's network for management. IDSs and IPSs both are able to build a profile of the types of attacks that are being tried against a network. This allows a stronger business case to be made for appropriate security measures, which can often be hard to justify. IPSs and IDSs can also provide evidence against attackers if litigation is desired.

- ▲ **Establishment of an overall defense-in-depth strategy**   IDSs and IPSs have become a critical part of a strong defense-in-depth security program, and their use shows due diligence on the part of the organization because the organization is being proactive in the expectation of and reaction to intrusions. Both technologies will help provide protection for network and application layer vulnerabilities, as well as help to correlate and validate information from other devices, such as antivirus programs, firewalls, and routers.

IDS AND IPS ANALYSIS SCHEMES

IDSs and IPSs perform analyses, and it is important to understand the analysis process: what analysis does, what types of analysis are available, and what the advantages and disadvantages of different analysis schemes are.

What Is Analysis?

Analysis, in the context of intrusion detection and prevention, is the organization of the constituent parts of data and their interrelationships to identify any anomalous activity of

Clinton Administration's Policy on Critical Infrastructure Protection

It is important to be familiar with the following legislative issues: *The Clinton Administration's Policy on Critical Infrastructure Protection: Presidential Decision Directive 63, May 22, 1998,* was designed to set forth a policy for protecting critical infrastructure in the United States.

The *Public Law 104-191 Health Insurance Portability and Accountability Act of 1996* helps improve portability and continuity of health insurance coverage in the group and individual markets. Among other things, it is designed to combat waste, fraud, and abuse in health insurance and health care delivery, to promote the use of medical savings accounts, to improve access to long-term care services and coverage, and to simplify the administration of health insurance.

The *Financial Modernization Act of 1999,* also known as the Gramm-Leach-Bliley Act or GLBA, includes provisions to protect consumers' personal financial information held by financial institutions.

interest. *Real-time analysis* is analysis done on the fly as the data travels the path to the network or host. This is a bit of a misnomer, however, as analysis can only be performed after the fact in near-real-time.

The fundamental goal of intrusion-detection and intrusion-prevention analysis is to improve an information system's security. This goal can be further broken down:

▼ Create records of relevant activity for follow-up

■ Determine flaws in the network by detecting specific activities

■ Record unauthorized activity for use in forensics or criminal prosecution of intrusion attacks

■ Act as a deterrent to malicious activity

▲ Increase accountability by linking activities of one individual across systems

Figure 1-4 illustrates the general idea of analysis. An IDS or IPS system will help identify those anomalous activities that fall outside the realm of what is considered normal baseline activity for the environment. This is considered the general goal, but there is still much debate over how much anomalous data falls outside the realm of normal baseline activity. Some believe the gap is large, while others see very little difference between the two.

The Anatomy of Intrusion Analysis

There are many possible data-analysis schemes for an analysis engine, and in order to understand them, the intrusion-analysis process can be broken down into four phases:

1. Preprocessing

2. Analysis

3. Response

4. Refinement

Preprocessing is a key function once data are collected from an IDS or IPS sensor. In this step, the data are organized in some fashion for classification. The preprocessing will help determine the format the data are put into, which is usually some canonical format

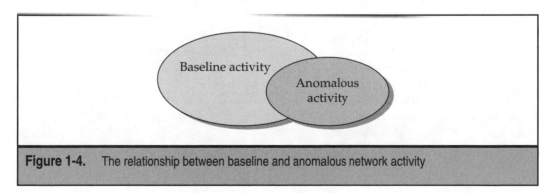

Figure 1-4.   The relationship between baseline and anomalous network activity

or could be a structured database. Once the data are formatted, they are broken down further into classifications.

These classifications can depend on the analysis schemes being used. For example, if rule-based detection is being used, the classification will involve rules and pattern descriptors. If anomaly detection is used, you will usually have a statistical profile based on different algorithms in which the user behavior is baselined over time and any behavior that falls outside of that classification is flagged as an anomaly. Both pattern matching and anomaly detection are covered later in this chapter.

Upon completion of the classification process, the data is concatenated and put into a defined version or detection template of some object by replacing variables with values. These detection templates populate the knowledgebase which are stored in the core analysis engine:

▼   Detection of the modification of system log files

■   Detection of unexpected privilege escalation

■   Detection of Backdoor Netbus

■   Detection of Backdoor SubSeven

■   ORACLE grant attempt

▲   RPC mountd UDP export request

Once the prepossessing is completed, the *analysis* stage begins. The data record is compared to the knowledge base, and the data record will either be logged as an intrusion event or it will be dropped. Then the next data record is analyzed.

The next phase, *response*, is one of the differentiating factors between IDS and IPS. With IDS, you typically have limited prevention abilities—you are getting the information passively after the fact, so you will have an alert after the fact. Once information has been logged as an intrusion, a response can be initiated. With IPS, the sensor is inline and it can provide real-time prevention through an automated response. This is the essential difference between reactive security and proactive security.

Either way, the response is specific to the nature of the intrusion or the different analysis schemes used. The response can be set to be automatically performed, or it can be done manually after someone has manually analyzed the situation. For example, Network Flight Recorder (a commercial IDS) offers a feature that can send a TCP RST packet and kill a session.

The final phase is the *refinement* stage. This is where the fine-tuning of the IDS or IPS system can be done, based on previous usage and detected intrusions. This gives the security professional a chance to reduce false-positive levels and to have a more accurate security tool. This is a very critical stage for getting the most from your IDS or IPS system. The system must be fine-tuned for your environment to get any real value from it. There are tools, like Cisco Threat Response (CTR), that will help with the refining stage by actually making sure that an alert is valid by checking whether you are vulnerable to that attack or not.

Rule-Based Detection (Misuse Detection)

Rule-based detection, also referred to as *signature detection, pattern matching* and *misuse detection*, is the first scheme that was used in early intrusion-detection systems. Rule-based detection uses pattern matching to detect known attack patterns.

Let's look at how the four phases of the analysis process are applied in a rule-based detection system:

1. **Preprocessing** The first step is to collect data about intrusions, vulnerabilities, and attacks, and put them into a classification scheme or pattern descriptor. From the classification scheme, a behavioral model is built, and then put into a common format:

   - **Signature Name** The given name of a signature
   - **Signature ID** A unique ID for the signature
   - **Signature Description** Description of the signature and what it does
   - **Possible False Positive Description** An explanation of any "false positives" that may appear to be an exploit but are actually normal network activity.
   - **Related Vulnerability Information** This field has any related vulnerability information
   - **User Notes** This field allows a security professional to add specific notes related to their network

   The pattern descriptors are typically either content-based signatures, which examine the payload and header of a packet, or context-based signatures that evaluate *only* the packet headers to identify an alert. Note that pattern descriptors can be atomic (single) or composite (multiple) descriptors. An atomic descriptor requires only one packet to be inspected to identify an alert, while a composite descriptor requires multiple packets to be inspected to identify an alert. The pattern descriptors are then put into a knowledge base that contains the criteria for analysis.

2. **Analysis** The event data are formatted and compared against the knowledge base by using a pattern-matching analysis engine. The analysis engine looks for defined patterns that are known as attacks.

3. **Response** If the event matches the pattern of an attack, the analysis engine sends an alert. If the event is a partial match, the next event is examined. Note that partial matches can only be analyzed with a stateful detector, which has the ability to maintain state, as many IDS systems do. Different responses can be returned depending on the specific event records.

4. **Refinement** Refinement of pattern-matching analysis comes down to updating signatures, because an IDS is only as good as its latest signature

update. This is one of the drawbacks of pattern-matching analysis. Most IDSs allow automatic and manual updating of attack signatures.

Profile-Based Detection (Anomaly Detection)

An anomaly is something that is different from the norm or that cannot be easily classified. *Anomaly detection,* also referred to as *profile-based detection,* creates a profile system that flags any events that strays from a normal pattern and passes this information on to output routines.

One key distinction between anomaly detection and other analysis schemes is that anomaly-based schemes not only define activities that are *not allowed,* but also activities that are *allowed.* In addition, anomaly detection is typically used for its ability to collect statistical behavior and characteristic behavior. Statistics are quantitative and characteristics are more qualitative. For example, "This server's UDP traffic never exceeds 25 percent of capacity" describes a statistical behavior, and "User Stan321 does not normally FTP files outside of the company" describes a characteristic behavior.

Anomaly-based schemes fall into three main categories: behavioral, traffic pattern, and protocol. *Behavioral analysis* looks for anomalies in the types of behavior that have been statistically baselined, such as relationships in packets and what is being sent over a network. *Traffic-pattern analysis* looks for specific patterns in network traffic. *Protocol analysis* looks for network protocol violations or misuse based on RFC-based behavior. Protocol analysis has the benefit of identifying possible attacks that are not yet publicized or that there is no known signature or remedy for.

NOTE Requests for Comments (RFCs) are a series of notes about aspects of the Internet, such as protocols. A document can be sent to the Internet Engineering Task Force (IETF), which is a standards organization for the Internet, and they will determine whether it becomes an RFC. See www.faqs.org/rfcs/ for more info about RFCs.

Again, let's review the analysis model in the context of anomaly detection:

1. **Preprocessing**   The first step in the analysis process is collecting the data in which behavior considered normal on the network is baselined over a period of time. The data are put into a numeric form and is then formatted. Then the information is classified into a statistical profile that is based on different algorithms in the knowledge base.

2. **Analysis**   The event data are typically reduced to a profile vector, which is then compared to the knowledge base. The contents of the profile vector are compared to a historical record for that particular user, and any data that fall outside of the baseline normal activity is labeled a deviation.

3. **Response**   At this point, a response can be triggered either automatically or manually.

4. **Refinement** The data records must be kept updated. The profile vector history will typically be deleted after a specific number of days. In addition, different weighting systems can be used to add more weight to recent behaviors than past behaviors.

Target Monitoring

Target-monitoring systems will report whether certain target objects have been changed or modified. This is usually done through a cryptographic algorithm that computes a cryptochecksum for each target file. The IDS reports any changes, such as a file modifications or program logon, which would cause changes in cryptochecksums

Tripwire software will perform target monitoring using cryptochecksums by providing instant notification of changes to configuration files and enabling automatic restoration. The main advantage of this approach is that you do not have to continuously monitor the target files.

Stealth Probes

Stealth probes correlate data to try to detect attacks made over a long period of time, often referred to as "low and slow" attacks. Data are collected from a variety of sources, and it is characterized and sampled to discover any correlating attacks. This technique is also referred to as wide-area correlation, and it is typically a combination or hybrid approach that uses other detection methods to try and uncover malicious behavior.

Heuristics

The term *heuristics* refers to artificial intelligence (AI). In theory, an IDS will identify anomalies to detect an intrusion, and it will then learn over time what can be considered normal. To use heuristics, an AI scripting language can apply analysis to the incoming data.

Heuristics still leave a lot to be desired at this stage, but development is progressing. What is needed is a pattern-matching language that can use programming constructs to learn and identify malicious activity more accurately.

Hybrid Approach

We have examined the fundamental analysis schemes. You will find that there is much debate on which is considered the best approach. In actuality, they all have their merits and drawbacks, but when they are used together they can offer a more robust security system. Products that use a hybrid approach typically perform better, especially against complex attacks.

Example IDS Rules

We have looked at the theory of IDS patterns and analysis schemes. It seems appropriate at this point to examine few IDS rules to illustrate those concepts.

The following is an IDS rule from an open source network IDS called Snort that detects whether the NetBus back door is running on a system:

```
alert tcp $HOME_NET 12345:12346 -> $EXTERNAL_NET any (msg:"BACKDOOR
netbus active"; flow:from_server,established; content:"NetBus";
reference:arachnids,401; classtype:misc-activity; sid:109; rev:4;)
```

From this rule, we can see that Snort will send an alert if a TCP packet on ports 12345–12346 come through. If that happens, Snort sends the message of "BACKDOOR netbus active" and the message is given a class type of miscellaneous activity and a signature ID of 109. The signature is on its fourth revision.

The following Snort IDS signature detects a DNS zone transfer request:

```
alert udp $EXTERNAL_NET any -> $HOME_NET 53 (msg:"DNS zone transfer
UDP"; content: "|00 00 FC|"; offset:14; reference:cve,CAN-1999-0532;
reference:arachnids,212; classtype:attempted-recon; sid:1948; rev:1;)
```

From this signature, we can see that Snort sends an alert if a UDP packet on port 53 comes through. Snort sends the message "DNS zone transfer UDP" with a class type of attempted reconnaissance and a signature ID of 1948. This signature is on its first revision.

IDS/IPS PROS AND CONS

As stated earlier, IDS and IPS are two separate technologies that can complement each other. The following sections list the pros and cons of both technologies.

Intrusion Detection

The pros of intrusion detection include the following:

▼ Can detect external hackers as well as internal network-based attacks

■ Scales easily to provide protection for the entire network

■ Offers centralized management for correlation of distributed attacks

■ Provides defense in depth

■ Gives system administrators the ability to quantify attacks

▲ Provides an additional layer of protection

These are the cons:

▼ Generates false positives and negatives

■ Reacts to attacks rather than preventing them

■ Requires full-time monitoring

- ■ Requires a complex incident-response process
- ■ Cannot monitor traffic at higher transmission rates
- ■ Generates an enormous amount of data to be analyzed
- ■ Requires highly skilled staff dedicated to interpreting the data
- ■ Susceptible to "low and slow" attacks
- ■ Cannot deal with encrypted network traffic
- ▲ It is expensive

Intrusion Prevention

The pros of intrusion prevention include the following:

- ▼ Protects at the application layer
- ■ Prevents attacks rather than simply reacting to them
- ■ Can use a behavioral approach
- ■ Provides defense in depth
- ▲ Permits real-time event correlation

The cons are as follows:

- ▼ Generates false positives that can create serious problems if automated responses are used
- ■ Creates network bottlenecks
- ■ It is a new technology
- ▲ It is expensive

INTRUSION-DETECTION AND INTRUSION-PREVENTION MYTHS

There are several untrue intrusion-detection and intrusion-prevention myths. These assertions repeatedly come up, even though some are diametrically opposed to others.

Myth 1: Intrusion detection and intrusion prevention are basically the same technology. Many believe that because some IDS systems have TCP kill and RESET capabilities that they are pretty much the same thing as IPS. The truth is that each of these technologies are separate in design and in function. An IPS device sits inline, and all the packets have to pass through it. If a suspicious packet has been detected, it can be dropped. With IDS this is not the case—the suspicious packets are sent on to the internal interface to be analyzed, an alert is then sent, and a response generated. The latency involved in an IDS often results

in a failed response. That is because an IDS is designed for detecting intrusions, not responding to them, though they do have some rudimentary response capabilities.

Myth 2: Intrusion-detection systems give too many false positives to be of any real value.   It is true that IDSs do give what appear to be false positives. Typically, signatures released by vendors are accurate, but sometimes legitimate traffic sets them off. You need to properly fine-tune the IDS for your particular network. What often happens is that an organization implements IDS and doesn't tune it, and soon the administrators feel overwhelmed by the alerts, which are mostly false positives. If an organization starts out on small segments of the network at a time and gets the IDS tuned to better understand what is and is not legitimate, the results will be better.

Myth 3: Intrusion detection will eventually replace firewalls.   *Wrong!* This will not happen. IDSs and firewalls perform separate and distinct functions on the network. We will likely see that most firewalls have some IDS and IPS capabilities, but IDS and IPS are just single layers in a security program, and they are not meant to replace firewalls.

Myth 4: IDS systems are on the way out, and IPS and firewalls are the wave of the future.   IDSs are far from becoming obsolete. We may see the integration of IDS and IPS capabilities within firewalls and routers, but the technology remains the same and the need is apparent. The wave of the future is seeing how the two can complement each other, not in debating which is better. There is some traffic that you do not want a response to, and that traffic is better passed off to an IDS.

Myth 5: IDSs are the wave of the future.   This is the opposite of the previous myth, but the answer is much the same. Both IDS and IPS technologies have a place in securing a network or host. There is no one "silver bullet" that will take care of everything. Intrusion detection is here to stay, but it is not the only technology in the game—IPS is also needed.

Myth 6: IDSs and IPSs will catch or stop all network intrusions.   This seems like a ridiculous statement to the technically minded, but it is often asked by management. Yes, IDS and IPS will help to prevent and deter some attacks, but they will never be able to catch everything.

Myth 7: When an organization implements IDS or IPS, it should need fewer security professionals. There is some truth to this myth in that automating intrusion detection can reduce the number of individuals needed to detect security breaches in systems and networks. At the same time, however, one of the big issues with IDS and IPS is that they do a good job at finding attacks, but there needs to be a trained professional on the other end who can interpret and react to the information. While this may seem like additional overhead, the attacks would be there whether or not you detected them.

Myth 8: You need real-time detection in order to get any real value from an IDS.   Real time is a bit of a misnomer, as the response and identification will always come after the attack has entered the network or host. A better approach is to ask whether the alert or response is accurate and is in time for the necessary response. While faster can be better, it also has

disadvantages, such as cost and more difficult data handling—data that are received in real time needs to be handled in real time.

SUMMARY

This chapter was an introduction to the basic concepts of intrusion detection. We looked at origins of intrusion detection and prevention and how it has developed over the years. We were able to examine the importance of intrusion detection in meeting many regulatory and legal needs as well as being a part of a defense in depth program. We examined the types of analysis schemes that can be used and how they are applied. We also discussed some of the various myths and realities of intrusion detection and prevention.

CHAPTER 2

Crash Course in the Internet Protocol Suite

As a consequence of the Internet's explosion of popularity, most networking protocols that competed with IP, the Internet Protocol, have been relegated to niche status, or have been made to work with IP (such as NBT, which is NetBIOS running under TCP, the Transmission Control Protocol). The IP family of protocols has been designed to provide a range of services, from low-level networking functions that touch the hardware, through data routing, reliability, and scaling capabilities, to application-level transparency in a layered approach.

As this book is focused on intrusion detection, we will, in later chapters, examine the security implications of both the lower-level communication protocols and the applications that depend on them. For now, it is important to take note of the trust relationships between the various components. Unfortunately IPv4, the current version of the Internet Protocol in use today, was designed with scant attention to security. Many of the mechanisms implicitly trust the information that they receive from others, permitting the possibility of subversion by malicious parties. Depending on the protocol involved, misleading information may be supplied to trusting hosts, which could allow for intrusion into those hosts.

Conceptually, the various functions that network hardware and software must perform can be understood as a series of layers of functionality, with each layer built on and depending on the proper functioning of the layers below it. Each additional layer brings greater functionality and a higher level of abstraction. This layered approach also gives applications a great deal of independence, because they do not need to be concerned with implementation details.

The Open Systems Interconnection (OSI) reference model describes such a framework for understanding these layers. It was originally developed to guide the implementation of the OSI network suite (of which some implementations have been developed), but due to the overwhelming success of TCP/IP, its main use currently is as an educational tool.

AN INTRODUCTION TO THE SEVEN-LAYER
OSI REFERENCE MODEL

The OSI reference model is a conceptual model that provides a framework for specifying and identifying the various network functions. There are seven layers within the OSI model that serve to differentiate the various hardware and software functions that a network provides. Each layer depends on the proper functioning of the layer immediately below it to provide its raw functionality, which is enhanced and then passed to the next higher layer. Status messages may be communicated up or down the various layers, although each layer only communicates with its immediate neighbors. As each layer is solely dependent on the layer below it for lower-level services, higher layers are shielded from system, hardware, and software implementation details. This leads to independence from specific systems and interoperability with many vendors' offerings.

The OSI model is very useful for developing and understanding a "big picture" view of network processes because it provides this independence. However, the model does

not claim to exactly match any specific network technology. Each layer must encapsulate the data it receives into a standard format for the next higher layer, thus incurring an overhead, and in the name of efficiency, the lines between one or more layers can be blurred. Some layers may not specifically have counterparts in an actual network implementation. However, as a tool for understanding the considerations involved in networking, the OSI model is unparalleled.

The OSI model's seven layers, from the physical hardware level up to the actual network application that users interact with are as follows: the physical layer, the data-link layer, the network layer, the transport layer, the session layer, the presentation layer, and the application layer. It is a rare individual indeed who has expertise in all of the layers.

The Physical Layer

The physical layer consists of the physical wiring that is used to connect the different systems on a network. To ensure interoperability between various vendor implementations, strict standards must be employed to ensure compatibility. These standards not only describe the electrical standards of the network cabling, but the physical jacks, connectors, taps, and so on, all of which must be physically compatible with each other. At this lowest level, a failure is catastrophic for network communications. An Ethernet adapter will conform to physical and electrical standards of the physical layer.

The Data-Link Layer

The data-link layer consists of the transmission standards that are used to transmit data over the physical layer. These typically will consist of the bit-level specifications and waveforms of the transmission standard. Note that this layer does not specify the actual voltages used, but the characteristics of the waveforms. If this layer detects a problem with the physical layer (usually identified by a partial or total failure to propagate the signal), it must attempt to retransmit the information or notify the network layer. At this layer, a network adapter will generate the waveforms appropriate to the physical media. On an Ethernet network, this layer will package the data into Ethernet frames, which will then be delivered to its destination via the physical layer.

The Network Layer

The network layer is responsible for the addressing, packaging, and delivery of data. It will format the data as appropriate for the data-link layer to deliver it to the physical layer. Typically, the network layer does not provide reliability mechanisms, such as error checking, but leaves this task to the transport layer. The partitioning of these two functions has proven to be useful, as some forms of network traffic don't have the same need for reliability as others. For our purposes, IP uses this layer.

The Transport Layer

The transport layer provides a mechanism for reliably transporting the data from its source to its destination. Built on top of the network layer, it provides the reliability that many network services require by using such strategies as checksumming packets and requesting retransmission if errors are detected.

Some network services may not avail themselves of all this functionality in the interest of efficiency. For instance, streaming audio can often get by at a somewhat degraded level with an occasional frame being dropped. If retransmission were expected of this traffic, a noticeable delay might be experienced. On the other hand, e-mail transmissions do not require the same timeliness of delivery, and can tolerate moderate delays in the interest of reliability. The reliability characteristics of TCP fall into this layer.

The Session Layer

The session layer is responsible for establishing communication sessions between various higher-level communicating programs, processes, or users. This layer creates a "virtual circuit" that communicating processes on network-enabled systems employ to transfer information. On a network with many systems, the data is multiplexed on the wire, but this layer creates the illusion of a dedicated circuit between the endpoints.

The Presentation Layer

The presentation layer provides a consistent interface to application programs that are using network services, and it is often termed an API (application programming interface). All programs using a particular API can be assured of a consistent programming interface. The session layer is thus not burdened with the responsibility of interpreting or formatting the data, but can simply act to manage the session.

One commonly used network-based API that resides at this layer is the X protocol, originally developed by MIT, which provides a consistent interface to application programs that use its services to manage graphical interfaces for Unix hosts.

The Application Layer

The application layer represents the high-level, abstracted network protocols that are directly used by application programs. Protocols such as HTTP, SMTP, FTP, and POP operate at this layer. The application layer is not concerned with what the application program itself does with the data—it simply provides the data to the application for processing and delivers generated traffic to the lower levels. The processing, because it does not interact with the network, is not in the scope of the OSI reference model.

TCP/IP VS. THE OSI REFERENCE MODEL

Although the OSI model is useful for understanding and describing the network functions that apply during communication, the IP suite of protocols does not conform to the model described by OSI. It was developed independently of OSI, and the IP designers used the simpler conceptual model shown in Figure 2-1. Generally, TCP/IP networking is split into four categories:

▼   **Network hardware**   This category covers the network hardware components (corresponding to the OSI model's physical and data-link layers) that are relied upon by TCP/IP. The network stack is coded to efficiently utilize these components, and unlike the OSI model, there is no distinct separation between the functions of these components. When a packet is to be sent down the wire, the IP software (often called the "network stack") will communicate with a device driver for the network card, which will encapsulate the data appropriately for the data-link layer, and send it out to the physical medium. In many cases (Ethernet, frame relay, and others), the network hardware performs a checksum on the data that it transports.

■   **IP**   The Internet Protocol works at the network layer to provide a routing and delivery mechanism for traffic. IP packets include a checksum that provides a reasonable assurance that a received packet has not been corrupted in transit. However, IP does not provide guaranteed delivery of packets or retransmission of corrupted or lost packets.

■   **Transport protocols**   TCP and UDP (the User Datagram Protocol) work at the transport and session layers. TCP provides for reliable "virtual circuits" with error correction. UDP provides no such reliability features, but does provide a lighter-weight mechanism for delivery of data, and it relies on application-level techniques to make provisions for lost packets. ICMP (the Internet Control Message Protocol), which provides feedback on network status, is also found at this level.

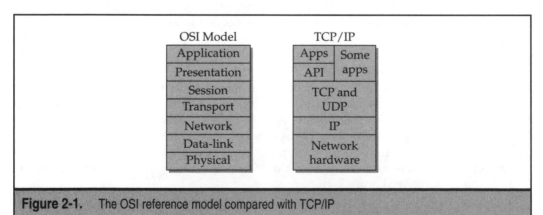

Figure 2-1.   The OSI reference model compared with TCP/IP

▲ **Presentation and application layers** The presentation and application layers are generally merged when the application receives the data, although some applications (X Windows being an example) act as presentation-level services on behalf of other application programs that employ their services. However, such services are not part of the networking layer—they provide a layering at the application level.

INTERNET PROTOCOL (IP)

IP (the Internet Protocol) provides a basic framework for the transport of traffic from source to destination on the Internet. (See RFC 1180 for a TCP/IP tutorial; www.faqs.org/rfcs/rfc1180.html). By design, it functions as an encapsulation (wrapper) and transport mechanism for this traffic. There is a header checksum to validate that the packet header, but not necessarily the data, has not been corrupted in transit. However, IP provides no facilities for retransmission or error correction.

Best-Effort Delivery

IP is responsible for the routing and delivery of packets on the Internet. If a packet is lost in transmission, as, for instance, during a period of congested activity, IP will not, of itself, trigger a retransmission. Instead, it is up to the higher-level protocol to detect that the packet has not been delivered and to take corrective action. IP will also be the transport mechanism for that corrective action, so it is possible that the first corrective action taken may, in turn, not be delivered. The higher-level protocols built on top of IP are expected to implement the necessary error-correction measures for that eventuality. TCP, for instance, has mechanisms to trigger multiple retransmissions. Only after repeated failures to communicate does TCP decide that the transport layer (IP) is fatally broken and, in this case, it provides a notification to the application requesting the communication.

Encapsulation

In the layered approach we have been discussing, each layer is embedded (or encapsulated) in a wrapper from the next lower-level protocol. On an Ethernet network, for instance, the actual wire protocol consists of Ethernet frames, which are addressed using 48-bit hardware addresses for the source and destination Ethernet adapters, and this includes a cyclical redundancy check (CRC) code to ensure reliability. Embedded in the data portion of this frame will be an IP packet, which encodes its source and destination using 32-bit IP addresses, and it also contains a checksum for reliability. Embedded as the data portion of the IP packet is a protocol-specific packet. In the case of TCP or UDP, this will contain source and destination ports, along with yet another checksum. The data portion of this packet will consist of the application or presentation layer data. Thus, each successive layer's message is treated as data by the layer below it, which provides an extensible framework (see Figure 2-2).

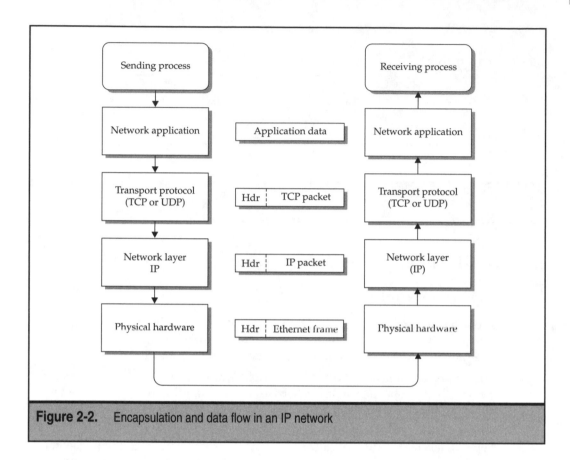

Figure 2-2.   Encapsulation and data flow in an IP network

Although having multiple checksums may seem redundant, the design actually allows each layer to detect faults emanating from the layer before it, and to take appropriate action. If the implementation employed only one check code, the traffic would need to travel completely from source to destination before any transmission faults could be detected. Using multiple checksums allows for detection of faults on the local Ethernet using the Ethernet CRC, faults in clean packet transmission between connected networks via the IP checksum, and faults in delivery to the final destination by the protocol-specific checksum. Corrective action can thus be taken at the point where the fault occurred. The redundancy contributes to the reliability and efficiency of the Internet, as well as assisting in failure detection.

The IP Header

The standard IP header is defined in RFC 791 and is shown in Figure 2-3. It consists of a minimum of 20 bytes and ranges up to a maximum of 60 bytes. Embedded in the data

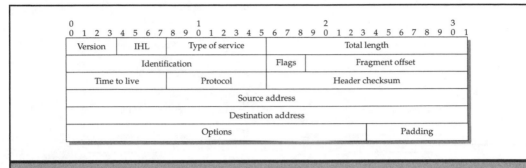

Figure 2-3. Internet datagram header

portion of the IP packet is the protocol-specific packet (such as a TCP or UDP packet), as discussed earlier.

These are the header fields:

▼ **Version number** A 4-bit field (values from 0 to 15) that specifies which version of IP the packet refers to. On the current Internet, this value will generally be 4, although the next generation IPv6 uses a value of 6.

■ **Internet header length (IHL)** A 4-bit field (values from 0 to 15) that specifies the length of the header in 32-bit (4-byte) words. Padding bytes are added to fill up the header to a multiple of 32 bits. Note that the maximum header length is thus 15×4 bytes = 60 bytes.

■ **Type of service (TOS)** An 8-bit field (values from 0 to 255) that encodes the service type desired for the packet. This field has been slowly gaining in usage. It encodes, via bit-level fields, the desired delivery characteristics of the packet from the following types: minimize delay, maximize throughput, maximize reliability, minimize monetary cost, and normal service. Routers can use this information to make routing decisions to conform to these requests.

■ **Total length** A 16-bit field (values from 0 to 65,535) that specifies the total length of the packet in bytes. There are few, if any, physical media that can directly transport a packet of the maximum size. If the packet is larger than the physical media can transport, the packet will be fragmented into multiple smaller packets that the media can transport. The next three fields support this fragmentation process.

■ **IP identification** A 16-bit field (values from 0 to 65,535), used to tie the fragments of a packet together. All fragments of an original packet will have this field replicated from the original packet to allow the fragments to be identified and reassembled into the original packet.

- **Flags**   A 3-bit field (values from 0 to 7) that contains three flags (most normal packets will have these 3 bits set to 000):
  - Reserved (should always be 0)
  - Do Not Fragment bit (D), which can have the following values:
    - **0**   Packet may be fragmented during transport
    - **1**   Packet is not to be fragmented (ICMP error message returned to the sending host if the packet reaches a router which needs to fragment the packet, but cannot due to this bit being set)
  - More Fragments bit (M), which can have the following values:
    - **0**   This is the last (or only) fragment
    - **1**   More fragments exist
- **Fragment offset**   A 13-bit field (values from 0 to 8,191) that when multiplied by 8 gives the offset into the reassembled packet of the current fragment. In an unfragmented packet, this field will be set to 0.
- **Time to live (TTL)**   An 8-bit field (values from 0 to 255) that specifies the lifetime of the packet in the Internet—each time a packet takes another hop through a router, this field is decremented by one. If the TTL value drops to zero, the packet is discarded, and an ICMP TTL exceeded message is sent back to the originating system. This field ensures that packets cannot persist on the Internet indefinitely in the event of a routing loop or other malfunction. Various operating systems have default settings for this field, but rarely is a value of more than 32 necessary in the current Internet.
- **Protocol**   An 8-bit field (values from 0 to 255) that identifies which protocol is being used by the message being transported in this packet. The data portion of the IP packet contains the protocol-dependent header, as well as the actual data being transported between the communicating systems. These are some common values:
  - **1**   ICMP
  - **6**   TCP
  - **17**   UDP
- **IP header checksum**   A 16-bit field (values from 0 to 65,535) that is a checksum of the IP header computed using ones-complement arithmetic. Each hop from one router to the next will cause this field to be recomputed as the header contents change, the most common change being that the TTL field will be decremented, although fragmentation, and some options, such as Record route, and Internet timestamp can also alter the header.

- **Source address**   A 32-bit field that contains the source IP address of the packet. The traditional dotted format (1.2.3.4) is a convenient designation for the four bytes that make up this 32-bit field.

- **Destination address**   A 32-bit field that is the destination IP address of the packet.

- **Options**   A 0- to 40-byte field. Multiple optional features are allowed in this field, some of which have security implications.

- **Padding**   A series of 8-bit bytes consisting of all 0's to pad the header up to the number of 32-bit words specified in the IHL field.

- ▲ **Data**   This field contains the data portion of the IP packet. Its length should be the difference between the Total length field and the IHL field (which, being a count of 32-bit words, must be multiplied by 4 to convert to bytes). Its contents are dependent on the protocol in use, but will typically consist of a protocol header and data bytes.

IP Fragmentation

It was understood by the developers of the IP protocol suite that a sending host might have little or no idea of the characteristics of the physical network through which traffic may be routed, and thus could not adjust packet sizes to fit the requirements of that network. Also, as traffic routing is an adaptive, dynamic process, a packet size appropriate for a known network may not be appropriate for an alternative routing pathway. If the preferred pathway goes down for any reason, routing protocols will attempt to develop alternative pathways, and they may not have the same Maximum Transmission Unit (MTU—the maximum packet size that the media will support).

These considerations drove the development of a packet fragmentation and reassembly process. The decision to fragment a packet is made by a router when the MTU of the next hop is smaller than the packet size. The packet can be flagged to disallow fragmentation, in which case an ICMP error message ("fragmentation needed, but Do Not Fragment bit set") is sent back to the originating host. Otherwise, the original packet will be split into two or more packets containing the fragments and the regenerated IP header with changes made to the appropriate fields and a recalculated checksum.

Fragmentation could take place several times, as one router may split a packet to match its MTU, then pass the fragments on to another router that may have an even smaller MTU, thus necessitating another fragmentation of the previously fragmented packet. Thus, the receiving host is the most reasonable place to reassemble the packet, although IDSs often perform reassembly as well, in order to examine packet contents.

Three fields in the IP header are used to support the fragmentation of packets:

- ▼ **IP identification**   This 16-bit field is the glue that binds the fragments together—every packet is stamped with this field, which on modern systems is generated via a pseudo-random process. For each IP packet thereafter, this number is generally incremented by 1. Each fragment of the original packet will contain

the same value in the IP ID field, and the receiving host will use this value to collect together all the fragments for reassembly. Note that since this field is only 16 bits long, the value must wrap around after 65,535 packets.

- **Fragmentation offset** This 13-bit field defines which portion of the original packet the current fragment references. As the maximum packet size in IP is 65,535 bytes, which is represented in 16 bits, it would seem that 16 bits would be required to identify a fragment offset, yet this field is only 13 bits long. The solution is to multiply the fragmentation offset field by 8 (2^3). This means that packets are only split on multiples of 8 bytes, which is certainly fine-grained enough.

- ▲ **Flags** This 3-bit field has three 1-bit flags: a reserved bit that should always be 0, a Do Not Fragment bit that indicates whether fragmentation is allowed for this packet, and a More Fragments bit that indicates whether further fragments are being sent or not.

For an unfragmented packet, the fragmentation offset will be set to 0, and the More Fragments bit will be cleared, indicating that the packet is complete.

The receiving system will collect the fragments, identified by the IP ID field, until the last fragment is received, which is signified by a 0 in the More Fragments bit. If there are no holes in the completed packet, the packet is ready for further processing. If a fragment was not received, there will be a hole in the buffer, and the system will have to wait until it is received. If a timeout occurs before IP has received every fragment, the received buffer will be discarded, and depending on the upper-level protocol, the entire packet may be retransmitted, with the possibility of fragmentation occurring again.

RFC 1122 recommends that the reassembly time be between 60 and 120 seconds, and that an ICMP time-exceeded error be sent to the source host if the timer expires and the first fragment of the datagram has been received. This ICMP message contains the first 64 bits of fragment 0 (or less if the fragment is less than 8 bytes long).

Fragmentation solves the problems of varying frame sizes between communicating hosts at a performance penalty, but, as we shall see in Chapter 3, security problems can result from fragments. Fragments have been used to evade firewalls and intrusion-detection systems. Wouldn't it be nice for systems to be able to determine the maximum size packets that could be transmitted on a link, and thus avoid the overhead of using fragmentation? There is, in fact, a process that determines the MTU between two hosts so that (unless the route changes) packets can be sent without resorting to fragmentation. It's called Path MTU discovery.

Path MTU Discovery

As was mentioned in the previous section, it would be desirable for systems to determine the maximum MTU they could use in communications to avoid the overhead of fragmentation. According to RFC 791, all devices talking to IP must support a minimum MTU of 68 bytes, so fragmentation can be avoided by transmitting IP packets of 68 bytes

which allows for an IP header of up to 60 bytes, and a fragment size of 8 bytes. Unfortunately, most useful packets will not fit into 68 bytes, so they may need to be fragmented anyway.

However, it is possible, by the use of some trickery, for a host to determine the maximum MTU that a link between two systems will support, as follows:

1. A host will assemble a maximum-size test packet (as defined by the interface MTU), set the Do Not Fragment bit, and send it on the wire to the destination.

2. If the packet reaches a router that would need to fragment the packet to forward it, but cannot, due to the Do Not Fragment bit, the router will send back an ICMP "fragmentation needed, but Do Not Fragment bit set" error message.

3. When the sending host receives the ICMP message, it will know that one of the links between the two hosts requires a smaller MTU, and thus can send a smaller test packet in the same manner. The appropriate size can be determined mathematically by dividing the packet size in half, or by successively trying popular default packet sizes for various media (4,352 for FDDI, 1,500 for Ethernet, 576 for X.25 and ISDN, and so on), until a suitable frame size is discovered that can accommodate the full end-to-end link without fragmentation.

4. If, on the other hand, no ICMP message is received after a suitable time delay, the sending host assumes that traffic can be sent to the target without danger of fragmentation.

Of course, this mechanism is not completely reliable. ICMP traffic is dependent on the best-effort delivery resources of IP. Although packet corruption is minimized by the use of a checksum, the message could be sent but dropped somewhere in the network, and the sending host would assume that the Path MTU is larger than it really is. Also, since routing is dynamic, the path could change, and the MTU might increase or decrease as a result. Some sites, for example, may have an emergency low-performance link to the Internet, for use when the main link fails. If this emergency link uses a different type of medium than the normal link, it likely will also have a different MTU. If the MTU is lower, traffic using the link will likely be fragmented, exacerbating the performance problems. Thus, it is important that ICMP traffic not be discarded at a network perimeter to allow these sorts of network issues to be signaled to hosts or internal routers for action.

More information on the process of Path MTU discovery can be found in RFC 1191 (www.faqs.org/rfcs/rfc1191.html).

TRANSMISSION CONTROL PROTOCOL (TCP)

TCP, the Transmission Control Protocol, can rightly lay claim to being the crown jewel of the IP protocol suite—it is by far the most widely used protocol, as well as the one that is responsible for carrying the majority of the Internet's useful content. TCP adds to the best-effort delivery capabilities of IP.

TCP Reliable Delivery

TCP, being embedded within an IP packet, paradoxically must employ the unreliable delivery mechanisms of IP to ensure reliability. Of course, perfect reliability is not possible in the real world, due to hardware, routing, and software failures, but TCP nevertheless achieves a high degree of reliability by employing three distinct, cooperating processes:

▼   **TCP checksum**   The TCP checksum is computed over the entire TCP packet, including the data portion. If the computed checksum does not match the packet contents, the receiving host discards the packet. In that case, the packet timeout mechanism (described below) eventually causes the sending host to retransmit the packet.

■   **Mutual acknowledgment of received data**   Each system maintains a count of bytes received properly from the other host (known as the acknowledgment or ACK number), as well as the number of bytes sent to the other host (known as the sequence or SYN number). Both systems thus know the expected amount of traffic that the other host should have seen. If a host fails to acknowledge data sent to it (by failing to increment the ACK number properly), the other host will resend that traffic again upon receipt of the next ACK number that is greater than the expected value (that is, if there is a gap in the sequence of numbers). Thus, each host acknowledges the traffic that the other host has sent, and each host is aware of the traffic that the other side has received.

▲   **Packet timeout**   As IP's non-guaranteed delivery may silently drop a packet, TCP will wait for an expected response to the sent packet for a given period of time, and then will retransmit the packet, on the assumption that either the packet or its response was lost. If a host receives a packet that it has already received and responded to, it will assume that the response was lost in transit and will retransmit its initial response.

Retransmissions may occur multiple times with varying timeouts before TCP decides that the IP layer is hopelessly broken—at that point, it will signal an error to the application.

TCP Communications Model

Each TCP connection is uniquely identified by four distinct items (a *four-tuple*): the IP addresses of the two communicating systems and the TCP ports used by each system. This does not mean that two systems cannot communicate using the same service on more than one connection—multiuser systems support multiple telnet connections from the same client. In such a case, the IP addresses will be the same, and the telnet service will be found on the standard TCP port 23. However, the client system will use a different port for each connection, thus keeping the traffic for each connection distinct.

Under normal conditions, a listening process must be running on the receiving host to accept and respond to TCP connection requests. If a TCP packet is received that is destined for a port with no listeners, a TCP RST packet will be sent back to the source by the receiving host.

TCP uses 16-bit port numbers, which means that there are 65,536 possible ports. These ports are normally divided into two distinct ranges: 0 through 1,023 represent the well-known services that are (on Unix systems) only accessible by the *root* account. Ports 1,024 through 65,535 are termed *ephemeral* ports, which user programs can access and use to provide services or use as client ports for establishing connections.

To reliably maintain a connection between two systems requires a well-defined process for session establishment, maintenance, and teardown. This process is described in the following summary of steps, and it is illustrated in Figure 2-4:

1. The receiving host socket is in a passive, listening state, awaiting an incoming connection request from the initiator.

2. The initiating system sends an initial TCP packet with the SYN flag set, and an initial sequence number (ISN) chosen pseudo-randomly. Each byte transmitted, as well as a few flags (SYN or FIN), will increment this sequence number. In effect, the initiator is signaling that it will start numbering the bytes transferred over the connection starting from the ISN. The SYN flag itself consumes the first sequence number.

3. The receiver will respond with a SYN/ACK packet, indicating its readiness to establish a connection, and acknowledging the initiator's SYN. In the response, the receiver puts the initiator's ISN+1 in the Acknowledgment field and sets up its own ISN in the SYN field.

4. The three-way handshake is then completed when the initiating system sends an ACK packet back to the responding system. The purpose of this packet is to let the responding system know that the connection is fully established.

5. At this point, the session is established. When either party wishes to send data to the other, it will send a packet with the ACK flag set, with an acknowledgment of the last sequence number (in the Acknowledgment field) received from the remote host, and with its own sequence number incremented to reflect the amount of data being transmitted. The actual data to be sent is included in the TCP data portion of the packet. If there is no data to be sent, and the host is merely acknowledging the data received from the other party, a packet with no TCP data portion is sent.

6. When a system is finished with the communication, it will send a FIN/ACK packet, signaling that it wishes to close the connection. However, a connection cannot be closed by only one side. Rather, by closing the connection, the system is indicating that it has no more data to send. The host receiving the initial FIN sends an ACK acknowledging the FIN, and if that system doesn't have any more data to send either, it sends a FIN as well. When the system that first closed the connection responds with an ACK of its own, the connection will be considered closed. Either party can also abort the connection by sending a RST/ACK packet, which will cause the connection to be immediately closed.

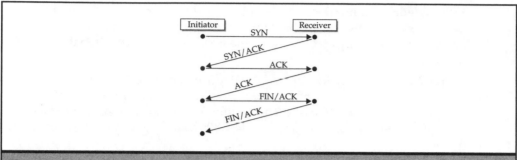

Figure 2-4.   Creating and tearing down a TCP connection

The TCP Header

The standard TCP header is defined in RFC 791 and illustrated in Figure 2-5. It consists of a minimum of 20 bytes and a maximum of 60 bytes. The application-specific information, which is delivered to the application program, is located in the data portion of the TCP packet.

The TCP header consists of the following fields:

▼   **Source port**   A 16-bit field (values from 0 to 65,535) that identifies the source port of the connection.

■   **Destination port**   A 16-bit field (values from 0 to 65,535) that identifies the destination port of the connection.

■   **Sequence number**   A 32-bit field (values from 0 to $2^{32}-1$) that identifies the current byte count (as of the end of this packet) relative to the initial sequence number (ISN), which is set in the initial SYN packet. Each byte transmitted, as well as the SYN and FIN flags, increment this value.

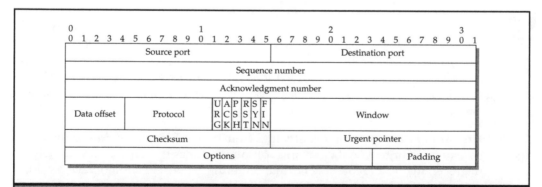

Figure 2-5.   TCP header

- **Acknowledgment number** A 32-bit field (values from 0 to 2^{32}–1) that holds the last sequence number of this communication transmitted by the other party and received correctly by the host. In the first packet sent (the initial SYN), this field is undefined.

- **Data offset** A 4-bit field (values from 0 to 15) that indicates the number of 32-bit words in the header portion of the packet. The maximum size of a TCP header is thus $15 \times 4 = 60$ bytes. The minimum size of a TCP header (a header without optional arguments) is 5 words, or 20 bytes. Values of 0 through 4 are invalid.

- **Reserved** A 6-bit field reserved for future expansion—it should always be 0.

- **Flags** A 6-bit field that contains the following six 1-bit flags:

  - **URG** Urgent

  - **ACK** Acknowledgment

  - **PSH** Push

  - **RST** Reset connection

  - **SYN** Synchronize connection

  - **FIN** Finish

- **Window** A 16-bit field (values from 0 to 65,535) that indicates the amount of receive buffer space available. This field has important performance implications, as it tells the remote system how much traffic the local host can accept, and thus how many packets the remote host can send before expecting an acknowledgment. The TCP Window Scale option modifies the behavior of this field.

- **Checksum** A 16-bit field (values from 0 to 65,535). This value is computed using ones-complement arithmetic over a pseudo-header, the TCP header, and the TCP data. The receiving system recomputes this value and drops the packet if the checksum is invalid—in this case, the TCP timeout mechanism will cause the packet to be retransmitted by the sender.

NOTE The pseudo-header used to compute UDP and TCP checksums includes the source and destination IP addresses, as well as the protocol specific header. At the packet's final destination, the checksum is recomputed using the source and destination addresses obtained from the header of the IP packet which transported the protocol-specific packet. If the checksums agree, then we can have a high degree of confidence that the packet reached the intended destination host, as well as the correct protocol-specific port.

- **Urgent pointer** A 16-bit field (values from 0 to 65,535) that points to the last byte of any "urgent" data that an application wishes to transfer immediately to the receiving host, bypassing normal buffering. This field should have a value of 0 unless the Urgent flag is set.

- ■ **Options**   This field can be used for various option capabilities that tune the behavior of the TCP communications. These are padded as necessary to bring the TCP header length to an even multiple of 32 bits.

- ▲ **Data**   The application data is placed here. The length of this field should match the total packet size identified in the IP header, minus the Internet header length, minus the TCP data offset (all scaled as appropriate to reflect bytes).

USER DATAGRAM PROTOCOL (UDP)

UDP, the User Datagram Protocol, is often used by applications that prefer to avoid the overhead of establishing a TCP connection (such as DNS, NFS, TFTP), or those that can tolerate occasional errors in the interest of efficiency (such as streaming audio or video). UDP is given the Internet protocol number of 17 and is defined in RFC 768 (www.faqs.org/rfcs/rfc768.html).

The UDP model is much simpler than that of TCP. There is no session-level error checking or retransmission built into the protocol. The packets do, however, contain a checksum. A receiving host can verify this checksum to ensure that the packet has not been corrupted during transit. The sending host, however, does not receive a protocol-level acknowledgment that the packet was delivered. If any such reliability is needed, it is left to be implemented at the application level.

An example of an application-level, reliable protocol built on UDP is the Trivial File Transfer Protocol, or TFTP (see RFC 1350, www.faqs.org/rfcs/rfc1350.html), which consists of server and client implementations. These two processes exchange crafted UDP packets that contain handshaking information along with the data being transferred. The application programs must handle this handshaking themselves, as well as extracting the data. Contrast this with TCP data transfers, where the application receives only the data bytes and needn't concern itself with the details of the data transfer.

UDP uses 16-bit port numbers, as does TCP, but UDP and TCP ports are distinctly different. As with TCP, there generally needs to be a listening process at the receiving host to accept and respond to the request. Under normal circumstances, the arrival of a UDP packet destined for a port with no listeners will cause the receiving host to respond with an ICMP "port unreachable" message.

UDP Header

The UDP header (shown in Figure 2-6) consists of four 16-bit fields, totaling 8 bytes in length. These fields follow immediately after the IP header:

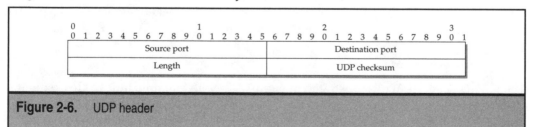

Figure 2-6.   UDP header

▼ **Source port**   A 16-bit field (values from 0 to 65,535).

■ **Destination port**   A 16-bit field (values from 0 to 65,535).

■ **Length**   A 16-bit field (values from 0 to 65,535). This field is the length of the UDP header and data bytes, and it does not include the IP header. Typically, the UDP packet length should be the difference between the IP total length field and the IP header length. If there is a discrepancy, most implementations will discard the packet as invalid.

▲ **UDP checksum**   A 16-bit field (values from 0 to 65,535). This value is computed using ones-complement math over a pseudo-header, the UDP header, and the UDP data. The checksum is actually optional in UDP, and if this field is set to 0, the checksum will not be examined by the receiving host. This field was originally put in place as a performance-enhancing measure, but currently all packets should have a checksum. Those that do not may bear further examination for possible intrusion attempts.

INTERNET CONTROL MESSAGE PROTOCOL (ICMP)

ICMP, the Internet Control Message Protocol, is the signaling mechanism used in IP networks to communicate error conditions and other control information about network conditions. As IP is a best-effort delivery protocol, failure to deliver a packet to its destination is not considered a network-level error. Protocols or applications need additional mechanisms to ensure reliability. For instance, as was mentioned earlier, TCP employs an acknowledgment protocol, along with retransmission of lost packets after a suitable time.

ICMP is given the protocol identifier of 1 in the standard IP packet, and it is documented in RFC 792 (www.faqs.org/rfcs/rfc792.html). All conforming implementations of IP must include ICMP, as it is integral to signaling error conditions on the network.

ICMP messages are of interest both to end-hosts and intermediate routers, although some messages are generally only sent by routers. It is never permissible for an ICMP error message to be generated as the result of receiving an ICMP error message—this avoids the infinite recursion of ICMP message generation (see RFC 1122, www.faqs.org/rfcs/rfc1122.html). It is also forbidden to send an ICMP message as the result of a datagram that references multiple hosts, such as a broadcast or multicast message, or upon receipt of a noninitial fragment (see the "IP Fragmentation" section earlier in the chapter). These restrictions are designed to prevent broadcast storms.

Broadly, there are two classes of ICMP messages: ICMP error messages and ICMP query/response messages. Each ICMP error message will be constructed from the Internet header, and (at least) the first eight bytes of the IP packet payload (which generally is data from the header of the lower-level protocol, such as TCP or UDP).

ICMP Packet Format

The ICMP packet format is illustrated in Figure 2-7. Note that it includes a checksum for reliability.

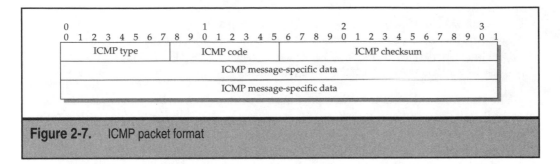

Figure 2-7. ICMP packet format

These are the fields in the ICMP packet:

▼ **ICMP type**   An 8-bit field (values from 0 to 255) that encodes the type of ICMP message being sent. These are some common values:

- **3** Destination unreachable
- **5** Redirect
- **4** Source quench
- **11** Time exceeded

■ **ICMP code**   An 8-bit field that encodes a subcategory of the type.

■ **ICMP checksum**   A 16-bit field.

▲ **ICMP message-specific data**   A variable length field. All ICMP error messages will store the Internet header and at least the first eight bytes of the Internet data (which typically will be the protocol header). This information allows the receiving system to identify the hosts and port numbers that the error message refers to.

ADDRESS RESOLUTION PROTOCOL (ARP)

IP addresses of 32 bits (or the upcoming 128-bit IPv6 standard) are *logical* addresses only. This means that the network adapter itself has no preconceived notion of what its IP address is, but rather is assigned an address by a hardware mechanism. This is an important distinction, since it would be difficult to replace a failed network adapter, or to change the IP address of an existing adapter, unless the hardware address were decoupled from the logical address.

Ethernet hardware addresses (called MAC addresses), by way of example, are 48 bits in length and are theoretically unique throughout the world. Vendors are assigned generous blocks of addresses out of this space so that each individual network adapter will have a unique address. To send a packet to another Ethernet card requires that the sender know the MAC address of the target system. At the IP level, though, the only information that the sender has is the IP address, which is not, as was mentioned, tied to a specific Ethernet card. Thus, a mechanism is needed to provide a mapping from the IP address to the hardware address of the card. ARP provides such a mechanism.

NOTE Although MAC addresses are supposed to be unique, in practice, some off-brand vendors have been known to use address space not allocated to them, or to randomly address cards. In the unlikely event that two network cards on the same subnet are utilizing the same MAC address, neither system will likely be able to successfully communicate with others.

When a system wishes to send a packet to a system whose hardware address is unknown, it will send out a network broadcast message that, in effect, asks, "Who, on this network, has this IP address?" The system that is using that IP address will respond with a message saying, "I have this address, and here's my hardware address." In order to increase the efficiency of the network, each system keeps a table of recently used hardware and IP addresses in memory, called the *ARP cache*. Typically, these recent addresses will expire after 20 minutes, in which case another ARP request will be made upon the next access to the system.

Diskless workstations suffer from an opposite problem—they know their hardware address but do not know their IP address. Reverse Address Resolution Protocol (RARP) is used to broadcast the request, and a RARP server will send a message back indicating the host's IP address. However, RARP has been mostly superceded by more advanced protocols, such as the Bootstrap Protocol (BOOTP) and Dynamic Host Configuration Protocol (DHCP).

ARP Packet Format

ARP was designed with the flexibility to handle different media with varying hardware address lengths, so length fields are included to allow differing field sizes. Figure 2-8 illustrates the ARP packet format.

The ARP packet contains the following fields:

▼ **Hardware type** A 16-bit field (values from 0 to 65,535) that encodes the type of hardware involved. The code for Ethernet is 1.

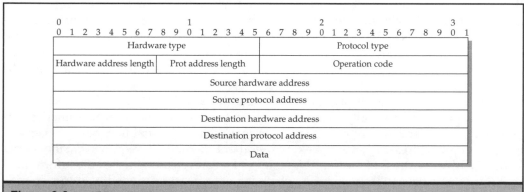

Figure 2-8. ARP packet format

- ■ **Protocol type**   A 16-bit field (values from 0 to 65,535) that encodes the type of addressing scheme being used. The value for IP addressing is 0x0800 (in hexadecimal).

- ■ **Hardware address length**   An 8-bit field (values from 0 to 255) that specifies the size in bytes of the hardware address. For Ethernet, this value will be 6.

- ■ **Protocol address length**   An 8-bit field (values from 0 to 255) that specifies the size in bytes of the protocol addressing being used. For IPv4, this value will be 4.

- ■ **Operation code**   A 16-bit field (values from 0 to 65,535) indicating the type of operation to be performed. These are some common values:

    - ■ 1   ARP request
    - ■ 2   ARP reply
    - ■ 3   RARP request
    - ■ 4   RARP reply

- ■ **Source hardware address**   A variable length field (the length depends on the value in the hardware address length field).

- ■ **Source protocol address**   A variable length field (the length depends on the value in the protocol address length field).

- ■ **Destination hardware address**   A variable length field (the length depends on the value in the hardware address length field).

- ■ **Destination protocol address**   A variable length field (the length depends on the value in the protocol address length field).

- ▲ **Data**   Any additional data that the protocol requires.

When an ARP or RARP packet is sent requesting information, the unknown fields are set to 0 by the sender and are filled in by the responding host.

Routing

Except when two communicating systems are part of the same subnet, they will not have any direct way to communicate with each other. Rather, they must forward their traffic through a router, which will forward the traffic on their behalf. The router, in turn, if not on the same subnet as the ultimate destination, will forward the traffic to another router, until the ultimate destination is reached. Each hop a packet takes results in the packet being subtly changed before it is forwarded:

- ▼ The TTL (time to live) field in the IP header is decremented by one. If this results in the value becoming 0, the router will send an ICMP error packet ("TTL exceeded") back to the sender of the packet, and the packet itself is dropped. There may also be some other header changes as a result of some IP options (record route, timestamp, or others).

■ If the packet is fragmented in order to traverse the next hop, multiple packets will be generated by the router.

▲ The IP checksum is recomputed to account for the header changes. The ones-complement arithmetic that is used allows for this to be done in a single step, rather than by rechecksumming the entire header.

Eventually, through this forwarding process, a packet will reach a router that has knowledge of the ultimate destination, and that will forward the packet to its destination. Of course, it is also possible that the destination system doesn't exist, in which case the packet will be dropped and an ICMP "destination unreachable" error packet will be sent back to the originator.

A Practical Example of Routing

Let's examine, in a little more detail, what happens to a packet as it traverses from host A to host B through a few routers. Suppose an application program on host A wants to initiate a TCP communication to an application on host B. We will assume that host A already knows the IP address of host B. (If this is not the case, the sequence of events described in the section on DNS applies.) The following are the steps that will be taken:

1. Host A constructs a TCP header using the operating system defaults (such as TTL) with the SYN flag set, checksums calculated, and includes the rest of the packet.

2. Prior to the packet actually being sent down the wire, the operating system on host A consults its routing table to determine what host is the next destination for the packet. Unless the two hosts are directly connected, this will be an intermediate router that can forward the packet to its next destination. Most systems have a default route to their local router, but many more complicated routing tables can be constructed.

3. The IP software on host A consults its ARP cache, which contains mappings between the high-level IP addresses and the low-level hardware addresses. If the hardware address of the next hop is unknown, an ARP request is made to determine this information.

4. The packet is encapsulated in the low-level framing appropriate for the physical medium (including low-level hardware addressing for the next hop), and it is sent on the wire.

5. Router 1 sees a packet addressed to its hardware address, picks it up, and checks the header for consistency. Packets with incorrect checksums are silently dropped, and the responsibility lies with the originating system (host A) to resend the packet if no response has been received after a suitable timeout.

6. Router 1 decrements the TTL, and if the TTL has reached 0, an ICMP error message is sent back to the originating host (host A) signaling this fact. Because

of the TTL change and other obscure options that can affect the packet contents, the checksum is recomputed.

7. Router 1 must make a decision about what to do with the packet by consulting its rule set—it may decide to drop the packet (with or without notification to the originating host), modify it, or forward it. If the packet is addressed to router 1 itself, it will be sent to the operating system of the router for processing.

8. If the packet is to be forwarded, router 1 will also decide whether the packet needs to be fragmented by comparing the size of the packet with the MTU that the next hop requires.

9. Router 1 consults its ARP cache, and issues an ARP request if the address of the next hop is unknown. In general, this will only need to be done for the first packet that is transmitted along a particular route, and periodically afterwards to ensure that the cache doesn't become stale.

10. Since the packet is to be sent on to host B, router 1 encapsulates the packet in the low-level framing appropriate for the physical medium (including the low-level hardware addressing for the next hop), and it is sent on the wire to router 2.

11. Router 2 will follow a sequence of events similar to those router 1 followed, and (if all goes well) will end up forwarding the packet to host B.

12. Host B receives the packet and examines the IP checksum and TTL. If those are okay, and if host-level firewalling is enabled, the packet will typically be examined by the firewall software and either be accepted or rejected, although some processing may occur later.

13. Assuming the packet has been allowed access to the TCP layer of host B, the TCP layer will ensure that the TCP checksum is valid.

14. Host B will then examine its table of connections, referenced by the *four-tuple* of source host, source port, destination host, and destination port, to see if this packet refers to an established connection.

15. In this example, host B sees that there is no established connection and will then check whether there is a listening socket on the destination port. If there is no such socket, a TCP RST packet will be constructed and sent back to the originating host, as an indication that the port on the destination is closed. Or, if the packet does not contain a SYN, a TCP RST will be initiated by host B, because a SYN packet must be the first packet of a connection.

16. If the packet passes these tests, a connection record will be established, options will be extracted (such as initial sequence number, desired window size, and so on), host B's options will be included, and a SYN/ACK packet will be created for transmission back to host A.

17. Host B will then send the SYN/ACK packet to host A using the same steps of events that host A used to send the original packet.

From this simple (!) example of transferring one packet between two hosts, it can be seen that Internet communication is a complex process that requires all cooperating hosts to adhere to defined standards. As Chapter 3 will show, though, there is enough wiggle-room in some of these areas for malicious activities to take place.

DOMAIN NAME SYSTEM (DNS)

DNS, the Domain Name System, is a worldwide distributed database whose most important function is to translate from the human-readable system names that we are all familiar with (such as www.osborne.com), into the simpler (but more rigid) 32-bit IP addresses. One benefit this database provides is that it is easy for web sites to migrate to different hosting companies, because only the DNS records need to be changed to reflect the changed IP address—all references to the host name will follow. As we shall see in later chapters, however, if the DNS records are modified or forged, an attacker can redirect traffic to an entirely different host than the expected legitimate host.

DNS was designed in 1984 to solve an escalating problem with the host-name-to-IP-address mapping system. Previously, all hosts needed to maintain a table (a file called *hosts*) with periodic updates. As the Internet grew, this host table became unwieldy and unmaintainable. DNS solves this problem by delegating the name service information to the owners of the domain, who maintain a table only of their own systems or subdomains.

DNS uses the concept of *domain name space*, which can be represented as an inverted tree, as shown in Figure 2-9. Each node on the tree represents a domain, and everything below a node is part of that domain, until the final leaf node is reached, which represents an individually named system. For example, in Figure 2-9 the system *gene* is part of the *bar* domain, which in turn is part of the *.com* domain, which along with the other "top-level" domains, are all subdomains of the Internet *root* domain.

To resolve a name to its IP address, a host will examine its host table (which still exists in most systems in a legacy form), and if the name is not found, the host will forward the request to its name server. (The order of this search is configurable on some systems). The name server, if it has recent knowledge of the name in question (all DNS records time out to ensure that the data isn't stale) will immediately respond with the IP address. If the name server is unfamiliar with the domain name, it will ask a server higher up the tree,

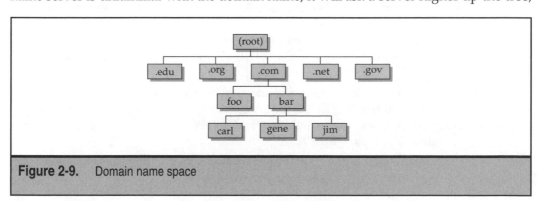

Figure 2-9.   Domain name space

which in turn will continue going up the tree until an answer is received. Under some circumstances, name resolution can take many seconds, thus appearing to the user as if the system has frozen. The recursive nature of the queries is one reason for these potential delays. Also, since DNS typically communicates over UDP (on port 53), it is possible that the packets could be lost, so multiple attempts are often made to resolve a name.

SUMMARY

We've explored the protocols and processes that drive the modern Internet: IP, the transport mechanism to deliver the traffic; TCP for the establishment of virtual circuits for two-way communication; UDP for lighter weight transport of data, without the overhead of creating a connection; and ICMP for transporting error or status conditions between hosts. We've also seen some of the infrastructure mechanisms, and examined how all of these mechanisms tie together to provide reliable delivery of data throughout the Internet. We've also discussed the complexity of the network infrastructure. It is a monument to the designers of the Internet that it functions so well. Complex systems, however, are often subject to damage or abuse by malicious parties.

In Chapters 3, 4, and 5, we will build on the foundations presented here, and delve into low-level network abuses, as well as specific application protocol abuses. We will also examine common programming errors that allow for attacks targeting network-aware programs. Get ready! The fun's just beginning…

CHAPTER 3

Unauthorized Activity I

In Chapter 2 we looked at the normal processes that occur in network communication. In this chapter, we will examine abnormal network traffic patterns and the problems that they can create or mask.

Some of the problems are intrinsic to the design of the Internet, which was not developed with security as a primary goal. The original Internet design was based on cooperating, friendly hosts communicating over secure lines. The main concern was robustness of traffic delivery in the face of outages, and routing protocols were developed to automatically reroute traffic when outages occurred.

Other network-level communication security problems occur in so-called "dark corners" of the specifications. Although much effort was devoted to specifying standard behavior for participating hosts, there is enough wiggle-room in some areas to allow for differing interpretations of the standards.

Also, not to be forgotten is the bug-prone nature of complex systems, of which the TCP/IP stack is a prime example. Some systems may crash or exhibit other anomalous behavior when confronted with illegal input. The Nmap tool has been developed for mapping operating systems, based on network stack behavior under these odd conditions, which can often distinguish between operating system patch levels, as bugs are corrected, and new or different behavior is noted.

Generally, there are two classes of network attacks of interest to an IDS. First, there are the network-level attacks, corresponding to the session layer and below on the OSI reference model, which attempt to subvert, disrupt, or gather information on the transport of data from source to destination. Some of these attacks are examined in this chapter.

The other main division of network attacks, corresponding to the presentation layer and above, are the application-level attacks, in which the transport mechanism is not subverted, but instead is used to transfer attack data to and from the target host. Again, the goal is to subvert, disrupt, or gather information on targeted systems. Some of these attacks will be discussed in Chapter 4.

GENERAL IDS LIMITATIONS

Some important applications straddle the line between the network level and the application level. These notably include IDS applications and firewalls, which are applications that must be intimately familiar with the lower-level workings of network protocols. As these applications exist to protect important computer assets (and, in fact, are important assets themselves), some attacks specifically target, disable, or evade these mechanisms. As a consequence, users of these applications expect them to be robust, as they need to be able to handle the onslaught of malicious traffic.

One type of attack that firewalls and IDS systems can be prone to is an attack based on resource exhaustion. Every system has memory, CPU, or bandwidth limitations, and by causing one of these limited resources to be completely expended, the operation of the system will be degraded, and it may possibly fail. This problem is not confined to these perimeter defense mechanisms, but because they are so critical, failures in these systems have a much more devastating effect on security than normal attacks.

In order to track connections, firewalls and IDS applications generally need to establish a connection record for each active connection as it is established. If excessive connection requests are made, one of the critical resources (memory, CPU, or bandwidth) may be entirely consumed. Hackers use the SYN flood technique to create this type of denial-of-service (DoS) attack.

In a perfect world, IDS and firewall applications would function without fail, within the limitations of their hardware. In practice, bugs have been discovered, and hackers have exploited them. One popular IDS had a vulnerability concerning fragmented packets that could result in an attacker gaining root access to the IDS box. Another less well-known IDS had a vulnerability in its memory allocation functions, such that specially crafted packets could cause it to crash by consuming excessive CPU cycles.

Many IDS systems make marketing claims in their sales literature about the maximum bandwidth that they can handle. As is common in the computer industry, such marketing claims need to be taken with a grain of salt—they typically describe ideal situations and generally do not reflect real-world usage. Currently there are no IDS systems that can keep up with a full gigabit connections, so flooding a network connection with traffic is another technique that can cause an IDS or firewall to fail, or to miss certain attacks.

NETWORK PROTOCOL ABUSES

This chapter focuses on abuses of the protocols that drive the Internet, from the bottom of the OSI model up to the session layer. (The presentation and application layers are covered in Chapter 4.) Because the higher layers depend on those below them, it is easy to imagine that a subversion of lower-level protocols will have a profound impact on the higher levels. Fortunately, though, most of these subversions cause a denial of service, meaning that some or all of the services depending on these lower levels will fail or will show degraded performance.

There are, however, classes of attacks that attempt to *spoof*, or fake, legitimate traffic. Under some circumstances, systems may believe that the traffic is indeed legitimate, and they may respond in a trusting manner to traffic that is, in fact, generated by a malicious party. We will look at attacks and abuses as they affect the various networking protocols: ARP, IP, UDP, TCP, and ICMP.

ARP Abuses

As was discussed in Chapter 2, ARP (Address Resolution Protocol) is used by hosts to determine the hardware address corresponding to a desired IP address so that systems can communicate. There is no authentication of either the request or the response, so it is fortunate that ARP requests are confined to the local subnet. However, if a system is compromised by an intruder, they may wreak havoc on that subnet with a variety of abuses, such as ARP flooding, MAC spoofing, and ARP spoofing.

ARP Flooding

Before we discuss why flooding a network with spoofed ARP packets has security implications, we should discuss the differences between *switched* and *unswitched* networks.

Unswitched networks, built on Ethernet hub technology, transmit all traffic to all ports on the hub. The hub itself is a relatively unsophisticated device that merely regenerates the traffic to all ports and resolves packet collisions. ARP packets go to all hosts connected to the hub.

A *switched network*, by contrast, uses an Ethernet switch, which attempts to deliver traffic to only those ports where the communicating hosts reside. The advantage of this, of course, is the decreased network traffic that hosts must deal with, because they only see the traffic addressed to systems on that switch port. The hosts do not see traffic destined for hosts on different switch ports. For practically all applications, this is an unalloyed win. The only applications that could possibly suffer under this system would be those that expect or desire to see all of the traffic traversing the switch.

The method that a switch uses to determine the routing of traffic is entirely passive—it maintains a cache of ARP responses that it has seen traversing the network, and it routes traffic addressed to a specific hardware address to the port that it saw the ARP response come from. When a switch is confronted with a packet addressed to a hardware address that it hasn't cached, it must temporarily revert to "hub" mode and send that packet to all ports on the switch. The port that responds is recorded in the ARP cache.

As with other real-world device, there are limitations on the number of entries that a switch can keep in its ARP cache. If the cache is full, and a packet referencing a previously unknown hardware address is seen, a switch has several possible strategies to continue functioning, albeit at a degraded performance level:

▼ The switch could simply revert to hub mode for those hardware addresses that aren't in its cache. Performance will suffer, but traffic will continue to be delivered.

▲ The switch can simply decide to flush its buffer and repopulate from new data received. Under this scenario, packets will be delivered in hub mode until the switch relearns the port locations of the hosts.

Under either of these scenarios, traffic destined to specific ports will "leak" and be seen by other ports. This traffic is of potential interest to attackers, who may run the type of application that benefits from this leakage—one that "sniffs" the wire for traffic destined for other hosts. A sniffer application will silently listen to all (or selected) packets on the wire and record them for later perusal by the hacker. Passwords, confidential information, or other sensitive data may be recorded. Clearly, this is a major problem, as a stealthy hacker could remain on a system and quietly record this information for an extensive period without detection.

All of this means that on a switched network a hacker can possibly gain access to more network traffic than you might expect by creating a flood of spoofed ARP reply packets, overflowing the switch's ARP cache, and thus forcing it into hub mode.

MAC Spoofing

Traffic can be disrupted on a network if two Ethernet adapters have exactly the same hardware (or MAC – Media Access Control) addresses. If all adapters are from major, recognized vendors, this problem is unlikely to occur, as each vendor is assigned a block of

addresses from which they assign a unique address to each card manufactured. However, bargain basement or offshore manufacturers have been known to hijack addresses from other manufacturer's address ranges. In practice, even this is unlikely to cause a conflict, as there are 2^{48} (over 280 trillion) separate hardware addresses available, and all that is required is that the hardware addresses of systems on the local subnet be unique.

Most people are surprised to discover that practically every Ethernet adapter can be reprogrammed to have any desired hardware address. Although this reprogramming is rarely done, except in cases where a software license is tied to the hardware address, hackers can reprogram the Ethernet adapter on a system to spoof that of another system on the network (hence the term MAC spoofing), which typically will result in neither system being able to communicate. If the hacker chooses the same hardware address as the local router, all communication outside the subnet will be disrupted.

ARP Spoofing

Along the same vein as MAC spoofing, ARP response packets can be spoofed to redirect traffic or disrupt it. Imagine that system A wants to communicate with system B, so it sends out an ARP request asking, in effect "Whoever has B's IP address, please send your hardware address." A hacker on system C who sees this request could spoof an ARP response packet saying "I'm B—here's my hardware address," but inserting C's hardware address instead. Of course, unless system B is prevented from responding, it is likely to respond as well. Which system A actually ends up communicating with depends on the timing of the responses seen by A.

Clever hackers can combine this ARP spoofing with a denial-of-service attack on system B to prevent it from responding, possibly using a SYN flood, or source-quench flood (both of which are discussed later in this chapter). By combining several network attacks in this manner, the hacker on system C may convince system A that system C is really system B, and may therefore be able to subvert system A. A hacker could also forward the (now snooped) traffic to system B, so that A and B are less likely to notice anything wrong. There are a number of tools that help in this sort of attack—one of the best is the dsniff arpspoof tool by Dug Song.

IP Abuses

IP is the unreliable transport protocol used to carry all the upper-level protocols on the Internet. IP provides the transport and delivery of datagrams but does not provide mechanisms to verify that datagrams from a host are actually from that host. In actuality, this is an almost impossible problem to solve, as nearly every host has the capability of acting as a router, and thus could be legitimately forwarding traffic on behalf of another system. This model, therefore, allows for the possibility of faking (or spoofing) the source or destination of packets.

IP Address Spoofing

In a perfect world, all ISPs would perform ingress and egress filtering to ensure that packets entering or exiting their network actually are addressed to hosts in their address

Ingress and Egress Filtering

There are some IP addresses which should not, under normal circumstances, be seen crossing the perimeter to or from the Internet. The term *ingress* filtering refers to the process of filtering out obviously bogus addresses entering into a network, while *egress* filtering refers to outbound traffic. A simple example would be that an enterprise with public IP space on the internet should reject all traffic claiming to be from their address space, but coming from the external Internet. Similarly, the same enterprise should filter all outbound traffic, and only allow traffic with source addresses in their IP space to exit the perimeter. Generally, the RFC 1918 addresses are also filtered in- and out-bound.

space. Unfortunately, improper configuration, among other factors, is responsible for the problem of IP address spoofing. Border routers are often not configured to reject traffic to or from the networks behind the router.

For instance, suppose your business uses an address range of 172.16.0.0 to 172.16.255.255 (the IP addresses involved would not be assigned to an actual business, as they are private addresses reserved for use in an intranet—see RFC 1918 for more information, www.faqs.org/rfcs/rfc1918.html). Accordingly, the border router should not allow inbound traffic addressed to anything but the 172.16.0.0/16 subnet. Outbound traffic should be rejected (and possibly investigated) if the source address is not from the 172.16.0.0/16 subnet.

One would think that ISPs and Internet backbone providers would perform this filtering on traffic traversing their networks. Typically, however, large ISPs cannot efficiently perform such traffic filtering, due to the continually changing nature of the address ranges that they service. The problem is even more intractable when packets enter the Internet backbone, since at that point the true source of the traffic is no longer known, and it thus must be assumed to be legitimate.

One set of addresses that should never be seen at a border are the private address spaces (as defined in RFC 1918), which are reserved for internal use by independent networks (such as the addresses in the previous example). These addresses are never routed on the Internet. Surprisingly, even these addresses are sometimes seen at network perimeters connected directly to the Internet. This is due to the fact that, for performance reasons, packets on the Internet backbone are often not filtered. However, it is an excellent idea to filter all the RFC 1918 address ranges at border routers, since they have no business coming in from the Internet at large.

The intent is that as a consequence of the lack of filtering on the internet at large, an inbound packet generally cannot (by itself) be proven to be from the host that it purports to be from. When two way communication is actually established, though, the confidence level that the host is who it purports to be goes up, but is not completely assured, as the possibility exists that an intermediate hop has been compromised, and is thus spoofing the traffic.

Because of this lack of filtering, a host has little assurance that a packet arriving from an untrusted link (such as a connection to the Internet) actually originates from the host that it purports to be from. Several software packages (such as hping and Libnet) exist that will craft packets precisely as an attacker intends.

An *IP address spoofing* attack, then, consists of packets injected into the network with an IP address that is different than the actual IP address of the system sending out these packets. One reason for using these spoofed addresses is clear: the actual attacker is shielded from the adverse consequences of these actions. The downside, of course, is that any return packets are sent back to the purported sender, rather than to the actual sender, which means that an attack using spoofed packets is a "fire and forget" attack, with no feedback directly going to the sender. This behavior may, indeed, be desired by the real attacker, since the return packets could be construed as an attack on the purported sender (see Figure 3-1).

Unless the attacker also controls a point on the return path to the alleged sender, they will have no knowledge of the critical information required to establish a TCP connection. In particular, without knowing the sequence number in the returned SYN/ACK packet, a valid connection cannot be established. If, however, the attacker has a system that can sniff the wire that the return packet travels, a valid packet could be synthesized. In general, however, established TCP sessions can be considered to be operating between the hosts they appear to be.

So, what would the system that is the alleged source of the packet see? Since the original packet wasn't sent from the host, the host would only see the return packet. In the case of a faked TCP SYN packet sent to a target, the SYN/ACK packet (assuming the target port has a listener) would be routed back to the alleged source, which, not having initiated the connection will respond with a RST packet. Even in this simple example, the traffic amplification possibilities of spoofing can be discerned—one spoofed packet caused two additional

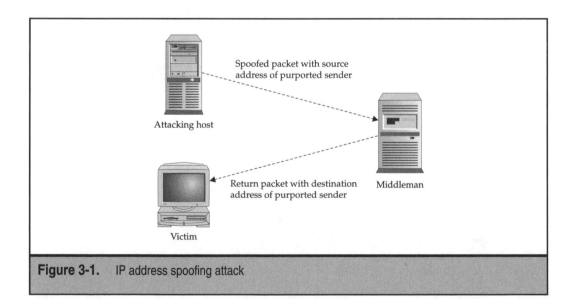

Figure 3-1.   IP address spoofing attack

packets to be broadcast on the Internet. Furthermore, both the (alleged) source and destination hosts could naively assume that the other host had engaged in an unsolicited, possibly hostile, connection. Due to this spoofing problem, counterattacking the apparent source of hostile packets is problematical, even aside from potential ethical and legal issues.

So far, with TCP, we can see that there will be a characteristic pattern when spoofed packets are used. When spoofing is used with connectionless protocols (such as UDP or ICMP) the activity is not so easy to detect, as the transaction often consists solely of an outbound request packet followed by an inbound reply packet. A spoofed packet arriving at an open UDP port, such as DNS which uses UDP port 53, could appear to be a perfectly normal request for name resolution. In that case, the name server would send its response back to the purported originating host, which would, most likely, reject the packet as never having been sent, and it would send an ICMP port unreachable packet back. Again, one spoofed packet caused two response packets. It is generally possible to assume that an unsolicited response is likely caused by spoofing.

A much more insidious attack is generated by sending spoofed UDP packets to port 7 (echo) or port 19 (chargen). This attack, called the *fraggle attack*, is generated by an attacker who sets both the source and destination ports to one or the other of these on two hosts that the attacker is targeting. As shown in Figure 3-2, an unending series of packets will be transmitted between the two systems as they ping-pong back and forth. When we examine specific amplification techniques in the "Traffic Amplification" section that follows, we will see how an attacker can use an attack of this type to wreak havoc throughout an entire subnet. Best practices generally recommend that these ports, and

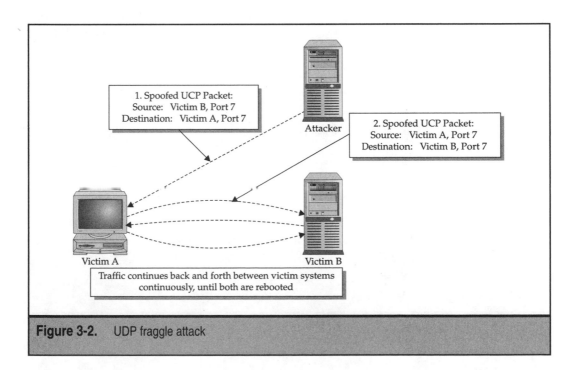

Figure 3-2.   UDP fraggle attack

others with little or no reason to be exposed on the Internet, be blocked at the perimeter. Hosts usually also have no need to expose these ports and generally should disable them.

Another similar attack (which most modern systems guard against) is the so-called *land attack*. In this attack, the source and destination IP addresses are both set to the victim's address, and the port is set to UDP 7 or 19, as in the fraggle attack. Of course, a packet of this nature is always synthetically generated, since no host will send a packet to itself over the network but would instead route the data internally. On a vulnerable host, this packet will cause it to ping-pong with itself, causing CPU utilization to zoom up to 100 percent.

Spoofing is problematic with ICMP traffic as well. Recall that the ICMP specifications specifically disallow responding with an ICMP error packet to an ICMP error packet to avoid an endless avalanche of error conditions. However, spoofed ICMP packets can be used to disrupt communications, as we will discuss in the "ICMP Abuses" section later in the chapter.

Traffic Amplification

Spoofed packets can also be used to cause an amplification effect if they are sent to a broadcast address. For instance, a typical private network might have a range of 192.168.1.0 to 192.168.1.255. Although there are a total of 256 addresses in this range, the lowest and highest addresses are reserved for network use. The broadcast address is the highest address (numerically) in the subnet, in this case 192.168.1.255. When a packet is sent to this address, it is delivered to all hosts on the subnet, which may (but are not required to) respond to this packet.

Since the one packet is communicating with multiple hosts, it is impossible to establish valid TCP connections to broadcast addresses, since TCP, by design, is strictly host to host. Thus any TCP connection directed to a broadcast address is either the result of a misconfiguration of the sender, or it is malicious in intent.

As UDP and ICMP are not connection oriented, each host may indeed respond, with potentially devastating results. In the *smurf attack*, the attacker spoofs an ICMP echo request packet (commonly used by the ping utility) with a source address indicating the intended victim, and a destination address that is the broadcast address of the network that will participate in the attack. When the echo request packet is processed by hosts on the network, many of them (those that respond to the broadcast address) will send an ICMP echo reply to the victim, which means that potentially hundreds, or thousands, of such replies will be sent at once. This poses not only a potential bandwidth problem for the target host, which receives many packets at once, but possibly a bandwidth issue for the participating network. Even worse, if the victim address is also a broadcast address, all hosts on the victim's subnet will receive all this unexpected traffic!

Another variation on the UDP fraggle attack has one or both of the addresses set to a broadcast address. Potentially, all hosts in one network could be ping-ponging messages with all the hosts on the other network, probably bringing both networks to their knees.

To defend against these sort of amplification attacks directed to broadcast addresses is fairly easy—border routers can be configured to reject traffic directed to the broadcast addresses in the subnet, and hosts can generally employ host-level firewalls to provide

an additional level of defense. Unless they are needed by applications, most hosts can safely firewall off the broadcast address of their subnets.

Packet Size Inconsistencies

As was discussed in Chapter 2, the IP header contains a 16-bit total packet length field, giving a maximum packet length of 65,535 bytes. Also in the header is the IHL field, which specifies the size of the header in 32-bit words. Logically, therefore, we would expect the data portion of the packet to be the difference between the values in these two fields.

As the data portion of an IP packet is the protocol-specific header and data, we would also expect the length fields in the protocol-specific headers to be consistent. In the case of TCP, for instance, there is a data offset field that specifies where the header ends and the data portion begins. Naturally there must be enough room in the total packet length to accommodate this offset field.

In the UDP header, there is the UDP length field, which is computed as the total size of the UDP packet, including the header and excluding the IP header. This field should exactly match the data portion computed from the previous IP header.

Packets with these inconsistencies should fail the sanity checks of most IP stacks, and thus will typically be silently rejected by most hosts.

IP Packet Fragmentation

All hosts must accept packets with a minimum length of 68 bytes, as was discussed in Chapter 2—this gives space for the maximum-sized IP header of 60 bytes and a data portion of 8 bytes. However, this doesn't mean that a fragment less than 68 bytes in length is considered invalid. The minimum size of the IP header is 20 bytes, and the last fragment could be as small as 1 byte if the unfragmented packet size was 1 greater than a multiple of 8. You could, therefore, theoretically see valid IP packets as small as 21 bytes.

IP fragments are an example of the dark corners in the IP specification.

Problems with Fragments   Packet reassembly resulting from fragmentation is not as straightforward as might be expected. There are several problems with fragments:

▼ **Duplicate fragments**   If duplicate fragments are received with differing content, which fragment is saved? The first? The second? Should both be discarded? Systems exist that implement all of these strategies.

■ **Overlapping fragments**   If a fragment is received whose contents partially overlap an already received fragment, should the new packet's contents take precedence over the original packet's contents? You might think that this would be obvious evidence of an intrusion attempt, since overlapping fragments should never occur in normal network operations. This, however, has proven not to be the case for traffic traversing the Internet. Recall that the routing path that traffic traverses may change in response to network conditions, including outages, and some network routes will have different MTUs than others. Thus, if a packet is retransmitted, it may travel over a different route and be fragmented differently.

If both sets of fragmented packets make it to the target host, they may indeed overlap. What would indeed be strange is for the overlapping sections to have differing contents, which would either indicate transmission difficulties or malicious crafting of packets. Overlapping fragments, however, are very rare in actual practice, and they generally should be investigated for malicious intent.

- ■ **Ping of death**   A fragment offset can be given along with a packet size that causes the total packet length to be greater than the maximum of 65,535 bytes. (This was famous several years ago as the aptly named *ping o'Death*, which used a crafted ICMP echo request packet of this nature to crash many systems.) For instance, the maximum offset that a fragment can have is 65,528. If a packet has this fragment offset, the data portion of the packet (computed as total length minus IHL) should not exceed 7 bytes, as this would cause the total packet length to exceed 65,535 bytes. In the case of Ethernet, which has a maximum data packet size of 1,500, an attacker could create a fragment with an offset of 65,528 and (assuming an IP header size of 20 bytes) a data portion of 1,480 bytes, giving a total (reconstructed) packet length of 67,008. If the system allocates a maximum 65,535-byte buffer for IP packets and fails to detect this overrun, it is possible that other data in the operating system will be overwritten by this malicious packet, potentially causing it to crash. When this problem was discovered, all major operating system vendors issued a patch to ignore packets that would cause this erroneous condition. Any packet with these characteristics is definitely malicious in nature and synthetically generated, as no TCP/IP stack will deliberately send these packets.

- ■ **Odd-sized packets**   Except for possibly the last fragment of a packet, it is highly suspicious if a fragmented packet has a length that is not an even multiple of 8, since packets are fragmented in multiples of 8.

- ▲ **Firewall evasion**   Fragments can be used for firewall evasion. Among other factors, firewalls will typically make access decisions based on the source and destination addresses and ports. Unless the fragment contains that part of the packet that contains the source or destination ports, the firewall may not have enough information to make the correct decision. Some firewalls solve this problem by not allowing fragments, or by performing packet reassembly before passing the packet along to its ultimate destination. Having firewalls reassemble packets adds its own potential for resource exhaustion by malicious parties.

An IDS is concerned with the effect that these problem packets will have on the end host, but most IDSs are currently not equipped with detailed knowledge of the ultimate destination hosts, so they can't create a fully accurate picture. Unfortunately, applying patches to a system will sometimes alter a system's fragment-reassembly characteristics, so acquiring and maintaining accurate data is difficult. However, even without detailed knowledge of how the traffic will affect the end host, an IDS can presume that packets of this nature are malicious and can alert the operator.

TTL Issues

Malicious hosts can use a combination of retransmission and TTL games to fool an IDS into believing that it has seen the traffic that a host has seen, when, in fact, the IDS could be mistaken. Ideally an IDS will know the packet-reassembly strategy of the target host. It also, ideally, should know the number of router hops between itself and the systems it is monitoring. This is an area of active research in the IDS field.

Let's assume the border IDS is five hops away from an attacker, and that a targeted system is two hops past that. Suppose the attacker sends a normal packet with a TTL of 6: the IDS will see the packet, since it has another hop left, but the packet will never make it to the target host. So far, no harm has been done, other than the IDS wrongly assuming that a packet was received by the target. Next, the attacker sends a similar packet, but with malicious content and a TTL of 7. If the IDS is acting under the assumption that the host will accept only the first of duplicate received packets, it may believe that nothing untoward has happened. The target host, however, only saw the second packet, which had malicious content (see Figure 3-3). This is an example of targeting an IDS specifically to evade detection. Ideally, even though the IDS does not correctly detect the nature of the

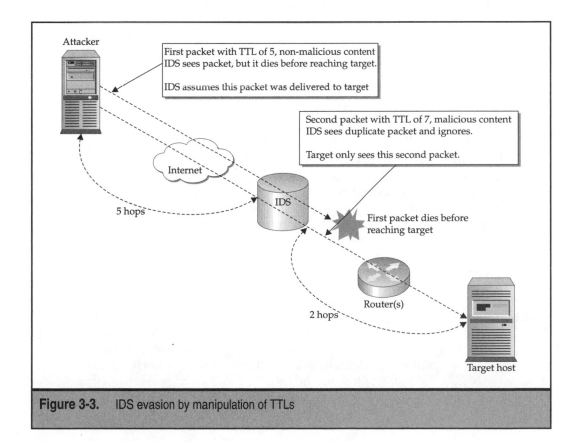

Figure 3-3.   IDS evasion by manipulation of TTLs

attack, it can infer malicious intent, due to the receipt of two differing duplicate packets, and it should report this anomaly.

IP Options

Several options in an IP header have security implications for the IDS analyst. Hosts are not required to implement option processing, but they are expected to forward those that they do not implement. The options that follow are obsolete, and packets containing them are generally considered malicious, and are often blocked at border routers.

Record Route   The *record route* option in the IP header was designed to provide a mechanism to determine the route that the packet took from source to destination. Each hop a packet takes will, if the header contains space, record the IP address of the router. This option has no obvious use, as modern tools, such as traceroute, are more capable of determining routes between hosts.

Loose and Strict Source Routing   *Loose and strict source routing* are used to specify the actual route that a packet is expected to take while traveling from source to destination. Strict source routing specifies the exact route, hop by hop, that the packet must take. Loose source routing also specifies the route that the packet must take, but there may be additional, unspecified hops between any two routers in the list.

The danger with source-routed packets is that it is not possible to trust the apparent source of the packet. If a hacker controls a router (which could be any device configured to act as a router, not just devices labeled as routers), then the hacker can control the routing of the packets, thus causing their system to appear to be have a legitimate address.

For this reason, hosts and border routers are well advised to drop source-routed packets, as no legitimate use for them exists. Indeed, many hosts, by default, are configured to ignore these packets. IDS sensors can assume that these packets are malicious in intent.

Internet Timestamp   The *Internet timestamp* option requests the timestamp from the system's perspective, in a return packet. This has limited value, but it may give a potential attacker an idea of the level of system administration on the target. With all the other malicious traffic out there, the use of this option is fairly benign, but in combination with other traffic it may be an indication of subtle probing.

Port 0

For both TCP and UDP, port 0 traffic is considered unusual, since it is officially a reserved port and shouldn't be used for any network communications. Any port 0 traffic is probably not legitimate, since the packets are probably generated synthetically.

Why the prohibition against using port 0? Although the original motivation for not allowing this port to be used is shrouded in the mists of time, it appears most likely to be due to the desire to have an in-band method of signaling the operating system to select a port. Instead of hard-coding port numbers, or writing code to find an open port, the Unix socket interface allows the programmer to specify port 0, which causes the operating system to select an ephemeral port for the communication. If all 65,536 port numbers were valid, an additional parameter would be needed to specify this option. Or, in other

words, if port 0 was not prohibited, all 65,536 port numbers could be valid parameters to the Unix socket interface, which would entirely use up the 16-bit field allocated to this parameter. Therefore, there would be a need to have an additional parameter, which would be an "I don't care" field. "this option" == "I don't care" or (another way of specifying it) "the system allocates a port." Having 0 as a magic marker meaning that the port number is unspecified is useful, and it does not measurably reduce the effectiveness of TCP or UDP. After all, very few hosts will actually be using all 65,535 ports at the same time!

Port 0 connections may be an attempt to fingerprint the host, as differing platforms respond in different ways. In general, hosts and firewalls should be configured to drop all port 0 UDP or TCP traffic.

UDP Abuses

The UDP header is so primitive as to appear impervious to abuse. After all, the header contains only source and destination ports, packet length, and checksum. It should be clear by now that these can all be spoofed by a malicious party, so further authentication is needed if the source of the packets is to be trusted. Furthermore, UDP can be used for traffic amplification, as was discussed earlier. But can the UDP header itself be abused?

UDP Checksum

Surprisingly, the UDP checksum is only optionally computed. If this 16-bit field is exactly 0, it signifies that the UDP checksum wasn't computed on transmission and shouldn't be checked upon reception. As UDP was originally intended as a lightweight protocol on much smaller and slower systems than modern equipment, a performance advantage was gained by not computing this checksum. However, without the checksum, there is no way to detect whether the packet was corrupted in transit.

Even inexpensive systems these days can completely fill a 100 megabit channel, and thus the reliability advantage of using a checksum greatly outweighs any minor performance gain in not computing it. Currently, there is really no legitimate reason for hosts to not compute the checksum, so any packets that have the UDP checksum turned off are questionable and may be subtle evasion attempts, although it is difficult to see what advantage would be gained by an attacker doing this.

TCP Abuses

We now turn to TCP-specific abuses. As we've seen, it is relatively difficult to spoof a full TCP connection, unless the hacker controls a router in the route between the two system, so traffic that travels on a fully established connection can be presumed to be between the two systems indicated. This means that an attacker can usually be identified if any abuses occur on an established TCP connection. We will reserve discussion of these types of abuses to Chapter 4, as abuses on an established connection are usually at the application level.

It is important to note, however, that there are certain network-level abuses that can be triggered by spoofed packets: TCP retransmission and TCP flags can be used maliciously; SYN floods and backscatter can overwhelm hosts; SYN or RST packets can but shouldn't contain data; and initial sequence numbers can sometimes be predicted.

TCP Retransmission

As discussed in Chapter 2, TCP retransmits packets to introduce a level of reliability to the unreliable IP transport mechanism. When TCP retransmits a packet, the retransmitted packet should be exactly the same as the original packet. Of course, it may be fragmented differently during transport, but the data portion of the reassembled TCP packet should exactly match the original packet. If an IDS sees a retransmitted packet (with correct checksums) that has different contents than the original packet, it can assume either a buggy TCP/IP implementation or a malicious attack.

TCP Flags

A close examination of the TCP header (shown in Figure 2-5 in Chapter 2) will reveal that it contains flags that are incompatible with each other in normal use. For instance, a SYN flag should never be seen with a FIN or RST flag, as the resulting combination does not correspond to any legitimate activity of the TCP stack.

Various TCP stacks react differently to these illegal inputs—in fact, the differences in reaction to various TCP flag combinations are used by programs such as Nmap or queso to identify the operating system type. Some stacks will, in fact, crash when confronted with this type of illegal input. In general, though, the main purpose of traffic of this nature is to perform recon on a network, for vulnerability analysis purposes. Table 3-1 shows some of the flag combinations that are often used for these purposes.

TCP Flags	Problem
(none)	A packet with no flags is neither Session Initiation (SYN), Midstream (ACK), nor Termination (FIN/RST). It is not part of any valid TCP transaction.
SYN/FIN	The flag combination indicates both Session Initiation (SYN) and Session Termination (FIN), an impossible condition.
SYN/RST	The flag combination indicates both Session Initiation (SYN) and Session Termination (RST), an impossible condition.
SYN/FIN /ACK	This flag combination indicates Session Initiation (SYN), Midstream (ACK), and Session Termination (FIN), an impossible condition.
SYN/RST /ACK	This flag combination indicates Session Initiation (SYN), Midstream (ACK), and Session Termination (RST), an impossible condition.
All Flags	Often called the Xmas Tree flag combination, this combines the problem of Initiation, Midstream, and Termination flags with the PSH and URG flags (which in themselves are valid).

Table 3-1.   Invalid TCP Flag Combinations

SYN Floods

Many TCP implementations are vulnerable to a resource-exhaustion attack known as *SYN flooding*, in which excessive requests are made to create sessions, thus causing memory utilization to explode. In an attack of this nature, numerous SYN packets are sent to an open TCP port. The target host will send back a SYN/ACK packet, create an entry in its pending-connection queue, and await the completion of the TCP three-way handshake. At this point, the connection is often termed *half open*. Queuing this connection takes a finite amount of memory, so if many SYN packets are received that fail to complete the three-way handshake, increasing amounts of memory will be consumed.

If these SYN packets are spoofed from addresses that do not exist, no response packet containing SYN/ACK will be received, and the pending connection queue will expand. As was explained in Chapter 2, TCP makes judicious use of timeouts, so eventually the pending connection will be torn down, and the memory will be freed, typically within three minutes. However, an enormous amount of spoofed traffic can be sent before this timeout occurs. Contributing to this potential problem is the fact that most systems typically have a fixed size for the pending-connection queue. When this queue fills, the system will be unable to accept new, potentially legitimate, connections, and may even crash.

To deal with this potential denial-of-service attack, hosts employ several strategies, either individually or in combination:

▼ **Limiting connection rate** Hosts can introduce rate-limiting software that permits only a certain number of pending connections in a given timeframe. Connection requests in excess of this limit are simply ignored by the host. The system can then be tuned to ensure that pending bogus connections are timed out at a rate greater than or equal to the maximum rate that they can enter, thus ensuring that the table doesn't overflow. The downside of this strategy is that legitimate connection attempts may also be rejected, although due to TCP retransmission, the originating host will attempt several transmissions, one of which may get through.

■ **Purging stale connections** Some hosts will purge a randomly chosen stale connection request from the pending-connection queue when a new request is made and the table is full. This neatly handles the problem, as old connection requests are likely to be from a SYN flooding attack, rather than legitimate connections. It is possible, though, that a legitimate connection could be discarded if its response time is slow, or if the rate of connection requests is extremely fast.

▲ **Using SYN cookies** The SYN cookie is a recently developed technique. In this technique, the initial sequence number is cryptographically derived from the IP addresses and port numbers of the connection, and a SYN/ACK packet is sent back with this initial sequence number, without retaining a pending connection queue. When an ACK packet is received at a host that implements SYN cookies, and it is determined not to be part of an established connection, that host will perform the same cryptographic calculation, and the value will

be compared with the received sequence number. If the two values correspond, the connection is then considered established, and normal communication takes place. Although this technique is a technical violation of RFC 792 (timeouts are not enforced as described in the RFC), it neatly solves the problem, as no memory is consumed to keep track of half-open connections. The biggest drawback is the requirement for the receiving host to compute this cryptographic sum for every unsolicited ACK packet received, thus potentially creating a CPU utilization problem for the host. At present, modern hosts can compute this checksum at network rates, but legacy hosts may be subject to a different denial of service via ACK packets if they implement this mechanism.

Backscatter

The term *backscatter* refers to the response SYN/ACK packets that a SYN-flooded host will send in response to receiving the SYN packets. If the source address of the original SYN packet is spoofed, the SYN/ACKs will be sent to that spoofed address, which may use all the network bandwidth for the spoofed host or network.

Backscatter can easily be detected as a flood of SYN/ACK packets without an initial SYN being sent. If the spoofed host exists, it will most likely send an RST packet back to the spoofed originating host, further increasing bandwidth utilization. However, the RST is an unexpected godsend to this spoofed host, since it can close down the connection and release the pending connection from the queue, thus avoiding some of the ill effects from the original SYN flood attack. For this reason, SYN floods are most effective (from a hacker's viewpoint) if the host that receives the backscatter (the spoofed source of the SYN flood) does not, in fact, exist, because the SYN flooded host must then wait for a timeout.

SYN with Data, RST with Data

Although it is not seen in normal traffic, RFC 792 does not disallow the transport of data in a SYN, FIN, or RST packet. Generally, the initial SYN packet and the return SYN/ACK are expected to be used solely for establishing a session. Similarly, a FIN or RST is expected to be used exclusively for session teardown. Normal TCP/IP stacks will not send data in these packets, and they may not process the data correctly if it is seen in these packets. Thus, IDSs that see such packets can generally assume that they are crafted, with the possible intent of evading or subverting normal mechanisms.

Initial Sequence Number Prediction

As has been mentioned, it is difficult to spoof a TCP connection, largely because of the difficulty in predicting the initial sequence number that the remote host will select. If this initial sequence number could be predicted, a reasonable facsimile of a connection could be spoofed. Of course, without knowledge of the return packet (which we're assuming here, since a hacker wouldn't need to predict the sequence number if the return packet could be directly observed), and particularly without knowing the number of bytes sent back, a continuous conversation would be difficult to maintain.

However, two factors work in favor of the attacker here:

▼ Many TCP services have easily predictable responses, and thus the byte count can be guessed with reasonable accuracy, although the actual response, in this case, won't be accessible. The attacker could even connect normally prior to the attack and empirically attempt to determine the size of the likely response.

▲ Many system compromises can be completed in a single packet, thus removing the necessity for seeing any responses. A favorite technique of hackers is to compromise a vulnerable service with the injection of some sort of back door in the same packet. The hacker later performs a normal connection to the back-door port, which has no apparent relation to the original attack.

The success of spoofing TCP connections, in these cases, would be predicated on the ease of predicting the initial sequence number used by the target host. In most cases on modern operating systems, this is an impossibly difficult task, as the 32-bit ISN is essentially chosen randomly. On some desktop operating systems, though, the ISN is a simple increment of the previous ISN, thus possibly allowing this type of attack to be successful. Often, too, TCP stacks in embedded devices (such as printers) will use predictable ISNs.

ICMP Abuses

ICMP packet spoofing can be used to create denial-of-service situations by falsely propagating error indications throughout the network. As ICMP is not session oriented, a received ICMP packet cannot be authenticated as actually coming from the alleged host. Usually ICMP errors are considered transient, so unless an attacker continuously spoofs network error messages, the disruption generally will cease when the packets stop arriving at the victim.

Destination Unreachable

There is an entire family of ICMP *destination unreachable* packets that indicate that a network, host, or specific port is unreachable for a variety of reasons. If a host receives such a packet alleging that a network service it wishes to access is unreachable, it may cease transmitting, thus causing a disruption of communication.

Host Quench

Host quench is a deprecated method of signaling to a sending system that the receiver cannot keep up with the flow of data. On receipt of a packet of this type, sending hosts are expected to slow down traffic to the receiver. If an attacker knows that host A and host B regularly communicate, spoofed ICMP host quench packets could disrupt such communication. It would be even more effective if the hacker spoofed these packets from each host to the other one, so that each host thinks the other one wants it to stop.

Minor ICMP Abuses

In general, security professionals hold that it is best to minimize the amount of information that is leaked to potential attackers. Several ICMP requests can be used for information-gathering purposes, although they are now somewhat antiquated, as much more sophisticated information-gathering mechanisms exist. However, for completeness, we will mention two ICMP information requests and responses:

▼ An ICMP timestamp request packet sent to a host is responded to with the time that the system understands it to be.

▲ An ICMP address mask request is responded to with the subnet mask that the host is using.

These items of information are of minor use to attackers. As mentioned before, the amount and type of information that a host leaks can give an attacker an idea of the level of care and skill of system administration. In particular, a significant discrepancy in the timestamp of the system with the true time is a negative indication of system administration ability. Just as in more traditional forms of illicit activity, attackers are much more likely to target the easy marks.

The functions of the ICMP mechanism are not generally accessible to application programs, whereas application programs do control which UDP or TCP services are offered. As ICMP has no such control mechanism, the recommended procedure is to firewall off these ICMP requests, either at the host or network level.

Covert Data Channels

Although by no means confined to ICMP, the problem of covert channels is more pronounced with ICMP because ICMP is often not examined as closely by IDSs as are other protocols. A covert channel can be defined as a hidden communications mechanism. When a system has been compromised by other means, some hackers will use these covert channels in an attempt to hide their activities.

There are a few basic things to know about covert channels:

▼ If the channel has a legitimate use, data can be hidden in unused fields or otherwise unassigned areas of the communications channel. ICMP traffic is ideal for this, as an ICMP packet generally is quite small (usually 36 bytes or less), and the remainder of the packet can be used for surreptitious data transport.

■ In general, the speed of the data transfer on a covert channel is inversely related to the ease of detection of the channel. If one errant byte is transmitted each week, the chances of detection are very low, but this rate of data transfer is probably too low for any but the most patient attackers. Except possibly in

long-term espionage situations, bit rates associated with interactive traffic and download would be expected, in which case ICMP packets would again be ideal.

▲ For added security, covert channels are often encrypted. The easy availability of encryption packages, such as PGP and SSL, provide this capability.

ICMP has been mentioned as a possible covert communications channel for hackers because tools are available for these communications that hackers have been known to use, such as loki, icmp-backdoor, and sneaky-sneaky-1.12.

Even more subtle and troubling covert channels exist, as in the Linux sucKIT tool, which waits quietly for specific packets in a specific sequence (or with a particular payload) to activate a back-door connection. If this tool is installed, it could be configured to activate if it saw a packet to port 4567, then another one to 6543, then another to 8765 from the same system. It could then wake up and initiate a root shell that the hacker could connect to. Detecting a sophisticated back door of this type is extremely challenging.

We haven't even scratched the surface of this topic, and clearly further study is needed by IDS vendors to counter these types of threats.

SUMMARY

That the Internet has been so robust is really a tribute to the genius of its pioneers, but it has begun to show its age. Various network level abuses have been discussed, which can disrupt or redirect normal traffic, and evade detection. We have seen how each of the major protocols used in the Internet Protocol suite can be misused, and suggested several mitigations or corrective actions, which can help to defend systems and networks from these abuses.

In Chapter 4, we will proceed to examine abuses of common applications built on top of these network services.

CHAPTER 4

Unauthorized Activity II

In this chapter, we examine some of the ways in which application programs can be attacked via the network. We have already explored the types of abuses that occur at the network level, but here we focus on how legitimate (from a network level) traffic can nevertheless be used to abuse or compromise applications. The term *application* runs the gamut from simple services (such as Telnet) installed as a matter of course when the operating system is installed, through the more complex network applications such as web servers, up to the custom application level.

One would expect that custom applications would not be as vulnerable as "off-the-shelf" products for the simple reason that hackers are not likely to be able to examine the inner workings of them for flaws. However, applications are often built on top of underlying foundations, such as databases, which may have exploitable security problems.

Unfortunately, even standard applications suffer from security vulnerabilities, in part due to bad programming practices, lack of awareness of exploitability, and configuration or other issues. When security issues are discovered in applications, operating system software, or utilities, bulletins are issued by various organizations (CERT, CIAC, and so on), vendors, and security professionals to alert administrators of the issues. Responsible vendors rapidly correct or mitigate security problems when they are discovered.

PROS AND CONS OF OPEN SOURCE

The movement toward open disclosure of software source code has made tremendous strides in recent years. Operating systems such as Linux and FreeBSD, and major applications that drive the Internet such as the Apache Web Server, Sendmail, and BIND (Berkeley Internet Name Domain) are completely open source, whereas other popular offerings such as Windows and Mac OS X are closed source. From a security standpoint, arguments can be made both ways about the security of open source versus closed source. In reality, whether or not the source is proprietary is secondary to other more important issues:

▼ Does the software design process embrace security as an important goal?

■ Are the software designers, developers, and engineers trained and aware of the importance of security in the development process?

■ Are the development tools also designed from a security perspective?

▲ Is the software sufficiently tested for security issues by competent testing personnel?

Systems designed with these criteria in mind are likely to have fewer security issues than those in which security is an afterthought. New security issues surface all the time, but except in extraordinary circumstances, they can generally be designed for or mitigated in the design process. Many software products do not live up to the maxim "Fail Gracefully" and contribute to security breaches by failing in a catastrophic fashion. Well-designed systems, on the other hand, have internal checks to detect "impossible" conditions and deal with them appropriately.

Most current systems, both open-source and proprietary, have grown organically from an insecure framework and thus have security "patched" in as an afterthought. This, of course, is not the preferred security model but is often necessary when original systems were designed in a much different world.

TYPES OF EXPLOITS

When we talk of application-level exploits, we are indicating those methods of taking control of, or denying, the usage to legitimate users of a service, process, or application which has a presence on the network, using normally crafted network packets. What we've seen in Chapter 3 are the sorts of misdeeds that a malicious party can perform by sending abnormal network traffic. In this chapter, we will examine those types of exploits in which the packets are legitimate in form and/or quantity, but where the contents of the traffic interact with the network application to provide unexpected access to the application by a malicious party, or denial of access to legitimate users.

Memory Buffer Overflow

The most common types of remote security breaches are due to memory buffers of various sorts being overflowed. A *buffer* is a contiguously allocated chunk of memory, in most cases on the computer's stack or in a memory heap. As this buffer has a defined size, if the bounds of this buffer are exceeded, other memory, not part of the buffer, will be overwritten. Hackers have been extremely clever in exploiting this flaw if possible. When a buffer overflow attack is successful, the execution path of the program is hijacked by the attacker, who therefore inherits the context of the exploited program, including access privileges, open files, and network connections. Thus, when a program running as root is exploited, the hacker code itself also runs as root, which enables complete control over the system. Often, the hacker code will execute an interactive command interpreter (*shell*) from which the hacker can then continue his compromise of the system.

A trivial C program that contains a buffer overflow will begin our exploration of this topic:

```
main()       {
    char buff[10];
    strcpy(buff, "This string overflows the buffer"};
}
```

This C program allocates 10 bytes on the stack for a buffer. It then copies a string whose size exceeds these 10 bytes into the buffer, thus overflowing the allocated size of the buffer. In C, each string is terminated by a zero byte, so the buffer in question can hold only nine characters and the zero byte.

This example is contrived, but programmers often make assumptions about the maximum length of input that anyone should ever make into a field. Hackers, however, are not constrained by what "should" be entered into a field, but by what "can" actually be entered. Let's examine, therefore, the effects of overflowing a buffer.

Memory Address Space

The memory required to run a program is called the *address space*. In modern operating systems, it is generally divided into the following memory sections (refer to Figure 4-1):

▼   **Text**   The binary code loaded from the executable, which is marked read-only. In many architectures, self-modifying code is supported by dynamically creating machine code on the stack or heap and branching to it.

■   **Initialized data**   A data area with data copied from the executable. This will contain variables whose values are initialized with a value but are subject to modification, and thus must be marked read-write.

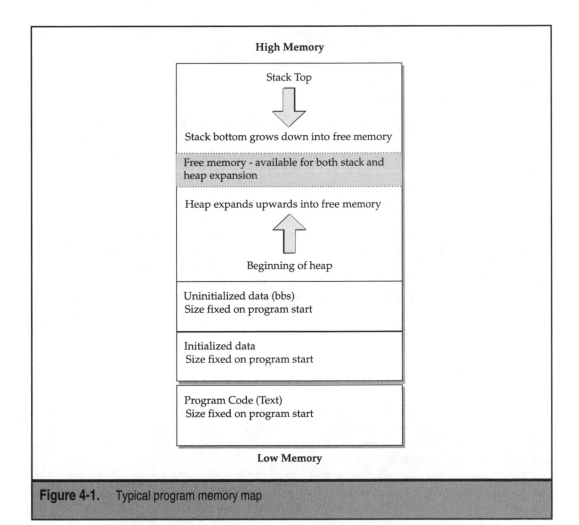

Figure 4-1.   Typical program memory map

- ■ **bss** An area for uninitialized data, although in practice this area is often initialized to binary zero. The term *bss* is an artifact from a long-obsolete operating system.

- ■ **Heap** This memory area is used for dynamically allocated variables whose lifespan must exist beyond the function that created it. This area can also expand or contract based on program memory demands, but it is structured different from the stack structure described next, since memory is allocated as needed without regard to the state of the stack.

- ▲ **Stack** The stack area is often likened to a stack of plates at a cafeteria, where the last plate pushed onto the stack is the first one taken out. In modern computer systems, the stack is allocated from the top of memory and grows downward, so that the data at the top of the stack has a lower memory address than the data at the bottom. The stack is used for storage of return addresses, as well as local variables for functions. The stack grows and shrinks in response to program memory demands.

NOTE Local variables are used by a function as it is running, but they are not needed once the function returns. Thus, the memory used by these local variables are available for other uses when they are no longer needed.

Most buffer overflows involve the stack, as the structure is simpler than the heap. Although our discussion focuses on the *x*86 family of processors, the concepts are similar in other processor families. A stack pointer (SP) points to the current "top" of the stack region. The term *top* is somewhat of a misnomer, since the stack region grows downward from the top of memory, and as it expands the SP decreases in value. When a function (or subroutine) is called, the parameters are pushed on the stack, along with the return address and a frame pointer (FP). Local variables (such as `buff` in the preceding code) are allocated on the stack below, as shown in Figure 4-2.

When a stack-allocated buffer is overflowed by excessive data, as in our example, it will overwrite data higher in memory, on the stack. This data, as described previously, includes the other local variables, the frame pointer, the return address, and data for other functions higher on the stack.

Classic Buffer Overflow

The classic buffer overflow exploit occurs when a buffer on the stack is overflowed, generally overwriting the return address of the function with a value supplied by the attacker. Additionally, the data entered into the stack will often be a machine language program that gains access to the system via this overflow, although, as we'll see in the section "Return to libc Buffer Overflows" later in the chapter, the data need only consist of a return address if useful code already exists in the program or included libraries. The return address is set to an address within this machine language program (often called *shell code*, as the object often is to gain access to an interactive shell). When the exploited function returns from its normal execution path, instead of returning whence it came, it returns to the shell code.

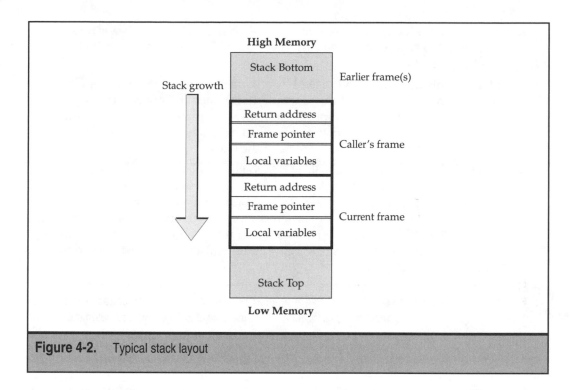

Figure 4-2.   Typical stack layout

When overflowing a buffer, it is often impossible to enter certain values in the buffer, which may cause greater, although not insurmountable, problems for the attacker. For instance, when overflowing an input buffer by entering data into it, it will not be possible to enter either a binary 0 or the end-of-line character (newline), as either of these characters would terminate the input. Some buffer overflows will have even more restricted capabilities, depending on the characteristics of the program involved. Although the point has been hotly debated, some believe that open-source software can be examined more closely by hackers to determine a precise vector of compromise, and it thus may be more vulnerable. Although this may be true, it is often also argued that open-source software benefits by having many (mostly nonmalicious) eyes examining, studying, and improving it.

Because some byte codes may not be entered into the shell code that is executed, hackers oftentimes need to perform various convolutions to generate those values, if needed. Our discussion here will not drift into specific hardware architectures, but methods are available for synthesizing these values programmatically without resorting to the forbidden values themselves. For instance, subtracting a hardware register from itself will generate a binary 0 in the register, without necessarily actually inserting a numeric zero into the shell code.

This classic type of buffer overflow exploit powered the Morris Internet worm of 1988, which caused large-scale disruption of the infant Internet of the time—we will discuss this in the section entitled "A Brief History of Worms".

A Certain Amount of Slop in Shell Codes

One technique that hackers typically engage in when generating buffer overflow shell codes is to allow for some slop in the return address. Sometimes the buffer being overflowed will not be in precisely the same location on the stack, due to intervening variables taking a different amount of space. Possibly, too, the shell code may target several variants of the vulnerable software and thus needs a method to adapt. If a hacker had unlimited time, he could try numerous combinations of addresses to enter into the stack. However, if the return address doesn't point to some genuine executable code, but rather some random data, the chances are great that the attack will simply crash the program—again, a possible attack, but not likely to be of interest to more ambitious hackers.

If the return address could possibly vary, how could the attacker hope to accommodate that? It turns out that this problem is often overcome by the use of what has been term as a NOOP "sled." Every processor instruction set contains at least one instruction that is in effect a null operation that makes no change to the state of the program, other than consuming a memory location. Most instruction sets will actually have a number of instructions that will operate as NOOPs. For instance, a binary OR operation of a register with itself will not change its value (although it may change processor flags) and thus likely also functions (for hacker purposes) as a NOOP.

Suppose the hacker shell code is preceded by 512 bytes of NOOPs. The return address merely needs to fall anywhere within this 512-byte window for the shell code to be activated. The processor will simply step through the NOOPs that it encounters until it reaches the actual shell code. Note, of course, that the NOOPs also need to follow the same rules about forbidden byte codes as the actual shell code.

In the x86 instruction set used on commodity PCs, the defined instruction for a NOOP is a hex code 0x90, although about 55 different hex codes could function in this capacity. In fact, depending on the actual shell code, additional instructions could also be used. For instance, if the shell code begins by storing a value in the AX register, any preceding instruction that may have changed the AX register is of no adverse consequence to the shell code. We will explore this issue further later in the chapter as we examine one of the more recent developments in this area, polymorphic shell codes.

Heap-Based Buffer Overflows

Another dynamically allocated memory region is the heap, which generally grows from the bottom of memory toward the top. This region is generally more difficult to exploit than the stack, as return addresses aren't stored in the heap, which make seizing control of the execution path of a vulnerable program more difficult. However, overflowing the heap can easily cause denial of service by causing memory allocation errors. The Code Red Worm that attacked Microsoft web servers in 2001 used a heap overflow technique to perform the compromise.

Return to libc Buffer Overflows

Instead of injecting shell code directly into a program, suppose that an attacker took advantage of code already known to be on the system. Unlike the standard stack-based or heap-based buffer overflows, this overflow modifies the return address to return to one of the functions in the standard library libc, which contains several functions to execute arbitrary commands. For any given version of the libc library, the addresses of these functions can be easily predetermined by an attacker. Additionally, traditional shell code is not needed, rather the overflowed variable is padded with extraneous data, and multiple copies of the return address, which is set to a known function in libc. This technique is typically used when for technical reasons the classic shell code injection techniques cannot be used, or when constraints exist on the size of the shell code that can be inserted.

Format String Overflows

One particular form of exploit that has achieved a level of popularity is the exploitation of a *format string* error. In the C programming language, a *template* string is used to format output. This template string can contain instructions to access variables on the stack that require formatting to output. A typical programming flaw that allows exploitation is that lazy programmers simply pass unchecked input directly as the format string. By injecting carefully crafted inputs, the format string forces the exploited program to access unintended data on the stack, thus potentially clobbering stack data that, although not technically a buffer overflow, has the same potential for abuse.

Recent Applications and Operating systems vulnerable to the format string overflow vulnerability include

▼ CERT Advisory CA-2002-10 Format String Vulnerability in rpc.rwalld

■ CERT Advisory CA-2002-12: Format String Vulnerability in ISC DHCPD

■ CERT Vulnerability Note VU#700575: Buffer overflows in Microsoft SQL Server 7.0 and SQL Server 2000

■ CERT-intexxia 12/20/2001: pfinger Format String Vulnerability

■ SuSE-SA:2002:037: 'heartbeat' Remote format string

▲ Securiteam.com 10/12/2000:PHP remote format string overflow

Polymorphic Shell Code

A continual arms race exists between those who protect systems from compromise and those who hope to harm them. Technology now exists to create "polymorphic" shell code, which actually mutates the code that is used to compromise systems. In 2001, an online tool (ADMutate) was released that (among other things) substitutes the NOOP codes generated in shell code with functional equivalents. As we saw earlier, approximately 55 byte codes are such equivalents. Thus, by changing NOOPs to random byte codes selected from this list, ADMutate attempts to evade IDSs that look for simple patterns.

ADMutate uses an application programming interface (API) and library that can be included by worm or virus authors to mutate the shell code, so that each attack uses a differing byte sequence.

Defense Against Buffer Overflow Attacks

Ultimately, the responsibility for systems being vulnerable to buffer overflow attacks rests with the vendors of vulnerable software. In the case of open-source software, especially those packages that are widely used, cooperative efforts arise in the open-source community to correct known vulnerabilities quickly. Generally, closed-source vendors will also be fairly responsive as well, as security issues have been raised to popular consciousness by high-profile exploits.

Although primary responsibility for providing security patches lies with the vendor, prudent system administrators can make some defensive measures to reduce or remove this exposure. Since it is unknown (by definition) what service may next be discovered to be vulnerable, it is wise to treat any network accessible service as potentially vulnerable. One mitigation that helps shield systems from exploitation is to restrict access to services only to authorized users by employing either network or host-level firewalling techniques.

In the case of publicly accessible services, such as web servers, anonymous FTP servers, or remote login services that must remain open to a significant portion of the Internet, the general recommendation is to stay on top of security problems for these products and patch when vulnerabilities are disclosed. Often, too, more secure alternatives to popular products do not suffer from the same reputation for security problems. For instance, a popular web server in the PC arena has been plagued with numerous security problems in the past. At some point, an honest appraisal of the total cost of ownership (TCO) might convince some enterprises to replace this product with a product whose security exposure is less problematic.

Systems can often be configured to harden themselves against buffer overflow attacks. Some architectures (such as Sparc) have the capability to make the stack "non-executable," so that shell code residing on the stack cannot be executed. An attempt to return into the stack on such systems will cause the program to abort, rather than be exploited. This can still pose a problem, albeit generally of less concern, as this changes a system compromise to a denial of service (DoS) attack. It is often possible to configure services to restart automatically if they exit, so this may prove to be acceptable.

Another recent development that has been implemented in the PaX Linux kernel patch and other systems is the idea of randomization of memory and stack allocation. As we have seen, shell codes can have some slop but need some idea of what to insert as a return address to wrest control away from the program. Absent some form of address randomization, these addresses are highly predictable, which allows easy exploitation of buffer overflows. With this patch, the stack is allocated at a random address that is selected when the program begins running. Along with the stack, this patch also randomizes the heap, shared libraries (such as libc), and each executable program executed in turn. As long as the randomization scheme is sufficiently strong, exploiting even a well-known vulnerability is unlikely to be successful. Even if an exploit is successful, the

same attack will fail the next time due to the differing addressing. More information on these and other techniques for host protection are available at these links:

▼ http://sourceforge.net/projects/stjude

■ http://people.redhat.com/mingo/exec-shield/ANNOUNCE-exec-shield

▲ http://www.grsecurity.net

Intrusion-detection system (IDS) defensive measures against polymorphic shell codes is proceeding. Current detection mechanisms are CPU intensive, as they employ regular expression matching on real-time data streams. No doubt that as more research takes place, IDS systems will be more capable of identifying these threats.

COMMONLY EXPLOITED PROGRAMS AND PROTOCOLS

Although the range of vulnerabilities is wide and rapidly expanding (Bugtraq lists newly-discovered exploits on a regular basis), there are applications and protocols which are as familiar as the "hit-parade" for the number of network exploitable vulnerabilities that they have historically exhibited. Problems may occur in programs that were designed during the early days of the Internet, before security became a significant issue; other problems are due to flaws in design or implementation. The following sections examine commonly exploited issues. (Space does not permit a full discussion of the myriad security issues extant on the Internet today.)

Cleartext Communications

Many protocols developed in the infancy of the Internet are still in use today. Those days, of course, were mainly concerned with getting the functionality of the infrastructure in place, as opposed to significant concerns about security. Some IP options did mark packets with security levels, but no attempt was made to embed encryption into the packet contents. This led to the development of cleartext protocols, of which the most widely used have been Telnet, Rlogin, and FTP.

While we will discuss other FTP security concerns in more detail later, all of these cleartext protocols suffer from the glaring weakness of transparency. Not only is the authentication step visible to anyone who is capturing packets on the wire, but the entire session is also available for inspection. In the early days, too, most Ethernet networks used shared media, where all packets were visible to anyone on the network. Thus, one compromised system anywhere on a network could be used to capture traffic from any connected system. In these days of switched networks, this problem isn't as severe, although, as we've seen in Chapter 3, it may be possible to subvert switches to allow sniffing of unintended packets. However, when a cleartext session is established across router boundaries, or across the Internet, the traffic is vulnerable to sniffing at multiple locations.

For these and other reasons, the use of these cleartext protocols should generally be restricted to internal routing at an enterprise. Most enterprises choose to filter the ports

associated with these protocols from inbound connections. As an alternative, IDS systems can monitor and flag these connections and examine them for malicious content. Many systems with embedded networking stacks, such as printers, conferencing equipment, and so on, allow configuration only via these cleartext protocols. In such cases, it is important to protect the system as much as possible by the selection of a strong password and strong access controls to the system. It is also important to change these passwords frequently, ideally from a nonremote location. Cleartext communication mechanisms with strong, one-time mechanisms (use of Kerberos or one-time passwords) can improve protection, as the password used for authentication, even if sniffed, cannot be easily reused by a hacker for later access.

Encrypted Communications

In contrast to the doom and gloom, the good news is that encryption now has taken an important place in Internet security. From encrypted web sites for e-commerce or other privacy-sensitive applications, and encrypted replacements for cleartext communications, to end-to-end Virtual Private Networks (VPNs), the future looks brighter for encrypted communications. However, such communications have their own security concerns. As we will delve into more closely when we discuss SSH, the Secure Shell, the "transparency" concern we mentioned earlier has advantages for IDS monitoring, in that session content can be monitored for attack signatures. In an encrypted connection, the IDS is essentially blind to traffic contents (unless it has a decoding module and access to decrypting keys).

VPN technology allows for the encrypted transfer of all traffic between two endpoints. Each individual connection is not itself specially encrypted; rather, the tunnel between the two sides is encrypted. Traffic enters the VPN tunnel unencrypted, is encrypted and transported securely over the Internet to the other end, and is then decrypted and transported to its destination. Although exciting, this is not a panacea for remote access inside an enterprise, since, in effect, the security perimeter is extended to include the VPN, which could be a CEO's virus-infested laptop in a hotel room. Thus, at the point of decryption, it is often recommended that an IDS monitor the (now decrypted) traffic for malicious content.

FTP

The File Transfer Protocol (FTP), defined in RFC 959, is used for unencrypted data transfer between systems, and authenticates users via a cleartext account and password authentication mechanism, similar to that used by Telnet. The same concerns about exposure of account names and passwords on cleartext passwords that we examined earlier are expected in the case of FTP. More modern authentication mechanisms also exist but have enjoyed limited success. FTP is unique among major protocols in that the control and data communication channels do not share the same port. In fact, it is not necessary for the two channels even to refer to the same system. An instruction can be sent down the command channel from the FTP client to the FTP server, initiating a data transfer to a third system. Although uncommon, this behavior is sometimes seen in normal traffic.

Generally, however, FTP transfers involving third parties are FTP *bounce attacks*. FTP allows the client to specify the IP address and TCP port on which the data transfer will occur. Under normal conditions, the IP address will be that of the client and the TCP port will be an ephemeral port. On the other hand, a malicious FTP client can use the PORT command to specify a system and service to attack, and then request that a file (already in place on the FTP server, perhaps uploaded previously by the hacker) be transferred to the victim. This file could contain commands relevant to the service being attacked, such as Simple Simple Mail Transfer Protocol (SMTP), Telnet, and so on. From the perspective of the attacked system, it would appear that the FTP server is attacking the victim. In actuality, though, the malicious FTP client is "bouncing" the attack off of the FTP server, hence the name of the attack.

Most current FTP servers avoid this problem either by refusing to accept PORT commands that do not refer to the actual FTP client or by disallowing PORT commands that refer to low ports (less than 1024), where most important services live. Note, as well, that the FTP bounce attack generally requires that the attacker be able to upload a file to the FTP server and then download it later to the victim system. Proper use of file permissions (that is, not allowing an upload directory to be readable as well as writable) will prevent this behavior. However, some services may be vulnerable to crashing when confronted with random binary data as well.

File permissions are also important for preventing improper use of system resources, particularly if the FTP server allows anonymous access. Hackers, file-sharers, and others have been known to use improperly configured FTP servers for storage and transfer of data. If an anonymous FTP directory intended for file upload also allows files to be downloaded, the potential for this type of abuse exists. Often, of course, system administrators may want to set up an area for files to be downloaded and uploaded without requiring authentication. To prevent abuse, it is recommended that two areas be set up—an upload area that is only writable, and a download area that is marked read-only. After reviewing files uploaded to the FTP server, the system administrator can move them to the download section for others to access.

An optional FTP command SITE EXEC, allows clients to execute commands on the FTP server. Clearly, if this feature is implemented on a server, the range of commands that can be executed needs to be configured with extreme care to avoid compromise of systems. Many IDSs are configured to trigger an alarm on SITE EXEC on FTP connections.

SSH

SSH, the Secure Shell, was developed as an encrypted replacement for cleartext protocols such as Telnet, Rlogin, and FTP. It provides for authentication and data transfer over an encrypted channel, and it thus provides an increased level of security for interactive data transfers. As such, it invaluable for remote system administration (especially those connections requiring privileged access) and transfer of sensitive data. However, the use of encryption comes at a cost: with cleartext protocols, evidence of intrusion can be determined by inspection of packet contents, while the contents of an encrypted connection are not available for inspection unless the IDS has access to the decryption keys.

Numerous security issues have occurred with various implementations of the SSH protocols as well as with the libraries (OpenSSL) that support encryption. As compromise is difficult or impossible to detect, due the encrypted nature of the connections; it is imperative that these services be patched whenever new vulnerabilities are announced. In addition, it is important that users not be lulled into a false sense of security by the use of the "encrypted connection" buzzword. Hackers have been known to install "keyboard sniffer" programs on compromised systems, which capture accounts and passwords for other systems directly from the keyboard of the compromised box, when the unsuspecting user logs into it. In this case, the encryption fails to assist, as the accounts/passwords are captured before they are encrypted. The encryption may actually detract from the detection of this compromise, since the IDS has no way of examining the connection for evidence of hacking activities.

SSH, if not already on a system, is sometimes installed by hackers, possibly on a non-standard port for precisely these reasons. Hackers can further their penetration essentially undetected under these circumstances, and reliance must be made on other detection mechanisms. Occasionally, the hacker may slip up and download tools via an unencrypted channel, or host-level detection mechanisms may provide some indication that the system in question has been compromised. In Chapter 5, we will discuss detection of SSH connections on these nonstandard ports, which provides evidence of possible compromise.

Web Services

The Hypertext Transfer Protocol (HTTP), in its initial incarnation developed in 1990, was small and somewhat inefficient, as each graphic required a separate connection to the web server. Due to the low bandwidth of the day, such inefficiency was tolerable. When dynamic pages became more prevalent, though, both the potential for abuse and the functionality of these web pages dramatically increased.

The common gateway interface (CGI) defined an early, and still quite commonly used method for the web server to interact with external programs that can vary their output based on the input they receive from the client browser. For security and performance reasons, many web servers include add-ons that will run CGIs in the web server itself. In general, this trend has proven to enhance security by disallowing dangerous actions (such as access outside of specified directories) within the framework of the web server itself, rather than relying on the expertise of the CGI author to provide these security features. On the browser side, both industry-standard and vendor-specific mechanisms exist to execute code on the browser with varying types of security controls.

The security considerations that exist are basically of two sorts (in addition to the network level risks we've explored earlier): web server bugs or misconfiguration that allow unauthorized remote attackers to

▼ Download data not intended for them

■ Execute commands on the server, or break out of the constraints of the commands allowed

■ Gain information on the configuration of the host or the software patch level, which will allow them to attack the web server

▲ Launch DoS attacks, rendering the system temporarily unavailable

The second type, on the browser side, includes the following:

▼ Active content downloaded from a malicious web page that damages the user's system, or damages confidentiality of user's data

■ Misuse of personal data provided by the user

▲ Eavesdropping of confidential information

SSL encryption is often used for web traffic that requires confidentiality. This does indeed provide protection against eavesdropping. However, as always, the security of such transactions are only as strong as the weakest link. Unless both browser and server sides are secured adequately, such information is still vulnerable to interception and misuse. It is important to keep in mind that the data is encrypted only during transit over the network, and is decrypted upon reaching its destination. Thus, the security of the encrypted data also, as always, is subject to the "weakest-link" principle, and attention must be given to host-level security of the server and the client.

In the following sections we will examine web security from the standpoints of both the server and the client.

Web Server Security

The two most popular web servers are Microsoft Internet Information Services (IIS) and the open-source Apache Web Server. Although many other servers exist, due to their popularity, these full-featured offerings dominate the web server landscape. However, as they include many components that some web pages may not need, and that may have security implications, prudent administrators will examine the feature sets of possible web servers and select a product based on the features that are needed. Unless esoteric web pages are needed, other web servers such as thttpd (available at http://www.acme .com/software/thttpd/) may be more appropriate.

Many optional features are also provided by modern web servers. These features allow increased convenience and functionality at the cost of increased security risk. In many cases, these additional features are not necessary, and should be turned off.

Directory Listing in the Absence of index.html   Unless a good reason exists for presenting a directory listing, this should be disabled, as it may reveal information of value to an attacker, such as misconfigured files or directories, source code to CGI scripts, log files, and other information. If an attacker can guess the name of a file, he may be able to download it anyway, but by making it more difficult, we can often deter attackers, who may seek more fruitful targets.

Symbolic Links   Following symbolic links can provide attackers with access to sensitive parts of the file system. This feature should be turned off. If it is desired to extend the directory tree, most modern servers allow this via an entry in the configuration file.

Server-Side Includes (SSIs)   SSIs are used to allow access to real-time data from the server by the inclusion of special commands in the web page. Some are relatively innocuous, such as displaying the current time, but others such as the "exec" server-side include may allow execution of arbitrary commands on the web server. In fact, in these days of plug-in CGI scripts and client-side software, the value of SSIs has been reduced to historical interest. Most web servers have no need to enable this obsolete and insecure feature.

Excessive Privileges   To bind a listening socket on TCP port 80 (the default web port) or 443 (the default encrypted web port) requires administrative-level privileges on most systems. Unless the web server restricts the directories that are publicly accessible, other unintended directories may also be available to web clients. For this reason, many web servers' privileges are dropped to a lower, less dangerous level, after binding to these ports.

Directory Traversal   This is seen in more contexts than web servers but is a common technique used by hackers to access files outside the desired directory structure. In this type of attack, an attacker will construct a request for a filename with a format similar to `../../../etc/passwd`. The `..` directory is a shorthand for the parent (or directory higher up). This construct goes up the directory tree, and then it goes down to the desired file to access it. Most current web servers reject requests with this sort of structure, as there is little if any legitimate use for this sort of access. However, Unicode encoding of this type of access may slip past unpatched servers. Most IDS systems will trigger alerts on directory traversal attacks.

Unicode   Unicode encoding allows for internationalization of web addresses, by encoding a 16-bit superset of ASCII standard web addresses, which are encoded in ASCII. It also allows for encoding of otherwise inexpressible characters, such as spaces, in web addresses. Unfortunately, some unpatched servers did not treat the same character in the same way, when expressed in Unicode form, as when it is expressed as a normal ASCII character. The `/` character, for example, used to separate directory components can be expressed in Unicode as `%c0%af`. Unfortunately, due to this bug, this allowed for successful exploitation of the directory traversal issue. Most IDSs *canonicalize* (convert to a standard form) Unicode data, so that it can be analyzed consistently. This is especially important, since Unicode provides multiple methods of expressing the same character.

CGI Security

One major source of web server compromise is the exploitation of vulnerable CGI programs. Quite a few canned CGI applications (many of them open source) exist for such diverse applications such as web guestbooks, bulletin board systems, feedback forms,

groupware, and many e-commerce applications. Unfortunately, many of these applications are not created with adequate attention to security matters for network enabled applications that must deal with untrusted input. This is a crucial security matter, as web-based applications must be prepared to accept input of any sort and any length, if they expect to be robust enough to survive in the Wild Web atmosphere of the Internet. In general, it is best to check for historical vulnerabilities before using a pre-made CGI package.

Some security concerns with CGI applications include the following:

Unchecked Input Causing Buffer Overflow or DoS   We've dealt with this at length earlier in the chapter. If a program allows a static buffer, and the hacker enters more data than the buffer has allocated, a buffer overflow occurs, potentially leading to a compromise of the system.

Command Injection   Many CGI functions build commands to be executed via a shell command. Sometimes, the full pathname to the command is not specified, thus allowing for the possibility that an unintended program of the same name may be executed in the context of the CGI program. Also, input containing shell metacharacters may cause unintended commands to be executed, and thus should be scanned for the standard shell metacharacters. See the man pages for your favorite shell for more information on metacharacters.

An Example of CGI Command Injection

Many web sites exist which allow "ping"ing of another site on the internet via a web browser. One such site recently implemented this functionality via a CGI, which tacked unchecked user input after the ping command, then executed the result. When run against an unknown site, the following was returned:

```
/usr/sbin/ping: unknown host noonehome.nothere
```

By appending a semicolon, and another command (in this case the "id" command) in the window for specifying the host to ping, the other (unintended) command was also run:

```
Pinging noonehome.nothere;id; from host.fictionalisp.net
uid=60001(nobody) gid=60001(nobody)
```

Obviously, something more destructive could also have been run. The problem here is that unchecked user input is passed from the CGI script directly to the command line. A simple command which filters out dangerous characters would have alleviated this problem. For example, the following Perl fragment will drop any input characters that are not alphanumeric, dashes, underscores, or periods:

```
$user_input  =~ s/[^A-Za-z0-9_-.]//g;
```

An Example of CGI Command Injection *(continued)*

As this web page was designed to simply ping remote sites, the character set described is adequate. Depending on the application, the valid characters that could be input to it would vary. The important point to remember is that only input that is valid for the application should be allowed.

Directory Traversal   If precautions are not taken with user supplied filenames, the CGI function may be tricked into accessing a file outside the expected file structure, as discussed earlier.

SQL Injection   This is a case of command injection that deserves special attention. Many e-commerce or other database applications that take input via a web form construct a SQL command from this input for query of a database. It is possible, with malformed unchecked input, to construct a valid SQL command that is significantly different from the desired command, and execute queries or other SQL commands that are unintended.

An Example of SQL Injection

Often, a secure web application will have a login page that allows access to the application. On this page, an account and password is provided by the user before access is granted.

In this scenario, the web designer has chosen to build a dynamic SQL statement which queries a database against the provided account and password. The following code provides an example of building the query:

```
System.Text.StringBuilder AccountInquiry = new System.Text.StringBuilder(
    "SELECT * from UserDB WHERE account = '")
    .Append(txtAccount.Text).Append("' AND passwd='")
    .Append(txtPassword.Text).Append("'");
```

Here, the account and password are used to build the query without any sanity checking. A malicious user who desires to gain access to the system and who knows a valid account could enter the following into the password field:

```
"' or '0'='0'"
```

This input will cause the code to create the following (valid, but unintended) SQL query:

```
SELECT * from UserDB WHERE account='validuser' AND passwd = '' or '0'='0'
```

An Example of SQL Injection *(continued)*

This command, when run against the database, could incorrectly grant access, as the '0'='0' portion of the query would cause the database entry for the account `validuser` to be returned, as if the correct password was entered.

As we saw when examining command injection, it is important to check untrusted input before using it to construct database queries. In particular, the use of quotes and hyphens should (unless necessary) be disallowed in input. We have just seen how quotes can be abused. Hyphens can be used in SQL queries to indicate comments, and allow an attacker to comment out part of a query and thus bypass access controls.

Excessive Privileges   CGIs often run in the context of the web server and thus may inherit the web server's privileges. Even if the application is considered secure, it is always important to take advantage of any mechanisms that help restrict access only to those resources that the applications need. Multiple application wrappers exist (cgiwrap, sbox, and so on) that enforce that CGI scripts be run as unprivileged users.

Browser Security

Client-side code (applets) has also been developed and become standard in browsers, beginning with relatively humble beginnings such as Java and JavaScript, up to the complex (and insecure) framework of ActiveX. Most of these client-side programs attempt to restrict the actions of a possible malicious (or simply buggy) web site by creating a "sandbox" where all actions of the untrusted applet are confined. Theoretically, this sandbox prevents the applet from making file, configuration, or other security-sensitive changes to the client system. In actuality, bugs in sandbox implementations and user-overrides (where the user is asked to override the sandbox controls, and accept the risk that the applet is not malicious or buggy) reduce the sandboxes' effectiveness. Vulnerabilities in both Java and JavaScript allow for the creation of a malicious applet that can bypass applet sandbox restrictions.

ActiveX takes a different approach to security and places no restrictions on what an ActiveX control (the equivalent of a Java applet) can do. The security of ActiveX is achieved through the trust-relationship that the user has with the vendor of the ActiveX control, which can be digitally signed by the vendor, who certifies that the software is virus and malicious content free. This certification ensures that the ActiveX control cannot be manipulated by a malicious third party, but it does not ensure that the control will be well-behaved.

A fully signed and certified ActiveX control called Exploder was developed by Fred McLain to prove this point. Exploder (whose certificate has since been revoked) caused Windows systems to shut down when run. It is available for inspection at http://www .halcyon.com/mclain/ActiveX. Although the certificate has been revoked, users can still choose to activate this control.

Uneducated users often download and install such software without a clear understanding of the risks that they are taking. Putting the onus to determine the security risks of installing unknown software on naïve users poses a severe security risk, one that is likely to increase with time. The emergence of a control that performs a subtle or stealthy action of transmitting confidential data to its creator, in addition to performing some legitimate action, can be expected in the next few years.

SNMP

The Simple Network Management Protocol, developed in 1988, is now the standard for network management. SNMP has had the derisive acronym "Security Not My Problem" due its unencrypted nature and lack of attention to security issues. Some of the most egregious SNMP security issues have been addressed in SNMP v3, however. Nearly all network hardware that supports remote management includes an SNMP agent for this purpose. The SNMP system is partitioned into two elements: management console(s), and multiple agents deployed on the managed network hardware (bridges, routers, hubs, firewalls, servers, and so on). Each managed device contains multiple managed objects, which may consist of hardware, software, or network performance statistics, configuration parameters, and so on These objects are arranged in a distributed virtual database, called a Management Information Base, or MIB. SNMP is the glue that allows management consoles and agents to communicate for the purposes of monitoring and modifying the objects in this database.

An SNMP community string is used to define the relationship among a management console and the agents, essentially a password to control access. The default access level is read-only, which allows inspection but not modification of data/configuration on the agent device. By default, most network devices come with a default read-only community string of *public* and a read/write community string of *private*. A surprising number of network devices are not reconfigured from these strings, which presents a severe vulnerability to the entire network to which they are connected.

Armed with knowledge of the read-only community string, a hacker can walk through the entire MIB of an enterprise by the use of the one-liner:

```
snmpwalk [-d] [-p port] -v 1 host community [variable_name]
```

where `host` is the name of a starting place to start the walk, and `community` is the community string. By utilizing an SNMP Get Next operation, this command will walk through the entire accessible MIB database and display configuration information highly useful for penetrating a network.

With knowledge of the read/write community string, an attacker can reconfigure at will the network configuration. It is critically important to change the community strings from their defaults and to protect these strings as appropriate.

SNMP has had several publicized vulnerabilities, so, as usual for important services, it is important to apply the appropriate patches. Generally, SNMP traffic shouldn't be allowed to traverse an organizational firewall, as outsiders have no need to access this important service. Blocking the following ports (TCP and UDP) at the border are recommended: 161, 162, 199, and 391.

VIRUSES AND WORMS

Everyone who has an e-mail account or Internet presence has been touched in some manner by the proliferation of viruses. (Note that in distinction to biological virii, generally the plural of a computer *virus* is *viruses*.) A virus, in the computer sense, is a piece of program code designed to replicate, or make copies of. itself, in an analogous manner to biological reproduction. Strictly speaking, it is not necessary that the virus do any damage, but its unwelcome nature makes eradication important. Recently, there has evolved a somewhat gray area between worms and viruses, but the following is generally true:

▼ If the malicious code automatically detects and spreads to another vulnerable system without human intervention, it is a *worm*.

▲ If the malicious code is transported to another system, but requires human intervention (such as opening an e-mail attachment) to activate it, it is considered a *virus*.

The key distinction is whether the malicious code requires some action to activate it, or whether it immediately begins running. Some viruses/worms straddle this line, as they incorporate several different infection mechanisms. For instance, the recent Nimda worm has several infection vectors:

▼ A viral infection mechanism of searching for and e-mailing itself to e-mail addresses found on the infected system

■ A worm-like infection mechanism of scanning for unprotected network shares and copying itself there

■ A worm infection mechanism of scanning for and infecting vulnerable IIS servers

▲ A viral mechanism of infecting both local and network accessible files on a compromised system; it also creates unprotected network shares for anyone on the Internet to access

Recent examples of pure viruses are "I Love You" and "SoBig," which propagate through e-mail attachments. Pure worm examples would be "Code Red," "Slammer," and "Blaster," which actively scan for and infect further vulnerable systems in a chain-reaction fashion.

Fortunately, up to this time, the worms and viruses seen on the Internet have been somewhat mild in their actions. Current worms/viruses have performed one or more of the following actions:

▼ Install back-door software for remote control of systems

■ Install an e-mail engine for relaying spam

■ Deface web sites

■ Conduct distributed denial of service (DDOS) attacks against targets

▲ Clog Internet bandwidth

Fears about future worms include the following:

▼   Corruption or deletion of data on systems. Paradoxically, those worms that perform this act slowly are considered to have more destructive potential, as they may spread more widely before completely crippling their victims. Of particular concern is the possibility of a "bit-rotting" worm that, over an extensive period of time, rots the data on the hard drive. Before its presence is detected, all data backups may themselves be copies of corrupted data as well.

■   Contrary to some beliefs, software can, in fact, damage hardware. A worm could overdrive a monitor and burn it out, or even scarier, reflash the BIOS of the system either to contain a permanent back door or render the system unusable.

■   Construct a large scale DDOS army of controlled computers, ready to be unleashed against targets, with crippling effect.

■   Espionage, both commercial and military.

▲   Personal information theft, such as credit card numbers, Social Security numbers, or other personal information of value.

A Brief History of Worms

In 1988, the Morris Internet worm made news by causing a disruption of the Internet for several days; it caused enormous slowdowns in the Internet, which had only 60,000 hosts at the time. Each successful worm in turn prompts, or popularizes, the correction of those bugs that it exploits. Although the Morris worm days are long past, it is worth reviewing the nature of this attack, as it is somewhat sophisticated. The Morris worm had three different attack vectors:

▼   **Attack on Sendmail**   The worm connected to another system's Sendmail process and invoked debug mode to download a 40-line C program to the target, which then was compiled on the target host. This compiled program downloaded additional code from the attacking system to create an executable called */usr/tmp/sh*.

■   **Attack on *fingerd*, the finger daemon**   A buffer overflow attack allowed for the execution of a shell on the fingerd port, which was then used to download the additional code, as in the Sendmail attack.

▲   **Attack using host trust relationships**   It accessed the *.rhosts* and */etc/hosts.equiv* files to determine which hosts were trusted by the infected hosts. To access these new victims, the worm attempted to guess passwords of accounts harvested from the */etc/passwd* file. It tried a number of combinations, as well as reading the entire */usr/dict/words* file (which contained an online dictionary). Once a password was successfully guessed, the worm would look for a *.rhosts* file and log into the next victim, downloading code, as in the other attack vectors, and continued the process again.

The bugs responsible for the first two vectors were quickly corrected, but variations of the third infection vector are still used to spread worms to this day. When a web of trust exists between hosts, the security of this web is only as strong as its weakest link.

These days, Unix worms are fairly uncommon, as Windows systems are the victims of choice for worm writers these days. This is not, per se, an indictment of Windows security, but it is an indication of the popularity of the operating system and the target-rich environment. Worms now propagate through Windows shares to infect additional systems, as well as attempting to guess remote access passwords. Unlike the Morris worm, modern worms do not generally download and compile source code, but instead target a particular architecture, although they sometimes are adapted to different versions of the Windows operating system.

The modern worm era pretty much began with the emergence of the Code Red worm in 2001, which employed a heap overflow to exploit vulnerability in Microsoft's IIS Web Server to deface web sites and scan for other victims. The original Code Red worm was entirely memory-resident, which means that rebooting the infected system would stop the worm's scanning action, but unless the system was patched for the vulnerability, it would rapidly become infected again.

The first variant of Code Red was released on July 12, 2001, and was relatively harmless, as each infected system attacked the same computed list of systems. On July 19, 2001, Code Red v2 was unleashed with an improved random number generator that rapidly infected an estimated 359,000 systems in 14 hours. At its peak, more than 2000 systems were being infected every minute. This worm was also programmed to launch a massive DDOS attack on http://www.whitehouse.gov. The IP address of this site was hard-coded into the worm, so the attack was foiled by moving the web site to a different IP address. Consequently, the programmed attack (which took place as scheduled) targeted an unused IP address. At the scheduled time, many backbone providers took the additional step of refusing to route traffic destined for the programmed address.

Code Red II (distinct from Code Red v2), discovered on August 4, 2001, exploited the same vulnerability that the original Code Red used, but it actually installed a back door for hackers to enter the system and remained on the system through reboots. Surprisingly enough, even as of this writing (October 2003), Code Red still exists in the wild on the Internet, and it still scans sites for vulnerable hosts.

The Nimda worm followed on the heels of Code Red to exploit another Microsoft IIS vulnerability and in fact attempted to spread via the back door created by Code Red II. It has numerous infection vectors, including e-mail, open shares, and the aforementioned IIS vulnerability. One interesting feature that other worm authors have emulated is that the Nimda worm disables common antivirus products on infected systems, thus increasing the difficulty of detection.

In 2003, the Slammer Worm hit, entirely enclosed in a single 376-byte User Datagram Protocol (UDP) packet. This worm was by far the fasted spreading worm to date, infecting every vulnerable system reachable on the Internet within 30 minutes of its release into the wild. The main effect of this worm was the enormous increase in traffic on UDP port 1434, clogging the Internet with high-speed scanning. As this worm was memory-resident, turning off the system removed the worm, but patching was required to prevent reinfection.

Later in 2003, the Blaster worm hit the Internet with a vengeance, exploiting a Windows Distributed Component Object Model (DCOM) vulnerability. Exploited systems began immediately scanning for other vulnerable systems and compromised them, and in turn lead the newly infected systems began scanningfor more vulnerable systems to infect. Fortunately, we have not seen malicious content in these worms, but researchers expect that to be merely a matter of time. The Welchia worm followed quickly on its heels, as a misguided attempt to install the Microsoft patch on vulnerable systems, but quickly achieved a life of its own and wreaked havoc in its own right.

It is clear that more virulent worms and viruses are to be expected. The goal of IDS is to detect and contain these incidents quickly so that they do not overwhelm enterprise security resources.

SUMMARY

We have seen some of the types of vulnerabilities in common software packages used on the Internet today. As the software industry matures further, we will see advances in application, system, and process security. We can also expect the hacking community to continue creatively challenging security professionals with new techniques and corresponding advances in IDS techniques to combat these threats. In Chapter 5, we will examine one of the seminal tools in IDS, TCPDump, and how it can be used to capture and foil attacks.

CHAPTER 5

Tcpdump

Tcpdump could well be called the first intrusion detection system—certainly when it was initially released in 1991 there were few, if any, other systems that could display network traffic. Even today, tcpdump is used as an adjunct to current intrusion detection products, providing a standard format for capturing and storing network traffic. As all IDS systems support tcpdump format files, it is useful when employing multiple IDS technologies. A file captured with tcpdump can be run through multiple IDS systems to contrast and compare the varying capabilities of the products.

In this chapter, we will explore some of the capabilities of tcpdump with a specific focus on intrusion detection uses. In addition, other useful programs in the tcpdump family will be briefly surveyed.

Tcpdump was originally developed by the Network Research Group at Lawrence Berkeley National Laboratory (LBNL), and it is currently maintained by and is available at www.tcpdump.org.

TCPDUMP COMMAND LINE OPTIONS

Tcpdump is capable of capturing, displaying, and storing all forms of network traffic (not just TCP traffic, despite the name) in a variety of output formats. Input packets can be captured from the network or read from a disk file. Tcpdump capture files are portable across architectures because all data is stored in network byte order.

The man page for tcpdump on a given system is the authoritative guide to its usage, but the main options are fairly standard. The syntax for the `tcpdump` command is as follows:

```
tcpdump [ -adeflnNOpqStvx ] [ -c count ] [ -F file ][ -i interface ] [ -r file ]
[ -s snaplen ] [ -T type ] [ -w file ] [ expression ]
```

The most commonly used options are described in Table 5-1.

Network Byte Order

When designing the TCP/IP protocol suite, attention was paid to standardizing the representation of multiple-byte quantities. Some processors (those from Sun and Motorola, IBM-370s, and PDP-10s, for instance) store the most significant bytes (that is, the bytes that hold the largest part of the value) first. These are known as *big endian* processors. Other processors (the x86 family, Vaxes, and Alphas, among others) store the most significant byte last. These are known as *little-endian* processors. A few older processors use a strange ordering called *middle-endian*, as well. Some modern processors can change their endian type programmatically.

Clearly, it was necessary to decide on a standard Internet format if systems with differing endian standards could hope to communicate. Possibly because early development took place on big-endian systems, the big-endian format was accepted as the standard *network byte order*. Systems that use other orders must convert the network data to their internal format on input, and convert it back to network byte order on outputting it to the network. Tcpdump, the TCP/IP stack in the operating system, and all network programs routinely perform these tasks so that a particular system's endian style does not affect their functionality.

Option	Description
-c	Capture *count* packets, then exit.
-e	Print the link-level header; usually the link-level (such as Ethernet) data is not printed.
-I	The name of the network *interface* to capture data from.
-n	Don't convert IP addresses or port numbers to names.
-O	Do not attempt to optimize the generated code; this is sometimes useful when specifying complex expressions.
-p	Don't put the interface in promiscuous mode.
-r	Read packets from the tcpdump capture *file* (created with the -w option, or IDS tcpdump format output).
-s	Capture *snaplen* bytes of data from each packet (the default is 68 bytes).
-S	Print TCP sequence numbers as captured 32-bit values, rather than relative to the beginning of the connection.
-t	Don't print any timestamp (not generally useful).
-tt	Print timestamp as standard Unix timestamp (number of seconds since the Unix beginning of time: Jan. 1, 1970), rather than human formatted.
-v	Produce more verbose output.
-vv	Produce even more verbose output.
-w	Write packets to *file*, in raw format.
-x	Print the packet in hexadecimal.

Table 5-1.   Tcpdump Options

A few of these options require special attention or caveats:

▼   **-n**   The -n option is used to specify that tcpdump should not attempt to resolve IP addresses or port names. In addition to the performance hit of invoking DNS, the use of this option may dramatically increase network traffic. Tcpdump, if it is examining the same network interface that the DNS queries and responses arrive on, could see those queries and responses too, thus potentially causing two additional packets for each input packet. Generally, therefore, this option is confined to offline use, such as when reading a file via the -r option.

■ **-O**   The *libpcap* library called by tcpdump compiles the given expression into code for the BPF (Berkeley Packet Filter) interpreter, which is either in the kernel or implemented in user space and optimizes the code for speed of execution. Unfortunately, bugs have been known to creep into this optimization process, so it is sometimes recommended to turn this flag on when using complex expressions. The optimizer's functionality can be verified by running a tcpdump capture file that thoroughly exercises the expression through tcpdump twice, with and without optimization. If the optimization is working correctly, the output in both cases should be identical.

■ **-p**   This flag instructs tcpdump to *not* enter promiscuous mode when reading packets from a network interface. When in promiscuous mode, which is the default for IDS purposes, a network interface card will pass all data seen on the network to the operating system kernel for processing. This feature is often termed *sniffing the network,* and it is used by hackers to capture data traversing the wire, such as cleartext accounts and passwords. With the –p flag set, the card will not be put into promiscuous mode, and only traffic destined for the host or sent to a broadcast address will be sent to the operating system for processing, and only that traffic will be seen by tcpdump. For security reasons, the ability to enter promiscuous mode is generally restricted to the root account or other trusted users. Some vendors have changed the meaning of this flag to its exact reverse—on those systems –p causes tcpdump to enter promiscuous mode. As usual, readers are advised to check the manual pages for their particular system.

■ **-s**   This argument is followed by a decimal number that specifies the maximum number of bytes to capture in each packet. Some applications, such as in network debugging, do not concern themselves with the packet data, but only with the protocol headers. In those cases, it is appropriate to only capture the beginning of the packet containing these headers. IDS applications are concerned with packet data as well, so the default of 68 bytes (enough, typically, for an IP header and a TCP header) will need to be overridden by the frame size of the media being used (for example, 1,500 for Ethernet). In many tcpdump implementations, using the shorthand –s 0 results in tcpdump autoconfiguring to the correct value to capture a maximum size packet appropriate to the transmission medium.

■ **-S**   The –S argument instructs tcpdump to *not* keep the state of TCP connections. By default, the initial sequence number from the original SYN packet of each side of the connection is saved by tcpdump. Each subsequent packet of that TCP connection will have the sequence number displayed as an offset from the initial sequence number. When the FIN or RST packet is seen, the final sequence number will be displayed, and the state of the connection will be torn down. As we will discuss later, this gives a direct indication of the number of bytes that were transferred in the connection. The –S option is appropriate when using a tcpdump filter that does not include both the beginning and the end of TCP connections, such as when looking only at SYN packets. If this is not

done, tcpdump will accumulate state information on sequence numbers, but since it never sees the end of the connection, this connection state will never be released, thus causing an apparent memory leak. Red Hat Linux 9 has an apparent bug that renders the use of this flag ineffective.

▲ **-tt**   This option causes tcpdump to print out the timestamp of the packet in Unix format. This format, although not directly human readable is often quite useful, as it allows direct arithmetic between timestamps to calculate connection timing. In some implementations, the date -r command can be used to convert this timestamp to a human-readable format.

TCPDUMP OUTPUT FORMAT

Tcpdump has two basic output formats: either a raw file, which consists of the packet contents along with accompanying information (such as timestamps), or various forms of human-readable output. In this section, we will explore the various human-readable formats that are of interest to the IDS analyst. To compare the formats, we will examine the effects of the various output formats on a sample packet, which is a mid-connection packet from a telnet connection.

By default, tcpdump will print one line per packet consisting of important packet data, including timestamp, protocol, source and destination hosts and ports, flags, options, and (for TCP packets) sequence numbers. We begin by using the following command to display our sample packet:

```
tcpdump -r demo.trace
```

This command produces the following sample packet:

```
03:00:44.919519 test.demo.com.3252 > help.demo.com.telnet: P
177:215(38) ack 331 win 62839 (DF)
```

In this example, we can see a timestamp shortly past 3 A.M., followed by the source hostname (test.demo.com), and the source port (3252). The greater-than symbol (>) indicates the direction of the packet. The destination host is indicated as help.demo.com on the telnet port. This packet contains the PUSH flag (P), indicating urgent data, followed by the sequence number at the beginning of the packet (177) and that of the packet end (215), followed by the difference, which will typically be the count of data bytes in this packet (38). In this default mode, the sequence numbers are normalized to 0, as we shall discuss later. We can also see that the packet is acknowledging (ack) relative sequence number 331 from a previous packet sent by help.demo.com. The transmission window (win) is 62839, and the Do Not Fragment flag (DF) is also set.

If we use the -tt flag described earlier, we will see the following output:

```
1063360844.919519 test.demo.com.3252 > help.demo.com.telnet: P
177:215(38) ack 331 win 62839 (DF)
```

Note that the timestamp is now expressed in Unix format, which is seconds since Jan. 1, 1970, 0:00 GMT. We can convert this to human-readable format by sending the numeric value thru date -r:

```
$ date -r 1063360844.919519
Fri Sep 12 03:00:44 PDT 2003
```

The Unix timestamp is valuable because direct arithmetic can be performed between timestamps. For instance, by taking the difference between the timestamp of the initial SYN packet that started a connection and the timestamp of the FIN or RST that ended it, the connection's total time in seconds can be directly computed.

We will now try the -n flag:

```
03:00:44.919519 192.168.3.3.3252 > 192.168.3.99.23: P 177:215(38) ack 331 win 62839 (DF)
```

The change from the original packet display is clear—neither the hostnames, nor the ports, are resolved to names. Some implementations of tcpdump require the use of -nn to achieve this result.

Using the -S flag gives us the following output:

```
03:00:44.919519 test.demo.com.3252 > help.demo.com.telnet: P
2053563889:2053563927(38) ack 3671890340 win 62839 (DF)
```

The display here gives the raw TCP sequence numbers. Previously, we saw sequence numbers relative to the beginning of the connection. We know from the previous displays that the relative sequence number of test.demo.com started at 177, and since the corresponding raw sequence number is 2053563889, we can by simple arithmetic conclude that test.demo.com started with a sequence number of 2053563712.

Combining the three options (tcpdump -n -tt -S -r demo.trace) gives no surprises:

```
1063360844.919519 192.168.3.3.3252 > 192.168.3.99.23: P
2053563889:2053563927(38) ack 3671890340 win 62839 (DF)
```

We can also increase the level of verbosity by using -v:

```
1063360844.919519 192.168.3.3.3252 > 192.168.3.99.23: P
2053563889:2053563927(38) ack 3671890340 win 62839 (DF) (ttl 126, id
36440)
```

Here, we additionally see the IP TTL (126) and the IP id field (36440).

In addition to the preceding display formats, tcpdump also provides the option to dump the packet in hexadecimal format by using the -x flag. In this format, the earlier flags still take effect, and the data is displayed as previously, along with a hex dump of the packet. For example, we can run this command:

```
tcpdump -x -n -tt -S -v -r demo.trace
```

The output of that command is as follows:

```
1063360844.919519 192.168.3.3.3252 > 192.168.3.99.23: P
2053563889:2053563927(38) ack 3671890340 win 62839 (DF) (ttl 126, id 36440)

                         4500 004e 8e58 4000 7e06 59d3 c0a8 0303
                         c0a8 0363 0cb4 0017 7a66 e5f1 dadc 99a4
                         5018 f577 2561 0000 594d 5347 000b 0000
                         0012 008a 0000 0000 db7f 11d4 30c0 8063
                         6861 726c 6573 686f 7761 7264 c080
```

What we see in the hex dump is the exact contents of the packet, starting with the IP header, which in this case is followed by the TCP header and the TCP data. As the previous data is in decimal format, and this display is in hex, a good programmer's calculator can be valuable as an aid in conversion.

Several things can, however, be easily gleaned from inspecting the hex dump and referring to the IP and TCP header formats that were discussed in Chapter 2. Each hex digit represents 4 bits, and the first 4 bits of the IP header represent the IP version, so we can easily see that this packet is using IP version 4. The next hex digit is the number of 32-bit words in the IP header, in this case 5. (This is by far the most common value, as it represents an IP packet with no options). Each set of 4 hex digits represents 16 bits, so after counting 10 (5 × 2) groups of 4, we reach the beginning of the TCP header, which starts with 0cb4, which is the source port (3252 in decimal).

It is important to read the manual for your version of tcpdump, as options and output formats vary. Our discussion has been based upon the original LBNL version of tcpdump, but there have been some additional changes made by the folks at www.tcpdump.org that are hugely useful. In particular, the -X option displays the packet in ASCII format for direct examination of cleartext protocols. See the man pages for your version of tcpdump for its particular details.

TCPDUMP EXPRESSIONS

The final argument to the tcpdump command is a Boolean expression against which packets are matched. The construction of the expression may seem somewhat obscure, but with practice it can be used to extract packets matching extremely precise characteristics. In fact, we will see how tcpdump expressions can be used in such diverse applications as detecting services running on nonstandard ports, determining whether users are using peer-to-peer applications, and keeping TCP connection records.

Basically, the Berkeley Packet Filtering (BPF) language used by tcpdump and most IDS products performs packet matching by using an expression that matches bytes within the packet. The expression can include bytes and the normal arithmetic and logical operators, generally matching those found in the C language. A packet that matches

the expression will be processed by the BPF application, whereas those that fail the pattern match are silently discarded.

Although tcpdump is capable of dissecting raw packets, we will examine the types of packets we've discussed earlier—namely IP and the higher-level protocols (TCP, UDP, and ICMP). Each byte in a packet can be addressed as an offset (starting at 0) from the beginning of the protocol header. The format of this basic form of addressing is *proto[offset]*, where *proto* is the protocol in question (IP, TCP, UDP, or ICMP), and *offset* is the byte count from the beginning of the protocol header. Multibyte fields can be addressed as *proto[offset:size]*, where *size* is 1, 2, or 4, indicating the number of bytes in the field. The IP *proto* is usually used to filter on specific fields in the IP header, while the TCP, UDP, and ICMP *protos* are used to filter on the protocol header and packet contents.

Numeric values in the BPF expression can be addressed in the familiar C syntax of *0xabcd* for hexadecimal (base 16) values, *01234* for octal (base 8) values, and the familiar decimal notation for decimal values. The following operators can be used to string these values together:

▼ **Standard C arithmetic and Boolean operators** +, −, *, /, &, |

■ **Logical operators** && (and), || (or)

■ **Relational operators** <, <=, = , >=, >

■ **Bit-shift operators** >>, <<

■ **The negation operator** !

▲ **Parentheses** ( )

Here are a few examples:

▼ **tcp[2:2] = 22** A TCP packet with a destination port of 22; bytes two and three of the TCP header are the destination port (later we'll see an easier way to do this)

■ **ip[8] = 1** An IP packet with a time-to-live value of 1; byte eight of the IP header is the TTL field

▲ **ip[0] = 0x45** An IPv4 packet with no options (the IHL field is five 32-bit words or 20 bytes, the minimum, hence no options); this is the most common first byte for IP packets

Rather than expecting casual users to remember that (for instance) the TCP destination port is addressed as tcp[2:2], users can use the shorthand tcp dst port 22 format instead of the more cumbersome tcp[2:2]=22 format. It is rather unfortunate that ranges are not expressible in this shorthand format, though. There is, for instance, no convenient way to express TCP ports from 20 to 30 other than the nonintuitive **tcp[2:2]>=20 and tcp[2:2]<=30.**

Expressions can be quite complex. To check that the first data byte of a TCP packet is a binary 1, we could use this expression:

```
tcp[(tcp[12]>>4)*4] = 1
```

Let's break down this rather complex expression from the inside out. First, we are taking byte 12 of the TCP header, which contains the header length (measured in 32-bit words) in the top four bits, and a reserved field in the lower four bits. We then shift this to the left by four bits, which will move the header length to the lower four bits, and fill the upper four bits with 0's. As this is a count of 32-bit (or 4-byte) words, we then multiply by four to compute the header length in bytes. This is the offset of the first data byte, whose value is then checked against 0.

NOTE If you've forgotten the details of the TCP header, see Chapter 2, particularly Figure 2-5.

Astute readers will note that we shifted four bits to the right, then two bits to the left in the multiplication by four, so if we assume that the reserved field is indeed filled with 0's, the expression could be simplified to this:

```
tcp[tcp[12]>>2] = 1
```

By performing an and operation on tcp[12] with a binary 11110000 (hexadecimal 0xf0, or decimal 240), the reserved field is masked out to zeros, so the final expression looks like this:

```
tcp[(tcp[12] & 0xf0)>>2] = 1
```

In IDS applications, it is probably safest to perform this extra step to avoid possible evasion attempts.

Shorthand Expressions

The somewhat tortured syntax we've just seen is often expressed more naturally with the use of shorthand expressions. When compiled, these shorthand expressions reduce to the comparisons of packet bytes we've looked at, but they are much more readable for human consumption. We'll briefly examine a few of the more useful shorthand expressions.

To specify hosts or networks, the qualifiers host or net are used, while to specify a port, the port keyword is used. These keywords are followed by a name or number that specifies what the keyword refers to. Here are some examples: host foobar, net 192.168/16, and port telnet.

To specify the direction of the transfer (in other words, to match the source or destination), the keywords src, dst, src or dst and src and dst are used. For example: src host bar, dst net 172.16.0.0/16, src or dst port ftp. If the directional keyword is omitted, src or dst (meaning either source or destination) is assumed.

The length keyword matches the length of the packet (excluding the link-level header), which includes the IP header length, the protocol-specific header, and the protocol data. For IP packets, this is equivalent to the much more cumbersome expression ip[2:2].

Here are a few examples using this more natural syntax:

▼ `host a or host b`   Matches all packets from either of the two hosts.

■ `host a and host b`   Matches packets that include both hosts; in other words, all traffic between the two hosts.

■ `host a and not host b`   Matches traffic between host a and all hosts except host b.

■ `src host a`   Matches traffic originating from host a.

■ `src host a and tcp port telnet`   Matches traffic originating from host a with a source or destination of the `telnet` port.

▲ `net `*`mynet`*` and not net `*`mynet`*   Matches traffic between *mynet* and other hosts or networks. The network can either be specified by referencing an entry in /etc/networks or using the standard network/netmask format.

BULK CAPTURE

Tcpdump is often used as an adjunct to IDS systems to capture traffic for later analysis. Utilizing tcpdump in this manner is often termed *bulk capture* to denote the process of capturing all (or a significant subset) of the traffic that the IDS sees for possible forensic analysis. In large sites, the size of these capture files are likely to be many megabytes or even gigabytes.

Why is this capture important? Several benefits accrue to sites that perform this additional data capturing: First, an IDS system must, of necessity, be lightweight enough to keep up with the traffic stream. Often, it is useful to perform more CPU-intensive analysis on the traffic offline. For instance, the IDS system Bro (available from www.icir .org/vern/bro.html) can detect encrypted stepping stones, where an incoming connection is used as a stepping stone to other systems. This detection mechanism is not lightweight enough to be performed in real time, and thus is performed offline using a bulk-capture file, which captures the same traffic that the IDS sees.

The use of a bulk-capture mechanism also allows experimentation with varying IDS rule sets and comparison between various IDS products in a controlled manner. As most IDS products can read input from a tcpdump file, their features can be compared by feeding each offering the same bulk capture file, and comparing results. Also, the effects of enabling various IDS options or detection features can be examined.

Probably the most compelling argument for utilizing a bulk-capture feature is for later forensic examination of traffic. An IDS alert can often be a later indication of a prior compromise of a system, and in cases like this, having prior tcpdump data can provide valuable clues as to the nature of the compromise.

Creating a bulk-capture facility is relatively simple, as the hardware and software requirements are generally relatively modest. The system needs hardware fast enough to support the capture and storage of the anticipated traffic. Disk storage requirements will be determined by the traffic load and the length of time that the traffic will be maintained

for archival and forensic purposes. Typical modern PC hardware generally has no difficulty with these requirements. Software requirements are, if anything, even more modest, requiring a modern operating system and the software described in this chapter.

To implement a simple bulk-capture system on a Unix system requires little more than the appropriate script, invoked periodically via cron:

```
#!/bin/sh
# bulk_capture.sh - to be invoked by cron periodically to perform bulk
# capture and rollover into periodic files

FILEPREFIX=/home/capturedir/trace.
PIDFILE=/home/capturedir/pid

# Determine filename for next capture
i=1
while true
do
        # Determine next free capture filename
        CAPTUREFILE=${FILEPREFIX}.$i
        [ -f $i ] || break
        i=`expr $i + 1`
done

# Get the process ID of the previous capture file
PID=0
[ -f $PIDFILE ] PID=`cat $PIDFILE`

# Start the next capture
#  Note that we don't kill the previous capture until after this
#  one has the opportunity to start, so that there is never a time
#  without coverage
tcpdump -s 1500 -i eth0 -w $CAPTUREFILE myfilter_expression &

# Save the new process ID away
echo $! >$PIDFILE

# Wait briefly to allow new tcpdump to start cleanly,
#  then kill the previous one
sleep 1
[ $PID -eq 0 ] || kill $PID

exit
```

The portions of the script in italics are to be customized by users for their installations. Note especially the use of the −s 1500 option to ensure that the full Ethernet packet is captured by tcpdump. This script can periodically be invoked via cron to roll over to a new file, which will be numbered in sequence, starting at trace.1. An additional script (not included here) that may be required is one that monitors disk space usage and purges old capture files when disk utilization reaches a predetermined value.

HOW MANY BYTES WERE TRANSFERRED IN THAT CONNECTION?

In Chapter 2, we examined the details of TCP communications. Each side of the communication establishes an initial sequence number, which is a randomly selected 32-bit number, and it is incremented with each byte transferred, or each SYN and FIN bit set. This means that if we know the sequence number of the packet that established the connection and the sequence number of the packet that ended the connection, we can easily calculate the actual number of bytes transferred. For each side of the connection, we simply subtract the initial sequence number from the final sequence number, and then deduct 1 for each SYN, FIN, and RST sent.

With that in mind, we will start with a tcpdump filter that captures TCP packets with SYN, FIN, or RST. tcp[13] contains the packet flags, and by masking out the lower three bits, which contain the flags we're interested in, and comparing it with zero, we can extract just the packets of interest:

```
tcp[13] & 7 != 0
```

When we use the −S flag with tcpdump, the raw sequence numbers are displayed, as mentioned earlier. When this flag is omitted, tcpdump does the arithmetic for us and computes relative sequence numbers, as shown in the following example:

```
1068422738.826406 HostA.2398 > HostB.23: S 1950934552:1950934552(0)
win 16384 <mss 1460,nop,nop,sackOK> (DF)
1068422738.908640 HostB.23 > HostA.2398: S 1373962008:1373962008(0) ack
1950934553 win 61440 <mss 1460>
1068422752.662658 HostB.23 > HostA.2398: F 4538:4738(200) ack 94 win 61440 (DF)
1068422752.665419 HostA.2398 > HostB.23: F 94:94(0) ack 4739 win 16319 (DF)
```

What we see above is an initial SYN from HostA with a value of 1950934552, with a relative sequence number of 0, the SYN/ACK from HostB with a sequence number of 1373962008, again with its respective relative sequence number of 0. At the end of the connection, we see HostB acknowledging HostA's relative sequence number of 94, and HostA acknowledging HostB's relative sequence number of 4739. By subtracting two from each, we see that HostA sent 92 data bytes to HostB, which sent 4737 data bytes.

In the upcoming section, "TCPDump as Intrusion Detection," we will see how to construct a TCP connection log based on this information.

There are a few minor limitations to this procedure, which are unimportant in most cases. First, the initial sequence number is randomly picked as a 32-bit number (offering over 4 billion possible values), and in a given connection, it can roll past the maximum value and begin counting up again from zero. By way of analogy, a 1,000 mile automotive trip, with the odometer starting at 99,500 will cause the odometer to roll past 99,999 and reach 500 by the end of the trip. In this case, we would recognize that the figure 500 really means 100,500, and that the top digit had not been recorded. This is easily dealt with by inserting an implied digit at the head of the number.

To continue with this analogy, though, unless we know how many times the odometer has rolled over, we cannot know for sure the mileage of the vehicle. An odometer reading of 10,000 could indicate a fairly new vehicle with 10,000 miles, or a vehicle with 210,000 miles that is past time for retirement. Similarly, because the sequence number range has a count of about 4 billion, any transfer in excess of this amount cannot be computed accurately by simply comparing the starting and ending sequence numbers—we also need to know how many times the "odometer" has rolled over.

Despite these minor objections, the captured data is generally extremely useful, as data transfers over 4 gigabytes in length are fairly uncommon, except perhaps in the supercomputer arena.

TCPDUMP AS INTRUSION DETECTION?

Can tcpdump be used as an intrusion-detection tool? Although tcpdump is strictly a packet-capture and archiving utility, the BPF language is capable of enough pattern matching to allow us to match some simple attacks. The early intrusion-detection tool Shadow used tcpdump to capture network traffic and pass it to scripts to process for anomalies. In this section, we will look at simple intrusion-detection capabilities along those lines.

The SQL Slammer worm hit the entire Internet with a vengeance on Saturday, January 25 at 05:30 UTC, and within 30 minutes had infected an estimated 75,000 vulnerable systems—the fastest propagating worm to date. This worm exploited the Microsoft SQL Server service on UDP port 1434. It was the first successful worm to propagate via UDP.

Key to the rapid propagation of this worm was the fact that it was entirely self-contained in one 376-byte UDP packet. The payload of this packet exploited the vulnerability, replicated itself, and generated random IP addresses that the newly exploited system would, in turn, send attack packets to. As the exploit is UDP-based, no handshake was necessary to complete the exploit, unlike TCP, which requires the three-way handshake to establish a connection. Compromised systems literally sent traffic as fast as their Internet connection could handle, thus clogging the entire Internet.

A tcpdump filter could help us be good neighbors on the Internet by notifying us immediately if any of our systems become infected, so that we could immediately take corrective action. A filter that matches the traffic that a worm on our network would send out can be constructed in several ways, depending on the precision in detection that is desired. We could look at the packet contents and verify that the packet contains the actual

Slammer byte codes, but in practice, any packet directed at UDP port 1434 with a data content of 376 bytes is highly likely to be the Slammer worm. Thus, we can construct a tcpdump filter like this:

```
udp[4:2] = 384 and dst port 1434 and src net mynet
```

This filter matches UDP packets with a payload size of 376 bytes (as explained in Chapter 2, the UDP header is 8 bytes long, so we add 8 to our desired 376 bytes, resulting in a packet 384 bytes long), a destination port of 1434, and a source IP within our home network.

By outputting matching packets through a simple filter that triggers on the first instance of a new source IP and that contacts our trusty sysadmin, we have created a detection mechanism for Unix that will alert us if any of our systems become infected with SQL Slammer:

```
#!/bin/sh

# This program monitors for SQL slammer traffic and alerts the admin
#  if any local sources are detected (only once per IP)

tcpdump -n -tt -i eth0 'udp[4:2] = 384 and dst port 1434 and src net mynet' |

awk '
BEGIN   { squote=sprintf("%c",39) }
{          split ($2,x,"."); ip=x[1] "." x[2] "." x[3] "." x[4];
           if (! addr[ip++] )    {
                temp="mail -s " squote " Slammer Source " ip squote
                temp=temp " " squote "admin@mynet.com" squote
                temp=temp " </dev/null >/dev/null 2>&1 &"
                system(temp)
           }
}'
```

Note that we do not need to use the -s option with tcpdump to capture more than the header in this case, since all of the data we're interested in is in the IP and UDP headers. Also note that we are not asking tcpdump to convert the timestamps or resolve hostnames, as this will simply slow down processing. The awk program extracts the source IP address, and sends an e-mail with the subject "Slammer Source *IP*" to *admin@mynet.com*, but only on the first appearance of a given IP address, since a Slammer-infected system will easily send out many thousands of packets.

Tcpdump can even be used to create connection records for TCP connections, with starting and ending timestamps, source and destination IP addresses and ports, and the number of bytes inbound and outbound. Such records can be enormously valuable for forensic use.

Although we will not go into detail here, we could begin by taking the tcpdump expression we used earlier to match TCP packets containing the SYN, FIN, or RST flags (tcp[13] & 7 != 0). The text output could then be run through a filter (not shown here) that matches packets with matching source and destination addresses and ports and outputs a connection log.

```
tcpdump -n -tt -S -r trace.1 'tcp[13] & 7 != 0' |
awk -f connection_log.awk
```

We have omitted the script that this tcpdump command feeds because this is an extremely inefficient method of producing connection logs—we are converting the data to ASCII format for processing, rather than directly examining the raw packets programmatically. For a robust, open source connection-logging package, consider using tcptrace, available at www.tcptrace.org.

Another interesting example is in the detection of Secure Shell (SSH) back doors. SSH is an encrypted replacement for older interactive network applications, such as telnet. SSH has a default port of 22, but hackers will often create an SSH encrypted connection on a nonstandard port so that they can enter the hacked system without detection. Tcpdump can be used to detect these hackers by detecting the distinctive SSH signature on a nonstandard port. Consider the following tcpdump expression:

```
tcp[((tcp[12] & 0xf0)>>2):4] = 0x5353482D
```

This filter matches any TCP packet whose first four bytes are 0x5353482D. By consulting an ASCII chart, we can see that 0x5353482D matches the string "SSH-". SSH uses this preamble during its negotiation of options when the session is being established. This is not a very foolproof detection mechanism, since the four characters could be part of a normal data transfer (for example, in a paper describing the SSH protocol). However, in practice, the false positive rate has been quite low. Packets that match this expression can be run through a short filter, similar to the preceding examples, to alert the IDS analyst.

NOTE In these days of peer-to-peer file-sharing abuse, the signature for the gnutella file-sharing program might be a target for filtering. Gnutella traffic has as its identifier the string "GNUTELLA."

From such humble beginnings as these, the first IDSs were built. Although they are now far advanced from their origins, we can see the roots of many of the current crop of IDS products in these simple examples. All IDSs can examine tcpdump-format traffic and store packet output in the same format. Tcpdump, along with packet reassembly, connection-state tracking, and advanced heuristics for pattern matching to the tcpdump engine (as manifested in the libpcap library), forms the basis of most modern IDSs.

TCPSLICE, TCPFLOW, AND TCPJOIN

TCPDump files are useful for forensic examination of traffic in the event of a system compromise. In many cases, due to the sheer bulk of data that may be captured in these files, auxiliary programs can be useful to prune, or otherwise process these files. In this section, we introduce three such programs: tcpslice—which can create smaller, bite-sized portions of tcpdump files, tcpflow—which can provide output of the data portion of TCP sessions recorded in tcpdump files, and tcpjoin—which provides pasting of several tcpdump files into one.

Tcpslice

At busy sites, tcpdump capture files can easily grow to many hundreds of megabytes, or even gigabytes. Extracting data of interest from these files can easily become quite time consuming. Since IDS systems will invariably give a timestamp for an event, tcpslice (another production of LBNL's Network Research Group, available for download at ftp://ee.lbl.gov/) comes to the rescue by providing slices (hence the name) of tcpdump data by starting and ending timestamp.

Frequently, the item that triggers an IDS alert will be preceded by other information of interest to the IDS analyst. For instance, TCP port 1524 is registered for use by the ingreslock service, but in practice it is almost never used. Thus, some IDS systems will flag successful inbound connections to that port as suspicious. Quite often, this will be evidence of a successful intrusion into the system. However, more than likely, it wasn't the ingreslock service itself that was compromised, but a vulnerable service running on another port, and the ingreslock port had simply been hijacked as a back-door method of access by the intruder.

In this scenario, it is critical to determine the actual service that was exploited so that appropriate action can be taken, not only on the compromised system, but on other potentially vulnerable systems in the organization. It is well-known that once a system has been hacked by exploiting a particular vulnerability, other systems in the institution may also be attacked in the same manner—the oversight that led to the first intrusion could indicate that additional systems are vulnerable in the same way.

Tcpslice lets us select a section of a capture file, perhaps from 10 minutes before the event to 10 minutes after, to reduce the amount of data that the IDS analyst needs to examine. Tcpslice takes a raw tcpdump file (created with the -w option) and the starting and ending times of the data to extract, and it creates another raw tcpdump file as output. The times can be specified in a variety of formats, including raw Unix format, and the more natural, human-readable timestamps.

Tcpslice is much faster than might be assumed, because it uses an intelligent algorithm to determine the slices to cut out of the trace file. It computes an assumed offset into the trace file by examining the first and last packet of the trace file, then refines the guess extremely rapidly. For instance, suppose the trace file contains data from 12 noon to 3 P.M., a period of three hours. If tcpslice were asked to retrieve data starting at 1 P.M., it would read the first packet and determine its timestamp (about 12 noon), and the last packet (3 P.M.),

then estimate that the 1 P.M. data would be a third of the way into the file, and read the packet at this offset. If, due to variations in traffic patterns, this packet doesn't match the timestamp, a revised estimate using the reduced range is used to quickly zero in on the starting point of interest. At that point, a sequential search and copy to the output file occurs until the ending timestamp is passed or the end of the trace file is reached. In practice, only a handful of probes into the file are generally necessary.

Tcpflow

Despite tcpdump's extensive capabilities, it is perhaps most useful for examining the types of network-level attacks we examined in Chapter 3. The logical streams that make up the attacks in the presentation and application layers that we looked at in Chapter 4 are crowded out with the network and transport layer data that tcpdump also displays. In these cases, we want to ignore such information and actually see the data bytes that were transferred via the virtual circuit.

Tcpflow is designed to do just that for TCP. Unfortunately, no similar open source package exists for UDP or ICMP traffic. Despite this limitation, tcpflow (available at www.circlemud.org/~jelson/software/tcpflow/) is an important tool for analyzing traffic, as it reconstructs the data streams of the TCP virtual circuit and stores each stream (or *flow*, in tcpflow parlance) in a separate file for IDS analysis. Tcpflow understands the TCP protocol and reconstructs the transmitted data, regardless of retransmissions and out-of-order delivery. However, tcpflow does not currently handle fragmented packets, a shortcoming that no doubt will be overcome in time. Additionally, as was noted in Chapter 3, there are ambiguities in the TCP specification that tcpflow does not attempt to disambiguate. Instead, it simply uses a default policy.

Tcpflow stores each data stream (*flow*) of the TCP conversation in a separate file, named with the source and destination IP addresses and ports. Each side of the conversation is stored in a separate file. For example, the telnet connection that we examined earlier (in the "Tcpdump Output Format" section of the chapter) would create two files named 192.168.003.003.03252-192.168.003.099.00023 and 192.168.003.099.00023-192.168.003.003 .03252. The first file would contain the traffic sent from the telnet client on the connecting host to the telnet service on the receiving host. The second file would contain the traffic sourced from the telnet server back to the telnet client. The data in the files is not interleaved, as we would expect in a typical interactive session, but rather, all the data for each side of the connection is placed sequentially in its file. In many cases, the sequence of events is fairly obvious, given a knowledge of the protocols involved, but in case of any questions, the packet timestamps in the tcpdump file can resolve any timing issues.

Tcpflow uses some of the same options as tcpdump. The man page gives the syntax as follows:

```
tcpflow [-chpsv] [-b max_bytes] [-d debug_level] [-f max_fds]
[-i iface] [-r file] [expression]
```

The most useful options are the following:

▼   `-i iface`   Network interface to collect data from.

■   `-r file`   Tcpdump-format file to read from; this could be a bulk trace file that was collected earlier.

▲   `expression`   The familiar tcpdump expression that was discussed earlier in the chapter. This allows us to specify which packets tcpflow should process. The default is for tcpflow to process all TCP packets that it receives.

Tcpjoin

We've now seen how tcpdump can be used to create a bulk data capture, how tcpslice can create slices from this bulk trace that contain data of interest, and how tcpflow can extract the data streams from the captured data. But suppose that the TCP connection we are interested in started in one bulk capture file but continued into another bulk capture file. Tcpflow cannot deal with input from two different files—to deal with this situation, we need a program that can paste multiple tcpdump files together.

Enter tcpjoin (www.algonet.se/~nitzer/tcpjoin/). Tcpjoin accepts two tcpdump files, pastes them together into a tcpdump file based on the packet timestamps, and sends the output file to the standard output, from whence it can be redirected to a file. (Tcpjoin also allows the use of a −w flag to specify an output file).

The steps to create a tcpflow of a connection that spans several bulk trace files is demonstrated by this example:

```
# extract the data we're interested in from the trace files into
temporary files.
tcpdump −s 1500 −r trace.1 −w tempfile.1 'host foo and host bar'
tcpdump −s 1500 −r trace.2 −w tempfile.2 'host foo and host bar'

# Paste the two files together
tcpjoin tempfile.1 tempfile.2 >mergefile.1

# Now run tcpflow on the merged file
tcpflow mergefile.1
```

In this case, tcpslice could have been used to paste the files together, as the timestamps of second file are after those of the first file. However, tcpjoin also merges files with interleaved timestamps. This can happen in high-traffic sites that devote two interfaces to capturing traffic, one inbound and the other outbound. In this case, to generate one complete tcpdump format file, the functionality of tcpjoin is necessary.

There is also another program, tcpdmerge, available on the Internet at various places (although its home page appears to have disappeared), which has similar features and functionality.

SUMMARY

A working knowledge of the tcpdump family of tools is essential for the IDS analyst. These tools and others (see www.tcpdump.org/related.html for tcpdump friends and relatives) provide important analysis features that are used every day to foil wily hackers.

We've now explored the basics of networking, the types of exploits to expect, and some of the ancillary tools used for IDS applications. We're now ready to embark on our exploration of specific IDS offerings.

PART II

Architecture

CHAPTER 6

IDS and IPS Architecture

Intrusion-detection and intrusion-prevention systems, at a minimum, actually require only one program or device. Someone might, for example, install a personal firewall with intrusion detection and IP source address shunning capabilities on a system used exclusively for home computing. Although doing so might be sufficient for a few purposes (such as home use or testing a particular IDS), deploying a single system or device is not sufficient for many organizations, such as global corporations, government agencies, and the military. These organizations typically use multiple systems and components that perform a variety of sophisticated intrusion-detection and intrusion-prevention functions. The roles performed by and relationships among machines, devices, applications, and processes, including the conventions used for communication between them, define an *architecture*. In its most fundamental sense, an intrusion-detection or intrusion-prevention architecture is a designed structure on which every element involved fits.

The architecture is one of the most critical considerations in intrusion detection and prevention. An effective architecture is one in which each machine, device, component, and process performs its role in an effective and (often) coordinated manner, resulting in efficient information processing and output, and also appropriate preventive responses that meet the business and operational needs of an organization. A poorly designed or implemented architecture, on the other hand, can produce a variety of undesirable consequences, such as data not being available or not being available when needed, networking slowdowns, or a lack of appropriate and timely responses.

This chapter covers intrusion-detection and intrusion-prevention architectures, and will look at tiered models, how servers are deployed, how sensors and agents function, and the roles and functionality of management consoles in an intrusion-detection and intrusion-prevention architecture.

TIERED ARCHITECTURES

At least three types of tiered architectures can be used: single-tiered, multi-tiered, and peer-to-peer architectures.

Single-Tiered Architecture

A *single-tiered architecture*, the most basic of the architectures discussed here, is one in which components in an IDS or IPS collect and process data themselves, rather than passing the output they collect to another set of components. An example of a single-tiered architecture is a host-based intrusion-detection tool that takes the output of system logs (such as the utmp and wtmp files on Unix systems) and compares it to known patterns of attack.

A single tier offers advantages, such as simplicity, low cost (at least in the case of freeware tools running on individual hosts), and independence from other components (an advantage if they should become compromised or disabled). At the same time, however, a single-tiered architecture usually has components that are not aware of each other, reducing considerably the potential for efficiency and sophisticated functionality.

Multi-Tiered Architecture

As the name implies, a multi-tiered architecture involves multiple components that pass information to each other. Many of today's IDSs, for example, consist of three primary components: sensors, analyzers or agents, and a manager.

Sensors perform data collection. For example, network sensors are often programs that capture data from network interfaces. Sensors can also collect data from system logs and other sources, such as personal firewalls and TCP wrappers.

Sensors pass information to *agents* (sometimes also known as *analyzers*), which monitor intrusive activity on their individual hosts. Each sensor and agent is configured to run on the particular operating environment in which it is placed. Agents are normally specialized to perform one and only one function. One agent might, for example, examine nothing but TCP traffic, whereas another might examine only FTP (File Transfer Protocol) connections and connection attempts. Additionally, third-party tools, such as network-monitoring tools, neural networks (which are covered in Chapter 17), and connection-tracing tools can be used if expanding the scope of analysis is advantageous.

When an agent has determined that an attack has occurred or is occurring, it sends information to the *manager component,* which can perform a variety of functions including (but not limited to) the following:

▼   Collecting and displaying alerts on a console

■   Triggering a pager or calling a cellular phone number

■   Storing information regarding an incident in a database

■   Retrieving additional information relevant to the incident

■   Sending information to a host that stops it from executing certain instructions in memory

■   Sending commands to a firewall or router that change access control lists

▲   Providing a management console—a user interface to the manager component

A central collection point allows for greater ease in analyzing logs because all the log information is available at one location. Additionally, writing log data to a different system (the one on which the manager component resides) from the one that produced them is advisable; if an attacker tampers with or destroys log data on the original system (by installing a rootkit tool that masquerades the attacker's presence on the system, for instance), the data will still be available on the central server—the manager component. Finally, management consoles can enable intrusion-detection and intrusion-prevention staff to remotely change policies and parameters, erase log files after they are archived, and perform other important functions without having to individually authenticate to sensors, agents, and remote systems. Figure 6-1 outlines the multi-tier architecture.

Advantages of a multi-tiered architecture include greater efficiency and depth of analysis. With each component of the architecture performing the function it is designed to do, often mostly independent of the other components, a properly designed multi-tiered

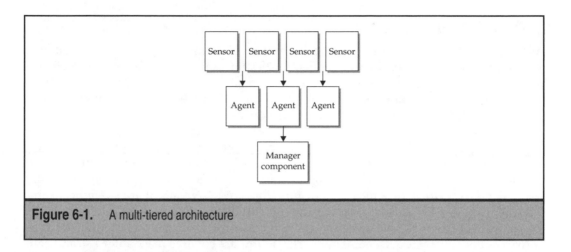

Figure 6-1. A multi-tiered architecture

architecture can provide a degree of efficiency not possible with the simpler single-tiered architecture. It can also provide a much more complete picture of the security condition of an organization's entire network and the hosts therein, compared to a single-tiered architecture. The main downsides include increased cost and complexity. The multiple components, interfaces, and communications methods translate to greater difficulty in setting up this architecture and more day-to-day maintenance and troubleshooting challenges.

Peer-to-Peer Architecture

Whereas the multi-tiered architecture generally takes raw information, processes it, then sends the output to a higher-order component, the peer-to-peer architecture involves exchanging intrusion-detection and intrusion-prevention information between peer components, each of which performs the same kinds of functions. This peer-to-peer architecture is often used by cooperating firewalls (and, to a lesser degree, by cooperating routers or switches). As one firewall obtains information about events that are occurring, it passes this information to another, which may cause a change in an access control list or addition of restrictions on proxied connections. The second firewall can also send information that causes changes in the first. Neither firewall acts as the central server or master repository of information.

The main advantage of a peer-to-peer architecture is simplicity. Any peer can participate in what is effectively a group of peer machines, each of which can benefit from the information the others glean. The main downside is a lack of sophisticated functionality due to the absence of specialized components (although the functionality is better than what is possible in a single-tiered architecture because the latter does not even have cooperating components).

A peer-to-peer architecture is well suited to organizations that have invested enough to obtain and deploy firewalls capable of cooperating with each other, but that have not

Critical Need for Architectures

Architectures make a critical difference in terms of the quantity and quality of the dividends that intrusion-detection and intrusion-prevention technology produce. At the same time, however, it is important to remember that "Rome was not built in a day." If you lack financial resources, starting with a simple single-tiered architecture is often the logical first step in developing an intrusion-detection and intrusion-prevention architecture. As more resources become available, and as the exact business and operational objectives of intrusion-detection and intrusion-prevention efforts become clearer, a migration to a more sophisticated architecture can occur.

invested much (if anything) in IDSs and IPSs. As discussed earlier, firewalls are, all things considered, the best single source of intrusion-detection data. Using them in a peer-to-peer manner to distribute information they have obtained and to make adaptive changes in access control lists or proxy rules can, at least to some degree, compensate for the absence of IDSs and IPSs.

SENSORS

Sensors are critical in intrusion-detection and intrusion-prevention architectures—they are the beginning point of intrusion detection and prevention because they supply the initial data about potentially malicious activity. A deeper look at sensor functionality, deployment, and security will provide insight into exactly what sensors are and how they work.

Sensor Functions

Considering all the possible intrusion-detection and intrusion-prevention components within a particular architecture, sensors are usually (but not always) the lowest end components. In other words, sensors typically do not have very sophisticated functionality. They are usually designed only to obtain certain data and pass them on. There are two basic types of sensors: network-based and host-based sensors.

Network-Based Sensors

Network-based sensors, the more frequently deployed of the two types, are programs or network devices (such as physical devices) that capture data in packets traversing a local Ethernet or token ring or a network switching point. One of the greatest advantages of network-based sensors is the sheer number of hosts for which they can provide data. In an extreme case, one sensor might be used to monitor all traffic coming into and out of a network. If the network has a thousand hosts, the sensor can, in theory, gather data about misuse and anomalies in all thousand hosts. The cost-effectiveness of this approach is huge (although critics justifiably point out that a single sensor is also likely to

miss a considerable amount of data that may be critical to an intrusion-detection and intrusion-prevention effort if the sensor does not happen to be recording traffic on the particular network route over which packets containing the data are sent). Additionally, if configured properly, sensors do not burden the network with much additional traffic, especially if two network interfaces—one for monitoring and the other for management—are used. A monitoring interface has no TCP/IP stack whatsoever, nor does it have any linkage to any IP address, both of which make it an almost entirely transparent entity on the network.

The programs that intrusion-detection and intrusion-prevention tools most frequently use as sensors are tcpdump (described previously in Chapter 5) and libpcap. To reiterate, tcpdump (www.tcpdump.org) captures data from packets and prints packet headers of packets that match a particular filter (or Boolean) expression. Packet parameters that are particularly useful in intrusion detection and prevention are time, source and destination addresses, source and destination ports, TCP flags, initial sequence number from the source IP for the initial connection, ending sequence number, number of bytes, and window size.

tcpdump is an application, but libpcap is a library called by an application. libpcap (http://sourceforge.net/projects/libpcap/) is designed to gather packet data from the kernel of the operating system and then move it to one or more applications—in this particular case, to intrusion-detection and intrusion-prevention applications. For example, an Ethernet card may obtain packet data from a network. The underlying operating system over which libpcap runs will process each packet in many ways, starting with determining what kind of packet it is by removing the Ethernet header to get to the next layer up the stack. In all likelihood, the next layer will be the IP layer; if so, the IP header must be removed to determine the protocol at the next layer of the stack (although it is important to note that in the case of the IP protocol, hexadecimal values of 1, 6, or 11 starting at byte position 40 within the packet header indicate that the transport protocol is ICMP, TCP, or UDP (User Datagram Protocol), respectively). If the packet is a TCP packet, the TCP header is also removed and the contents of the packet are then passed on to the next layer up, the application layer. libpcap provides intrusion-detection and intrusion-prevention applications with this data (payload) so that these applications can analyze the content to look for attack signatures, names of hacking tools, and so forth. libpcap is advantageous not only in that it provides a standard interface to these applications, but also because, like tcpdump, it is public domain software.

Many other sensors are also used. Some IDS vendors, for example, develop and include their own proprietary sensors in these systems. These sensors sometimes provide more functionality than tcpdump and libpcap have, and sometimes have substantially scaled-down functionality so they are more efficient.

Host-Based Sensors

Host-based sensors, like network-based sensors, could possibly also receive packet data captured by network interfaces and then send the data somewhere. Instead of being set to promiscuous mode, the network interface on each host would have to be set to capture

only data sent to that particular host. However, doing so would not make much sense, given the amount of processing of data that would have to occur on each host. Instead, most host-based sensors are programs that produce log data, such as Unix daemons or the Event Logger in Windows NT, 2000, XP, and Windows Server 2003. The output of these programs is sent (often through a utility such as scp, secure copy, which runs as a cron job, or through the Windows Task Scheduler) to an analysis program that either runs on the same host or on a central host. The program might look for events indicating that someone has obtained root privileges on a Unix system without entering the su (substitute user) command and the root password—a possible indication that an attacker has exploited a vulnerability to gain root privileges.

Sensor Deployment Considerations

Many sensors require that a host be running one or more network interfaces in promiscuous mode. In many current Unix systems, entering this command

```
ifconfig <interface>
```

will produce standard output that displays the IP address, the MAC address, the net mask, and other important parameters, including "promisc" if the interface is in promiscuous mode. Note that if there is only one network interface, it is not necessary to enter the name of the interface in question.

Sensors can be placed outside of exterior firewalls, inside them, or both. Sensors outside exterior firewalls record information about Internet attacks. Web servers, FTP servers, external DNS servers, and mail servers are often placed outside of the firewall, making them much more likely to be attacked than other hosts. Placing these systems within an organization's internal network potentially makes them lesser targets, because being within the internal network at least affords some protection (such as one or more

More Considerations for Network-Based Sensor Functionality

Ensuring that a network interface is in promiscuous mode is critical for network-based sensor functionality, but there are other important technical considerations, too. For one thing, programs that capture data or read these data need certain privileges or access rights. In most versions of Linux, for example, root privileges are necessary for accessing captured data in files such as /var/log/messages. Running windump, the Windows version of tcpdump, requires Administrator-level privileges on systems such as Windows 2000 or XP. Running tcpdump (or, in the case of Windows systems, windump) sets the network interface in promiscuous mode. Disk space management is another important consideration. Capturing raw packet data off the network can quickly eat up precious disk space. Having a huge amount of disk capacity, regularly checking how full the disk is, and archiving and then purging the contents of files that hold raw packet data is usually a necessary part of operations associated with intrusion detection and prevention.

filtering barriers provided by firewalls and screening routers). At the same time, however, having these servers within the internal network will increase the traffic load for the internal network and will also expose the internal network more if any of these servers become compromised. Given that servers placed outside of the internal network are more vulnerable to attack, it is a good idea to place at least one network-based sensor in one or more demilitarized zones (DMZs; see Figure 6-2).

Installing host-based sensors provides better precision of analysis, because all data gleaned by each sensor are for a particular host, and because the data indicate what traffic that host actually received (and also possibly how that host reacted to the input). In contrast, sensors placed at intermediate points on the network will record data about traffic that may or may not have actually reached the host. Additionally, host-based sensors are far more likely to provide information about insider attacks, especially if the attacker has had physical access to the target host.

Although network-based sensors (especially those deployed at external gateways to networks) provide a wide range of data, effectively covering many hosts, network-based sensors have a number of limitations.

One major concern is throughput rate. A sensor may receive so much input that it simply cannot keep up with it. Many types of sensors (such as those based on bpf) have difficulty handling throughput much greater than 350–400 Mbps, and a few have trouble with even lower input rates. Although a sensor may react by dropping excess packets, the sensor may also crash, yielding no data whatsoever until it is restarted. Alternatively, an overloaded sensor may cause excessive resource utilization on the machine on which it runs.

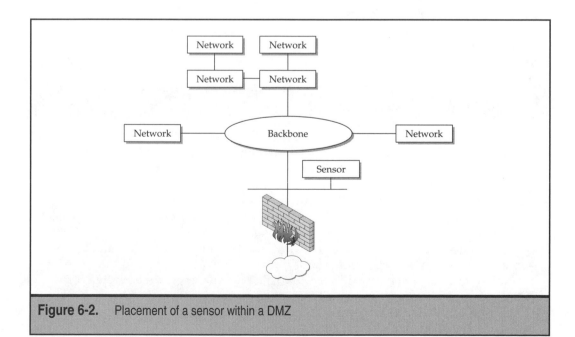

Figure 6-2.   Placement of a sensor within a DMZ

Additionally, in switched networks, network-based sensors cannot capture packet data simply by putting an interface in promiscuous mode—switched networks present significant hurdles to capturing packets. Obtaining packet data in switched networks thus requires that one or a number of potential special solutions be used. One such method is deploying a special kind of port known as a *spanning port* between a switch or similar device and a host used to monitor network traffic. Another is to place a hub between two switches, or between a switch and a router, or to simply tap the network traffic using a vampire or other type of tap.

Encrypted network traffic presents an even further level of complication. The most frequently used solution is placing a sensor at an endpoint where the traffic is in cleartext.

Capturing packet data in switched networks is thus anything but a simple matter, but solving this issue is well described elsewhere. If you need more information concerning this issue, see Chapter 6 of *Incident Response: A Strategic Guide to Handling System and Network Security Breaches,* by Eugene Schultz and Russell Shumway (see www.newriders.com).

One possible solution for bandwidth problems in sensors is to install filters that limit the types of packets that the sensor receives. In our experience, of all the transport protocols (TCP, UDP, and ICMP) that can be captured and analyzed, TCP is the most important to examine because of its association with attack activity. In other words, given a choice between analyzing TCP, UDP, or ICMP traffic, TCP would often be the best single choice for intrusion-detection and intrusion-prevention purposes. A filter can be configured to limit input for one or more sensors to TCP traffic only. This solution is, of course, not optimal from an intrusion-detection perspective because it misses other potentially important data. But if sensors are becoming overwhelmed with traffic, this is a viable strategy.

A variation on this strategy is to install a filter that accepts only TCP traffic on a few sensors, to install a filter that accepts only UDP traffic on others, and to install still another filter that accepts only ICMP packets on yet other sensors. Alternatively, sensors can be removed from points in the network with very high throughput—removed from the external gateway and moved to gateways for internal subnets, for example (see Figure 6-3). Doing this helps overcome any throughput limitations in sensors, but it also diminishes the value of sensors in terms of their breadth of intrusion-detection data gathering.

Still another possibility is to modify sensors to sample input according to a probabilistic model if they become overloaded with packets. The rationale for doing so is that although many packets may be missed, at least a representative set of packets can be analyzed, yielding a realistic view of what is occurring on the network and serving as a basis for stopping attacks that are found at gateways and in individual hosts.

Host-based sensors can be placed at only one point—on a host—so the point within the network where this type of sensor is deployed is not nearly as much of an issue. As always, the benefits should outweigh the costs. The costs of deploying host-based sensors generally include greater financial cost (because of the narrower scope of host-based as opposed to network-based sensors), greater utilization of system resources on each system on which they are deployed, and the consequences of being blind to what is happening on a host due to unauthorized disabling of the sensor on the host (especially if that host is a sensitive or valuable system). Although network-based sensors are generally

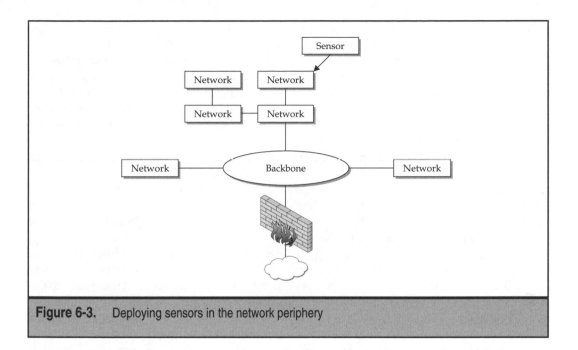

Figure 6-3. Deploying sensors in the network periphery

used in DMZs, for example, deploying a host-based sensor on a particularly critical public web server within a DMZ would be reasonable.

A hybrid approach—deploying network-based sensors both at external gateways as well as at gateways to subnets or within virtual local area networks (VLANs) and using host-based sensors where most needed—is in many cases the best approach to deploying sensors (see Figure 6-4). This kind of sensor deployment ensures that packet data for traffic going in and out of the network, as well as at least some of the internal traffic, will be captured. If a sensor at an external gateway becomes overwhelmed with data, data capture within the network itself can still occur. Furthermore, although the network-based sensors at external gateways are unlikely to glean information about insider attacks, the internal network-based sensors are much more likely to do so. At the same time, deploying host-based sensors on especially sensitive and valuable servers is likely to yield the information necessary to determine whether inside or outside attacks have occurred and, in the case of IPSs, may possibly stop malicious code from executing or unauthorized commands from being run in the first place. Finally, if host-based sensors fail, there will at least be some redundancy—network-based sensors (especially the internally deployed network-based sensors) can provide some information about attacks directed at individual systems.

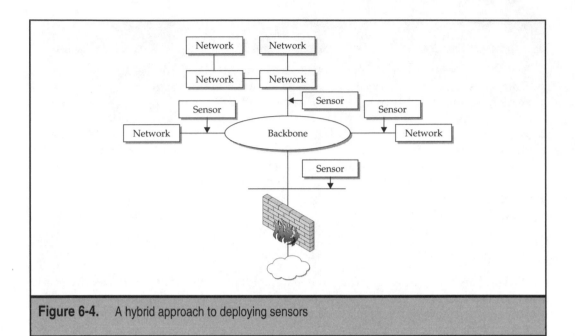

Figure 6-4.   A hybrid approach to deploying sensors

Sensor Security Considerations

Both the placement and sophistication of sensors vary considerably from one intrusion-detection or intrusion-prevention implementation to another. The security considerations associated with sensors thus also vary considerably. Despite these variations, of the three major components of a multi-tiered architecture, sensors are the most frequently attacked.

In the case of low-end sensors that can only capture network traffic, the normal worst case if they become compromised is that they yield a lower hit rate. Conceivably, an ingenuous attacker could also subvert a low-end sensor to inject false data to be sent to clients or to cause denial of service by flooding them with input. However, in the case of high-end sensors, such as sensors that have embedded policies and that may also preprocess data sent to agents, the range of outcomes in case of subversion is potentially more diverse. Injection of bogus data and denial of service are just a few of the outcomes if one or more high-end sensors become compromised. One of the worst possible outcomes is subversion of the entire IDS or IPS itself. In other words, the other components of the system may be compromised because the sensors are under the control of attackers. Dependencies between systems and devices may enable someone who has gained unauthorized access to one component (in this case, sensors) to more easily gain access to others. Sensors may contain information concerning the configuration of other systems, they may have dependencies that allow trusted access to other systems, they may identify hosts of which the sensors are aware, and so forth. Ideally, each component in a

Component Independence

Lack of independence of components in an IDS can spell big trouble. An interesting example is the remote procedure call (RPC) reassembly bug in earlier (version 1) versions of Snort. It is possible for an attacker to gain unauthorized access to the node running Snort with the privileges of the process under which it is running by sending specially crafted packets. Even if the process is not root, the IDS will nevertheless be able to control data flow and records. This is actually an agent-specific problem, but the vulnerability that allows access to a process spawned on behalf of the agent can allow more widespread access. The major lesson here is that there needs to be as much independence between the components of an architecture as possible. Additionally, countermeasures need to be built in, such that if one component is compromised, the others will not be more at risk.

multi-tiered architecture will be relatively independent of the others, but in reality this is often not true.

The bottom line is that sensors need at least a baseline level of security, perhaps even higher in many cases. At a minimum, the host on which each sensor resides needs to be hardened by tightening file permissions (especially permissions for files that the sensor uses and creates), restricting privileges, restricting access to the system itself, running as few services as possible, installing patches, and so on. Each sensor should normally be placed where it is most needed, but if a sensor is not very hardened, it might be best to move it behind a firewall so that the firewall can at least repel some of the attacks that originate from the Internet. Many vendors of IDSs provide sensors that are surprisingly vulnerable to attack; hopefully, these vendors will start providing much more attack-resistant sensors in the future.

Additionally, it is very important to be notified immediately if the sensor fails. Losing one or two sensors results in a somewhat lower hit rate and impaired intrusion prevention, but losing even more sensors can prove catastrophic if an organization is highly dependent on intrusion-detection and intrusion-prevention. An IDS or IPS that attempts to contact all sensors at frequent, scheduled times to discover failed sensors is very advantageous in this respect.

Finally, a secure communication channel between each sensor and the other components is highly desirable. The interception of communications between sensors and other components could lead to a range of undesirable outcomes, such as attackers being able to discover whether their attempts to evade intrusion detection have been successful, or it could lead to a compromise of privacy if personal information is contained in the packets that sensors capture. Having an authenticated, encrypted channel between sensors and other components is a reasonable solution to this problem.

AGENTS

Agents are the next consideration in intrusion-detection and intrusion-prevention architectures. This section discusses the functions, deployment considerations, and security considerations associated with agents.

Agent Functions

Agents are relatively new in intrusion detection and prevention, having been developed in the mid-1990s. As mentioned previously in this chapter, their primary function is to analyze input provided by sensors. Although many definitions exist, we'll define an *agent* as a group of processes that run independently and that are programmed to analyze system behavior or network events or both to detect anomalous events and violations of an organization's security policy. Each agent should ideally be a bare-bones implementation of a specialized function. Some agents may, for example, examine network traffic and host-based events rather generically, such as checking whether normal TCP connections have occurred, their start and stop times, and the amount of data transmitted or whether certain services have crashed. Having agents that examine UDP and ICMP traffic is also desirable, but the UDP and ICMP protocols are stateless and connectionless. Other agents might look at specific aspects of application layer protocols such as FTP, TFTP, HTTP, and SMTP as well as authentication sessions to determine whether data in packets or system behavior is consistent with known attack patterns. Still others may do nothing more than monitor the performance of systems.

Our definition of agent states that agents run independently. This means that if one agent crashes or is impaired in some manner, the others will continue to run normally (although they may not be provided with as much data as before). It also means that agents can be added to or deleted from the IDS or IPS as needed. In fact, in a small intrusion-detection or intrusion-prevention effort, perhaps only a few of two dozen or so agents may be deployed. In a much larger effort, perhaps all of the agents may be deployed.

Although each agent runs independently on the particular host on which it resides, agents often cooperate with each other. Each agent may receive and analyze only one part of the data regarding a particular system, network, or device. Agents normally share information they have obtained with each other by using a particular communication protocol over the network, however. When an agent detects an anomaly or policy violation (such as a brute force attempt to su to root, or a massive flood of packets over the network), in most cases, the agent will immediately notify the other agents of what it has found. This new information, combined with the information another agent already has, may cause that agent to report that an attack on another host has also occurred.

Agents sometimes generate false alarms, too, thereby misleading other agents, at least to some degree. The problem of false alarms is one of the proverbial vultures hovering over the entire intrusion-detection and intrusion-prevention arena, and cooperating but false-alarm-generating agents can compound this problem. However, a good IDS or IPS will allow the data that agents generate to be inspected on a management console, allowing humans to spot false alarms and to intervene by weeding them out.

The Advantages and Disadvantages of Agents

The use of agents in intrusion detection and prevention has proven to be one of the greatest breakthroughs. Advantages include:

▼ **Adaptability**   Having a number of small agents means that any of them can potentially be modified to meet the needs of the moment; agents can even be programmed to be self-learning, enabling them to be able to deal with novel threats.

■ **Efficiency**   The simplicity of most agent implementations makes them more efficient than if each agent were to support many functions and to embody a great deal of code.

■ **Resilience**   Agents can and do maintain state information even if they fail or their data source fails.

■ **Independence**   Agents are implemented to run independently, so if you lose one or two, the others will not be affected.

■ **Scalability**   Agents can readily be adapted to both large- and small-scale intrusion-detection and intrusion-prevention deployments.

▲ **Mobility**   Some agents (believe it or not) may actually move from one system to another; agents might even migrate around networks to monitor network traffic for anomalies and policy violations.

There are some drawbacks to using agents, too:

▼ **Resource allocation**   Agents cause system overhead in terms of memory consumption and CPU allocation.

■ **False alarms**   False alarms from agents can cause a variety of problems.

■ **Time, effort, and resources needed**   Agents need to be modified according to an organization's requirements, they must be tuned to minimize false alarms, and they must be able to run in the environment in which they are deployed—this requires time, effort, and financial and other resources.

▲ **Potential for subversion**   A compromised agent is generally a far greater problem than a compromised sensor.

At a bare minimum, an agent needs to incorporate three functions or components:

▼ A *communications interface* to communicate with other components of IDSs and IPSs

■   A *listener* that waits in the background for data from sensors and messages from other agents and then receives them

▲   A *sender* that transmits data and messages to other components, such as other agents and the manager component, using established means of communication, such as network protocols

Agents can also provide a variety of additional functions. Agents can, for example, perform correlation analyses on input received from a wide range of sensors. In some agent implementations, the agents themselves generate alerts and alarms. In still other implementations, agents access large databases to launch queries to obtain more information about specific source and destination IP addresses associated with certain types of attacks, times at which known attacks have occurred, frequencies of scans and other types of malicious activity, and so forth. From this kind of additional information, agents can perform functions such as tracking the specific phases of attacks and estimating the threat that each attack constitutes.

Although the types of additional functions that agents can perform may sound impressive, "beefing up" agents to do more than simple analysis is not necessarily advantageous. These additional functions can instead be performed by the manager component (to be discussed shortly), leaving agents free to do what they do best. Simplicity—in computer science jargon, *Occam's razor*—should be the overwhelming consideration with agents, provided, of course, that each agent implementation embodies the required functionality. Additionally, if resource utilization is already a problem with simple agents, think of the amount of resources multifunctional agents will use!

Agent Deployment Considerations

Decisions about deployment of agents are generally easier to make than decisions concerning where to deploy sensors. Each agent can and should be configured to the operating environment in which it runs. In host-based intrusion detection, each agent generally monitors one host, although, as mentioned before, sometimes sensors on multiple hosts send data to one or more central agents. Choosing the particular hosts to monitor is thus the major dilemma in deciding on the placement of host-based agents. Most organizations that use host-based intrusion detection select "crown jewel" hosts, such as servers that are part of billing and financial transaction systems, more than any other. A few organizations also choose a few widely dispersed hosts throughout the network to supplement network-based intrusion detection.

In network-based intrusion detection, agents are generally placed in two locations:

▼   **Where they are most** *efficient*   Efficiency is related to the particular part of a network where connections to sensors and other components are placed. The more locally coresident the sensors and agents are, the better the efficiency. Having an agent in one network and the sensors that feed the agent in another is an example of inefficiency.

▲ **Where they will be sufficiently** *secure*   Security of agents is our next topic, so suffice it to say here that placing agents in secure zones within networks, or at least behind one or more firewalls, is essential.

Finally, tuning agents is a very complicated issue. It is highly desirable that each agent produce as high a hit rate (positive recognition rate) as possible, while also producing as low a false-alarm rate as possible. When agents are first deployed, however, they usually perform far from optimally in that they yield output with excessively high false-alarm rates. Fortunately, it is possible to reduce the false-alarm rate by eliminating certain attack signatures from an analyzer, or by adjusting the statistical criteria for an attack to be more rigorous, thereby reducing the sensitivity of the sensor. Doing so, however, may lower the positive recognition rate, causing other problems. Many intrusion-detection experts would rather have more false alarms than false negatives (misses). Each false negative, after all, represents a failure to notice ongoing events that may quickly proliferate catastrophically if you don't have the opportunity to intervene. Each false alarm represents extra effort, but experts can quickly dismiss false alarms. Most commercial IDSs have management consoles that enable those with sufficient privileges to make whatever adjustments in agents are necessary.

Agent Security Considerations

The threat of subversion of agents is a major issue. Agents are typically much smarter than sensors; if an agent is successfully attacked, not only will the attacker be able to stop or subvert the type of analysis that the agent performs, but this person will also be able to glean information that is likely to prove useful in attacking the other components of the IDS or IPS. Compromised agents thus can rapidly become a security liability.

Fortunately, the way agents are typically deployed provides at least some level of defense against attacks that are directed at them. Agents (especially in network-based IDSs and IPSs) are generally distributed throughout a network or networks. Each agent must therefore be individually discovered and then attacked. This substantially increases the work involved in attacking agents, something that is very desirable from a security perspective. The diversity of functionality within agents also provides some inherent security—each is to some degree unique, and attacking each presents unique challenges to the attacker. Additionally, mobile agents are becoming increasingly popular, and agent mobility makes discovery of agents by attackers considerably more difficult.

Nevertheless, agents need to be secured by doing many of the same things that must be done to protect sensors—hardening the platform on which they run, ensuring that they can be accessed only by authorized persons, and so on. Here are a few guidelines:

▼ **Dedicate the hardware platform**   Dedicating the hardware platform on which agents run to agent functionality is essential. If other applications run on the same platform as one that houses one or more agents, attackers may be able to access the platform via the other applications and then escalate privileges to the point where they gain control over all the agents.

- **Encrypt traffic**   Because of the high importance of agent security, encrypting all traffic between agents and other agents and possibly also between agents and other components is also advisable. Including a digital signature that must be validated before any message is processed is another good measure.

▲ **Filter input**   Additionally, to guard against denial-of-service attacks, filters that prevent excessive and repetitive input from being received should be deployed. Many vendor agent implementations have this kind of filtering capability built in.

Other interesting approaches to agent security include using APIs (application programming interfaces) to control data transfer between agents. In this approach, one of the most important considerations is sanitizing the data transferred between agents to guard against the possibility of exploiting vulnerabilities to gain control of agents and the platforms on which they run by passing specially crafted data.

MANAGER COMPONENT

The final component in a multi-tiered architecture is the *manager* (sometimes also known as the *server*) component. The fundamental purpose of this component is to provide an executive or master control capability for an IDS or IPS.

Manager Functions

We've seen that sensors are normally fairly low-level components and that agents are usually more sophisticated components that, at a minimum, analyze the data they receive from sensors and possibly from each other. Although sensors and agents are capable of functioning without a master control component, having such a component is extremely advantageous in helping all components work in a coordinated manner. Additionally, the manager component can perform other valuable functions, which we'll explore next.

Data Management

IDSs and IPSs can gather massive amounts of data. One way to deal with this amount of data is to compress (to help conserve disk space), archive it, and then periodically purge it. This strategy, however, is in many cases flawed, because having online rather than archived data on storage media is often necessary to perform the necessary ongoing analyses. For example, you might notice suspicious activity from a particular internal host and wonder if there has been similar activity over the last few months. Going to a central repository of data is preferable to having to find the media on which old data reside and restoring the data to one or more systems.

Having sufficient disk space for management purposes is, of course, a major consideration. One good solution is RAID (Redundant Array of Inexpensive Disks), which writes data to multiple disks and provides redundancy in case of any disk failing. Another option is optical media, such as worm drives (although performance is an issue).

Ideally, the manager component of an IDS or IPS will also organize the stored data. A relational database, such as an Oracle or Sybase database, is well suited for this purpose. Once a database is designed and implemented, new data can be added on the fly, and queries against database entries can be made.

Alerting

Another important function that the manager component can perform is generating alerts whenever events that constitute high levels of threat occur (such as a compromise of a Windows domain controller or a network information service (NIS) master server, or of a critical network device, such as a router). Agents are designed to provide detection capability, but agents are normally not involved in alerting because it is more efficient to do so from a central host. Agents instead usually send information to a central server that sends alerts whenever predefined criteria are met. This requires that the server not only contain the addresses of operators who need to be notified, but also have an alerting mechanism.

Normally, alerts are either sent via e-mail or via the Unix syslog facility. If sent via e-mail, the message content should be encrypted using PGP (Pretty Good Privacy) or some other form of message encryption. Attackers who discover the content of messages concerning detected intrusions or shunned IP addresses can adjust their strategies (such as using a different source IP address if the one they have been using is now blocked), thereby increasing their efficiency. The syslog facility's main advantage is flexibility—syslog can send messages about nearly anything to just about everybody if desired. Encrypting syslog content is a much bigger challenge than encrypting e-mail message content, however. Fortunately, a project called syslog-ng will sometime in the future provide encryption solutions for syslog-related traffic. Additionally, the syslog server will ideally keep an archive of alerts that have been issued in case someone needs to inspect the contents of previous alerts.

Event Correlation

Another extremely important function of the manager component is correlating events that have occurred to determine whether they have a common source, whether they were part of a series of related attacks, and so forth. Event correlation is so important that Chapter 12 is devoted to the topic.

High-Level Analysis

Still another function that the manager component may perform is high-level analysis of the events that the intrusion-detection or intrusion-prevention tool discovers. The manager component may, for example, track the progression of each attack from stage to stage, starting with the preparatory (doorknob rattling) stage. Additionally, this component can analyze the threat that each event constitutes, sending notification to the alert-generation function whenever a threat reaches a certain specified value. Sometimes high-level analysis is performed by a neural network or expert system that looks for patterns in large amounts of data.

Monitoring Other Components

We've seen previously in this chapter how having a monitoring component to check the health of sensors and agents is important. The manager is the ideal component in which to place this function because (once again) this function is most efficient if it is centralized.

The manager can, for instance, send packets to each sensor and agent to determine whether each is responsive to input on the network. Better yet, the manager can initiate connections to each sensor and agent to determine whether each is up and running. If the manager component determines that any other component has failed, it can notify its alerting facility to generate an alert.

In host-based intrusion detection, the manager can monitor each host to ensure that logging or auditing is functioning correctly. The manager component can also track utilization of system and network resources, generating an alert if any system or any part of the network is overwhelmed.

Policy Generation and Distribution

Another function that is often embedded in the manager component is policy generation and distribution. In the context of the manager component, *policy* refers to settings that affect how the various components of an intrusion-detection or intrusion-prevention system function. A policy could be set, for example, to activate all agents or to move an agent from one machine to another.

Nowhere is policy more important than in IPSs. Based on data that the manager component receives, the manager component creates and then distributes a policy or a change in policy to individual hosts. The policy might tell each host to not accept input for a particular source IP address or to not execute a particular system call. The manager component is generally in charge of creating, updating, and enforcing policy.

Security Management and Enforcement

Security management and enforcement is one of the most critical functions that can be built into the manager component. This function is covered in the "Manager Security Considerations" section later in this chapter.

Management Console

Providing an interface for users through a management console is yet another function of the manager component. This function, like most of the others covered in this section, makes a huge difference in terms of the value of an IDS or IPS to an organization. The management console should display critical information—alerts, the status of each component, data in individual packets, audit log data, and so forth—and should also allow operators to control every part of an IDS or IPS. For example, if a sensor appears to be sending corrupted data, an operator should be able to quickly shut down this sensor using the management console.

The importance of human-factors engineering in the design of a management console cannot be overstated. Management consoles are almost invariably designed to be the sole

The Importance of Being Able to View Packet Data

Management consoles should allow operators to readily access all data that an IDS or IPS gathers, sends, and processes. A type of data not available in some implementations of IDSs and IPSs is packet data. Saving packet data, after all, requires huge amounts of disk space. But packet data are often one of the most useful types of data for operators. Errors in applications, the universal tendency for IDSs to produce false alarms, and tricks played by attackers can, for example, cause erroneous output or may prompt further questions. Going directly to packet data often resolves these issues and questions.

Suppose, for example, that an IDS reports a distributed scan from a certain range of IP addresses. Going to the IP portion of each packet will yield information such as the indicated IP source address, the version of the IP protocol, and the TTL (time-to-live parameter). If the apparent IP source addresses for the distributed scan are 15 hops away (as revealed by the output of the "traceroute or "tracert command), but the TTL parameter of most packets is equal to four or five, something is wrong. Many operating systems and applications assign an initial TTL value of 64 or 128 to IP packets they create. In this case, packets from hosts that are 15 hops away on the network should have TTL values equal to 115 (or perhaps 51) or so. The illogically low TTL values indicate that these packets have almost certainly been fabricated (spoofed).

The bottom line is that you should think twice if you are considering buying an IDS or IPS that does not allow you to easily access packet data.

means through which operators and analysts interact with IDSs and IPSs. Display formats should be easy to comprehend, and interaction sequences should be intuitive. In short, the possibility of human error should be minimized. The major problems with management consoles in IDSs and IPSs today include excessive complexity, nonintuitive navigation methods, and cluttered displays, resulting in unnecessarily long learning times, confusion, and elevated error rates.

Manager Deployment Considerations

One of the most important deployment considerations for the manager component is ensuring that it runs on extremely high-end hardware (with a large amount of physical memory and a fast processor) and on a proven and reliable operating system platform (such as Solaris or Red Hat Linux). Continuous availability of the manager component is essential—any downtime generally renders an IDS or IPS totally worthless. Using RAID and deploying redundant servers in case one fails are additional measures that can be used to help assure continuous availability.

Decisions concerning where within a network to deploy the management console should (like the deployment of agents) be based on efficiency—the management component

should be in a location within the network that minimizes the distance from agents with which it communicates—and on security, as discussed next.

Manager Security Considerations

Of the three major components of a multi-tiered architecture, sensors are attacked most often, and compromised or disabled agents can cause considerable trouble, but a single successful attack on a management console is generally the worst imaginable outcome. Because of the centrality of the manager component to an entire IDS or IPS, such an attack can quickly result in all components in a multi-tiered architecture becoming compromised or unusable, and it can also result in destruction of all data and alerts that are centrally collected. It is thus advisable to devote considerable effort to hardening the host on which the management console runs.

Hardening includes implementing measures that prevent denial-of-service attacks, such as installing a properly configured firewall or TCP wrapper on the box that houses the manager component, ensuring that all vendor patches are installed, and not running unnecessary services. The server should also be protected by one or more external and possibly also internal firewalls, and it should not be located in a portion of a network that has particularly high levels of traffic. The hardware platform on which the manager component runs must also be dedicated solely to this function, and it should have a special sensor—a watchdog function that is independent of the built-in logging capabilities—to provide specialized monitoring of all activity on that host.

Unauthorized physical access is always a major concern in any system, but unauthorized access to the management console is even more critical. Putting suitable physical access controls in place is thus imperative. Implementing measures such as a keyboard lock and a locking encasement over all hardware used in connection with the manager component, and placing the system in a server room with restricted access (through a combination lock or badge reader), is a good starting point. Assigning a CMOS boot password or, in the case of Unix and Linux systems, protecting against unauthorized single user boots is also essential. Auditing all access to the room in which the manager component resides and enabling a password-protected screensaver that activates shortly after each user's session becomes inactive are further effective physical security measures. Protecting against fire and water hazards and providing suitable temperature control are also highly advisable.

Authentication is also a special consideration for the manager component. Given that password-based authentication has become increasingly ineffective in keeping out unauthorized users, you should require third-party authentication for access to any part of the manager component, but especially the management console. Smart cards and tokens (such as SecurID tokens by RSA) are two of the currently popular forms of third-party authentication. Although biometric authentication is still in its infancy, some forms of biometric authentication, such as facial recognition, are also becoming sufficiently reliable to merit their strong consideration in contexts such as management console access.

Finally, providing suitable levels of encryption is critical. All communications between the manager component and any other component need to be encrypted using

strong encryption, such as 192- or 256-bit Advanced Encryption Standard (AES) encryption. Sessions from remote workstations to the management console, in particular, need to be encrypted. If not, they could be hijacked, or their contents could be divulged to unauthorized persons. Any kind of data about individuals that is stored on the manager component should also be encrypted to avoid privacy breaches and to conform to state and local laws.

SUMMARY

This chapter has covered intrusion-detection and intrusion-prevention system architectures. The term *architecture* refers to the functions supported by and relationships among machines, network devices, programs, and processes, and the communications between each. Three major types of architectures—single-tiered, multi-tiered, and peer-to-peer—are generally used in intrusion detection and intrusion prevention.

A *single-tiered architecture* consists of one component that performs all of the functions. A *multi-tiered architecture* has more than one component, and each component communicates with some or all of the others. Components are hierarchical, and they include the sensors (which tend to be at the low-end), the agents (which are more sophisticated, but usually are dedicated to one type of analysis), and the manager component, which typically embodies many centralized functions. The final type of architecture considered in this chapter is the peer-to-peer architecture, an architecture in which there are multiple components, such as firewalls, each of which is a peer (not a subordinate or superordinate) of the others.

Of the three major types of architectures, multi-tiered architectures are used more than any other. *Sensors* perform data collection, *agents* take the information they obtain from sensors and possibly also from other agents and analyze it, and the *manager component* provides centralized, sophisticated functionality, such as data aggregation, data correlation, policy creation and distribution, and alerting. Operators and analysts generally interact with the management console, which is the user interface portion of the manager component, to control the entire IDS or IPS.

Many decisions about deployment and security need to be made for each component. In general, the higher the level of the component, the more need for high levels of security. Sensors, for example, generally can be deployed anywhere on the network without causing undo concern, whereas agents need greater levels of protection and should reside where they operate most efficiently and are the most secure. Manager components need the most security and should be afforded the same protections that agents receive, as well as having additional controls, such as physical security measures, strong authentication, and strong encryption.

CHAPTER 7

IDS and IPS Internals

IDSs and IPSs can be as simple or as complex as you want them to be. At the simplest level, you could use a packet-capturing program to dump packets to files, and then use commands such as egrep and fgrep within scripts to search for strings of interest within the files.

This approach is not practical, though, given the sheer volume of traffic that must be collected, processed, and stored for the simple level of analysis that could be performed. Yet, even at this rudimentary level, more would be happening than one might imagine. Packets would be collected, and then decoded. Some of these packets would be fragmented, requiring they be reassembled before they could be analyzed. TCP streams would often need to be reassembled, too.

In a more complex IDS or IPS, additional sophisticated operations, such as filtering out undesirable input, applying firewall rules, getting certain kinds of incoming data in a format that can be more easily processed, running detection routines on the data, and executing routines such as those that shun certain source IP addresses would occur. In this latter case, even more sophisticated internal events and processes would occur.

This chapter covers the internals of IDSs and IPSs, focusing on information flow in these systems, detection of exploits, dealing with malicious code, how output routines work, and, finally, how IDSs and IPSs can be defended against attacks against them.

INFORMATION FLOW IN IDS AND IPS

How does information move internally through IDSs and IPSs? This section answers this question.

Raw Packet Capture

IDS and IPS internal information flow starts with raw packet capture. This involves not only capturing packets, but also passing the data to the next component of the system.

As explained in Chapter 6, *promiscuous* mode means a NIC picks up every packet at the point at which it interfaces with network media (except, of course, in the case of wireless networks, which broadcast signals from transmitters). To be in *nonpromiscuous* mode means a NIC picks up only packets bound for its particular MAC address, ignoring the others. Nonpromiscuous mode is appropriate for host-based intrusion detection and prevention, but not for network-based intrusion detection and prevention. A network-based intrusion detection/prevention system normally has two NICs—one for raw packet capture and a second to allow the host on which the system runs to have network connectivity for remote administration.

Most packets in today's networks are IP packets, although AppleTalk, IPX, SNA, and other packets still persist in some networks. The IDS or IPS must save the raw packets that are captured, so they can be processed and analyzed at some later point. In most cases, the packets are held in memory long enough so initial processing activities can occur and, soon afterwards, written to a file or a data structure to make room in memory for subsequent input or discarded.

Solving Problems

IDSs and IPSs typically experience all kinds of problems, but one of the most-common problems is packet loss. A frequent variation of this problem is that the NIC used to capture packets receives packets much faster than the CPU of the host on which the IDS/IPS runs is capable of despooling them. A good solution is simply to deploy higher-ended hardware.

Another problem is this: the IDS/IPSs itself cannot keep up with the throughput rates. Throughput rate is a much bigger problem than most IDS/IPS vendors publicly acknowledge—some of the best-selling products have rather dismal input processing rates. One solution is to filter out some of the input that would normally be sent to the IDS or IPS, as discussed shortly. Another more drastic solution is to change to another, different IDS or IPS. High-end IDSs/IPSs can now process input at rates up to 2GB (see http://enterprisesecurity.symantec.com/products/products.cfm?ProductID=156 for information about Symantec's ManHunt firewall, for example).

Yet another manifestation of the packet-loss problem is misdirected packet fragments on connections that have an intermediate switching point with a smaller maximum transmission unit (MTU) than that of the remote system. In this case, the problem could, once again, simply be a CPU that is too slow—the problem may not be fragmentation per se. Or, the problem could be inefficient packet reassembly, which is discussed in the section "Fragment Reassembly."

Whatever the solution to any of these problems might be, it is important to realize that packet loss is a normal part of networking—not exactly anything to panic about (unless, of course, the loss rate starts to get unacceptably high).

Chapters 5 and 6 covered the details of how programs such as tcpdump and libpcap work in connection with packet capture. These programs run in an "endless loop," waiting until they obtain packets from the network card device driver.

Filtering

No need for an IDS or IPS to capture every packet necessarily exists. Filtering out certain types of packets could, instead, be desirable. *Filtering* means limiting the packets that are captured according to a certain logic based on characteristics, such as type of packet, IP source address range, and others. Especially in very high-speed networks, the rate of incoming packets can be overwhelming and can necessitate limiting the types of packets captured. Alternatively, an organization might be interested in only certain types of incoming traffic, perhaps (as often occurs) only TCP traffic because, historically, more security attacks have been TCP-based than anything else.

Filtering raw packet data can be done in several ways. The NIC itself may be able to filter incoming packets. Although early versions of NICs (such as the 3COM 3C501 card) did not have filtering capabilities, modern and more sophisticated NICs do. The driver

for the network card may be able to take bpf rules and apply them to the card. The filtering rules are specified in the configuration of the driver itself. This kind of filtering is not likely to be as sophisticated as the bpf rules themselves, however.

Another method of filtering raw packet data is using packet filters to choose and record only certain packets, depending on the way the filters are configured. *libpcap*, for example, offers packet filtering via the bpf interpreter. You can configure a filter that limits the particular types of packets that will be processed further. The bpf interpreter receives all the packets, but it decides which of them to send on to applications. In most operating systems filtering is done in kernel space but, in others (such as Solaris), it is done in user space (which is less efficient, because packet data must be pushed all the way up the OSI stack to the application layer before it can be filtered). Operating systems with the bpf interpreter in the kernel are, thus, often the best candidates for IDS and IPS host platforms, although Solaris has an equivalent capability in the form of its streams mechanism (see http://docs.sun.com/db/doc/801-6679/6i11pd5ui?a=view).

Filtering rules can be inclusive or exclusive, depending on the particular filtering program or mechanism. For example, the following tcpdump filter rule (port http) or (udp port 111) or (len >= 1 and len <= 512) will result in any packets bound for an http port, or for UDP port 111 (the port used by the portmapper in Unix and Linux systems), or that are between 1 and 512 bytes in length being captured—an inclusive filter rule.

Packet Decoding

Packets are subsequently sent to a series of decoder routines that define the packet structure for the layer two (datalink) data (Ethernet, Token Ring, or IEEE 802.11) that are collected through promiscuous monitoring. The packets are then further decoded to determine whether the packet is an IPv4 packet (which is the case when the first nibble in the IP header is 4), an IP header with no options (which is the case when the first nibble in the IP header is 5), or IPv6 (where the first nibble in the IP header will be 6), as well as the source and destination IP addresses, the TCP and UDP source and destination ports, and so forth.

It is quite important to realize just how broken a good percent of the traffic on the Internet is. Everyone agrees on the steps for the so-called TCP three-way handshake, but numerous instances exist where the RFCs have not done a perfect job of defining behavior for certain protocols. Also, in many other cases, RFCs have been at least partially ignored in the implementation of network applications that use these protocols, so some kind of "sanity check" on these protocols is thus needed. Packet decoding accordingly examines each packet to determine whether it is consistent with applicable RFCs. The TCP header size plus the TCP data size should, for instance, equal the IP length. Packets that cannot be properly decoded are normally dropped because the IDS/IPS will not be able to process them properly.

Some IDSs such as *Snort* (covered in Chapter 10) go even further in packet decoding in that they allow checksum tests to determine whether the packet header contents coincide with the checksum value in the header itself. Checksum verification can be done for one, or any combination of, or all of the IP, TCP, UDP, and ICMP protocols. The downside of

performing this kind of verification is that today's routers frequently perform checksum tests and drop packets that do not pass the test. Performing yet another checksum test within an IDS or IPS takes its toll on performance and is, in all likelihood, unnecessary. (Despite this, the number of IP fragments per day is large).

Storage

Once each packet is decoded, it is often stored either by saving its data to a file or by assimilating it into a data structure while, at the same time, the data are cleared from memory. Storing data to a file (such as a binary spool file) is rather simple and intuitive because "what you see is what you get." New data can simply be appended to an existing file or a new file can be opened, and then written to.

But writing intrusion detection data to a file also has some significant disadvantages. For one thing, it is cumbersome to sort through the great amount of data within one or more file(s) that are likely to be accumulated to find particular strings of interest or perform data correlation, as discussed in Chapter 12. Additionally, the amount of data that are likely to be written to a hard drive or other storage device presents a disk space management challenge. An alternative is to set up data structures, one for each protocol analyzed, and overlay these structures on the packet data by creating and linking pointers to them.

Taking this latter approach is initially more complicated, but it makes accessing and analyzing the data much easier. Still another alternative is to write to a hash table to condense the amount of data substantially. You could, for example, take a source IP address, determine to how many different ports that address has connected, and any other information that might be relevant to detecting attacks, and then hash the data. The hash data can serve as a shorthand for events that detection routines can later access and process.

Fragment Reassembly

Decoding "makes sense" out of packets, but this, in and of itself, does not solve all the problems that need to be solved for an IDS/IPS to process the packets properly. Packet fragmentation poses yet another problem for IDSs and IPSs. A reasonable percentage of network traffic consists of packet fragments with which firewalls, routers, switches, and IDSs/IPSs must deal. Hostile fragmentation, packet fragmentation used to attack other systems or to evade detection mechanisms, can take several forms:

▼ One packet fragment can overlap another in a manner that the fragments will be reassembled so subsequent fragments overwrite parts of the first one instead of being reassembled in their "natural" sequential order. Overlapping fragments are often indications of attempted denial-of-service attacks (DoS) or IDS/IPS or firewall evasion attempts (if none of these know how to deal with packets of this nature, they would be unable to process them further).

■ Packets may be improperly sized. In one variation of this condition, the fragments are excessively large—greater than 65,535 bytes and, thus, likely to trigger abnormal conditions, such as excessive CPU consumption in the hosts

that receive them. Excessively large packets thus usually represent attempts to produce DoS. An example is the "ping of death" attack in which many oversized packets are sent to victim hosts, causing them to crash. Or, the packet fragments could be excessively short, such as less than 64 bytes. Often called a *tiny fragment* attack, the attacker fabricates, and then sends packets broken into tiny pieces. If the fragment is sufficiently small, part of the header information gets displaced into multiple fragments, leaving incomplete headers. Network devices and IDSs/IPSs may not be able to process these headers. In the case of firewalls and screening routers, the fragments could be passed through and on to their destination although, if they were not fragmented, the packet might not have been allowed through. Or, having to reassemble so many small packets could necessitate a huge amount of memory, causing DoS.

▲ Still another way of fragmenting packets is to break them up, so a second fragment is contained completely within the first fragment. The resulting offsets create a huge program for fragment-reassembly process, causing the host that received these fragments to crash. This kind of attack is known as a *teardrop* attack.

A critical consideration in dealing with fragmented packets is whether only the first fragment will be retained or whether the first fragment, plus the subsequent fragments,

Evading Intrusions

As new and better systems to detect and prevent intrusions emerge, the black-hat community is devoting more effort to discover more effective ways to defeat them. Many network-based IDS and IPS tools go through a plethora of data trying to identify signatures of known exploits in the data. Evasion focuses on fooling signature-based attack detection by changing the form of an attack. *Fragroute* is a tool that works in this manner—it breaks packets into tiny fragments in extremely unusual ways before transmitting them across the network. A network-based IDS or IPS collects these fragments, and then tries to decode and reassemble them before detection routines analyze their data, but it will not be able to do so properly. In particular, older IDSs are vulnerable to fragroute attacks.

Although many types of packet fragmentation attacks exist, most of them are currently passé. Most OS vendors have developed patches for the vulnerabilities on which fragmentation attacks capitalized soon after the vulnerabilities were made public. Meanwhile, new releases of operating systems have been coded in a manner so they are not vulnerable to these attacks. The same applies to IDSs, IPSs, and firewalls, all of which are likely to detect ill-formed fragments, but not process them any further. So, knowing about packet fragmentation attacks and their potential perils is important, usually nothing special must normally be done to defend systems against them, provided you use recent versions of IDSs/IPSs and network devices.

will be retained. Retaining only the first fragment is more efficient. The first fragment contains the information in the packet header that identifies the type of packet, the source and destination IP addresses, and so on—information that detection routines can process later. Having to associate subsequent fragments with the initial fragment requires additional resources. At the same time, however, although some of the subsequent fragments are unlikely to contain information of much value to an IDS or IPS, this is not true for many types of attacks, such as those in which many HTTP GET command options are entered, and then the packets are broken into multiple fragments. Combining fragments is necessary if you want a more thorough analysis of intrusion detection data.

Fragment reassembly can be performed in a number of ways:

▼   The OS itself can reassemble the fragments.

■   A utility can perform this function.

▲   The previously discussed filtering capability can reassemble fragments. The main advantage of this approach is that reassembly can be selective. UDP packets, especially those used in Network File System (NFS) mount access, tend to fragment more than do other packets, for example. Packet reassembly requires a good amount of system resources, so selecting only certain kinds of packets (such as TCP packets) to be reassembled is often best.

Stream Reassembly

Stream reassembly means taking the data from each TCP stream and, if necessary, reordering it (primarily on the basis of packet sequence numbers), so it is the same as when it was sent by the host that transmitted it and also the host that received it. This requires determining when each stream starts and stops, something that is not difficult given that TCP communications between any two hosts begin with a SYN packet and end with either a RST (reset) or FIN/ACK packet.

Stream reassembly is especially important when data arrive at the IDS or IPS in a different order from their original one. This is a critical step in getting data ready to be analyzed because IDS recognition mechanisms cannot work properly if the data taken in by the IDS or IPS are scrambled. Stream reassembly also facilitates detection of out-of-sequence scanning methods.

According to RFC 793, FIN packets should be sent only while a TCP connection is being closed. If a FIN packet is sent to a closed TCP port, the server should respond back with an RST packet. So, stream reassembly is critical in recognizing situation such as these (such as when an ACK packet is sent for a session that has not been started. Additionally, determining which of two hosts has sent traffic to the other is a critical piece of information needed by analyzers.

Stream reassembly results in knowing the directionality of data exchanges between hosts, as well as when packets are missing (in which case a good IDS/IPS will report this as an anomaly). The data from the reassembled stream are written to a file or data structure, again, either as packet contents or byte streams, or are discarded.

Stream reassembly may sound simple but, in reality, it is rather complicated because many special conditions must be handled. Policies based on system architecture usually dictate how stream reassembly occurs under these conditions.

From an IDS/IPS point of view, it is critical to know what the policy for overlapping fragments is—whether only the first fragment or all fragments are retained, for example—on each target host. One host TCP may drop overlapping fragments, whereas another may attempt to process them. Retransmissions in TCP connections pose yet another problem. Should data from the original retransmission or the subsequent one be retained?

The issue of whether the target host handles data in a SYN packet properly is yet another complication in stream reassembly. According to RFC 793, data can be inserted into a SYN packet, although this is not usually done. This also applies to FIN and RST packets. Should these data be included in the reassembled stream? Failure to include them could mean the detection routines to which the stream will be sent could miss certain attacks.

The packet timeout is another issue. What if a packet from a stream arrives after the timeout? How does the reassembly program handle this? Once again, the program doing the session reconstruction needs to know the characteristics of the target host to understand what this host saw. You might think the session has been properly reassembled when, in fact, it has not. The saving grace is that you can assume something is wrong whenever you see overlapping fragments. Reacting to overlapping fragments is, usually unnecessary; simply flagging the fact that they have been sent is sufficient, at least for intrusion-detection purposes.

A type of stream reassembly with UDP and ICMP traffic can also be done but, remember, both these protocols are connectionless and sessionless and, thus, do not have the characteristics TCP stream reassembly routines use. Some IDSs/IPSs make UDP and ICMP traffic into "pseudosessions" by assuming that whenever two hosts are exchanging UDP or ICMP packets with no pause of transmission greater than 30 seconds, something that resembles the characteristics of a TCP session (at least to some degree) is occurring. The order of the packets can then be reconstructed. This approach to dealing with UDP and ICMP traffic is based on some pretty shaky assumptions but, nevertheless, useful analyses could be subsequently performed on the basis of data gleaned from these reassembled pseudosessions.

NOTE In general, the current generation of IDSs and IDPs actively reassemble IP fragments and TCP streams. Accordingly, certain types of fragmentation attacks against these systems that used to be able to evade these systems' recognition capabilities no longer work. Other attacks are based on how differing operating systems put fragments back together but, even these types of attack are being thwarted by IDSs and IPSs that are aware of the flavor of the OS at the destination and that reassemble the stream appropriately for each particular OS.

Stateful Inspection of TCP Sessions

Stateful inspection of network traffic is a virtual necessity whenever the need to analyze the legitimacy of packets that traverse networks presents itself. As mentioned previously,

attackers often try to slip packets they create through firewalls, screening routers, IDSs, and IPSs by making the fabricated packets (such as SYN/ACK or ACK packets) look like part of an ongoing session or like one being negotiated via the three-way TCP handshake sequence, even though such a session was never established.

IDSs and IPSs also have a special problem in that if they were to analyze every packet that appeared to be part of a session, an attacker could flood the network with such packets, causing the IDSs and IPSs to become overwhelmed. An IDS evasion tool called *stick* does exactly this.

Current IDSs and IPSs generally perform stateful inspections of TCP traffic. These systems generally use tables in which they enter data concerning established sessions, and then compare packets that appear to be part of a session to the entries in the tables. If no table entry for a given packet can be found, the packet is dropped. Stateful inspection also helps IDSs and IPSs that perform signature matching by ensuring this matching is performed only on content from actual sessions. Finally, stateful analysis can enable an IDS or IPS to identify scans in which OS fingerprinting is being attempted. Because these scans result in a variety of packets sent that do not confirm to RPC 793 conventions, these scans "stand out" in comparison to established sessions.

Firewalling

Earlier in this chapter, you learned that part of the internal information flow within an IDS and IPS includes filtering packet data according to a set of rules. Filtering is essentially a type of firewalling, even through it is relatively rudimentary. But, after stateful inspections of traffic are performed, more sophisticated firewalling based on the results of the inspections can be performed. While the primary purpose of filtering is to drop packet data that are not of interest, the primary purpose of firewalling after stateful inspection is to protect the IDS or IPS itself. Attackers can launch attacks that impair or completely disable the capability of the IDS or the IPS to detect and protect. The job of the firewall is to weed out these attacks, so attacks against the IDS or IPS do not succeed. Amazingly, a number of today's IDSs and IPSs do not have a built-in firewall that performs this function. Why? A firewall limits performance.

Putting It All Together

Figure 7-1 shows how the various type of information processing covered so far are related to each other in a host that does not support bpf. The NIC collects packets and sends them to drivers that interface with the kernel. The kernel decodes, filters, and reassembles fragmented packets, and then reassembles streams. The output is passed on to applications.

Figure 7-2 shows how information processing occurs when an operating system supports bpf. In this case, a program such as libpcap performs most of the work that the kernel performs in Figure 7-1, and then passes the output to bpf applications.

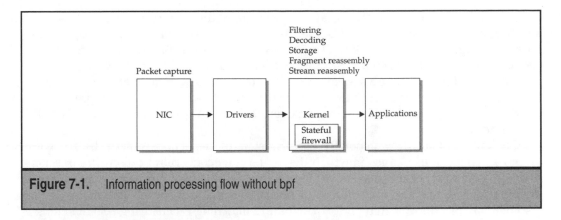

Figure 7-1. Information processing flow without bpf

DETECTION OF EXPLOITS

We turn our attention next toward how IDSs and IPSs detect exploits. After defining various kinds of attacks that IDSs and IPSs are designed to detect and prevent, we consider several matching methods: signature matching, rule matching, profiling, and others.

Types of Exploits

The number of exploits with which an IDS or IPS potentially must deal is in the thousands. *Snort*, a tool discussed in Chapter 10, has over 2000 exploit signatures, for example.

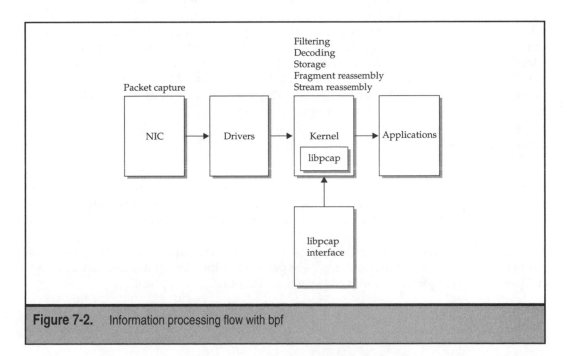

Figure 7-2. Information processing flow with bpf

Although describing each exploit is not possible in this book, the SANS Institute (http://www.sans.org) has helped the user community become acquainted with the most frequently exploited vulnerabilities by publishing the "SANS Top 20 Vulnerabilities" at http://isc.sans.org/top20.html. Consider the top 20 vulnerabilities at press time.

Top Vulnerabilities in Windows Systems

A list of Windows systems' top vulnerabilities follows:

▼ Buffer overflows in Internet Information Server (IIS) script mappings and WebDAV that can be exploited by sending specially crafted excessive input, resulting in DoS, execution of rogue code, and other outcomes.

■ Multiple vulnerabilities in Microsoft SQL Server that can allow unauthorized read and write access to database entries, execution of rogue commands and code, and control of the server itself by attackers (in the last case because the SQL Server administrator account is unpassworded by default).

■ Weak and crackable passwords that can result in unauthorized access to systems and resources therein.

■ A variety of vulnerabilities in Microsoft Internet Explorer (IE) that can allow execution of rogue commands and code, control of systems that run this browser by attackers, disclosure of cookies, and other negative outcomes.

■ Unprotected shares, anonymous logons, remote Registry access, and remote procedure calls that can allow unauthorized access to and subversion of systems and resources therein.

■ Vulnerabilities, such as buffer overflow conditions in Microsoft Data Access Components, such as Remote Data Services (RDS) that can allow unauthorized execution of rogue commands and code.

■ Multiple vulnerabilities in Windows Scripting Host (such as in the autoexecution feature, which can be made to run unauthorized Visual Basic scripts) that can allow execution of rogue code.

■ Vulnerabilities in embedded automation features in Microsoft Outlook and Outlook Express that can allow execution of rogue code.

■ Peer-to-peer file sharing that can result in unauthorized access to systems and legal troubles.

▲ Vulnerabilities in the Simple Network Management Protocol (SNMP) that can lead to DoS and unauthorized configuration changes in systems.

Top Vulnerabilities in Unix Systems

A list of Unix systems' top vulnerabilities follows:

▼ Vulnerabilities in the Berkeley Internet Name Domain (BIND) program (particularly in nxt, qinv, and in.named) that can result in DoS and execution of rogue code.

- Multiple vulnerabilities in the remote procedure call (RPC) that can lead to DoS.

- Multiple bugs in the Apache web server (such as a heap buffer overflow vulnerability in the apr_psprintf() function) that can result in DoS, unauthorized access to information, defacement of web pages, and root-level compromise of the host that runs Apache.

- Unpassworded accounts or accounts with weak passwords that can allow unauthorized access to systems (sometimes with root privileges).

- Cleartext network traffic that can lead to unauthorized reading of information and unauthorized access to systems (because cleartext passwords are exposed).

- Vulnerabilities in sendmail (such as an error in the prescan() function that enables someone to write past the end of a buffer) that can result in DoS, unauthorized execution of rogue code with root privileges or unauthorized spam relay.

- SNMP vulnerabilities that can lead to DoS and unauthorized configuration changes in systems.

- Bugs in Secure Shell (ssh) that can lead to unauthorized root access and other outcomes.

- Misconfiguration of the Network Information Service (NIS) and the Network File System (NFS) that can result in unauthorized access to files, unauthorized access to systems, and other outcomes.

- ▲ Bugs in Open Secure Sockets Layer (SSL), such as improper integer overflow handling and insecure memory deallocation, that can cause unauthorized execution of rogue code and unauthorized root access.

Although these 20 vulnerabilities are currently the most exploited ones, an IDS or IPS that recognized nothing more than the exploits for these vulnerabilities would be a dismal failure. But, because of the frequency with which these vulnerabilities are exploited in real-life settings, failure to recognize any of these 20 vulnerabilities would also be catastrophic.

The SANS Top 20 List: How Current?

The SANS Top 20 List has proven extremely useful, but it is not always updated as quickly as it needs to be. At press time, for example, the SANS Top 20 List did not include an at-the-time new, serious vulnerability in Windows systems that the MSBlaster worm and its variants exploited. The problem is in an RPC function that deals with TCP/IP message exchanges, particularly in the manner it handles improperly formed messages. The Distributed Component Object Model (DCOM) interface with RPC listens for client requests for activating DCOM objects via TCP port 135. An attacker could forge a client RPC request with a group of specially crafted arguments in a packet, causing the server that receives this packet to execute the arguments with full privileges. This vulnerability will undoubtedly be included in the next SANS Top 20 List.

Signature Matching

We'll start with the simplest type of matching, signature-based matching.

How Signature Matching Works

As discussed previously, a signature is a string that is part of what an attacking host sends to an intended victim host that uniquely identifies a particular attack. In the case of the exploit for the ida script mapping buffer overflow vulnerability (see the sidebar "How Vulnerabilities Are Exploited"), `.ida?` is sufficient to distinguish an attempt to exploit the buffer overflow condition from other attacks, such as exploiting a buffer overflow condition in the idq script mapping.

Signature matching means input strings passed on to detection routines match a pattern in the IDS/IPS's signature files. The exact way an IDS or IPS performs signature

How Vulnerabilities Are Exploited

How are vulnerabilities exploited? Consider the first vulnerability from the SANS Top 20, buffer overflows in IIS script mappings. One of the script mappings that the IIS Indexing Service Application Programming Interface (ISAPI) uses is ida (Internet data administration). This script mapping has an unchecked buffer when it is encoding double-byte characters. Whoever wrote this script mapping did not consider what would happen if this kind of input were sent to it. ida.dll should not accept this kind of input at all. An attacker can exploit this problem in an IIS server that has not been patched by sending the following input to the server:

```
GET /default.ida?NNNNNNNNNNNNNNNNNNNNNNNNNNNNNNNNNNNNNNNNNNNNNNNNNNNN
NNNNNNNNNNNNNNNNNNNNNNNNNNNNNNNNNNNNNNNNNNNNNNNNNNNNNNNNNNNNNNNNNNNNNNN
NNNNNNNNNNNNNNNNNNNNNNNNNNNNNNNNNNNNNNNNNNNNNNNNNNNNNNNNNNNNNNNNNNNNNNN
NNNNNNNNNNNNNNNNNNNNNNNNNNNNNNNNNNNNNNNNNNNNNNNNN%u9090%u6858%ucbd3%u7801%
u9090%u6858%ucbd3%u7801%u9090%u6858%ucbd3%u7801%u9090%u9090%u8190%u
00c3%u0003%u8b00%u531b%u53ff%u0078%u0000%u00=a

HTTP/1.0
```

240 or more Ns (or any other character—this does not matter) overflow the buffer, at which point the remaining input spills over into memory where the commands—the portion of the previous input after the string of Ns (note, they are in Unicode format) will be executed. A similar vulnerability also exists in the Internet data query (idq) script mapping. Interestingly, these vulnerabilities are the ones exploited by the Code Red worm family.

matching varies from system to system. The simplest, but most inefficient, method is to use fgrep or a similar string search command to compare each part of the input passed from the kernel to the detection routines to lists of signatures. A positive identification of an attack occurs whenever the string search command finds a match.

More sophisticated types of signature matching exist, however. For example, Snort, an IDS covered in Chapter 10, creates a tree structure of attack patterns and uses a search algorithm that results in only patterns relevant to the particular packets being matched in a particular branch of the tree being used in the matching process. This produces a far more efficient search process.

Evaluation of Signature Matching

Signature-based matching is not only simple, it is also intuitive. People who understand little about intrusion detection quickly understand that certain input patterns, if picked up by an IDS or IPS, indicate an attack has occurred. But few additional advantages of signature-based matching exist.

Some of the major limitations of signature-based matching include the following:

▼ Numerous variations of an attack often exist, each with its own signature. For example, in many versions of Washington University (wu) ftp, a SITE EXEC vulnerability exists in which an attacker can gain root access to an ftp server. The attacker can initiate a SITE EXEC attack by connecting to a wu-ftp server and entering the following:

```
quote site exec exec echo toor::0:0::/:/bin/sh >> /etc/passwd
```

The previous character string constitutes a signature for one version of the SITE EXEC attack, so having only this signature in a file or database would result in numerous missed attacks if other SITE EXEC attack methods were used. A hacker tool, *ADMutate* (see http://www.nwfusion.com/news/2002/0415idsevad.html), starts with a single buffer overflow exploit and creates a plethora of functionally equivalent exploits, every one with a unique signature.

■ Signature-based IDSs have gotten well behind the proverbial power curve given the variety and pace of discovery of new attacks. Adding a new signature to an IDS or IPS's signature library before that system is capable of recognizing an attack pattern is necessary. Thus, signature-based IDSs and IPSs initially miss new types of attacks.

■ Signature databases or flat files storing lists of signature tend to get cluttered with archaic signatures (so the vendors can "beat their chests," claiming their products can detect more attacks than their competitors' products). This not only hurts performance (because the more signatures there are, the slower detection becomes), but also causes those who deploy IDSs and IPSs to become falsely optimistic about detection rates.

▲   Signature-based IDS and IPSs tend to generate unacceptably high false alarm rates. The reason is that some types of input patterns such as

```
vipw /etc/passwd.adjunct
```

can constitute attacks, but may sometimes also constitute legitimate usage (for example, by system administrators). Signatures are all-or-none in nature—in and of themselves, they reveal virtually nothing about the *context* of the input. Any time one of the predesignated signatures comes along, a signature-based IDS or IPS issues an alarm.

Rule Matching

We'll next turn our attention to rule matching, another matching method.

How Rule Matching Works

Rule-based IDSs and IPSs are, as their name implies, based on rules. These types of IDSs hold considerable promise because they are generally based on combinations of possible indicators of attacks, aggregating them to see if a rule condition has been fulfilled.

Signatures themselves may constitute one possible indication. In some cases (but not usually), a signature that invariably indicates an attack may be the only indicator of an attack that is necessary for a rule-based IDS or IPS to issue an alert. In most cases, though, particular combinations of indicators are necessary. For example, an anonymous FTP connection attempt from an outside IP address may not cause the system to be suspicious at all. But, if the FTP connection attempt is within, say, 24 hours of a scan from the same IP, a rule-based IDS should become more suspicious. If the FTP connection attempt succeeds and someone goes to the /pub directory and starts entering cd .., cd .., cd .., a good rule-based IDS or IPS should go crazy. This is because what we have here is most likely a *dot-dot* attack (in which the intention is to get to the root directory itself) with the major antecedent conditions having been present. This example is simple, yet it is powerful. Real rule-based systems generally have much more sophisticated (and thus even more powerful) rules.

Evaluation of Rule Matching

The main advantages of rule matching are as follows:

▼   A relatively small set of rules can cover many exploits, exploits for which perhaps scores of signatures would be needed for signature matching.

■   Rule matching has considerable robustness—minor variations in string patterns are also normally no problem in rule matching. Consider the previously covered IIS ida script-mapping buffer-overflow attack. A rule-based system might ignore the .ida? signature and, instead, focus on any input with large numbers of repeated characters, regardless of what the particular characters are.

The Pros and Cons of Protocol Analysis

Using rules based on protocol behavior has become increasingly popular (especially in IDSs) over the years and for good reason. Deviations from expected protocol behavior—each protocol is supposed to behave according to RFC specifications (although, as mentioned before, these specifications are not always as "air tight" as they should be)—is one of the most time-proven and reliable ways of detecting attacks, regardless of the particular signature involved. Many consecutive finger requests from a particular IP address are, for example, almost always an indication of an attack, as is a flood of SYN packets from a particular host. Excessively large packet fragments and improperly chunked data sent to a web server are other indications of anomalous protocol behavior. Most of the systems with the highest overall detection proficiency use a variety of protocol analysis methods. On the downside, protocol analysis can result in a substantially elevated false alarm rate if a network is not working properly. For example, a malfunctioning router may spray packets, causing protocol anomaly routines to go berserk.

▲ Rule matching is a good way to detect new, previously unobserved attacks (although no rule-based system is anywhere near perfect as far as this goes). New rules have to be added and existing ones must be updated, but not nearly at the rate that signature-based systems require.

The main limitations of rule matching include the following:

▼ Rules are better suited to detecting new variations of exploits than radically new types of exploits. Like signatures, new rules need to be added to IDSs and IPSs, although they generally need to be added much less often.

▲ In rule-based systems, packet data are generally stored in data structures, and then compared to representations of the rules. If hash tables are used to store the data, hash values are usually calculated for the portions of the packet that represent each event of potential interest. If the hash function uses XOR operations to combine one part of its input with another, and if a relatively weak hashing algorithm is used, it is possible to determine in what manner and when incoming packets are handled before hash table entries for them are created. Once this determination is made, it is possible to send floods of specially created packets to the rule-based IDS or IPS that will produce identical hash values as normal packets, creating hash table "collisions." The CPU becomes massively overloaded trying to resolve these collisions, resulting in DoS or a substantial slowdown.

Profile-Based Matching

Next we'll look at profile-based matching methods.

How Profile-Based Matching Works

Information about users' session characteristics is captured in system logs and process listings. Profiling routines extract information for each user, writing it to data structures that store it. Other routines build statistical norms based on measurable usage patterns. When a user action that deviates too much from the normal pattern, occurs the profiling system flags this event and passes necessary information on to output routines. For example, if a user normally logs in from 8:00 A.M. to 5:30 P.M. but, then, one day logs in at 2 A.M., a profile-based system is likely to flag this event.

Evaluation of Profile-Based Matching

Profile matching offers the following major advantages:

▼ Profile-based systems are the best way to detect insider attacks. Profiles are typically constructed on a user-by-user basis, making the IDS or IPS capable of detecting specific "eccentricities" in special users' usage patterns. Conventional IDSs and IPSs, which do not focus on particular individuals and their actions, simply "miss the mark" when it comes to insider attacks. Profiling is the most effective way to identify perpetrators of insider attacks.

▲ Profile-based systems are well suited for discovering new kinds of attacks. These systems do not look at specific characteristics of attacks, but rather at deviations from normal patterns. No one but a few individuals (in all likelihood, a few members of the black hat community) may be aware of a signature for a new attack, making that attack impossible to detect using conventional methods, such as signature matching. But, if the attacker uses the new exploit to break into a user's account, the usage characteristics of this account are likely to change radically, something a profile-based system is likely to pick up.

Some major downsides of profile-based intrusion detection include the following:

▼ Profile-based intrusion detection is based on a limited number of simplistic types of usage patterns, such as time of usage or the number of privileged commands entered. Accordingly, profile-based systems also tend to generate high false alarm rates.

■ A clever trusted insider can make reasonable guesses concerning how much "deviance from normal" will be tolerated and cause his/her profile to become broader and broader over time, making the IDS or IPS miss deviant actions that occur later.

▲ An attacker who knows the basic usage patterns of a user can break into that user's account, and then use compromised credentials to engage in a wide variety of unauthorized actions. Unless the attacker does something far from the ordinary (such as surf a hacking tools site), these actions are not likely to be discovered.

Other Matching Methods

Many other types of matching or, more properly, detection methods, too numerous to cover here, are also used. *Tripwire-type tools* compare previous and current cryptochecksum and hash values to detect tampering with files and directories. Another method uses *Bayes' theorem,* which allows computation of the probability of one event given that another has occurred, providing a way of calculating the probability that a given host has been successfully attacked given certain indications of compromise.

MALICIOUS CODE DETECTION

Malicious code is so prevalent and so many different types of malicious code exist, antivirus software alone cannot detail with the totality of the problem. Accordingly, another important function of intrusion detection and intrusion prevention is detecting the presence of malicious code in systems. The next section discusses this function.

Types of Malicious Code

According to Edward Skoudis in *Malware: Fight Malicious Code* (Addison Wesley, 2003), major types of malicious code include the following:

▼ **Viruses**   Self-replicating programs that infect files and normally need human intervention to spread

■ **Worms**   Self-replicating programs that spread over the network and can spread independently of humans

■ **Malicious mobile code**   Programs downloaded from remote hosts, usually (but not always) written in a language designed for interaction with web servers

■ **Backdoors**   Programs that circumvent security mechanisms (especially authentication mechanisms)

■ **Trojan horses**   Programs that have a hidden purpose; usually, they appear to do something useful, but instead they perform some malicious function

■ **User level rootkits**   Programs that replace or change programs run by system managers and users

■ **Kernel level rootkits**   Programs that modify the operating system itself without indication that this has occurred

▲ **Combination malware**   Malicious code that crosses across category boundaries

How Malicious Code Can Be Detected

IDSs and IPSs generally detect the presence of malicious code in much the same manner as these systems detect attacks in general. This is how these systems can detect malicious code:

▼ Malicious code sent over the network is characterized by signatures such as those recognized by antivirus software. IDSs and IPSs can match network data with signatures, distinguishing strings of malicious code within executables, unless the traffic is encrypted.

■ Rules based on port activation can be applied. If, for example, UDP port 27374 in a Windows system is active, a good chance exists that the deadly SubSeven Trojan horse program (that allows remote control by perpetrators) is running on that system.

■ Worms often scan for other systems to infect. The presence of scans (such as TCP port 135 scans by Windows system infected by the MSBlaster worm and its many variants) can thus also be indications of malicious code infections for rule-based IDSs and IPSs.

■ Tripwire-style tools can detect changes to system files and directories.

▲ Symptoms within systems themselves, as detected by host-based IDSs and IPSs, can indicate malicious code is present. Examples include the presence of certain files and changes to the Registry of Windows systems (particularly to the `HKEY_LOCAL_MACHINE\Software\Microsoft\Windows\Current Version\Run` key, in which values can be added to cause malicious code to start whenever a system boots).

Challenges

Although IDSs and IPSs can be useful in detecting malicious code, relying solely on these kinds of systems to do so is unwise. Instead, they should be viewed more as an additional barrier in the war against malicious code than anything else. Why? First and foremost, other types of detection software (at least antivirus software for Windows and Macintosh systems) is more directly geared to serving this kind of function. Antivirus vendors generally do better in writing malicious code detection routines in these systems in the first place. The situation with Unix, Linux, and other systems is quite different, however. In these cases, IDSs and IPSs should be considered one of a few first-line defenses against malicious code. This is because antivirus software for these systems is not as necessary as for Windows systems and it is not as freely available. This is not to imply that malware detection software in these systems is useless. The chkrootkit program, for example, is simple to use and quite effective in detecting the presence of rootkits on Unix and Linux systems. It can even detect when something in a system is not behaving correctly that might indicate the presence of a rootkit. Additionally, network encryption presents a huge obstacle to detection of malicious code on systems on which this code runs. Finally, symptoms of possible

malicious code attacks often turn out to be nothing more than false alarms. Suppose, for example, an IDS or IPS detects that a host has received packets on UDP port 27374. This could possibly indicate the host is running the SubSeven Trojan horse, but this could also simply mean a network program has sent packets to this port. It may transmit packets to a different port next time and still another port the time after that. The behavior of many network applications with respect to ephemeral ports is, at best, weird.

The bottom line is this: IDSs and IPSs can help in numerous ways in the war against malicious code. Many of the indications of incidents jibe with indications of the presence of malicious code. In and of themselves, however, IDSs and IPSs are not likely to be sufficient

OUTPUT ROUTINES

Once detection routines in an IDS or IPS have detected some kind of potentially adverse event, the system needs to do something that at a minimum alerts operators that something is wrong or, perhaps, to go farther by initiating evasive action that results in a machine no longer being subjected to attack. Normally, therefore, calls within detection routines activate output routines. Alerting via a pager or mobile phone is generally trivial to accomplish, usually through a single command such as the

```
rasdial <phone_number>
```

command in Windows systems. Additionally, most current IDSs and IPSs write events to a log that can easily be inspected. Evasive action is generally considerably more difficult to accomplish, however. The following types of evasive actions are currently often found in IDSs and IPSs:

▼ Output routines can dynamically kill established connections. If a connection appears to be hostile, there is no reason to allow it to continue. In this case, an RST packet can be sent to terminate a TCP connection. One important caveat exists, however: sending an RST packet may not work. Systems with low-performance hardware or that are overloaded may be unable to send the RST packet in time. Additionally, ICMP traffic presents a special challenge when it comes to terminating ICMP "sessions." The best alternatives for stopping undesirable ICMP traffic are one of the following ICMP options: icmp_host (meaning to transmit an "ICMP host unreachable" message to the other host), icmp_net (resulting in transmitting an "icmp network unreachable" to the client), or icmp_port (causing an "ICMP port unreachable" to be sent to the client). Unfortunately, terminating UDP traffic from a hostile host is usually not feasible. The best alternative is to temporarily block the ports to which this traffic is sent.

■ Systems that appear to have hostile intentions can be blocked (shunned) from further access to a network. Many IDSs and IPSs are capable of sending commands to firewalls and screening routers to block all packets from designated source IP addresses.

▲ A central host that detects attack patterns can recognize a new attack and its manifestations within a successfully attacked system. The central host can change a policy accordingly. It can, for example, forbid overflow input from going into the stack or heap. It can also prevent recursive file system deletion commands from being carried out, given that commands to do either are entered on a system, and then send the changed policy to other systems, keeping them from performing these potentially adverse actions.

A major limitation to taking evasive action (other than the fact that, with UDP traffic this is, for all practical purposes, impossible) is the action may not be appropriate. Only heaven knows the number of packets daily transmitted over the Internet that have spoofed source IP addresses. Blocking traffic from these apparent hostile addresses can block legitimate connections, causing all kinds of trouble. Additionally, evasive action by IPSs can readily result in DoS in systems. IPSs can prevent systems from processing commands and requests that may be necessary in certain operational contexts, but that are identical or similar to those that occur during identified attacks. Critics of intrusion prevention technology are in fact quick to point out that they are ideally suited to the purposes of insiders (and possibly also outsiders) intent on causing massive DoS attacks.

DEFENDING IDS/IPS

Most of the currently available IDSs and IPSs have little or no capability of monitoring their own integrity. This potentially is an extremely serious problem given the importance that intrusion detection and intrusion protection play in so many organizations. An attacker who wants to avoid being noticed can break into the host on which an IDS or IPS runs, and then corrupt the system, so it will not record the actions of the attacker (and also possibly anyone else!). Or, the attacker can send input that causes an IDS or IPS to process it improperly or that results in DoS. Countermeasures against these kinds of threats include the following:

▼ Filtering out any input that could cause the IDS/IPS to become dysfunctional. Stateful firewalling often best serves this purpose.

■ Stopping further processing of input if some particular input could result in partial or full subversion of the IDS or IPS. This is an extreme measure given that intrusion detection and prevention functions are temporarily suspended while this option is in effect.

■ Shunning apparently hostile IP addresses, as discussed previously.

▲ Building an internal watchdog function into the system. This function may determine whether the IDS/IPS is doing what it is supposed to do. If this function determines the system is not performing its functions normally, it sends an alert to the operator.

SUMMARY

This chapter has covered the topic of IDS and IPS internals. These systems almost always process information they receive in a well-defined order, starting with packet capture, filtering, decoding, storage, fragment reassembly, and then stream reassembly. The packets are then passed on to detection routines that work on the basis of signatures, rules, profiles, and possibly even other kinds of logic. IDSs and IPSs can also detect the presence of malicious code, although antivirus software (if available for a particular operating system) is likely to be the more logical first line of defense against this kind of code. Detection routines can call output routines that perform a variety of actions, including alerting operations staff, resetting connections, shunning IP addresses that appear to be the source of attacks, and/or modifying intrusion prevention policy for systems. IDSs and IPSs are a likely target of attacks, so they need to have adequate defenses. Defensive measures include filtering out any input that could cause the IDS/IPS to become dysfunctional, terminating further processing of input if that input could cause partial or full subversion of the IDS or IPS, shunning ostensibly malicious IP addresses, and incorporating an internal watchdog function into the system.

PART III

Implementation and Deployment

CHAPTER 8

Internet Security System's RealSecure

Internet Security Systems (ISS) has been the market leader in intrusion detection software for the better part of a decade now. With the original creation and release of Real Secure, ISS had grabbed the technological advantage for a small, but quickly growing, niche within the security market. According to the 2003 Information Security magazine IDS report, ISS owned nearly 36 percent of the entire IDS market. At press time, Real Secure was on its seventh major release, also known as Real Secure 7.0. All of the following information, screen shots, and tips are for Real Secure 7.0.

The chapter is divided into five main areas. The first area is an overview of the product, Real Secure's history, its capabilities, and its inherent issues. The second areas is installation, and architecture tips and recommendations. The third area covers location and deployment. As with all intrusion detection systems, these are key because information that isn't collected can't be analyzed. In the fourth area, the chapter dives right into a collection of configuration tips and tricks that can and, quite frankly, should be implemented to ensure all crucial attacks are identified and reported. And, in the fifth area, the chapter describes the different reporting options and methods to enable attack signatures or even create custom attack signatures.

INSTALLATION AND ARCHITECTURE

One of RealSecure competitive advantages over other commercially available intrusion detection products is its inherent flexibility and scalability for technically diverse networks. RealSecure comes with the capability to be installed on numerous platforms to include multiple versions of Windows server-based platforms, multiple flavors of Linux, Solaris, and Nokia appliances. Whether it be remote or manual, Windows' installations are the most complicated and detailed installations compared to other platform installations. This, in part, is because of the intricacies within Microsoft platforms, creating Windows services, and the general complexity of the file system and registry in comparison with Linux and Unix systems. At the end of this section, you should be able to install RealSecure quickly and automatically, in a somewhat customized fashion. You also learn how to automate the installation process, so multiple sensors can quickly be deployed throughout your environment.

NOTE   Installation procedures for installing RealSecure on Nokia appliances will not be covered. Please refer to ISS documentation for installation procedures on network sensor installation and gigabit installation with Nokia at http://documents.iss.net/literature/RealSecure/RS_NetSensor_IG_7.0.pdf.

Architecture Considerations

As with every other intrusion detection system, intrusion-detection system location is the most critical aspect when planning an intrusion-detection system deployment. RealSecure is no different, yet the management systems designed for use within RealSecure's deployment could prove to be somewhat different, especially when compared to something like the freeware version of Snort. *Snort* uses a three-tier architecture to

capture, manage, and access the stored data on the RealSecure sensor, as seen in Figure 8-1. The first tier is the RealSecure sensors themselves, the second tier is SiteProtector, and the third and near-virtual tier is the management consoles. These management consoles include security and network administrator stations that are used to access SiteProtector. You should consider management communications when you deploy these systems within the environments.

While it is true most communication occurs over HTTP and HTTPS, TCP ports 3998 and 3999 are also used for communication between SiteProtector and the RealSecure Sensors. Firewalls, routers, and VLANs should be configured to ensure the proper communication channels are opened, but that holes haven't been created to weaken the overall security posture of the network. One popular configuration is to have a security management network to house all security management devices and administrator systems, and then enforce access control lists (ACLs) throughout your network to disallow direct traffic to the security devices, unless it was initiated on the security network. The only downside to this type of configuration is a spoofed attack from a system residing in the route may be able to sniff or collect sensitive data between the sensors and management console.

Because you already learned about network locations IDS sensors, we assume you understand the benefits, advantages, and disadvantages of deploying your sensor inside the network's outmost perimeter versus outside. Refer to earlier chapters if you have any questions about sensor placement.

Network mapping tools are excellent resources that can lessen some of the burden during the initial architecture-design periods for deployment. Logical and geographical network maps can be used to determine how many sensors are needed and combined with network administration statistics on bandwidth consumption. This may also prove helpful with identifying hardware requirements for the individual sensors. One last note before moving forward, geographical locations are an extremely useful guide to assisting with device naming schemas.

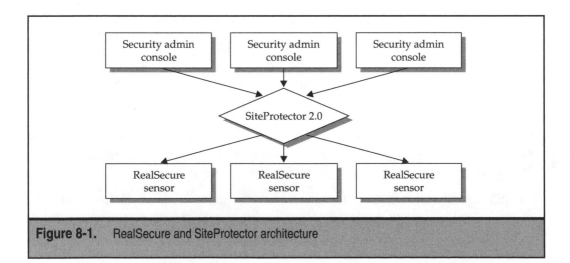

Figure 8-1.   RealSecure and SiteProtector architecture

Windows Installation

If you've ever installed a Windows application, the typical sensor installation is straight-forward. In this section, the focus is on the intricacies of going through a potentially atypical or custom installation on Windows systems. The graphical interface appears like any other Windows installation walkthrough and, with the corresponding directions, navigating through the installation quickly should be easy.

After you ascertain the main setup.exe program, double-click it and the installation will start. The installation GUI should pop up and begin to lead you through the installation program. Click Next to begin, and then accept the software license agreement to proceed to the rest of the installation.

Once the actual setup program begins after the license agreement, click Custom. Even if you don't want a custom installation, this provides you with the knowledge of what is being installed on your sensor and what options you can modify from the onset. Plus, if you use the Autorecord and Autoinstall features, you will only have to do this once. After you select the RealSecure Network Sensor option, you must enter a sensor name. As a reminder, there is no specific requirements for a sensor's name but, as nearly every IT department has learned, naming schemas is key to keep your administrator's sanity intact.

RealSecure enables you to modify the default location for the sensor programs (C:\Program Files\ISS\issSensors\network_sensor_name). In general, there is no reason to modify the installation directory unless, for some reason, you want to put it on another drive or you implemented an atypical directory structure for your Windows' systems. The daemon location can also be modified from the default location at C:\Program Files\ISS\issDaemon.

The next portion of the installation procedure is to configure your sensor's authentication. The recommendation is that you implement a secure management communication tunnel for all traffic to and from your sensors. Select Yes on the dialog box, and then proceed to import the desired key you want to use. As a side note, if you intend to manage this RealSecure system with the SiteProtector suite, this option is required. Importing the keys is made easy through the Allow Auto-Import key feature.

ISS has conveniently built local system hardening into the installation process for sensor and daemon deployment. A good idea is to use their hardening guidelines as a first step in locking down your system, but this should only be the first step! Supplement their hardening techniques with that of your enterprise-hardening policies. Both SANS www.sans.org and the NSA www.nsa.gov have good security best-practice guides, although each may seem a bit over the edge at times.

 Local security-hardening techniques for the network sensors and management can, and should, be frontloaded onto any intrusion-detection deployment plan.

Public key administrators can be added and, in nearly every production installation, only one key administrator needs to be added. Addressing this issue now is best because, if you wait, you will have to reinstall the entire module. The last item to configure during

installation is the cryptographic provider, in addition to archiving the private keys. In general, this should not have to be modified. Archiving the private keys is critical to ensure you have keys in the case of a disaster. Make certain you don't lose the passphrase you use to protect the folder that contains these keys.

The last screen should have appeared now, so click Finish and call it a day. Take the following steps to quickly install Windows:

1. Run the RealSecure setup.exe program.

2. Agree to the Software License Agreement, and then click Custom.

3. Select RealSecure Network Sensor, and then click Next.

4. Enter a sensor name with standard alphanumeric characters, dashes, or underscores, and then click Next.

5. Enter installation folders for the Sensor and Daemon, respectively.

6. Use secure communication and authentication for the sensors and console.

7. Determine if you want to autoimport the keys.

8. Lock down the system using ISS's autolock-down feature.

9. Add the administrator's public key.

10. The cryptographic provider is secure and should be fine.

11. Archive the private keys, as appropriate.

Voila! You're finished

Automating the Windows Installation

The three types of systems being covered and addressed in this RealSecure chapter—Windows, Solaris, and Linux—each come with different mechanisms for automating installations. These automation techniques only recognize their true value if more than one sensor is being deployed in your environment, however. Obviously, you will realize more return on the investment in creating custom install files using the Autorecord and Autoinstall programs included within RealSecure.

 NOTE The National Security Agency created a set of .inf security templates for all major versions of Microsoft Operating Systems in 2001 that are freely available at www.nsa.gov.

Two chief steps are required to automate the process for installing sensors. The first requires that you use the Autorecord feature to save your installation configurations into the ISS response file. Then you use that response file within the Autoinstall process to restore the configurations of the first installed system on to the other to-be-installed sensors. These Microsoft configuration files will look alarmingly similar to .inf files that have a range of uses to include housing configuration settings for other Windows applications or even Local Security Policy settings for a particular system.

> **NOTE** AbortIfNoHotFix, Trace, and Upgrade configurations are not stored within the generated response files during the Autorecord process. All hope is not lost though. You can use any text-based editor to open the file and append the desired corresponding lines to the end of the file. If you are a command line guru, you could also use the command `echo AbortIfNoHotFix = 1 >> myResponseFile.rsp` from Microsoft's command prompt.

Take the following steps to autorecord:

1. Locate your setup.exe file from your Microsoft command prompt (usually CMD or COMMAND from the Start | Run prompt.

2. After you locate the file, enter the following command, and then click OK:

   ```
   C:\ISS\setup.exe -pC:\Windows\temp\myResponseFile.rsp
   ```

3. The Installation wizard for RealSecure pops up and, from here, you want to Record the remainder of the installation for later use on other sensor installations.

4. At the completion of the installation, you will have a Response file that can be used via the Autoinstall feature to decrease the installation time for the remaining sensors.

Take the following steps to autoinstall:

1. Similar to the Autorecord command, you must first locate the setup.exe file again on the sensor.

2. After you locate the file, enter the following command, and then click OK:

   ```
   C:\ISS\setup.exe -gC:\Windows\temp\myResponseFile.rsp
   ```

3. That's it. The remainder of the installation should be completely automated. To verify if the installation was successful, check the autoinstall log.

During the installation and setup of RealSecure, differing applications automatically create log files with unique names. Table 8-1 displays the log filenames for the major applications used within the RealSecure product suite.

Solaris Installation

The Solaris installation comes with a few more installation options and, as a user, you should realize a significant decrease in the time required to install RealSecure compared to a Windows platform. As the most popular Unix operating platform, Solaris installations are quite popular within large commercial and government organizations. For nearly a decade, Solaris was the operating system (OS) of choice within the Department of Defense and it still has a healthy following. Like the installation of most applications on Unix systems, this is rather straightforward and quick. In general, with the release of

Application Name	Log Filename
Network Sensor	RealSecure_Network_Sensor_7.0_X...X_install.xml
Server Sensor	RealSecure_Server_Sensor_7.0_X...X_install.xml
Workgroup Manager	RealSecure_Workgroup_Manager_7.0_X...X_install.xml
RealSecure Utilities	RealSecure_Utilities_7.0_X...X_install.xml

*The ... stands for a continuation of a variable amount of characters that could be included within the filename depending on the major and minor version of the product and service packs installed.

Table 8-1.   RealSecure Log Files

RealSecure 7.0, five options are available for configuration during the installation process. The following are the five configuration options.

▼   RealSecure Daemon to Automatically Import Communication Keys

■   Daemon Installation Path

■   Daemon Cryptographic Provider

■   RealSecure Sensor Key Management

▲   Sensor Location Directory

These five options provide the basic capabilities during installation, such as where the files should reside and key management issues. Notice the similarity to the options available that are during the Windows installation.

NOTE   It's pertinent for you to assess and verify that you have a properly working system (local and network responses achieved successfully) before you install RealSecure.

When you are ready to install RealSecure, you must untar, or uncompress, the tar file that contains the two bundled packages and installation shell script. The following command will untar the file, while displaying the contents of the file to the screen in a list format. The Xs represent version-specific information included within the file schema that ISS ships.

```
Command: tar -xvf rsns7.0.XXXX.XXX-sparc-solaris.multi.tar
```

After you uncompress the file, you will be left with three files on your local file system. The two large files are the actual installation packages to be used to install the sensor and the daemon on the IDS box, while the third file is a quick bash shell script created to help automate sensor installations by combining the sensor and daemon installation.

This is different from automating Solaris installations, which is covered in the section "Automating the Solaris Installation."

▼ **pkgISSXnsinstall.sh** Automatically install the daemon and the sensor

■ **pkgISSXdmn** Only install the daemon

▲ **pkgISSXrsns** Only install the sensor

The pkgISSXnsinstall.sh script automatically installs both the sensor and daemon packages. As root, run the script from its local directory by typing in **.\pkgISSXnsinstall .sh** at the shell prompt, and then press ENTER. Next, type in the same command but, this time, add the word "all" to the end of the command line, so it reads **.\pkgISSXnsinstall .sh all**, and then press ENTER again. You will then be prompted with a message asking if you want to accept the RealSecure license agreement and to install the packages with the default options. We recommend installing the packages with the default options initially because, then, you have the capability to go back and add other key management systems later if you choose. Options outside the default options are rarely implemented within production environments. Type **Y** for yes, and then press ENTER to continue.

The installation script will continue to install the packages by running multiple scripts that complete single tasks. If the system has never before had RealSecure installed on it, you will be prompted to see if it is okay to create the installation directory of opt/ISS. Accept by entering **Y** for yes. We recommend installing all the packages shipped with RealSecure's daemon. Once the daemon finishes installing, another license screen appears, asking if you agree to the Sensor license agreement. After you enter **Y**, the package will continue to install several binaries and text files to your file system. Depending on the speed of your system, this may take a few minutes but, if you purchased a "beefy" system, that should knock this out quickly.

Finally, you will now have the capability to create additional key management administrators for your system. If you choose to create additional administrators, type **Y** and create the names for these administrators. Any name will suffice. Just make sure you pick one that makes logical sense for your environment. After this, or if you typed **N** for additional key administrators, the installation will run through its clean-up cycle. The installation program will remove all the temporary files and directories created throughout the installation program before reminding you, in one final note, that you should run the keyadmin_setup.sh script to configure your administrative key.

The entire installation process for the Solaris installation for a single sensor with the daemon should take under ten minutes, if you have a server with a good amount of memory and processing capability. Take the following steps to install Solaris:

1. Prepare for installation with appropriate files.

2. Run pkgISSXnsinstall.sh script (you will install both the sensor and the daemon).

3. Accept the license agreement and default parameters.

4. Allow directory creation and install all files.

5. Accept the license agreement.

6. Rename the sensor to reflect the enterprise-naming convention.

7. Add additional key administrators.

Automating the Solaris Installation

Even with the evolution and advanced in relational-database computing, text-based configuration files seem to maintain their popularity in commercial application installations. The RealSecure installation for Solaris enables you to create what ISS refers to as a text response file to save all your configuration information by using the `pkgask` command. This response file will be used and distributed to the other sensors on which you want to install the RealSecure sensor and daemon.

 If this is your first time installing the sensor or daemon on this particular platform, you must first untar the two packages, using the command stated at the beginning of this section.

Before we begin creating the response files for the sensor and daemon, let's first create the Admin file necessary to house the data. The following three lines are the only required lines in the admin file gabriel_admin_file for the quick installation.

gabriel_admin_file
```
        action=nocheck
        conflict=nocheck
        instance=overwrite
```

After the admin file is ready, installing the daemon only takes two commands to complete the execution. The first command generates the response file with a filename that corresponds to whatever is supplied in the myResponseFile variable location. The second command must use the same filename specified in the first command, plus the name of the admin file created previously.

```
Daemon Step 1: pkgask -r myResponseFile -d ./pkgISSXdmn
Daemon Step 2: pkgadd -n -r myResponseFile -a gabriel_admin_file -d
./pkgISSXdmn all
```

As with every RealSecure network sensor, it is highly recommended that you always install the daemon before you install the sensor. The sensor installation does not require you to create a new admin file, but it does require the serial execution of three commands using the response and admin files created during the daemon setup. By default, the first command installs the temporary sensor data in the /tmp/ directory, and then the second command creates the response file. The command that follows "Note:" on line 2 removes the temporary file in case you need to remove the files abruptly during installation. The last command installs the sensor package, using the original admin file and the newly updated response file.

```
Sensor Command 1: pkgadd -n -a gabriel_admin_file -d ./pkgISSXrsns
Note:   pkgrm ISSXrsns
Sensor Command 2: pkgask -r myResponseFile -d ./tmp/pkgISSXns
Sensor Command 3: pkgadd -n -r myResponseFile -a gabriel_admin_file -d
/tmp/pkgISSXns all
```

 TIP   Keep the names of the response and admin files the same throughout the sensor and daemon installations. This should decrease the time required to install a single sensor to under a few minutes, including unpacking and installation time.

Linux Installation

Yes, we saved the easiest for last. For all intents and purposes, the Linux installation is the most straightforward RealSecure installation when dealing with single sensor installations that you can find. Let's hope all your sensors are lucky enough to be Linux.

As with any system, first prepare your Linux system for the RealSecure installation by backing up any business-critical data, verifying the proper drivers and hardware specifications are as recommended, ensuring kernel and supporting applications are running the most current versions, and testing basic connectivity and activation before you attempt to install. These should be in addition to any custom system checks that seem appropriate based on your custom configuration. After the system is ready for installation, the first step is to install the Common Library.

NOTE   All of the following package installations must be done with root privileges.

The RedHat Package Manager (RPM), also known as the RPM Package Manager (RPM), was designed to assist with the quick installations of software on Linux systems. It only takes one command to install the ISS Common Library RPM file for RealSecure 7.0. This command is as follows:

rpm—Uvh ISS-RealSecure-common-lib-7.0-XXXX.XXX.i386.rpm

After ISS's Common Library is installed, you need to install the ISS daemon using a similar command, as shown here:

rpm—Uvh ISS-RealSecure-ns-daemon-7.0-XXXX.XXX.i386.rpm

The last package that must be installed is the ISS sensor package. This is the main package and it may take several minutes to install. After the program completes its installation, it informs you that you must now run the ./setup.sh script for additional configuration and policy creation.

rpm—Uvh ISS-RealSecure-ns-sensorx-7.0-XXXX.XXX.i386.rpm

After you take these steps, you will have a fully installed RealSecure sensor that is all but useless. Only after properly configuring this sensor is it of any use or benefit

within your environment. The following is a quick recap of the Linux installation procedures:

1. Prepare to install.
2. Install the Common Library.
3. Install the ISS Daemon (issDaemon).
4. Install the ISS Sensor (issSensor).
5. Continue to configure your sensor.

Automating the Linux Installation

The Linux installation is cut-and-dry regarding the steps required to automate the typical installation process. Because the Linux installation is only three commands that have to get executed on the remote system, these commands can be easily put into a shell script to run and install serially. Another route you could take is simply to pipe each command on to the end of the first, and then run them all from a Linux shell.

```
#!/bin/sh
rpm -Uvh ISS-RealSecure-common-lib-7.0-XXXX.XXX.i386.rpm;
rpm -Uvh ISS-RealSecure-ns-daemon -7.0-XXXX.XXX.i386.rpm;
rpm -Uvh ISS-RealSecure-ns-sensorx-7.0-XXXX.XXX.i386.rpm;
```

CONFIGURING REALSECURE

Congratulations, you are now well on your way on to setting up your RealSecure intrusion-detection infrastructure deployment. Now that you have installed at least one RealSecure network sensor, you are ready to move on to configuring that monster.

Configuration of your sensor will take a significant investment of your time to ensure it is configured in the most efficient and accurate method possible. Anything—from configuring the proper alerts, to minimizing false positives on attack signatures, to increasing the efficiency of your logging policy, to the use of certain protocols, to the decision on how much data should be collected for any given event—will prove important as you move forward. The "little things" can certainly make your IDS deployment a giant hole that constantly requires resources in terms of hours of maintenance costs to monitor and investigate insignificant alerts. Or, those little things can make your IDS deployment one of the most important tools, which quickly alert you and take action on malicious traffic heading inbound for your environment, of your security organization.

Increasing Efficiency

One of the easiest methods for increasing the performance of you sensor is to purchase more than you need. Let us explain. If your network has a 100MB backbone that can spike at rates near 80 to 90 percent saturation then you may want to get a gigabit sensor. With the release of RealSecure 7.0 came the first true commercial gigabit-capable network IDS

sensor. Also, if you believe a beefy single CPU with 1Gb of memory will suffice, spend a little extra money to buy the dual CPU 4Gb of memory system. This type of overkill may seem unrealistic initially, but during network traffic spikes is when the most malicious traffic and attacks seem to go unnoticed by the IDS systems because of dropped packets or packet loss.

Another route to increase the potential workload for your IDS sensors is to install multiple sensors in a cluster via a load balancer. RealSecure 7.0 comes with the capability to create multiple similar sensor deployments with the automatic installation procedures. Coupled with the option-implementing load balancers, any environment should have the option of being safe and secure. By purchasing "extra" hardware via a single strong system or multiple lesser systems in a cluster, you will have the capability to avoid dropped packets.

Outside of hardware considerations, features such as the Protocol Anomaly Detection (PAM), traffic filters, event filters, and upfront network configurations can be set to ensure that only the appropriate traffic is capture and analyzed. This allows the sensor to spend its CPU processing power on the packets that matter.

Enabling PAM

RealSecure PAM can be used to ensure that network services residing or using atypical ports for communication do not get missed by the analysis engine. For instance, if a rogue HTTP server was using port 62, instead of port 80, it is quite possible some of your signatures relying on HTTP analysis may miss attacks on this server. Another example is that internal FTP servers use port 22 instead of 21, in addition to changing their banners to mimic Secure Shell (SSH) servers. This type of technique currently throws off nearly 98 percent of all network port and vulnerability scanners, and it has a high potential to misconstrue your IDS signatures if it is not accounted for properly.

Table 8-2 lists the default values configured within PAM. Each module has a name, a value type, a value, a priority, and an administrative description. You will soon learn the available options for creating new PAM rules to add to this somewhat small default coverage.

Name	Value	Description
pam.http.heuristic	true	Identifies HTTP traffic via proprietary anomaly-detection techniques looking for HTTP requests and responses on atypical ports. The value can only be true or false.

Table 8-2.   Default PAM Configurations

Name	Value	Description
pam.login.any	Ex: foster:foster, testuser:password	An extremely useful module, login.any enables you to enter general authentication credentials. The module then detects if these credentials are used for any type of remote service logon.
pam.login.maxpass	100	Aids with password attacks leveraging long password strings. The default numerical length is 100, which can be modified via the creation of another module.
pam.login.vnc.count	4	A specific module that monitors the number of VNC remote authentication failures for any given session. If the number of failures is greater than the numerical value entered, an alert is generated.
pam.tcpport.ftp	21	This module defines the one port used as a trigger to analyze FTP traffic. The default value is 21.
pam.tcpport.http	80	The default configuration, or port number, for the HTTP service and web server communication.
pam.tcpport.pop3	110	The default configuration, or port number, for the POP3 server.
pam.tcpport.smtp	25	The default configuration, or port number, for the SMTP server.

Table 8-2. Default PAM Configurations *(continued)*

RealSecure's PAM has one extremely significant downside as far as the product feature is concerned: only one port or value can be assigned to each name. For instance, if you want to analyze FTP traffic or data on ports 21, 22, 23, and 92, then you must create four different rules on your sensor, instead of allowing multiple values specified within a single rule. That alone could make this feature more tedious and allow it to become a maintenance nightmare, instead of providing true administrative value.

Creating new PAM rules should be done with the knowledge that each additional rule can affectively decrease overall system performance. These rules take a good deal of CPU resources during packet analysis and should only be implemented if you concretely know that your at-risk internal services reside on atypical or custom ports.

Take the following steps to configure custom PAM modules:

1. Click the Tuning tab within the policy for the sensor that you want to modify.

2. From this window, you now have two options. You can either Add a new module or Edit an existing module. Remember, you can only edit custom modules you created.

3. After entering the desired data into the rules, press ENTER twice, and then go on to saving and applying the new or modified rules.

Table 8-3 lists some additional PAM modules that can be created to enhance the overall effectiveness for identifying HTTP services running on the common atypical ports. These ports often house custom vendor-specific management interfaces for a range of network devices. Such devices include wireless access points, switches, mail relays, DNS servers, and custom application servers to name a few. Plus, one rule is at the bottom to identify Telnet traffic destined for the common SSH port of 22.

NMAP Can Help!

The latest version of NMAP (www.insecure.org/nmap) comes with what is quickly becoming known as *remote service identification,* which can be leveraged to find services residing on atypical ports on target systems. While this feature may seem somewhat valuable for attackers or hackers, it can also prove extremely valuable for network and security administrators. Capturing snapshots of your network in a regular cycle can be

Name	Value	Description
pam.tcpport.http	7001	Additional port for HTTP modules
pam.tcpport.http	7070	Additional port for HTTP modules
pam.tcpport.http	8001	Additional port for HTTP modules
pam.tcpport.http	8080	Additional port for HTTP modules
pam.tcpport.http	9000	Additional port for HTTP modules
pam.tcpport.http	9001	Additional port for HTTP modules
pam.tcpport.Telnet	22	Additional port for Telnet modules

Table 8-3. Additional Custom Examples HTTP Modules

used to ensure your sensor is properly configured to identify what RealSecure defines as protocol anomalies.

If the command is

```
C:\nmap\nmap.exe -sV -P0 www.mcgraw-hill.org
```

Then the output would be

```
Starting nmap 3.45 ( http://www.insecure.org/nmap ) at 2003-10-28 05:28 Pacific Standard Time
Interesting ports on 198.45.18.151:
(The 1655 ports scanned but not shown below are in state: filtered)
PORT     STATE   SERVICE VERSION
80/tcp   open    http    Netscape Enterprise httpd 6.0
Nmap run completed -- 1 IP address (1 host up) scanned in 260.695 seconds
```

The previous NMAP usage ran a port scan against www.mcgraw-hill.org with two flags specified via the command line, as seen prefacing the domain name. The -P0 flag tells NMAP not to rely on the ping responses when port-scanning the system. This ensures every default gets scanned, even if perimeter devices are blocking ICMP or the standard ports used for NMAP's TCP ping sequence. The second flag—sV—stands for version scan. In addition to looking for common open ports, sV also conducts tests on the service for the remote system to identify the underlying protocols, in addition to grabbing any available application banners.

NMAP with service detection is relatively new, and it is in the process of being enhanced via the signature database and bugs within compilation. We recommend visiting Insecure.org to retrieve the latest information on NMAP's version scanning feature.

Customizing the Sensor for Your Environment

Customizing the sensor for your environment is absolutely critical because every large organization is bound to be different. A combination of custom applications, network topology, and the onslaught of available commercial applications can also make an environment unrecognizable from other networks. Two RealSecure features stand out as being excellent resources for customizing general traffic that is transmitted across the wire. The first feature focuses on customizing the network protocols used in your environment. The second feature focuses more on atypical services or applications that may be implemented within your environment.

Configuring custom ports to be associated with protocols is extremely simple, given the graphical nature of RealSecure. The following Quick Guide walks you through the necessary appropriate steps to add or remove target port associations with a corresponding protocol:

To modify protocol ports take the following steps:

1. Open the Network Events tab from within the policy you want to modify for your environment. Unfortunately, you can only modify or edit one policy at a time.

2. After you select the group of protocols you want to edit, a list will appear and enable you to select the particular protocol you want.

3. Select Edit.

4. Enter the additional ports you want associated to that protocol. You also have the capability to remove any ports you do not want specifically associated with that protocol. This is not a recommended practice, however. Just because your network may not use certain ports for communication, for example, if you do not use 7070 for HTTP communication, this does not mean you should disassociate that port from the HTTP protocol. Ports can be added to the configurations in one of two methods. The first method enables you to add the ports one at a time separated by single spaces. The second method lets you specify a port range with a single dash or a hyphen.

> Example of #1: 80 443 7001 7070 8001 8080
> Example of #2: 32200-33400

5. Click OK twice to return to the policy editor.

6. Apply these new settings for your protocols to ensure the new settings take place.

7. Repeat steps 1 through 6 for any other protocol policies that need modification.

The second major option you have when configuring your sensor to become more appropriately tied to your environment is within the network services feature. As you just learned, you have the capability to modify the ports associated with a protocol. Yet, to take that feature one step further, RealSecure also provides you with the capability to add or edit a network service: for all intents and purposes, this is a protocol. In terms of RealSecure 7.0, a network service associates a defined service name with a combination of a protocol and at least one port. The procedure instructs you to add a new network service to your sensor policy. Note, this will only take effect on the policy you are modifying.

To create a new network service follow these steps:

1. Select the appropriate event or filter for the network service you want to edit from within the Sensor Policies window.

2. Click the proper Connection Events or Packet Filters tab, select the service or ICMP type, and then click Add.

3. If you selected a TCP or UDP service, you must now distinguish between the two of them.

4. Select a suitable name for this custom service. For example, fosters_worm.

5. Now, enter the port or ports this service will use in the same way you create custom ports (separated by single spaces or with a hyphen).

6. Click OK and Save until you are presented with the next screen, which lets you Apply the policy to your sensor.

7. Applying the policy to your system will take effect in real time, yet there will not be any signatures that use this service.

After you create custom network services, you may require the capability to modify them later. RealSecure does enable you to change the settings of any custom service, yet it does not let you modify any default services found within the product to include popular services, such as Telnet, FTP, or HTTP.

The following abbreviated steps are required to modify a custom network service:

1. Select the appropriate event or filter for the network service you want to edit from within the Sensor Policies window.

2. After clicking Customize, click the Connection Events or Packet Filters tab.

3. You now have the capability to modify the source address for the service or the protocol (ICMP, IP, TCP, or UDP).

4. Save the configurations, and then Exit.

Implementing Filters

RealSecure filters were created to minimize the amount of unnecessary packets being analyzed by the analysis engine, as well as to make the alerting engine more effective and accurate. Numerous scenarios exist where the potential for false positives or false negatives can be realized. These bugs or issues within a RealSecure sensor can completely make or break the maintenance process of your IDS deployment.

Two core types of filters are implemented within RealSecure: specifically packet filters and event filters. If you have been in the IT community a while or if you are familiar with network technologies, packet filters should sound familiar. RealSecure *packet filters*, different from Berkeley Packet Filters (BPF) implemented within numerous programs to include the popular TCPDUMP (www.tcpdump.org), enable administrators to assign a special action to occur on packets analyzed and flagged with corresponding source and destination addresses. *Event filters* are completely different from their seemingly similar packet-filter counterparts because they process events the sensor has triggered after the packet-analysis phase. In case an event filter is triggered, it will disregard the corresponding event that would normally have taken action.

Creating and Implementing Packet Filters

RealSecure packet filters can leverage and filter packets based on certain values and flags within the IP, TCP, UDP, and ICMP protocols. The TCP/IP suite of options available to use outside the ICMP extensions are standard-packet filter options. Note, understand these filters only disregard packets that match the configurations specified and there is no place to customize or specify a different output or action once a filter is created. Those type of desired actions can be configured within the product using IDS signatures. Table 8-4 details the types of filters with their corresponding protocols that can be implemented within RealSecure.

TCP	UDP	IP	ICMP
Source, destination, network, or range of IP addresses	Source, destination, network, or range of IP addresses	Source, destination, network, or range of IP addresses	Source, destination, network, or range of IP addresses
Source, destination service, or port	Source, destination service or port		Destination ICMP code
			Source ICMP type

Table 8-4. Options for Creating a Packet Filter

The RealSecure packet filters get executed before the signature engine is launched to analyze the current queue of packets. This is critical because any packets generated from trusted sources can automatically be taken out of the equation and lessen the burden on the CPU during analysis. Other areas commonly focused on for creating packet filters include outbound traffic generated from SMTP, DNS, and even FTP servers.

After you determine the parameters you want to use in creating one more multiple packet filters, the next step is to learn to create and implement or apply them. From within your RealSecure console, select the Properties from the Sensor menu in the Managed Assets window. You should now be presented with a tab titled Packet Filters. Click Add, type in the name for the new packet filter, and then click OK to move onto the next step.

Now, you are ready to configure the packet-filter payload-match criteria. You have no reason to worry about adding too many packet filters because the CPU resources used to parse and check these filters are far less than those required to parse and analyze against thousands of attack signatures. As you know, the only real concern is disregarding malicious packets. To start with the match criteria, first select the protocol you want to use for the filter: you can only select one protocol per filter. Depending on the protocol, you can now enter the corresponding types, codes, or addresses for the filter. Don't forget, the key here is to test these rules and deployments with a plethora of network tests and simulated attacks from ranging source and destination addresses.

After the match criteria is entered, save the configuration from the File menu and close the current window.

The following guide can be used as a high-level reference to assist in the process of creating new packet filters:

1. Select the desired policy.

2. Click Customize, and then Add from within the Packet Filter tab.

3. Decide on, and then enter the filter name.

4. Enter packet filter option-specific data (such as, source IP address – 10.0.3.203).

5. Save and apply the new filter configurations.

CAUTION   RealSecure packet filters *only* disregard packets and can not be made to invoke alerts!

Table 8-5 displays a variety of custom packet filters that are commonly implemented in enterprise-class intrusion detection systems. These configurations can be used as additional references when it comes time to customize and localize your sensor to run more

Name	Protocol	Type & Value	Description
Dns	TCP	Source IP: 10.0.*.* and Destination IP: 10.0.1.4 and Destination Port: 51	Disregard internal traffic going toward our DNS server.
dmz_email	TCP	Source IP: 10.0.*.* and Destination IP: 10.0.1.4 andDestination Port: 25	Disregard internal traffic going toward our DMZ e-mail server.
outbound_ping	ICMP	Source IP: 10.*.*.* and ICMP Type: 8	Disregard outbound ICMP echo requests.
ip_trusted_net	IP	Destined: *.*.*.*	Disregard all IP traffic to include both TCP and UDP from the trusted administrator network.

Table 8-5.   Example Packet Filters

Name	Protocol	Type & Value	Description
icmp_trusted_net	ICMP	Destined: *.*.*.*	Disregard ICMP traffic from the trusted administrator network.
10-3-0-203	IP	Source: 10.3.0.203 or Destination: 10.3.0.203	Disregard all IP traffic to and from a particular IP address.
a_snmp_net	UDP	Destination Port: 161	Disregard all UDP traffic traveling across the common SNMP port: 161.
intranet_http	TCP	Source IP: 10.*.*.* Destination: 10.4.5.70 Destination Port: 80 or 443	Disregard all TCP traffic destined toward our internal intranet web server for both HTTP and HTTPs.

IP address ranges are depicted using asterisks for space and aesthetic purposes. You should assume the address 10.0.1. is the same as 10.0.1.1–10.0.1.255.

Table 8-5.   Example Packet Filters *(continued)*

accurately within your environment. Examples are provided for each of the four protocol options that you have as an administrator within RealSecure.

The ip_trusted_net filter uses the IP protocol because its underlying goal is to disregard both TCP and UDP protocols. Remember, the TCP/IP suite of protocols communicates over multiple layers of the OSI model. Specifically, TCP and UDP use the underlying IP protocol to encapsulate their payloads.

CREATING AND IMPLEMENTING EVENT FILTERS

Event filters help administrators sort through the tons of "useless" alerts that can quickly become a nuisance. These filters should be created for systems you know consistently produce false positives. For instance, you may notice a huge increase in attack-alert false positives because of the setup of your test network and the recent installation of a particular peek-a-booty server. This issue could be remediated in multiple ways to include a packet filter or an event filter.

Take the following steps to create an event filter on your RealSecure sensor:

1. After opening the policy you want to add an Event Filter to, click the Event Filter tab, and then click Add.

2. Enter a filter name, and then open that filter from within the Filters list.

3. From within the Filter properties, modify the corresponding protocol, intruder, and victim information as appropriate.

4. Save and Apply these filters.

Removing and customizing event filters is almost identical to the process of creating event filters. Instead of clicking Add, click Customize or Edit, and then modify the corresponding properties for that event filter. The properties could be anything from an alert for a given IP address or network range of IP addresses.

Handling Network Devices

Network devices to include DNS, FTP, Database, and SMTP servers are ever-increasingly becoming more tedious to maintain because of the increase in application functionality and overall number of differentiating implementations by vendors. Most commonly, these types scenarios are handled in one of four ways.

▼ *Create a packet filter.* Packet filters are probably your best bet, but realize these are potentially the riskiest because all packets that satisfy your match criteria will be ignored and will not be passed to the attack-signature analysis phase.

■ *Create an event filter.* An event filter parses all the traffic as normal, but it suppresses any event action that would normally be triggered by a particular network packet or packet sequence.

■ *Create a special rule.* Special rules, aka custom signatures or rules, are easily created within RealSecure to enable you to trigger rules on particular responses, and then report on them in a selection of your choice.

▲ *Modify the action for a particular rule.* The final option is to modify the action or reporting for a particular rule. Such a response could be used to send the output to a different logging mechanism.

Getting Acquainted with Your Network

One last bit of advice for when you put the finishing touches on your sensor configuration. Run NMAP over your entire address space (during off-peak hours), so you can find the specifics of your network and so certain realized vulnerability alerts don't come as a

shock. The best option for running this scan is to scan for common ports using a stealth TCP SYN scan with the timing set to Aggressive and an output selection of your choice.
Typically NMAP Usage:

```
nmap -sS -T Aggressive 10.*.*.* > myOutput.txt
```

Using SiteProtector for Central Management

ISS's RealSecure uses the SiteProtector management console to centralize a management for large deployments containing multiple sensors or deployments that want to use the advanced correlation features included within the vulnerability assessment line of products. Their vulnerability assessment products include the popular Internet Scanner, and Wireless, System, and Database Scanners. The major benefits of SiteProtector include the capability to manage all your sensors from one console to include automatic product installs and updates, view real-time reporting trends for an entire enterprise network, correlate vulnerability data with intrusion attempts, integrate vulnerability identification with intrusion prevention, and manage any of ISS's new Proventia security appliances.

Complementing Your Deployment with Proventia

The Proventia appliance series created by ISS includes everything from vulnerability assessment systems to intrusion detection boxes to the new all-inclusive network perimeter appliance that houses antispam technology, firewall capabilities, vulnerability assessment, intrusion detection and prevention, and antivirus.

So what's the difference between the Proventia's RealSecure appliance and a software installation conducted by my engineering team? The ISS marketing department will tell you a significant difference exists in configuration and speed to deployment and potentially performance. The real-world differences that would be noticed by an organization are few, but direct. Deployment costs and time-to-implementation are significantly reduced because the appliances come preloaded and configured on Linux platforms with hardened kernels, a local firewall, and multiple other local security-hardening techniques. Point blank, even with minimal IDS experience, these systems can be up and running in under 15 minutes. And, if you're unlucky, they can be connected to the SiteProtector appliance and functional in an hour or two! That said, if you or your team have the hardware and experience to install RealSecure on a Linux systems, then it is quite possible you can replicate nearly everything included on this appliance for less cost, but not much less. The real questions are as follows:

How much time do you have to spend on deployment?

Do you want to buy ISS's hardware or use what you already have?

REPORTING

ISS has always been a market leader in technology, reporting to include all their legacy product lines: Real Secure, Internet Scanner, and System Scanner. In general, each of the ISS flagship products come with three levels of reporting. The highest level is geared for executives who are not intimately familiar with the daily operations or technology. The second option and, often the most useful level, is designed to be informative for technical managers. Security managers, CISOs, administrators, and engineers can use these reports for quick analysis purposes. These reports are also commonly used for trending purposes. The third, and last, general reporting level is the technical reports, which are for those people who are intimately familiar with intrusion detection technology.

 Reporting is significantly different from attack alerting. Understanding the differences is critical because even the lowest level of reports is geared toward a higher level of understanding than those of the detailed packet-specific alerts.

Executive Reporting

Several reports are generated with high-level graphs and diagrams that can be easily integrated into executive reports or presentations. In general, these reports are excellent me diums for communicating security trends from your IDS sensors and can be used to help strategize for future architectural deployments. Figure 8-2 details attack trends for a seven-quarter analysis period with the count equaling the number of realized "high-rated" attacks directed toward the three different organizations within a large

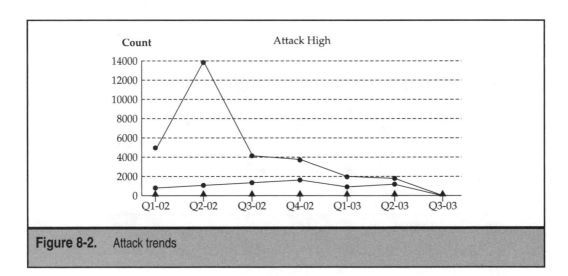

Figure 8-2.   Attack trends

organization. The red line is the Tech_grp and, as you can see, they have consistently had the highest volume of attacks although, in general, perimeter security appears to be slowly improving.

Technical Management

RealSecure's centralized management system—SiteProtector—provides the bulk of the analytical, trending, and correlation CPU-processing capabilities and responsibilities. Within the Enterprise Dashboard, numerous graphs and charts can present daily attack trends for any given environment. In particular, the *dashboard* is an excellent medium for technical managers, such as security managers, intrusion detection management, or even a broader perimeter security group. Two of the most valuable metrics for any security organization are to measure how well vulnerabilities are managed and the number of successful attacks. The image in Figure 8-3 graphically shows the number of the attacks directed at vulnerable systems within a one-week time period. This is an extremely useful metric for weekly status reports.

Engineering Reports

Now for the nitty-gritty of the reporting families. The more technical reports can assist in a multitude of initiatives. They can track employees who are testing the new hacking tool they found on the Internet, monitor abuses by an individual that can be used as a reference for an incident response case, become reference guides when adding to the packet filters on the outermost perimeter devices, or any other of a large range uses. Figure 8-4

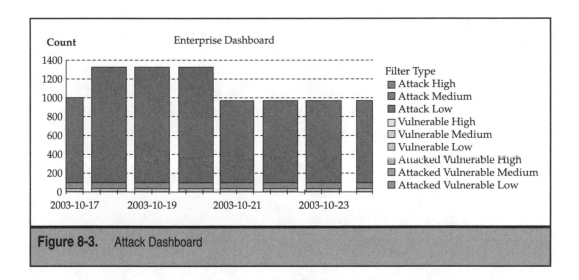

Figure 8-3. Attack Dashboard

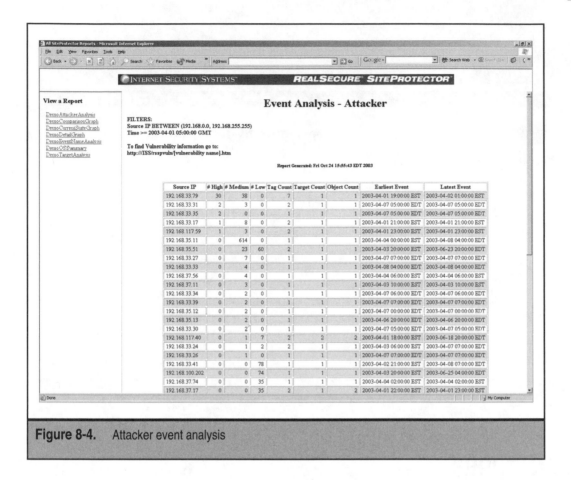

Figure 8-4. Attacker event analysis

lists a group of attackers and the corresponding attacks that were identified and logged from a particular source system. The source is sorted and displayed by its IP address.

The last report to cover here is somewhat unique in that RealSecure provides you with the quick capability to list the number of unique OSs that were attacked. This could prove important in a real-world environment if you know a new vulnerability was just discovered in one of your Unix systems but, because of time constraints and prioritization issues, the systems have not been compromised. A sudden spike in attacks by OS could be caused by anything from automated malicious code, such as worms or viruses, to exploit code being released for a major vulnerability that has been in the mainstream. Figure 8-5 is an example of the OS report that SiteProtector can provide to you in a near real-time situation.

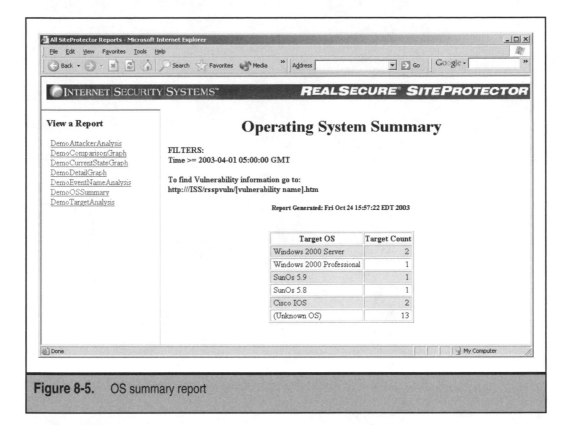

Figure 8-5. OS summary report

SIGNATURES

As you probably knew before you opened this book, the intrusion detection signatures are the core modules for all IDS products. Reporting, trending, varying alert mechanisms, interfaces, and even correlation to vulnerability scanners should be considered nice-to-have add-on features but, if the signatures implemented within the product are of poor quality, nothing else matters. Poor-quality attack signatures will yield inaccurate attack results, false positives on attacks, slow responses, and, worst of all, missed attacks. This should be unacceptable to a security engineer, manager, or C-level executive when discussing intrusion detection networks.

Throughout this section, we cover the details of creating custom attack signatures and implementing these signatures within RealSecure 7.0. The emphasis is on the implementation of the custom signatures, yet a few tips and tricks from the pros might teach you something about creating these from scratch. As any signature engineer will tell you, the research leading up to the signature is the hard part. Creation and implementation is easy after you have done it more than a few times.

NOTE RealSecure has almost double the attack signatures of ISS's product acquisition NetworkICE. These increases in product signatures have given more customers the capability to trust the comprehensive nature of RealSecure over every other product, including the freeware power player, Snort.

In most cases, the creation of an accurate attack signature requires you have access to the exploit, a vulnerable system, and an invulnerable system. Yet, as with most technological theories, there is the proper way, an easier way, and a "potentially risky, but it may get the job done" way. In the realm of IDS signatures, the last and most risky choice is by far the easiest. Depending on the application being attacked, it is potentially possible to profile the remote system, and then determine what the anticipated response may be for a vulnerable system to determine if an attack was successful.

The easiest type of attack to fingerprint or create a signature for is known as static attacks. These *static attacks* come in the form of novice attackers using prewritten public exploits, worms, viruses, and scanners. These attacks are extremely simple to replicate because the source or binary, depending on the tool, is usually available for download. The following is our custom signature creation methodology:

1. Ascertain the malicious code.

2. Set up the vulnerable and invulnerable systems.

3. Adequately prepare and start a network sniffer.

4. Launch the attack.

5. Analyze the malicious traffic.

6. Analyze the response differences between the vulnerable and invulnerable systems.

7. Find the unique tokens in the attack traffic to create the initial attack signature.

8. Determine if the unique tokens are available within the compromised system's response to create a compromised alert signature.

9. Create and document the signatures.

10. Implement the signatures into production systems.

Implementing Custom Rules

ISS's X-Force research group creates intrusion detection signatures for all critical vulnerabilities, although some of these signatures could take more time to create, test, and deploy than your organization is willing to wait. Other reasons you may want to create custom attack signatures can range from custom applications with known vulnerabilities, malicious activity from an internal user that needs to be monitored, or even vulnerabilities that could be important to your organization, yet deemed unimportant for most other organizations. RealSecure enables users to create custom attack signatures in two methods. The first method is through their Graphical Attack Signature wizard and the second method enables you to import Snort rules as the signature.

Throughout this section, the focus is on the first option, creating signatures using RealSecure's graphical engine. We also briefly touch on implementing Snort rules within RealSecure. For a more comprehensive solution on creating Snort-formatted rules, please refer to Chapter 10.

Creating RealSecure Signatures

As advanced as the capability may seem, the capability to create and implement custom attack signatures has always been a mainstream feature within the IDS product industry. Why? The answer is simple. Snort has been an extremely tough competitor within the intrusion detection community even though it is a freeware product, has fair technical documentation, and, in general, has always lacked enterprise scalability, yet it provided users with the capability to create attack signatures easily and implement other publicly available signatures from Day 1. Any commercial vendor that truly desired to enter the market did not have an option to do this.

Whether you are managing one or 50 network sensors, it is still possible to have multiple IDS policies on an individual system. You must first open the policy you want to create the new signature for, and then open the Policy Editor window. After opening that window, you will presented with multiple tabs to include the one that should be selected: the User-Defined Events tab. When you navigate to this point, click the Add button that lets you create a blank custom signature. Enter the desired name for this new signature, and then click the OK button to indicate you finished entering the name. You should now be able to notice the new signature has been added to the signatures list on the current page displayed.

Open the new signature you created, so you can now edit the signature specifics in the right pane of the window, known by ISS as the signature properties. After setting the priority of the signature (completely dependant on how important this is in your environment), you must choose which part of the packet should be analyzed and used for matching purposes.

As mentioned earlier, the hardest part of creating any new attack signature is determining what the unique tokens or identifiers within a malicious packet should be. This can be entered into the RealSecure signature in one of two forms: a ASCII text search string or a regular expression. The last step is to decide on is the response the sensor should take after it detects this attack or anomaly. For instance, you need to set the property to e-mail you, log the packet, generate an alert, and so forth. Enter the desired response, and then save the signature and apply these settings to the sensor or sensors you want to affect.

Take the following steps to create a signature:

1. Within the Policy Editor window of the desired policy, select the User-Defined Events tab.

2. Click Add, and then type and enter the desired signature name.

3. Navigate to User Defined Signatures and open signature.

4. Set Priority.

5. Configure packet-field specifics.

6. Create a payload token.

7. Enter the signature response event.

8. Save and apply the updated policy.

After the signature or signatures are created, it is critical to test them. Your IDS infrastructure is only as good as these are, so put the time! The following are our top three tips or pointers for testing attack signatures on sensors:

▼   Replay the attacks against vulnerable and invulnerable systems to ascertain unique vulnerable system responses.

■   Test the breadth of your signature on other protocols or ports that could be leveraged in an attack. For example, make sure your HTTP signature works on 80 and 8080, or even over HTTPS on 443.

▲   Test regular expressions by modifying useless customizable attack packets, but leaving the "kill payload" intact. For example, change HTTP headers and immaterial fields within an MDAC buffer overflow that can be leveraged through IIS over HTTP.

Using Trons

The *Trons* feature, coincidently spelled Snort backward, can parse in most Snort attack signatures, so they can be used on a RealSecure sensor. ISS took the road of "we can't beat the Snort community, so we'll join them" with this feature. This lets you quickly enable this feature with a trons=enabled line within the configuration file, and then specific a local file on your file system where the desired Snort-formatted attack signatures resides. The file configuration line could be something as simple as trons.filename=c:\snort\apache_rules.conf.

 Bugs have been identified within Trons in the past to include properly formatted Snort rules that are not functioning properly within Trons because of negation flags, binary used in regular expressions—new features within Snort that had yet to be implemented within ISS's parsing engine. Testing signatures added within RealSecure's Trons feature is critical.

UPGRADING

Two types of upgrades are considered for RealSecure 7.0 because of ISS's acquisition of NetworkICE Corporation. The most common upgrade is RealSecure 6.x to 7.0. As a previous NetworkICE customer, however, you also have the capability to migrate from Sentry to RealSecure 7.0. Throughout this section of the chapter, we refer to upgrading for the 6.x RealSecure software and migration for Sentry. First, the focus is on the procedures for

upgrading RealSecure, and then it delves into migrating, with a quick guide on the critical points to remember when you migrate.

Upgrading from the RealSecure 6 Series to 7.0

ISS has enabled its users with two potential options when upgrading their sensors. The first, and obvious, choice for most enterprise deployments is to upgrade the product remotely. This is done in a rather automatic fashion and nearly completely behind the scenes—usually an excellent choice for your average setup and somewhat simple configuration. As with nearly every software installation, the other choice is a manual install, conducted locally at the console of the sensor. The second options is much less scalable for large product rollouts or geographically robust networks.

NOTE Manual installations are more simple in nature and all come with rather easy-to-follow onscreen instructions for a step-by-step walkthrough for upgrading. Because of this, all our attention is focused here on installation notes for remote upgrades. For detailed instructions on upgrading locally or manually, refer to ISS's documentation found at http://www.iss.net/support/documentation.

Preface for Remote Upgrades

In most enterprise environments, upgrading a RealSecure sensor remotely should only take you several minutes because of the extended effort put forth by ISS in the upgrade automation technologies. As system or security administrators, it is critical to quickly upgrade or continuously update your security product investments. In most cases, these investments make significant technological advancements with every major product release because the market is still emerging and remains rather immature. As far as the updates go, these are the bloodlines of the products. In today's hash environment, these vulnerability signatures must be updated as soon as they are available and, in some cases, sooner (see the previous writing custom-signatures section of this chapter.)

Some reminders before you get started:

▼ Download or save the product upgrades to a safe, yet accessible, location that can be accessed by SiteProtector.

■ Upgrade all management components to the latest version. This includes SiteProtector's WorkGroup Manager, Databases, and Event Collectors.

■ As with any software upgrade, back up any pertinent data before you begin the upgrade process.

▲ You will be taking down production intrusion-detection systems and, as such, the correct timing is critical. You have the capability to select the best time for upgrading the sensors in your environment. Most people select the time in which the least amount of attacks are realized within your environment. This type of data can be ascertained from the RealSecure Dashboard or a trending report based on High Vulnerable Attacks.

Upgrading Windows Sensors

ISS's SiteProtector saves the day again, while letting administrators to remotely upgrade one or many sensors simultaneously via the WorkGroup Manager. Provided that the appropriate configurations are in place as stated previously, upgrading Windows systems should be a no-brainer.

Nearly all this upgrade will take place within the SiteProtector Workgroup Manager (from here on, this is called the Workgroup Manager.) Open the Workgroup Manager and select the sensors you want to upgrade. Right-click the desired sensor or sensors, and then select X-Press or Product Update on the pop-up box that appears. Two options should be presented to you at this time. The first options asks if you want to install X-Press Updates. The second option asks if you want to install an Upgrade or a Service Release. In this case, select Upgrade or Service Release.

After selecting Upgrade or Service Release, the option prompts you to specify the location of the installer package. Navigate to the location and select the package, and then click Next. After you select the appropriate package, select the available update that you want to install. Agree to the Strong Encryption Export Agreement, which is mandated by United States Federal Law. The update program will now initiate the download of the package and could take several minutes, depending on the download speed and size of the package. Click Continue on the pop-up message, which tells you this could take a considerable amount of time to finish and you should only proceed if the remote sensor is already at 6.5 or higher.

Shortly thereafter, you will notice some changes within the sensor. The component status will change to Unknown and the control status will show several errors related to the sensor daemon. Specifically, these errors include the following:

▼   Sensor not running

■   Connection refused or closed by remote host

▲   Sensor restarting

After the upgrade is complete, which could be several minutes, the component status changes back to Active. This is your ticket or acknowledgement that the upgrade is complete and everything finished successfully. Additional Windows sensors can be upgraded in this same fashion.

Take the following steps to quickly upgrade Windows:

1. Open WorkGroup manager and select the sensor you want to upgrade.

2. Right-click and select X-Press or Product Update.

3. Click Upgrade or Service Release.

4. Navigate to the upgrade package and select the corresponding product upgrade.

5. You are now home free! Click through the rest of the installer until the installation is complete.

Upgrading Unix and Linux Sensors

Similar to the Windows Upgrade process, the majority of the remote upgrade procedures are conducted through the SiteProtector Workgroup Manager interface (Workgroup Manager.) A key differentiator in ease of maintenance, the process to upgrade Linux and Unix systems is identical. Open the Workgroup Manager and select the sensors you want to upgrade. The Workgroup Manager permits you to stop the sensor or sensors being upgraded on the remote system—stop them! You will notice the component status remains in a Connected state, yet the sensor status has changed to Stopped.

Right-click the desired sensor or sensors and select X-Press or Product Update on the pop-up box that appears. Two options should be presented to you at this time. The first option asks if you want to install X-Press Updates. The second options asks if you want to install an Upgrade or Service Release. In this case, select Upgrade or Service Release(1). After selecting Upgrade or Service Release, it prompts you to specify the location of the installer package. Navigate to the location and select the package, and then click Next. After you select the appropriate package, select the available update that you want to install. Agree to the Strong Encryption Export Agreement mandated by United States Federal Law. The update program now initiates the download of the package and could take several minutes, depending on the download speed and size of the package. Click Continue on the pop-up message, which informs you this could take a considerable amount of time to finish and you should only proceed if the remote sensor is already at 6.5 or higher. Shortly thereafter, you will notice some changes within the sensor. The component status will change to Unknown and the control status will show several errors related to the sensor daemon. Specifically these errors will include the following:

▼ Sensor not running

■ Connection refused or closed by remote host

▲ Sensor restarting

You will know the upgrade is complete for the sensor when the state returns to Connected. Do not worry, the sensor state should still be set to Stopped. In case you have any additional sensors that need to be upgraded, now is the time. Go back to the Workgroup Manager and right-click on the corresponding systems you want to upgrade and repeat the previous instructions.

NOTE   If you remember or have logically named your sensors, the recommended is that you upgrade the sensors in the same order as you originally installed them.

After you successfully upgrade all the desired sensors, go to the Workgroup Manager and restart all the sensors. Last, but definitely not least, verify all the sensors are connected and active.

Take the following steps to upgrade Unix:

1. Open WorkGroup manager and select the sensor you want to upgrade.

2. Stop the sensor(s).

3. Right-click and select X-Press or Product Update.

4. Click Upgrade or Service Release.

5. Navigate to the upgrade package and select the corresponding product upgrade.

6. Repeat steps 3 through 5 on any additional sensors.

7. Start the sensor(s).

Migrating from Sentry to RealSecure

As you learned, SiteProtector is used to centrally manage all the RealSecure sensors via HTTP and HTTPS. The first consideration to make when you are attempting to upgrade is architecture. Your network architecture must be modified to support the new platform and software. In general, network location is the same, but RealSecure leads the market in enterprise-class sensor deployment speeds. RealSecure was the first to offer functional gigabit processing capabilities and the first to implement dropped packet alerts. The following is a checklist that can be used to assist in migrating from the outdated NetworkICE's Sentry to RealSecure 7.0:

▼   **Location**   SiteProtector can go in the same location as that of ICEcap Manager, while Sentry can also be replaced with RealSecure. In general, the location needn't change. Running tests on a regular basis is critical, however, to ensure that all potentially dangerous traffic is being captured and analyzed.

■   **Management routes**   Sentry utilizes ports 8081, 8089, 9091, and 9089 to communicate to and from ICEcap, whereas RealSecure uses the standard web ports of 80 and 433, in addition to 3998 and 3999 for the application server. It is pertinent to ensure the network devices between your sensors and management systems are configured to securely allow SSL communication between the systems on the previously specified ports.

NOTE   Port 80 is not required if you only allow encrypted communication over 443.

■   **Hardware**   In general, the hardware requirements for both applications are extremely similar and dependant on networks the residing and supporting sensors. The only two differences we acknowledge are disk space and CPU recommendations. RealSecure recommends a minimum of 9GB of hard disk space and Pentium II processing capabilities, obviously created with enterprise networks as the focus point. NetworkICE has a minimum of 10MB and does

not require as much processing power. One of the big reasons for these differences is reporting options and increased policy rules within RealSecure.

- **Successful installation of RealSecure**   Detailed RealSecure installation tips and tricks can be found earlier in the chapter, but we did want to include that a working version of RealSecure is necessary for a "happy" transition.

- **Tasks**   All scheduled tasks should be migrated to the new sensors before they roll into production status. You can view your created tasks in ICECap by navigating to and clicking the Scheduled Tasks tab. The SiteProtector tasks can be viewed by clicking the Sensor tab. Unfortunately, no easy method exists to migrate these tasks. The best solution is to reenter one from the other. Take your time because these steps are critical!

- **Events**   Events are also extremely important when configuring your sensor. You have the capability to view and verify your sensor events by clicking the Sensor Analysis tab. This provides you with the capability to look at all the events. If you click on the top of the Events column, you have the capability to see the events ordered by the number of times they have been executed. This is one of the quickest and easiest methods to determine attack trends.

- **Configuration responses**   E-mail, audio alerts, visual pop-ups, and logging are only some of the options users must be alerted to when vulnerabilities are triggered. These are some of the most time-consuming tasks, but they are equally important to any of the other tasks listed.

- **System accounts**   In general, RealSecure and SiteProtector implement two types of application accounts. Both operator- and administrator-level accounts are used to allow the appropriate permissions to Sensor users. Administrators have full control of the system.

- ▲ **Alerting policy**   Configuring your alert policy to be effective requires that you also ensure it is efficient. Too many alerts decrease the effectiveness of each alert and increase the overall cost of ownership for your intrusion detection deployment. Because of the number of signatures included within RealSecure, this can take some time to set and configure properly.

These steps are meant to be used as a complementary guide to your ISS documentation, which can assist in your transition to RealSecure from Sentry and ease your deployment frustration.

SUMMARY

Throughout this chapter, we covered ISS's latest revision of the market-leading RealSecure intrusion detection system. RealSecure was created to minimize the complexities and intricacies of installing and engineering an intrusion detection network within enterprise environments. The minimal effort required during installation permits the

security administrators to focus their time and resources on ensuring that the system is configured and customized properly, so all critical attacks and attempted attacks are identified and quickly alerted. We also discussed the multiple reporting options that provide the appropriate amount of detail to each target audience: executive management, management, and technicians. SiteProtector, ISS's product line for central management of security products, was briefly touched on to the extent that you now should have an understanding of how it can make your job easier. Last, and, by far the most important section of the chapter, described the process taken and details required to write accurate and efficient attack signature rules. The IDS rules are the bloodline for all intrusion detection products and Real Secure is no different. Real Secure comes with attack signatures, but it also provides you with the capability to design your own attack signatures if you choose to do so.

CHAPTER 9

Cisco Secure IDS

Cisco offers a compelling product line in the IDS and IPS space based on the availability of NIDS, HIPS, and strong software management capabilities. Cisco refers to its product line as the Cisco Intrusion Detection System (IDS), made up of the various NIDS and HIDS solutions offered. Given the wide acceptance of Cisco's technology solutions, many real-world organizations (businesses, governments, universities, and others) have found effective solutions using the Cisco product line. Further, recent improvements to deployment options and the acquisition of the leading host-based, intrusion-prevention provider Okena show Cisco's commitment to being a significant player in the IDS/IPS space.

Cisco focuses on four goals in its product line:

▼   Accuracy

■   Enabling Investigation and Response

■   Comprehensive Management

▲   Flexible deployment

The "current" (at press time) Cisco product line includes appliance-based NIDS, modules compatible with many routers and switches, and software-based solutions for certain releases of the Cisco IOS. These combine to create a flexible offering that allows each organization to tailor the product offerings to meet their needs. The CiscoWorks VPN/Security Management Solution (VMS) version 2.2 manages all the different platforms. Prior to the release of the 2.2 version of VMS, Cisco had been working to consolidate the number and type of management solutions for the suite of products. In most cases, Cisco has acquired technology for its IDS/IPS line. Each acquired product has had its own management software, which Cisco has integrated under the CiscoWorks umbrella. Cisco Threat Response (CTR) is a new software solution released last year by Cisco. CTR enables investigation by quickly assessing victim hosts to determine if they're vulnerable to attacks they've received. CTR adds an automated investigation component to the product mix.

The Cisco IDS Sensor 4200 series are appliance-based network equipment carefully constructed for fast and efficient networking monitoring to enable detection and response. The hardware is Intel-based PCs, with fast Pentium processors, and large amounts of RAM and disk space. The products support up to five monitored interfaces, while always using a separate interface for command and control. The 4250 and 4250 XL support fiber interfaces, while the rest of the product line supports standard Ethernet (copper).

Cisco produces the Cisco Catalyst 6500 Series Intrusion Detection System (IDSM-2) Services Module. This module is again a PC style appliance, but Cisco designed this option on a board that allows it to integrate into the 6500 series chassis in exactly the same way a module with fast Ethernet ports is integrated. This module runs the same codebase including the same Red Hat Linux based kernel and uses a Pentium 3 processor with a 232 MHz IXP 32-bit StrongARM policy processor on the built-in accelerator. Currently

the IDSM-2 is rated for 600 Mbps of monitored traffic. From a pure software perspective, the IDSM-2 is identical to the 4200 sensors.

Cisco's offering for its routers include hardware modules and an IDS feature set implemented in software. This software feature set allows the router to monitor for 59 unique attacks. Cisco chose which signatures based on factors such as severity and real-world likelihood. The IDS feature set allows the router to take real-time action once it discovers an attack. It can take three actions: alarm, drop packets, or reset a TCP connection. This creates the option for a proactive defense in situations where little protection was previously unavailable. The router modules are once again an Intel chip with Linux, and the same code as the appliance and switch module.

The recent addition of the Okena product line as Cisco's Security Agent (CSA) is a significant step forward for the network equipment maker. The CSA enables the host-level implementation of a fundamental security strategy: "That which is not expressly allowed, is denied." This means that product enforces a strict policy governing the actions of a particular piece of software, where the normal activities of the application are allowed, and everything else is denied. This is an example of an anomaly based approach to IPS. Cisco has integrated the CSA management software into the CiscoWorks VMS 2.2 allowing for even greater advantage of the common management platform.

The VMS platform version 2.2 represents the first time that Cisco allows control from a single product suite, including control of VPNs, routers, and network- and host-based IDS. CiscoWorks VMS 2.2 allows configuration management, monitoring, device inventory, and software release (version) management features. VMS 2.2 allows administrators to configure network, switch, and host IDS sensors, and can also capture, view, and report on events from these IDS sensors, as well as from Cisco PIX and Cisco IOS devices. More importantly, one can obtain notification of events and alarms. In the near future, the Threat Response module will allow automated investigation. Current CTR is a stand-alone product offered as a free beta.

The VMS 2.2 suite runs on both Solaris- and Windows-based infrastructures. IT managers typically view deciding between platforms as a challenge in some organizations. Selecting the platform that will be easiest to support is best, as the best-operated management center will also produce the best-operated infrastructure. For organizations already standard on Windows or Solaris, it's best to continue with the platform of general choice. For large enterprise environments where excellent support for either platform exists, experience has shown that Solaris is better suited for large installations, and security administrators can more easily secure that platform. Please note, minor differences exist between some the reporting and minor features in the releases across the platforms. Cisco documented these differences in the release notes, and we discuss them in the section "Collecting Requirements."

DESIGNING YOUR CISCO-BASED SOLUTION

In every environment, several key factors contribute to the success of an IDS/IPS infrastructure. Many experts agree that the processes for infrastructure management and incident response are the most critical success factors. While these are clearly important, you

can't fully use these processes unless they're applied based on a sound infrastructure. Given the wide adoption of the Cisco product lines in today's enterprises, many organizations are making the choice to use a single vendor to product IDS/IPS infrastructure. Based on the mix of products and the strong support through the Technical Assistance Center (TAC), Cisco becomes a viable choice for a single vendor solution.

The best place to start the design process is with a clear plan. We generate this plan typically from stated goals or objectives and combined with requirements. Determining up front how you will use the IDS/IPS system is important. In some environments, they provide detailed, near real-time records of current network activity. Other environments want the infrastructure to provide proactive defense leveraging capabilities to block attackers and stop malicious activity as soon as possible. Often overlooked is how to divide operational responsibilities for the maintenance, use, and operation of IDS/IPS infrastructure.

Collecting Requirements

Accurate requirements can be difficult to collect in many organizations. Table 9-1 contains example requirements that can be used to drive this process. This table discusses specific areas requiring careful consideration. Analysis of these requirements will allow the proper design and implementation.

Defense in Depth

Designing the solution is the combination of applying the technology to the existing infrastructure, while considering the requirements generated. Cisco has defined its SAFE Blueprint for designing, implementing, and tuning a Cisco-based IDS/IPS solution. The reference architecture presents an excellent guideline and you should consider that starting point for a sound design. The SAFE Blueprint breaks down the components of a corporate network into modules. Each module is a self-contained set of infrastructure (routers, switches, firewalls, IDSs, and so forth) working together to perform a specific network function. Modules are mixed together to build an enterprise network.

The SAFE blueprint recommends placing network IDS sensors at

▼ Corporate Internet Access

■ Remote Access

■ Major LAN Interconnections

■ Server Farms

■ Management LANs

■ Extranets and DMZs

▲ Data Centers/E-Commerce

In choosing where to start first, you should consider factors such as criticality of assets, robustness of design, and accessibility of assets. While Assets deemed to be critical infrastructure because of their business value clearly will benefit from IDS deployment,

Area	Component	Intrusion Detection Requirements IDS System Characteristics	Where Cisco's Product Line Stands
IDS system characteristics	Comprehensive set of intrusion signatures	Signature-based IDS systems suffer from a fundamental flaw. They only identify events that can be described (in detail) before they take place. However, the majority of intrusion detection systems operate by recognizing signatures of network attacks. These signatures can describe the details of violations of network protocols, packets destined for suspicious ports, the presence of particular byte sequences in the data payload of a packet, suspicious packet sequences, and so forth. The number and type of signatures available is a key requirement of an IDS system.	Cisco has a comprehensive set of signatures developed by its Cisco Countermeasures Research Team (C-CRT). The C-CRT is made up of engineers from the WheelGroup acquisition. They develop signatures based on years of experience in both commercial and government roles.
IDS system characteristics	High performance on sensors	The IDS sensors must be able to process packets at a rate fast enough to keep up with network load. If the sensor becomes overloaded, it might begin to drop packets, and those dropped packets could lead to a significant increase in false negatives. Therefore, it's important to build network sensors capable of handling the traffic load on the segment they'll be monitoring.	Cisco offers a comprehensive product line with solutions to fit most needs. This includes stand-alone appliances, router and switch modules, host-based intrusion prevention, and integration into existing Cisco infrastructure.
	Capability to create custom filters	One might want to identify specific events of interest for which monitoring is required, but public-domain activity signatures don't exist. The capability to create custom filters gives us the capability to record and analyze these events.	Cisco provides the capability to create highly detailed custom signatures through a comprehensive wizard.
IDS system characteristics	Acceptable false-positive and false-negative rates	While this rate (ratio of false positives to false negatives) is entirely dependent on the type of network traffic seen by the IDS, managing these failure rates is essential. The false-negative rate can be reduced through a well-designed engine that recognizes a large number of attack signatures. The false-positive rate can be reduced through an engine that supports threshold tuning and well-defined filters.	Cisco's TAME is a leading engine based on years of development. In addition, Cisco offers customization of all signatures to increase accuracy.
Architecture	Network-based IDS component	Network-based IDS places a crucial role in appropriately covering an environment. Network IDS is best at covering aggregated network segments, places where different portions of a network architecture meet.	Cisco offers several options for network-based deployment with flexible options for integration into existing infrastructure.

Table 9-1. IDS Best Practice Requirements

Area	Component	Intrusion Detection Requirements IDS System Characteristics	Where Cisco's Product Line Stands
Architecture	Host-based ILS component	Host-based IDS provide protection of critical assets. Host-based IDS (HIDS) takes advantage of the existing processing on each host process, packet, and data stream, adding a small overhead for inspection. Typically, these operate at the kernel layer of a host, and are given an excellent vantage point into attempted operations on a host. Because network-based IDS must account for the multiple ways that hosts reconstruct network traffic, HIDS holds a distinct advantage in terms of accuracy.	Cisco's acquisition of the Okena product line provides best in class host-based intrusion prevention for Windows, Solaris and (soon) Linux.
Architecture	Distributed architecture	The most common (and most effective) design for an IDS is that of a distributed system, with remote sensors deployed throughout the network, a central data collection facility, and one or more analyst consoles on the analyst's desktop.	Cisco offers a highly scalable distributed system for event processing from detection to alerting and response.
Architecture	Communication architecture	In a "push" communication architecture, the sensors feed their data into the analysts console as events of interest are identified. This gives us a near real-time intrusion-detection capability. This is in contrast to a "pull" communication architecture, in which the analyst console polls the sensors periodically for newly identified events of interest.	Cisco has recently switched from a push-based to a pull-based architecture.
Analysis support	Intrusion reporting, response, and recovery policies and procedures	The IDS is a tool that will provide a skilled analyst with the information needed to identify network intrusion attempts. The analyst is ultimately responsible for decisions regarding response and recovery. The use of software to automate these steps, however, is attractive in some scenarios. To ensure these actions are carried out in a manner both consistent and acceptable, specific policy elements should be implemented to govern response and recovery.	Cisco offers a comprehensive set of reporting and response options. These are the free Event Viewer and CiscoWorks VMS. Also, Cisco is automating investigation with the release of the Threat Response software.
Analysis support	Integrated console and database -or host- and network-based components	An integrated console and database provides several advantages to the intrusion analyst. The integrated database gives the analyst the capability to do thorough event correlation through database queries, reducing the need for manual correlation. The integrated console allows the analyst to identify and respond to alerts from a single interface, improving the efficiency of their work.	CiscoWorks VMS 2.2 offers the capability to manage events from all Cisco IDS products, including the Cisco Security Agent and the Network IDS.

Table 9-1. IDS Best Practice Requirements (*continued*)

Area	Component	Intrusion Detection Requirements IDS System Characteristics	Where Cisco's Product Line Stands
Analysis support	Significant drill-down capability to provide detailed information on demand	A well-designed IDS console will provide basic information at first glance, and allow the analyst to "drill down" to important details. On request, the IDS should give the analyst significant and complete data for analysis and classification of the event.	Cisco provides drill-down capability all the way to captured packets from attacks. Views are customizable and filterable to ensure the right data is presented.
Analysis support	Relational database back end	An RDB back end can be queried, giving the analyst the capability to mine the IDS data for trends, patterns, and detailed information about events of interest. A database back end can also be used for building reports and archiving data.	Cisco uses a MySQL backend for the Event Viewer with export capability. VMS uses an MS SQL run time (a.k.a. MSDE) back end.
Analysis support	Report generation capability	IDS should give the capability to create reports. This capability, directly from the system itself, removes the requirement to add additional software to the solution. The system would ideally provide some canned reports and should offer the capability to create customized reports.	Cisco provides comprehensive reporting in both the Event Viewer and VMS products. These features are maximized on the Windows version of the CiscoWorks Monitoring Module. Some areas aren't supported on Solaris yet. There's no support for events from the Management Center for Cisco Security Agents, version 4.0. Also, the Cisco IDS Network Module for routers IDS version 4.1 isn't supported, but IDS 4.0 is supported. No additional reports are available for firewall and Cisco Security Agents. Also, there's no support for saving the preferences of column ordering in the Event Viewer on the Solaris version.
Analysis support	Well-built analyst console	A well-built analyst console is important. A console that isn't reliable and robust can render the work done by the sensors. Advanced features for distributing administration responsibilities and required access are also important factors in the construction of the console.	The VMS console is a mature product with a world-class software-engineering group developing it. CiscoWorks VMS offersCentralized Role-Based Access Control (RBAC).

Table 9-1. IDS Best Practice Requirements (continued)

Area	Component	Intrusion Detection Requirements IDS System Characteristics	Where Cisco's Product Line Stands
Analysis support	False-positive management	False positives can be a time-consuming failure mode for the intrusion analyst. To combat this problem, the IDS should offer a mechanism for false-positive management. Common techniques include adjustable alarm thresholds and console enhancements to facilitate information management.	Cisco offers fully tunable signatures and alarm thresholds.
Analysis support	Event correlation capability	Network activity that triggers IDS alerts could be more than a traffic anomaly or a single attack. Some of the events of interest identified by the IDS might, in fact, be part of a coordinated (possibly distributed) attack. The IDS should offer tools to identify any correlation in these events of interest. If the back end is a relational database, then this correlation can be done through database queries. If the back end isn't a relational database, it might be possible to achieve this correlation through custom scripts or other techniques.	Cisco's Security Monitor (part of VMS's Monitoring Center) supports basic event correlation. It does this by allowing the analyst to leverage the Event Viewer, the Event Rule, and Reporting subsystems.
Analysis support	Database stores raw data	The database should store be able to store completed packets. because complete packets providee a much more powerful trend analysis/correlation capability particularly as new features are added.	Cisco's network IDS products have the capability to perform packet capture when a signature fires. This means that the entire packet or stream of packets can be analyzed at a later time when required.
Internal (IDS) security	Encrypted traffic between sensor and console	Because IDS management traffic is the "key to the kingdom," the capability to protect this data is crucial.	Cisco's RDEP uses SSL/TLS to protect network communications.
Internal (IDS) security	Hardened agent and console hosts	The IDS is a key component in the defense of the network. If the IDS is easily compromised, not only do we lose this critical piece of our security solution, we run the risk of the IDS giving up valuable information about the network environment. To mitigate this risk, we must protect ourselves from attacks against the IDS itself. An essential component of this protection is hardening of the OSs on machines hosting IDS sensor and console components. These hosts should be completely dedicated to their IDS functions, running nothing other than that required by the IDS software.	Cisco provides the capability to use the CSA to protect the VMS station. The network IDS line is difficult to attack on the network because it doesn't have an IP address.
Response and recovery capabilities	Intrusion response capability	An attractive approach to intrusion response would be for the IDS to generate a real-time "recommended response" to a detected intrusion. This assists the analyst in quickly responding to intrusions, but provides the opportunity to sanity-check the response to avoid disaster.	Cisco is adding the threat response software to automate investigations and speed response. With the highly accurate data this produces, response options are clear.

Table 9-1. IDS Best Practice Requirements (*continued*)

systems not processing millions of dollars of transactions aren't likely to be first in line for protection. You'll want to consider the robustness of design, meaning the protections already in place when deciding between assets. Systems already built to withstand attacks might not be in urgent need when compared to systems without protections, such as network firewalls and application proxies. Accessibility of assets is a key measure of the level of risk. Systems not exposed to large portions of internal networks could present a lower risk profile. Clearly the converse is true: highly critical systems, systems you haven't built to withstand attacks, and systems connected to large numbers of networks or the Internet need IDS protection.

Packet Capture Options

The Cisco Network IDS product line is no different from any other NIDS product, in that it can only detect attacks in traffic that it can "see." This means capture must be given to monitoring interface using techniques like adding a hub, using port mirroring, or using a tap.

Management and Operations

In general, three options exist for managing a Cisco IDS infrastructure: local interfaces (web and command-line access), CiscoWorks VMS, and third-party tools. Most organizations will find that overall management is best accomplished using a clearly defined suite of tools and not relying on any single tool to be the best fit in all situations. While the Cisco Security Agent requires the use of CiscoWorks VMS, the NIDS products (4000 series, router modules, and switch modules) can be managed either locally or remotely.

For local management, this means two options: the command line interface (CLI), which Cisco revamped as of version 4.0, and a local web interface called the IDS Device Manager (IDM). For Cisco IOS-based solutions, Cisco provides management via both CLI and VMS. In all but the smallest deployments, CiscoWorks VMS will be required to achieve the best possible results. In particular, this will decrease the amount of time spent tuning individual sensors or sensor groups by allowing changes to be applied to groups of sensors. third-party software tools mostly concentrate on pulling events and alarms from the sensors.

Event Viewer

Cisco also provides the Event Viewer application for small installations. The Event Viewer is capable of remotely pulling data from Cisco NIDS products, such as the 4200 series and IDSM-2 running 4.0 or later. The Event Viewer allows quick and powerful analysis of the status of events analyzed by the IDS infrastructure. The Event Viewer is a powerful tool that contains drill-down capability down to view captured packets from real attacks.

The Event Viewer presents both real-time reports of activity and historical viewing of data. The primary mechanism for helping sort through this data is the use of filters. You can create *filters* to match particular sets of events based on characteristics such as Severity, Source or Destination Address, Signature or Sensor Name, or Time and Status. When you create filters, it's important to document what filters you created and what purpose they serve. This assists in the response process because incident handlers can reliably understand the context of events from the IDS system. Typically, organizations develop a

set of filters over time that meet their needs, so it's equally important to ensure that documentation is kept current.

Some typical filters that we've found to be useful in separating data are as follows:

▼ Using **Source** and/or **Destination Address** to isolate systems serving a particular function, such as Enterprise Resource Planning (ERP) or E-Commerce.

■ Using **Source** and/or **Destination Address** combined with Signature Name to look for signatures of attacks when a particular set of systems is known to still be vulnerable.

▲ Using **Time** to help isolate a specific series of events noticed in other data, such as firewall logs or Syslog events.

The Event Viewer enables the use of customized Views to control what data is displayed related to a specific event. Because the Event Viewer can display over 40 data elements for a single event, it's important to customize what information is displayed to allow accurate analysis. The Event Viewer ships with the following five default views:

▼ **Destination Address Group**   Shows events sorted by Destination Address (typically the victim host). This allows quick analysis to determine which machines are most significantly under attack.

■ **Sensor Name Group**   Shows events generated by a specific sensor. This shows where in the network the IDS sensors are finding attacks. This enables comparisons that can validate assumptions, such as that Internet-connected networks are more dangerous.

■ **Severity Level**   Shows the alarms sorted by criticality.

■ **Signature Name Group**   Shows activity sort by specific Signature names. This is extremely useful during widespread attack, such as during worm outbreaks.

▲ **Source Address Group**   Shows activity by source address, typically attacking hosts. This can be compromised or infected hosts.

Network IDS

The centerpiece of the Cisco lineup is the IDS built around the Threat Analysis Micro Engine (TAME) and its accompanying policy language. Cisco has unified the underling code base in version 4.0 across all the NIDS deployment options. This means you can expect similar features and performance from all the product line. This solution is widely considered simply as "signature based," but Cisco has identified that it uses a hybrid approach to combine different detection techniques to achieve maximum results. Primarily protocol decodes are used because of the number of Cisco's signatures that have been written this way.

Heuristic-based signatures are the second most-often used. Cisco uses pattern matches almost as much as heuristic-based signatures. Cisco doesn't currently use classic anomaly detection (in its NIDS product line) outside of protocol anomaly detection but, let's remember, this is only protocol decoding. Cisco doesn't use anomaly detection primarily because

it hasn't found a solution it views appropriate for its customers. Clearly, Cisco's R&D team will continue to look for better ways to detect malicious activity and examine all avenues.

System Features

Cisco NIDS offer the capability to capture packets, log, and alert events, and to take proactive action to stop attacks. The Cisco NIDS can capture packets for historical records, troubleshooting, and forensic analysis. The primary function for IDS in the eyes of many people is to log an alert on events, so the incident response process can initiate quickly. Clearly the capability to take proactive action by resetting connections (session sniping) and blocking attacking devices (shunting) is a powerful tool in the protection of critical infrastructure.

The NIDS can capture packets either when firing signatures or when manually configured to find packets associated with a particular IP address. For either scenario of starting a packet capture (a.k.a. IP Log), a specific number of bytes, length of time, or a specific number of packets binds it.

Assigning Packet Capture to Signatures

All signatures can result in IP Logging. This includes Cisco provided signatures or custom-developed signatures. To configure the Cisco NIDS to start an IP Log for a specific event, the signature parameter "EventAction" must to set to "Log". Because data is exchanged via XML-based RDEP, this is accomplished by a specific name/value pair. In this case, "EventAction=log". Using the IDM, you can configure from the screen Configuration | Sensing Engine | Virtual Sensor Configuration | Signature Configuration mode. From this screen, you must drill down to the specific signature in question.

Let's assume you want to add an IP Log for all the times there are fail logins to a critical HTTP server.

First, start by selecting Service HTTP from the Signature Configure Mode screen. Next, drill down and click the check box next to the line number for signature ID #6256 HTTP Authorization Failure. Then, select Edit across the bottom. Now, you're presented with the screen for Signature Configuration. From here, change the EventAction to Log by selecting that menu item.

Session Sniping and Shunning

Instructing the IDS to take proactive action is sometimes considered a controversial topic. IT managers cite concerns on the impact of false positives. In many cases, this is a valid concern and certainly must be addressed. You learn about reducing false positives in the section "Tuning." Assuming these concerns have been appropriately addressed, let's discuss how these features work.

Session Sniping is a method of stopping attacks by closing the TCP session associated with that attack. The Cisco NIDS accomplishes this by sending a TCP RST (reset) packet from the command and control interface to the identified attacking host and to the victim or target host. For this to work properly, it's important to ensure that the IDS command and control interface (typically interface 0) have IP connectivity (be able to route packets)

to the attacker and victim hosts. In particular, if network firewalls are in the path, it could be difficult to implement this without changes to the policy applied to the firewall.

Shunning is the process of applying access control lists (ACLs) to nearby routers or switches to block individual connections or hosts to stop attacks. Cisco supports shunning on all IOS devices, the Catalyst 6500 line, and the PIX firewall. This is enabled by configuring the IDS Sensor with a user name and a password to specific devices where ACLs will be applied (see Figure 9-1). This must be carefully configured and managed in concert with other tools, such as configuration management and troubleshooting.

TAME

Cisco's architecture for the Network IDS products is based on the TAME microengine. The *TAME microengine* processes individual engines for different traffic types. These engines are a comprehensive set of network protocols used today, and they encompass network, transport and application levels, as shown in Table 9-2.

Signatures

Cisco's IDS sensors work by examining network traffic against its knowledge of malicious traffic types. Each time the sensor finds a match, the sensor takes an action, such as logging the event or sending an alarm to IDS Event Viewer. Sensors enable you to modify existing signatures and define new ones. Cisco ships a comprehensive database of signatures. While you can't delete or change the names of built-in signatures, you can disable them. Cisco enables most signatures by default.

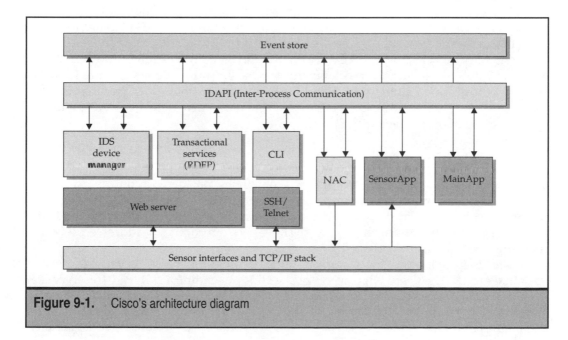

Figure 9-1. Cisco's architecture diagram

Engine	Description
ATOMIC.ARP	Analyzes ARP packets both individual packets and groups.
ATOMIC.ICMP	Analyzes ICMP packets for the following parameters Type, Code, Sequence, and ID.
ATOMIC.IPOPTIONS	Analyzes IP packets for IP options in the layer 3 header.
ATOMIC.L3.IP	Analyzes layer 3 IP headers.
ATOMIC.TCP	Analyzes TCP headers for these parameters: Port, Destination, Flags, and single packet Regex.
ATOMIC.UDP	Analyzes UDP headers for these parameters: Port, Direction, and DataLength.
FLOOD.HOST.ICMP	Detects ICMP floods for a single victim.
FLOOD.HOST.UDP	Detects UDP floods for a single victim.
FLOOD.NET	Detects multiprotocol floods for a single victim subnet.
OTHER	Available for changing common parameters to groups of signatures.
SERVICE.DNS	Protocol breakdown for DNS service.
SERVICE.FTP	Protocol breakdown of FTP service.
SERVICE.GENERIC	Cisco recommends for expert use only.
SERVICE.HTTP	HTTP protocol breakdown based on a string engine. Includes capability to normalize URLs.
SERVICE.IDENT	Analyzes the IDENT service.
ERVICE.MSSQL	Analyzes Microsoft SQL.
SERVICE.NTP	Protocol decode of Network Time Protocol.
SERVICE.RPC	Analyzes the RPC service.
SERVICE.SMB	Cisco's SMB SuperInspector signatures. Cannot be used in custom signatures.
SERVICE.SMTP	SMTP protocol decode.
SERVICE.SNMP	Analyzes SNMP packets.
SERVICE.SSH	SSH header decode signatures. Cannot be used in custom signatures.
SERVICE.SYSLOG	Analyzes syslog messages.
STATE.STRING.CISCOLOGIN	Analyzes Cisco Login's (via telnet).
STATE.STRING .LPRFORMATSTRING	LPR protocol decode.
STRING.ICMP	ICMP-based string search engine.

Table 9-2.   Microengine Details

Engine	Description
STRING.TCP	TCP-based string search engine.
STRING.UDP	UDP-based string search engine.
SWEEP.HOST.ICMP	Detects a single host performing discovery ICMP.
SWEEP.HOST.TCP	Detects TCP port scans.
SWEEP.MULTI	Detects cross-protocol sweeps.
SWEEP.OTHER.TCP	Detects fingerprint scans.
SWEEP.PORT.TCP	Detects port sweeps for a pair of hosts.
SWEEP.PORT.UDP	Detects UDP port sweeps between two hosts.

Table 9-2.   Microengine Details *(continued)*

A signature can be made up of several variants known as a subsignature, which allows parameters for the subsignatures to be modified without affecting each other. Changes to event action such as log vs. shun will affect only the specific signature (or subsignature) being modified.

Cisco provides a comprehensive capability to create your own signatures. The sensor will be assign them to a specific ID range (2000) and are flexible to model nearly any known traffic type. Custom signatures use the same engines as the built-in signatures. This enables you to create signatures that work as well as the Cisco shipped database.

Sensor Models

The current lineup of IOS sensors includes the 4200 series of appliances, as well as IDS modules for routers and switches. The 4200 series are stand-alone appliances built as effective IDS sensors. Currently, Cisco offers four models: 4215, 4235, 4250, and 4250-XL. Sharing similar PC-based platforms, they offer increasing amounts of performance and support for gigabit interfaces, although only the 4250-XL supports 1000 Mbps performance. All come standard with a single command and control interface, and one monitoring interface.

Table 9-3 provides a brief comparison between models.

The performance ratings for each assume packet sizes of 445 bytes for TCP-based connections, but the ratings for the 4250-XL assumes 595 byte packets. These assumptive packet sizes might not be realistic for many network environments, however, this doesn't mean they're inaccurate. One clearly prudent planning step would be to analyze packet sizes and network use before deploying the IDS sensors. Also, Cisco provides a dropped-packet signature that alarms when the IDS drops packets. This signature can be used to monitor for overloaded sensors. As with all signatures, it can be applied to any model, including the router and switch modules.

Feature	4215	4235	4250	4250-XL
Performance rating	80 Mbps	250 Mbps	500 Mbps	1000 Mbps
Max Ethernet monitoring interfaces	5	5 (with support for gigabit)	5 (with support for gigabit) Use of all Ethernets eliminates capability to support fiber	1 (with support for gigabit)
Max Fiber monitoring interfaces	0	0	1	1

Table 9-3.   4200 Series Options

Catalyst Switch Module The IDSM-2

The IDSM-2 is the module for the Catalyst 6500 line. You can use it in any of the entire 6500 line of switches. It takes up one slot and you can use multiple modules in a single chassis. B The IDSM-2 can be expected to operate identically to the 4200 series. The main difference is this: the IDSM-2 is able to acquire packets directly from the switch backplane using VACLs. One common misconception is that the IDSM-2 monitors all packets going through the switch. Instead, you must tailor your VACLs to monitor the traffic that required IDS detection. Because the ISDM-2 offers 600 Mbps of performance, careful consideration to what traffic it monitors is required to prevent overloading. The IDSM-2 can push ACLs for blocking to the switch that hosts.

When the IDS is oversubscribed, it will drop (not process) individual packets. These packets will, most likely, be part of TCP streams and affect context for most signatures, as well as the capability to normalize data. Because you cannot control what traffic can be dropped first with the sensor, avoiding oversubscription altogether is important. Because oversubscription is a significant concern in many environments, you can take several steps to avoid it. First, you can enable Cisco's SigID993. This signature fires when dropped packets reaches a high-enough rate. The default for this signature is to fire on any percentage higher than zero. Typically, you want to monitor for anything over the zero level, and take action as it approaches 5 percent or higher. Because the IDS sensor family uses the same code throughout, oversubscription is handled identically across the product family.

Router Modules

One of the newer additions to the Cisco product line is the Cisco IDS Network Module for the Cisco 2600, 3600, and 3700 series routers. These modules provide "IDS on a card," which can be deployed in existing Cisco routers. Given the wide deployment of these routers, this presents an attractive option in many cases. Because Cisco has unified the

code base, once again, exactly the same features are available from the router modules as from the 4200 sensors and IDSM-2. The router modules support significantly less performance (as low as 10 Mbps in the 2600XM and 45 Mbps in the 3600), so this isn't an issue because these routers aren't typically passing more traffic than these ratings. These cards include a 20GB hard drive.

Router and Firewall Sensors

Cisco rounds out the product line with software-based solutions for its IOS routers and Firewall IOS. This software supports a subset of signatures (total of 59), however, it uses the same TAME-based architecture. Cisco selects signatures from its database, enabling you to customize which of the available signatures to apply.

Alerting

In versions below 4.0, Cisco used the PostOffice Protocol (POP) to exchange messages between the IDS sensors and management platforms. Cisco replaced POP with Remote Data Exchange Protocol (RDEP). *RDEP* is an XML-based protocol that uses a subset of HTTP/1.1 for network communications. RDEP is a major shift from POP because it changes from a push to a pull method of data exchange. This means management stations "subscribe" to feeds from the sensors, and "pull" or request updates. This places the responsibility to ensure alerts are received on to the management platform. Cisco does support backward compatibility, so version 4.*x* managers (such as VMS) can pull events from 3.*x* sensors. Cisco requires that older managers be upgraded to support 4.*x* sensors.

Tuning

Tuning your IDS infrastructure is a critical step to ensure it operates effectively. *Tuning* consists of taking steps to adjust the configuration to ensure the right data is analyzed and, when it is analyzed, that it's analyzed correctly. Issues like false positives, false negatives (missed attacks), dropped packets, and data overload must be considered together to devise an effective tuning strategy. Tuning can be a time-consuming process, however, the author found in several scenarios that it's significant enough to warrant concern. The author's experience shows 80 percent of most tuning efforts happen during pilot or test phases of a new IDS system and ongoing tuning activities can either be a small portion of a daily administration process or bunched into weekly, or even monthly, analysis sessions.

The following process shows the typical lifecycle for tuning your IDS:

1. Select signatures
2. Adjust signature properties

   - Parameters
   - Severity

3. Eliminate traffic
4. Monitor and reevaluate

Signature Selection

Depending on the type of network and network traffic expected, not all of the 3000+ signatures in Cisco's Network Security Database (NSDB) make sense to apply. Signatures that detect vulnerabilities that cannot exist in the environment are the first candidates. For instance, attacks specific to Solaris infrastructure might not be of interest. Although the first reaction of many is to consider that any attack is meaningful, when tuning the IDS to provide clear data, some compromises must be made.

Cisco enables the selection and deselection of groups or individual signatures. Because some signatures have subsignatures (IE variants on a specific attack), reviewing the subsignatures also makes sense. Some environments might not expect certain protocol types, such as ICMP traffic or HTTP traffic. This allows quick elimination of these protocol types. (I know you're still worried you'll miss attacks, but don't worry. You're managing risk!)

Adjust Signature Properties

One of the greatest strengths in the Cisco NIDS product family is the capability to tune signature properties easily. With roughly 30 editable properties for each signature, the capability to customize signatures creates a powerful tool to increase accuracy. Each signature can be customized to change its behavior, such as changing the AlarmDelayTimer to a longer value to increase the sensor's capability to consider events with a long delay between them. That capability is crucial to look for events such as slow port scans.

Signature Properties Detail

Table 9-4 is a review of the properties in a typical signature from Cisco. Some of these properties go all the way back to the NetRanger product aquired from the WheelGroup. Cisco appears to have taken a solid foundation from the WheelGroup and expanded it over time.

The first step in tuning your IDS is to manage the amount of traffic "seen" by the sensor. This is important to perform first because the IDS cannot send an alert on traffic it doesn't see. Next, you need to address normalization. *Normalization* is the process used by the IDS to ensure it reconstructs packets the same way the target systems do. Finally, individual parameters are changed or "tuned" to improve accuracy and reduce false positives.

The most basic decision to make in choosing which traffic the sensor monitors is placing the sensor. It's important not to oversubscribe the sensor by attaching it to networks carrying more traffic than the sensor is rated to handle. This is particularly important when using the module for the 6500 family of switches. These switches can handle significantly more traffic than the module itself.

Cisco provides the capability to reconstruct or normalize traffic by host type. Cisco's 4.1 sensors support Windows NT, Solaris, Linux, and BSD. This can be applied using the Device Manager and selecting Configuration | Sensing Engine | Virtual Sensor Configuration | IP Fragment Reassembly. On this screen, you can select the reassembly mode.

Property	Information
AlarmDelayTimer	Time in seconds to wait to continue inspection after an alarm is generated. Used either to make sure a single event isn't lumped in with multiple events or used to lump multiple events together. Think two failed logins vs. ten: sometimes two matter, but, sometimes, only ten matter.
AlarmInterval	Amount of time to consider firing a signature-related events, such as, – "Fire this signature for five hits in AlarmInterval ten seconds."
AlarmSeverity	The preassigned severity of the signature.
AlarmThrottle	This parameter is for limiting alarm firings. You can select "FireAll" to send all alarms; "FireOnce" to send one alarm, and then start the inspecting again; "Summarize" to send alarms at the rate prescribed in "IntervalSummary"; or "GlobalSummarize" to send a GlobalSummary alarm.
AlarmTraits	Signature-specific value for extra information about the alarm.
ChokeThreshold	Value used to determine when the AlarmThrottle action should be taken.
Enabled	Used to tell the sensor to apply the signature.
EventAction	Determines which action (Log, Reset, ShunHost, or ShunConnection) the sensor should take. A Log event is stored for events Reset, ShunHost, and ShunConnection.
FlipAddr	Use this when the traffic that fired the alarm is response traffic from the host being attacked. The IDS would normally show the source address as the attacker, however, this signature allows this to be reversed when needed. One example is looking for a directory listing on a DMZ that should support a custom web application. If the web application never needs to send a directory listing, seeing one could mean a compromise occurred. A custom signature looking for a directory list, when fired, would show the attacker as the web server unless you use the FlipAddr property.

Table 9-4. Configurable Engine/Signature Properties

Property	Information
MaxInspectLength	Here you can control the number of bytes that need to be inspected.
MaxTTL	This can be used to configure signatures that look for patterns over time. This can enforce a global limit when inspecting a series of events.
MinHits	This sets the low-water mark for hits to cause a signature to fire. Many times MinHitswill be set to one but, for instance, when looking for port scans, setting MinHits higher can be useful to decrease false positives.
Protocol	What type of traffic does the signature inspect?
ResetAfterIdle	Length of time (in seconds) for a signature to reset counters after watching traffic go idle.
ServicePorts	Used to specify ports (or lists of ports) to inspect for a signature. Comma-separated for lists.
SigComment	Comment/Info.
SIGID	Number used to identify signatures. 993–19999 is used for Cisco shipped signatures. 20000–50000 used for custom signatures.
SigName	Name used for signature.
SigStringInfo	Text information sent with alarm.
StorageKey	Used to determine how to store persistent data.
SubSig	Subsignature ID number.
SummaryKey	Defines the type of storage used for the signature.
ThrottleInterval	Used to control the throttling of alarms. Defines the duration of an AlarmThrottle event.
WantFrag	Seldom used parameter to determine if a fragment is needed. Can be set to True, False, or ANY.

Table 9-4. Configurable Engine/Signature Properties *(continued)*

The last step in this process is changing signature parameters. Because this will vary widely for signature types and different networks, following a consistent generalized process is best. First, examine an alarm to determine why the sensor issued it. Many times, alarms are considered false positives without fully understanding the signature

that matched the traffic type. Read Cisco NSDB and analyze the traffic. Next, consider the need for the traffic itself. Many times. traffic that is the result of a misconfigured system matches a signature and causes an alarm. The last step is to identify the specific pattern that matched the signature and decide to change the signature itself. Sometimes it's best to change severity, but not to change the underlying signature.

Cisco Security Agent   Cisco has added the Cisco Security Agent (CSA) as Cisco's in-house entry in the host-based intrusion prevention space. This product comes from the acquisition of the Okena System. CSA is widely considered to be extremely effective protection. In the wake of the Blaster worm, many companies have turned to CSA to protect critical hosts. With the capability to lessen the impact of these worms, many companies have found CSA to be well worth the investment.

Endpoint Protection

In the past few years, it's been apparent that signature-based products on the endpoints are no longer sufficient in protecting against the increasing amount of malicious code circulating in the wild, including viruses, worms, and malicious mobile code. These types of technologies also forced you to use numerous different agent-based technology, such as personal firewalls, host intrusion detection (HIDS), file integrity products, and malicious mobile code products. Also, the OS had to go through a rigorous hardening process.

The CSA is a behavior-based approach to security. This single agent is proactive compared to the reactive nature of signature end-point security, for example, Virus Scanner and Host IDS. CSA protects your endpoints, that is, laptops, desktops, and servers from known, new, and unknown attacks. The technology looks like all the products previously mentioned because it has this functionality built in already.

The CSA currently supports NT, Windows 2000, and Solaris 8 (64 bit) on servers and NT, Windows 2000, as well as XP Corporate Desktop (Professional). The CSA MC is part of Cisco Works VMS 2.2 management solution and supports up to 5000 agents.

All agents are created and maintained on the management console (CSA MC). All the rules and policies are enforced locally on the agents. The agents contact the MC at their appropriate polling interval, which you can set, anywhere from ten seconds to once a day. They also send the logs back to the MC in case they're experiencing an attack.

Kernel Mode

The CSA agent gets installed in kernel mode, which is similar to your standard antivirus products and VPN drivers. The kernel itself has no modifications, it only has a module loaded. When an application or process wants to do something, such as open a file or establish a network connection from *A* to *B*, it must go to the kernel and ask for resources. The application that's running in user mode is making a call to the kernel that's in kernel mode. This call is funneled through the CSA shims, which are similar to print drivers or VPN drivers. These shims then forward the calls to the CSA rules engine, which makes allow or deny decisions based on your rules and policies.

System Shims

The CSA agent has numerous shims placed to make sure it can look at all these calls.

▼ **Lower-level network shim at the NDIS layer**   This is the shim that protects your hosts against network-/IP-based attacks like ping scans, syn floods, malformed IP packets, and any other RFC-type violations.

■ **Network shim at the TDI layer**   This is the shim in charge of the interaction between applications and the network. This is the personal firewall-type functionality, that is, which application is allowed to talk to which IP address over which port.

■ **File shim**   The shim watches for file and directory access. The agent provides you with File Monitoring, as well as with File Integrity, ensuring important files can't be changed.

■ **Configuration shim**   This shim watches the registry for read or write access, as well as access to configuration files, such as the rc files or any other files in / etc on Unix.

■ **Execution space shim**   The execution space interceptor is worth an explanation. While this doesn't refer directly to a specific resource like file or network, it deals with maintaining the integrity of each application's dynamic run-time environment. Requests to write to memory not owned by the requesting application are detected and blocked. Attempts by one application to inject code (for example, by injecting a shared library like a DLL) into another are also detected and blocked. Finally, buffer overflow attacks are detected as well. The result is this" not only is the integrity of dynamic resources like file system and configuration preserved, but the integrity of highly dynamic resources, such as memory and network I/O are also preserved.

■ **HTTP shim**   This shim uses dataset variables (strings of data) to match against Uniform Resource Identifier (URI) information in a HTTP request either to allow or deny the action. These datasets can include the following:

■ Known exploits classes

■ Association of metacharacters ("or")

▲ Specific attacks against web servers

The CSA ships with predefined datasets that you can use out of the box or change to your environment. New ones can also be added.

Proactive Security on the Endpoint

New and unknown attacks need to be stopped cold, as do new variants of old, known attacks. This introduces an interesting problem on your endpoint. Can you keep up with all

the patches and updates mandated by the OS and application vendors? And are you ready for the next zero day exploit or virus? This dependence on reactive technology is causing considerable grief and has cost many companies millions of dollars.

The CSA introduces a security paradigm shift from reactive signature-based technology to proactive intrusion-prevention technology. The agent uses policies and rules to ensure good behavior is allowed and bad/malicious behavior will be stopped. It also can enforce your corporate security policy. You can make sure the employees can do their work, but you can prevent them from downloading or installing software, as well as prevent them from listening to music or watching videos at work. You can also enforce application control: instant messenger applications are allowed, but only Yahoo! and, within that instant messenger application, you can only use the chat functionality, but not the file transfer, e-mail, or audio/video features.

Security functionalities include the following:

▼ **Application Related**

- Application run control
- Executable file-version control
- Protection against code injection
- Protection of process memory
- Protection against buffer overflows
- Protection against keystroke logging

- **Resource Related**

- File access control
- Network access control
- Configuration access control
- Execution space access control

- **Control of Executable Content**

- Protection against e-mail worms
- Protection against automatic execution of downloaded files or ActiveX controls

- **Network Related**

- HTTP filtering to remove bad behavior before it gets to the web server
- Connection rate limit where you can make sure your server only receives so many connections in a certain timeframe from a single host or from all the hosts Outbound limitations as well

- Detection
  - Packet sniffers and unauthorized protocols
  - Network scans
  - Monitoring of OS event logs

Implementation—A Safe Approach

The CSA infrastructure is already part of Cisco's SAFE architecture. Make sure the MC is deployed in a physically safe environment because it's the key to the kingdom. As with any other security product it is important to have a deployment strategy, this deployment strategy includes getting familiar with the product by evaluating it first, deploying it in test mode, and then, when you're satisfied, putting it in production.

Installation

Insert the Cisco Works VMS 2.2 CD into the drive. If autorun is enabled, the installation will begin automatically. If not, go to My Computer and double-click the CD. VMS 2.2 provides you with the management capabilities for IDS, PIX, and VPN Routers, as well as the CSA agents. We suggest you install the CSA MC on a separate machine. You must install both the Common Services and the Managing Cisco Security Agents. After you install the Common Services, the Managing Cisco Security Agents installation prompt you for the typical information, such as what directories to use. It will also install and configure the Microsoft SQL Server run-time engine (MSDE) for you.

In case you already have Microsoft SQL Server installed with Service Pack 3, the CSA will use that. At the end of the installation, the VMS/CSA MC agent will be installed to ensure utmost security. Because SQL has been the center of attention lately with the SQL Slammer exploit, the suggestion is that you fully patch the SQL server with the latest

---

System Requirements for the VMS 2.2 Installation

These are the system requirements for the Windows version of the VMS platform.

- ▼ Minimum of Intel Pentium 1 gigahertz or higher and up to two processors
- 1 gigabyte of RAM Memory (more memory will give you better results)
- 1 gigabyte of Virtual Memory
- 9 gigabytes of HDD Space
- ▲ 1 NIC Card only

security patches and hotfixes. Remember, the agent service will protect the SQL Server from being exploited, so it's good security practice to be fully patched.

Getting Started

1. Log on to VMS2.2 by going to Start | Programs | Cisco Works | Cisco Works
2. Acknowledge the certificate
3. Type **admin** and your password in the login prompt
4. Click VPN Security Management Solution (VMS2.2)
5. Click Management Center
6. Click Security Agents

The CSA MC will open a new window in your browser. Let's examine the interface and the options available. Table 9-5 gives an overview of each option and how it can be used.

Monitor	Status Summary	Quick Network overview. This view shows you the alerts, the active agents, and the agents that need to be updated or haven't polled.
	Event Log	The Event Log displays a snapshot of the current events.
	Event Log Management	This option lets you manage your event log by setting up jobs to delete old events you no longer want.
	Event Monitor	This is the same as Event Log, but it cycles every 15 seconds to give you the latest event information.
	Alerts	You can have alerts sent to you via pager, e-mail, or SNMP.
	Event Sets	Event Sets are information you want to be alerted about, such as Trojan events or mission critical events.
System	Groups	Groups are setup by functionality, such as HR or web servers. See the following for more information on groups.
	Hosts	When a host registers with the MC, it appears in this view. You can click on it and get detailed information about the host as to what OS, which groups it belongs to, and so forth.

Table 9-5. Overview of Menu Options

Configuration	Policies	The CSA ships with over 30 policies for applications that are commonly used. You can use these or add new ones. The default policies are a great start.
	Variables	These are variables. The CSA uses variables like $email-clients to make administration of policies easier. Instead of writing executables over and over, you use a File Set. File Sets include Applications, Registry, COM and Network addresses, and Services.
	Application Classes	*Application classes* are groupings of application executable files that you combine under one name, generally as part of a File Set Variable.
	Application Class Management	You can manage all your Application classes here.
	Global Event Correlation	The CSA has built-in event correlation for network scans, potential worms, Event Log messages, as well as antivirus events.
	Audit Trail	The *audit trail* keeps track of all changes that were made and who made them.
	Export/Import	The Export/Import feature lets you move data from one MC to another by exporting the data and importing it on the other MC.
	Registration Control	The MC can set restrictions on who can register with the MC. This is done by IP addresses.
	Agent Kits	The CSA ships with pre-built agent kits that can be deployed. You can also create new ones from groups you created.
	Software Updates	You have two options: Available Software Updates and Scheduled Software Updates. After the management console is upgraded or updated, this new version will display under Available Software Updates. You then schedule updates for the agents under Scheduled Software Updates to execute when this is convenient for you.
	License Information	You can see your licensing information here, as well as apply a new license if you made additions.
	Backup Configuration	Backing up your database is important because all your information is saved in the SQL database.

Table 9-5.   Overview of Menu Options *(continued)*

Profiler	Analysis Job	Create a new profiling job to analyze an application to create a new policy.
	Analysis Report	This provides you with a report of what the profiler has seen, for example, what files were accessed, which network ports were used, and so forth.
Reports	Events by Severity	This report shows you all the events sorted by severity.
	Events by Group	This report shows you all the events sorted by group.
	Host Detail	This report gives you the host detail, name, OS, and which groups and policies it uses.
	Policy Detail	This report gives you a detailed list of all the policies.
	Group Detail	This report gives you a detailed overview of all the groups.
Search	Hosts	You can search for specific hosts here.
	Groups	You can search for groups here.
	Policies	You can search for policies here.
	Rules	You can search for rules within policies here.
	Variables	You can search for Variables, such as File Sets, and so forth.
	Application Classes	You can search for Application Classes.
	All	This lets you search for everything.
Help	Online Help	Online Help will bring you to the help of where you're located right now. If you're in Policy creation, it displays step-by-step instructions on how to do that.
	Technical Support	This gives you the contact information for technical support.
	About...	Information about the agent for example, version is displayed.

Table 9-5. Overview of Menu Options *(continued)*

Agent Kits

Agent kits are the actual binary that will get installed on the laptops, desktops, and servers. These agent kits contain groups. The CSA ships with predefined kits for you to use for both Windows and Unix systems.

To create new agent kits, go to maintenance, and then click on agent kits. Choose new and, when prompted, choose the OS for which you want this kit. Add a description and

choose the groups you want to be part of this agent kit. Agent kits can be part of more then one group, that is, web and database server.

The agents are created on the MC, and then are deployed via your software distribution method of choice, such as logon script, ftp, Tivoli, SMS, CA, link to pull it from the MC or ghost images. Ensuring that the agent can talk to the MC over SSL is also important. Otherwise, it can't register.

Groups

This is the streamlined process to assign policies to numerous hosts at once. These groups are collections of policy modules with specific behavior enforcement for the functionality of the host.

Make sure your group hosts according to the following criteria:

▼　System functionality, such as web or database servers. You would create a policy that corresponds specifically to the needs of your web and database servers, and distribute it to that group.

■　Business groups, such as HR, finance, operations, security, and marketing. Tailor policies based on each business group's individual needs. Allow your security group to make its own decisions, but not your other groups.

■　Geographical or topological location. For example, group hosts based on their subnet designation for reporting purposes.

▲　Importance to your organization. Place mission-critical systems into a common group to apply critical alert-level configurations to them.

Policies

Every corporate enterprise should have security policies in place. The policies you create on the CSA MC should enforce these guidelines. CSA ships with over 30 preconfigured policies you can use. Additional policies can be created manually, as well as via the profiler.

Table 9-6 shows a list of a few policies already included.

Unix	Windows
Apache	Apache
IPlanet	IIS
IDS Systems	IDS Systems
Default Server	Default Server
Mission Critical System	Default Desktop
Sendmail	Restrictive DNS/DHCP

Table 9-6.　Preconfigured Policies in CSA

Rules

Rules give you control over all the different shims. They make sure good behavior is allowed and bad behavior is stopped. Table 9-7 lists the types of rules you can create.

Agent service control	Controls who can suspend security, as well as turn off or uninstall the agent. Options are Administrators, everyone, or a certain application.	Unix and Windows
Application control	Enforces which application can start another application.	Unix and Windows
COM component access control	Controls which application can access COM objects.	Windows
Buffer overflow	Controls specific buffer overflow. Windows has built-in control.	Unix
Connection rate limit	Creates a rule that enables you to limit how many concurrent connections from a single host or from all the hosts it can receive. This also works for outbound traffic.	Unix and Windows
Data access control	Lets you filter out behavior before it hits the web server.	Unix and Windows
File access control	Creates rules that controls read and write access to files. You can control the download or installation of any file.	Unix and Windows
File monitor	Monitors for file changes.	Unix and Windows
File version control	Enforces which versions are allowed to run on the endpoint. IE version 6.2 is allowed, but not the next beta release.	Unix and Windows
Network access control	Controls which application can act as a client or server talking to what IP addresses over what service.	Windows
Network interface control	Controls whether an interface can be put in promiscuous mode.	Unix
Network worm protection	Protects against worm damage and propagation.	Windows

Table 9-7. Rules to Create

Network shield	Protects against network-based exploit, such as malformed IP packets, and so forth. This is a built-in rule under Windows.	Unix
NT Event log	Enables you to control which event log information you want to collect.	Windows
Resource access control	Controls access to system resources.	Unix
Registry access control	Governs which application can read or write which registry keys.	Windows
Rootkit/Kernel protection	Protects against root kits and kernel modification.	Unix
Service restart	Lets you have services, such as IIS, to restart automatically, in case it doesn't respond to the user or the system.	Windows

Table 9-7. Rules to Create *(continued)*

Rules are enforced by six different action levels, as shown in Table 9-8. Rules are created as follows:

1. Go to Configuration.
2. Go to Policies.
3. Choose a policy you want to add rules to or create a new one.
4. Click modify rules.

Add Process to Application Class	Priority 1
High-Priority Deny	Priority 2
Allow	Priority 3
User Query (Default Allow)	Priority 4
User Query (Default Deny)	Priority 5
Deny	Priority 6

Table 9-8. Action Levels

5. Click add.

6. Chose a rule from the drop-down menu.

7. Add a description.

8. Choose an action level from the drop down menu.

9. Only deny and user query rules are logged by default.

10. Choose application class, that is, network application, all applications (see Figure 9-2).

11. Depending on the rule you have chosen, make the appropriate choices.

12. Save and generate the rules.

These rules are automatically sent out to the groups they're associated with.

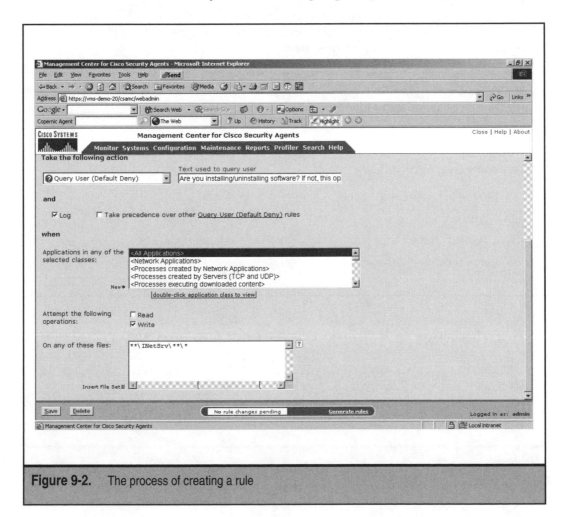

Figure 9-2.   The process of creating a rule

Evaluation

Cisco provides you with an evaluator's guide that shows you how to test this type of technology. This guide is available at http://www.cisco.com/en/US/partner/products/sw/secursw/ps5057/index.html. This will prompt you to log in with your CCO account. It's important for you to test this technology completely. Make sure you use at least two desktops and servers, so you're comfortable deploying these agents. You'll quickly discover the difference between a personal firewall, an IDS, file integrity, and malicious mobile code product and the CSA technology. Understanding the defense in-depth that the CSA uses is important. Reactive products usually only use a single line of defense.

Train/Learn

CSA offers you the capability to create custom policies for any applications. This could make such a system fairly complex. Because the default policies cover any application—store-bought or homegrown—you should start by using the default server and default desktop groups, make copies of them, and then create the agent kits you want to deploy. These default policies are what Cisco believes should be your basic security measures. Agents always should be deployed in *test mode*, which is a nonintrusive way of observing how the agent is going to impact your system. Instead of preventing the action, test mode lets you know what it would have done if it had been in prevent mode. You should run in test mode until you've adapted to your environment. After a few weeks of running in test mode, you can change to prevent mode.

NOTE   Always deploy in test mode first

The CSA also has an add-on product called the *profiler*, which lets you take any executable and run an analyzer against it. The profiler is a snap-in to the CSA MC that turns on functionality in the agent itself. It uses the same technology used to prevent the malicious behavior by using the shims (network, file, configuration, execution space) to collect all the behavior of the application, such as what network connections the application is performing, what files and directories it's touching, which registry keys are read or written, and what COM objects were used during the run. That information is then analyzed and a policy is created that can be imported into the MC and deployed to the agents.

▼   **Test**   Make sure you run all your applications to check if they trigger any of the default rules. Common mistakes are things like monthly backups get forgotten and denied because backup.exe tried to touch all the files. Check the event log periodically to make adjustments by using the wizard functionality. The wizard lets you create exceptions right from alerts that were reported to the MC.

- **Promote to production** After you run the agents in test mode for a few weeks (most people run it for two to four weeks in that environment), move a few machines in to prevent mode. Beware, though, because prevent mode is done by group. If you create agent kits with more than one group, if one group is in test mode, the agent kit will be in test mode. Let these systems run and observe them. When you feel comfortable, move the rest of the agents over to prevent mode.

- **System maintenance** The CSA doesn't require constant changes and updates as you're used to from other signature-based reactive technologies. There are no signature updates or pattern updates because this system doesn't use any. Therefore, changes are much less frequent then you usually would see. These changes might include the following:

  - **Configuration changes** These types of changes are usually changes in your environment. A database server is now located at a different IP address, so the policy needs to reflect this change to make sure your web server now points to the new IP address. Other changes might be if you want to introduce a new application and you want to make sure it's secure. The CSA MC includes over 30 default application policies of applications commonly used in the corporate environment, such as Microsoft Office, SQL, ISS, DNS/DHCP, Apache, IPlanet, and so forth. These policies give you more granular control over these applications.

  - **Application patches** Patches to the applications usually don't require any changes made to the policies or rules. If you feel you need to make sure of that, run the profiler against the patched application. In that case, you can quickly see if something has changed.

  - **OS patches** Unless some fundamental changes exist, they don't require you to make any changes to the policies and rules or the CSA agent code itself. Service Packs usually are tested by Cisco, and then officially supported in the next release. Service Pack 4 is officially supported in CSA version 4.01. No changes were made to the agent because of the Service Pack. You can install this OS patch in two ways: one is simply to turn the agent service off while you install it. The reason is the agent would prompt you because of the behavior of the patch-overwriting system files. The other way to install the OS patch is to create a job with the profiler. The profiler would analyze the patch as to what it does and how it behaves. After it finishes, you can then deploy this policy to all the endpoints before you patch. In that case, the behavior is expected.

- ▲ **OS upgrades** OS upgrades usually require changes made to the agents because some fundamental differences exist between OS releases. Changes from NT to Windows 2000 were quite fundamental, as are the changes from Windows 2000 to Windows 2003. The procedure for an OS upgrade suggests the agent kit be removed first, and then the upgrade be performed. At the end, deploy a new agent kit to the machines.

Agent Maintenance

The agent has two different versions of maintenance: one is a new version upgrade and one is patches. These upgrades are all made to the Management Server.

New Versions

Cisco releases upgrades periodically where it introduces new functionality, as well as new OS support. This happens about once a year. Version 4.0 introduced the following new functionality:

▼ Policies for CiscoWorks, VPN Client, Unity, Call Manager, and Personal Assistant

■ HTTP shim

■ Connection rate limiting

▲ Integration into Cisco's SecMon

Patches

Patches are released as needed. Remember, no pattern or signature updates are necessary at any time. The CSA doesn't use them.

▼ **Upgrading the management server**   After a new upgrade or patch is released, you can go to www.cisco.com. Log in your CCO user name and password, and then download the new software. First, uninstall the agent running on the CSA MC. To upgrade the Cisco Security Agent, run the setup.exe file on the CSA MC system. When you run the setup file, follow the instructions that appear onscreen. After the installation is complete, install a new agent kit.

Application Forensics

The CSA offers security for store-purchased applications, as well as homegrown applications. By using the profiler functionality, the CSA enables you to create specific policies for that critical application you were worried about.

▼ **Learning what your applications are "really" doing**   A great benefit of running the profiler against any of your applications is that it will tell you exactly what this application is doing. For example, you have a legacy application that was written for NT many years ago. The programmer left the job and you need to make sure you understand the application and that proper security is deployed. This is, indeed, a difficult task because that programmer probably used classes or modules from other programmers for functions that someone already created before him. This leaves you with many potential security holes. The CSA Profiler is a snap-in to the CSA MC. It turns on functionality in the agents to collect all the information about the behavior of an application. The CSA Profiler uses the shims the CSA technology uses to collect this data. After the data is collected, it's

then sent back to the MC for analyzing. A report is generated, so you can see all the different behavior, such as file access, network access, and so forth.

▲ **Ensuring software performs are promised**   The profiler can also help you to make sure all the applications perform as designed. You could quickly see if an application is spawning off processes to start other applications or use COM objects to send out information over e-mail or IRC.

Patching

Patching has become an increasing nightmare. It's a constant race to stay on top of the latest updates mandated by the OS vendors. Rolling out patches requires a strict change management control system to be in place.

▼ **Take control of the patch process**   The CSA gets you out of the constant race of keeping up with patches. You can take control of the process by testing the patch rigorously before you deploy it out to the hosts, making sure you aren't breaking anything. The behavior enforcement ensures these hosts are protected at all times.

Integration with Other Cisco Products

▼ **SecMon**   The CSA agent has been fully integrated with the security monitoring offered by VMS2.2. This enables you to collect and view logs from your IDS devices and Pix firewalls, as well as VPN Routers and CSA agents. When you compare the network-related events to the events reported by the hosts, you can quickly analyze this data to see where threats came in.

■ **VPN Client 4.0**   The CSA integrates with the Cisco VPN Client version 4.0. The initial integration currently offered is the VPN Client will check for the presence of the CSA agent. If the agent isn't running, the VPN Client will be unable to establish a tunnel. Because of the nature of the CSA agent, you can ensure end-to-end protection by controlling which application on which server the VPN users are allowed to use.

▲ **SIMS**   The CSA MC offers full integration with all the major Security Information Management Systems, including Netforensics, Microsmuse, Arcsight, and so forth. It can also forward any events to SNMP Collectors. These Security Information Management Systems try to support all vendors. They enable you to collect information for all different network devices, as well as different hosts agents.

SUMMARY

This chapter focused on the Cisco product line of IDS products uncluding appliance-based NIDS, compatible modules for routers and switches, and software-based solutions for certain releases of the Cisco IOS. The chapter also covered the Cisco safe architecture and how it has evolved. We also examined implementation issues and how the products should be maintained.

CHAPTER 10

Snort

Many IDSs, some commercial, some in the public domain, are currently available. Of all the IDSs, few have generated as much enthusiasm within the user community as has *Snort*, a public domain tool. Originally developed by Marty Roesch, Snort has, in many respects, become synonymous with new IDS capabilities. Many individuals have contributed code that has provided new functions and enhancements. Snort is now the most widely deployed IDS of all. This chapter covers the basics of Snort, its IDS components and functions, Snort rules, Snort output, special hardware and software requirements, some of the enhancements in Snort 2.0, and the advantages and limitations of this tool.

ABOUT SNORT

Snort (see http://www.snort.org) is a rule-based IDS. Snort uses signatures to identify types of attacks that occur but, unlike a pure signature-based IDS, Snort does not stop there. It also uses and provides considerable additional contextual information, including how attacks have transpired and what the origin of each attack appears to be (thus leading to its being classified as a "rule-based" IDS). In version 2.0, the current version, it provides extensive protocol analysis, as well as other more sophisticated detection capabilities. This tool runs on a variety of operating systems (OSs), including Windows NT and 2000, Unix (Solaris, HP-UX, IRIX, OpenBSD, NetBSD, Free BSD, and Mac OS X), Linux, and even on PowerPCs. Although mainly known and deployed as a NIDS, Snort can serve as a HIDS if it is configured to analyze only traffic to and from an individual host. Its detection engine depends on a rudimentary language that serves as a basis for recognizing input patterns that characterize attacks. Snort deploys rules for decoding data within packets as well as packet headers, helping it recognize data-driven attacks, such as buffer overflow and improperly encoded web server chuck attacks. This IDS also provides quick and easy access to raw packet data to support inspecting network traffic more closely or reporting Snort's findings. You can download Snort from http://www.snort.org/dl.

TIP   Although this chapter is intended to provide a working knowledge and a birds-eye view of Snort, a single chapter cannot do justice to the many details related to it. Obtaining a book on Snort, such as Brian Caswell's *Snort 2.0: Intrusion Detection* (published by Syngress Press) is the best course of action for someone who wants to thoroughly understand the in's and out's of Snort.

Snort was originally developed not to be an end-all IDS but, rather, as a simple and flexible supplement to be run in parallel with other IDSs. The goals of Snort include to:

▼   Cause minimal interference with system and network performance. Accordingly, Snort 2.0, the latest version at press time, contains only about 75,000 lines of code.

■   Run within numerous parts of networks, gathering data that can be collected at a single point.

■   Optimize the hit rate, while keeping the false alarm rate at a minimum.

- Offer easy-to-use reporting functions.
- Work in real time in detecting incidents and providing alerts.
▲ Provide packet capture capabilities. As mentioned previously in Chapter 6, being able to get to packet data quickly is a critical feature in IDSs.

SNORT MODES

Snort runs in three different modes: sniffer mode, packet logger mode, and intrusion detection mode. This section discusses all three modes.

Sniffer Mode

Running Snort in Sniffer mode allows you to dump data in the header and body of each packet to the screen. To start Snort so that it displays all application data, enter the following:

```
./snort -d (this works in most versions of Snort)
```

   or

```
./snort -dv (in the current version—you need to enter the "-v" option
to keep from getting an error message)
```

To display packet headers for IP (layer 3) and TCP, UDP, and ICMP (layer 4) packets to the screen, enter the following:

```
./snort -v
```

To display both the layer 3 and 4 packet headers, and the application data, enter the following:

```
./snort -dv OR ./snort -d -v
```

Note, entering the –e flag causes the link layer (level 2) headers also to be displayed to a screen.

Packet Logger Mode

Packet logger mode is different from Sniffer mode in that in the former, packet data and/or headers are written to the hard drive of the host on which Snort runs. To write to a directory named log on the hard drive, enter the following:

```
./snort -dev -l ./log
```

To ensure logging captures data for a local network, it is also necessary to enter the IP address range of the network, as follows:

```
./snort -dev -l ./log -h 10.1.1.0/24
```

Note, in this example, once again, the source and destination IP addresses are private addresses—addresses that would not work for moving packets over the Internet—to avoid calling attention to any particular real-world addresses. The −h flag and the following argument ensures that Snort will log the packets for which the destination IP address is in the range from 10.1.1.0 to 10.1.1.255. A separate subdirectory under log will be created for each address. If Snort runs on a high-speed network, entering the −b switch, which will cause binary output, all of which goes to a single directory, is a good alternative. Other flags such as −d, -e, and −v are unnecessary because, in binary mode, *everything* in the packet—header and application data—is dumped. Note, also, that entering the −r flag causes Snort to play back the data in any specified tcpdump-formatted file. Finally, to view only one type of data (such as TCP data only), you can use bpf's capabilities to filter out unwanted traffic by entering the following:

```
./snort -dvr packet.log tcp
```

 If Snort is started with the -b flag, any packet in which Snort becomes interested is recorded. If you have tagged a stream to be examined, it, too, will be recorded in a libpcap-style file.

Network Intrusion Detection Mode

Sniffer or packet logger modes are appropriate for bulk data capture, but sorting through volumes of packet data to determine whether a security breach has occurred is not practical. Snort's network intrusion detection mode does not record packets but, rather, allows rules that you select to be applied. (Rules are covered in the section "Snort Rules.") snort.conf is the file that, by default, contains these rules (although nearly any file you specify could be used instead). Snort will inspect only the traffic defined in snort.conf's rule set.

A basic way to start Snort in intrusion detection mode is to enter the following:

```
./snort -dev -l ./log -h 10.1.1.0/24 -c snort.conf
```

Failing to enter an output directory will result in the output being written to /var/log/snort. Note, also, that the previously discussed flags can be entered in this mode, although the usefulness of entering some of these flags, such as the −e flag, which results in a dump of each link layer header, in the context of this mode is questionable.

SNORT'S IDS COMPONENTS

Snort has four main IDS components: the packet capture engine, the preprocessor plug-ins, the detection engine, and the output plug-ins, as illustrated in Figure 10-1. We'll start with the packet capture engine.

Packet Capture Engine

The first component is the *packet capture engine* that picks up traffic using libpcap or WinPcap (both of which will from now on be collectively referred to simply as "pcap").

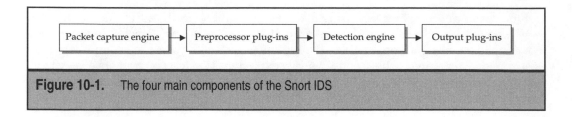

Figure 10-1.   The four main components of the Snort IDS

pcap is a library that enables applications to receive *datagrams*, parcels through which datalink-level data (data at level two of the seven-layer OSI model) are carried. The network interface card (NIC) physically captures the network traffic and passes it on to drivers that interface with the OS kernel. After the kernel processes the data, pcap then takes the data from the kernel and passes them on to Snort applications, which are normally drivers that interface with the third Snort component, the preprocessor plug-ins. For example, the data go through a bpf interpreter if the kernel supports it. The interpreter decides to which applications the data will be passed. If the no interpreter exists, pcap sends all the packets to the applications, which need to have filters to avoid being bombarded with data.

 As discussed in Chapter 6, someone who wants to capture network traffic normally has to put at least one network interface on a host in promiscuous mode. One nice thing about pcap, however, is it is not necessary to put the network interface(s) through which network traffic will be captured in promiscuous mode—pcap does this automatically.

Preprocessor Plug-Ins

Snort's preprocessor plug-ins test and inspect packet data they receive from pcap, determining what to do with each packet—whether to analyze it, change it, reject it, and/or generate an alert because of it. The preprocessor plug-ins are highly advantageous because they establish a structure for dealing with packets before they're sent to the next component. Preprocessors modify URIs and URLs to conform to a standard format, provide stateful analysis of TCP/IP traffic, detect portscans, decode RPC packets, decode telnet packets, as well as serve other functions. They also alleviate having to deal with a wide range of undesirable and potentially malicious packet data, including data that could crash Snort or radically deteriorate its performance. Unless a preprocessor plug-in has rejected certain input, it passes it to the next component, the detection engine.

Detection Engine

The third major component is the detection engine. Packets are first decoded in a manner that defines the packet structure for layer two protocols, and then layer three protocols, and so on. This enables the *detection engine* to systematically compare data within every packet it receives to the rule options. This engine then conducts basic tests on whatever part(s) of each packet contain(s) a particular string or value associated with a rule, and

then performs another such test using the next rule, and so forth until tests for all rules Snort knows about have been done. Any match is a "hit." The detection engine then moves on to the next packet. A variety of plug-ins (which at the latest count numbered 22, as of version 2.0.2) can also be used to conduct extra detection tests on packets. Every key-word option in every rule is, in fact, associated with a plug-in which, if used, increases the detection engine's capability to identify attacks.

Output Plug-Ins

The final major component of Snort is the output plug-ins, the major purpose of which is to produce information to be displayed to intrusion detection analysts. Snort creates alerts based on alerting rules within the preprocessors, the decode engines, and the detection engine. An example of the output of the output plug-ins appears in section "Snort Output." Other output plug-ins perform a variety of other functions, as discussed in the following technical note.

NOTE   Although the Snort IDS has four major components, new development efforts have resulted in new functions that are likely to prove as important as the four components covered in this chapter. A flexible response plug-in, flexresp2, for instance, enables Snort users to set up rules that result in dropping undesirable connection attempts—a "shunning" capability that makes Snort not just an IDS, but also now (at least to some degree) an IPS.

SNORT RULES

The rules Snort uses are at the heart of its IDS functionality. This section explores the nature of these rules, considerations related to the ordering of rules, and how to write rules.

The Nature of Snort Rules

Among the many types of rules are those for FTP and web attacks, distributed DoS attacks, attempts to exploit weaknesses in the Server Message Block (SMB) protocol in Windows systems, and Remote Procedure Call (RPC) attacks. Each rule corresponds to a number, a Sensor ID (SID) that enables everyone to distinguish one from another easily. For example, the following code listing shows the rule for the Apache web server chunked-encoding memory-corruption vulnerability exploit. When processing requests coded with a type of encoding mechanism called the "chunked encoding" mechanism, Apache incorrectly determines buffer sizes needed. Consequently, specially formulated input from a malicious browser can cause a buffer overflow that could result in the execution of rogue code on an Apache server. Note, the signature is in the second through fifth lines. The Common Vulnerabilities and Exposures (CVE)—see http://www.cve.mitre.org) numbers (both of which start with CAN) are in the eighth and ninth lines. The SID for this attack is 1807, as an inspection of line 9 shows.

```
alert tcp $EXTERNAL_NET any -> $HTTP_SERVERS $HTTP_PORTS \
(msg:"WEB-MISC Transfer-Encoding\: chunked"; \
flow:to_server,established;\
content:"Transfer-Encoding\:"; nocase; \
content:"chunked"; nocase; \
classtype:web-application-attack; \
reference:bugtraq,4474; \
reference:cve,CAN-2002-0079; reference:bugtraq,5033; \
reference:cve,CAN-2002-0392; sid:1807; rev:1;)
```

Over time, the number of available rules has increased substantially as more exploitation methods have been developed. As a result, Snort's rules have become organized on the basis of type of rule, with related rules having SIDs within a certain numerical range. For example, the NetBIOS attack rules currently have sequentially numbered SIDs 529 through 539 (and a few others not within this range), as do telnet attack rules (which currently have SIDs 709 through 714, plus a few others outside this range). Anyone who deploys Snort can choose to use all the rules or can select only a subset of all the rules. Using all the rules results in a more complete detection capability, but at the disadvantage of slower performance. The more rules Snort must find and test, the slower Snort works. On the other hand, someone might want to use Snort for a special purpose, such as detecting only attacks directed at Windows systems. In this case, you might want to include only NetBIOS, MS-SQL, virus, web-IIS, and a few other rules.

NOTE One potential problem with a signature and rule-based intrusion detection system is keeping signatures and rules current. Snort goes a long way in solving this problem by supporting the most recent rules only on the most current version. For example, the most recent rules work only on Snort 2.0, the most recent version at press time.

Rule Order

The Snort 2.0 detection engine examines five rule chains: Activation, Dynamic, Alert, Pass, and Log (as shown in Figure 10-2). By default, Activation rules (which generate an alert, and then activate some other dynamic rule) are applied first, and then Dynamic rules (which cause a packet to be logged when they're triggered by an Activation rule), and then Alert rules (which issue an alert, and then log a packet), followed by Pass rules (used for ignoring certain kinds of packets, such as traffic from DNS servers, as well as to cause the use of the bpf filter language when Snort starts), followed by Log rules (which cause a packet to be logged, but without any alert). The ordering of any rule chain can easily be modified, however. To start Snort with full logging only (as indicated by the –l flag) and also to have Snort read the default configuration file for applying rules, enter the following:

```
./snort -l ./log -c snort.conf
```

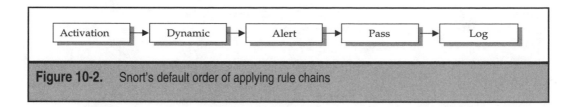

Figure 10-2. Snort's default order of applying rule chains

The –l flag means to use full logging and the ./log argument means to log to a file named log in the current directory. The –c flag means to read Snort's default configuration file, which is snort.conf.

In Snort 1.*x*, if you want one rule applied before another, simply ensure the flag for that rule is to the left of the flag for another when you start Snort via the command line. In Snort 1.*x*, flags are always read and processed sequentially, left to right. Things are different in Snort 2.0, however. The rule-optimization mechanism in Snort takes apart the individual parts (flags, content requests, and so forth), and then creates an optimized list of rules that normally needs to be checked only once or, under unusual conditions, twice. The pattern-matching algorithm for content searching has also been changed to the Wu-Manber or Aho-Corasick algorithm (the choice is yours), resulting in much greater efficiency.

Once Snort 2.0 has applied a rule chain, it goes to the Rule Tree Nodes, further protocol-specific rules to be applied. The *Rule Tree Nodes* analyze TCP, UDP, ICMP, and IP traffic. Within each Rule Tree Node are options, one for Content, which results in a pattern-matching algorithm being applied to packet data and the other for Flow, which results in a detection plug-in being applied.

Writing Snort Rules

Another nice thing about Snort is that it is so extensible. Anyone who uses Snort can create custom rules that are not in the default rule set. Each rule consists of two parts: the rule header and rule option. The *rule header* contains the rule's action (alert, log, pass, activate, or dynamic, as discussed previously, or also custom for home-built rules), type of protocol, source and destination IP addresses, masks, and source and destination port. The *rule option* has the content of alert messages, as well as information concerning the portion of each packet that will be analyzed to decide if the action specified will be carried out. In the following example, if the signature (06 4a 05 42) for a Windows NET SEND message is found in a UDP packet, regardless of the particular source IP address, an alert labeled Windows messenger service message is issued.

```
alert udp any any -> 10.1.1.0/24 135 (content:"| 06 4a 05 42|" ; msg:
"Windows messenger service message";)
```

Given all the possible variables that can be specified in each Snort rule, the number of potential rule options is mind-boggling.

Snort Filters

To help control the volume of traffic with which Snort must deal, Snort also provides filters. Filters control what data Snort does and does not dump. For example, if you wanted Snort to pick up all DNS-related traffic, UDP traffic destined for port 53, you could define the following filter:

```
udp and dst port 53
```

Then you would have to enter a command to activate this filter:

```
# tcpdump udp and dst port 53
```

The effect would be to examine a file that tcpdump writes to for every access to port 53.

SNORT OUTPUT

The Snort-alerting function allows alert data to be sent as SNMP trap data (as covered first in this section) or to be appended to a log file or a database (such as a MySQL and Postres database).

Alerts

Understanding the format of Snort alerts and the various alert modes is essential for using alerts effectively. This section covers both of these issues.

Alert Format

Each detect is shown in double-spaced log files, as shown in the following code:

```
[**] SCAN-SYN FIN [**]
11/02-16:01:36.792199 10.0.0.1:21 -> 192.168.0.1:21
TCP TTL:24 TOS:0x0 ID:39426
**SF**** Seq: 0x27896E4 Ack: 0xB35C4BD Win: 0x404
 [**] SCAN-SYN FIN [**]
11/02-16:01:36.803980 10.0.0.1:21 -> 192.168.0.1:21
TCP TTL:25 TOS:0x0 ID:39426
**SF**** Seq: 0x27896E4 Ack: 0xB35C4BD Win: 0x404
```

Snort always shows the rule that was applied at the top, followed by summary information concerning the packet. In this example, Snort has labeled both of the TCP packets as part of a scan in which SYN-FIN packets have been sent to the destination host. These packets have been fabricated, as shown by the fact that the ID, sequence number, and acknowledgement number do not change from one packet to the next, as well as the fact that the source port (TCP port 21) is the same as the destination port, something that does

not happen in real life. Whoever ran this scan may have been interested in discovering FTP-related vulnerabilities in the host at the destination address. Sending SYN/ACK packets without a previous SYN packet is a hacker trick designed to get the packets through firewalls that do not do stateful analysis of traffic. Nonstateful firewalls will accept SYN/ACK packets at face value, allowing them through, thinking the three-way TCP handshake sequence can be completed with a subsequent SYN packet from the client.

Alert Modes

Snort offers several Alert modes, each with its own special flag:

▼ **–Full** In this mode, Snort prints both the alert message content and the entire packet header for each packet. This is the default mode.

■ **–fast** Choosing this mode results in a simplified format that contents the time, the message itself, and source and destination IP address and ports.

■ **–socket** This option results in alerts being sent to a Unix socket to allow the data to be passed to a program.

■ **–syslog** This option results in the syslog facility in Unix and Linux (or even Windows systems in which this facility has been implemented) to be used to send the alerts. One of the greatest advantages of this option is that alerts from various Snort boxes can be sent to a central console.

■ **–smb** SMB is the Server Message Block, a protocol used by Windows systems (and also by SAMBA running on Linux and Unix) to transfer information from one host to another. Choosing the –smb option causes this protocol to be used to send alerts.

▲ **–none** Entering this option shuts off alerting altogether.

Log Files

Snort has two output options for writing to log files: ASCII (default) and binary. Although ASCII is sufficient most of the time, binary output is desirable when you need Snort to run as fast as possible and when interoperability with other tcpdump output is desirable. In fact, if you start Snort using both the –b (binary) and –A ("fast") options, Snort can keep up with fairly high throughput rates. The syntax is as follows:

```
./snort -b -A fast -c snort.conf
```

The result will be that packets will be logged in tcpdump format with few alerts generated. The more alerts, the slower Snort runs.

SPECIAL REQUIREMENTS

Snort, like any other IDS, has certain kinds of hardware and software requirements. This section discusses these requirements.

Hardware

In many respects, Snort is what you make it. You can run a bare bones deployment of Snort with most features disabled. If you do this, you will not need much in the way of disk space and special hardware. But most Snort deployments are much bigger. In this case, disk space is critical. Sufficient disk space is necessary for keeping all the data Snort's detection engine uses to look for rule matches. Additionally, Snort can archive packet data (which, as those who have used tcpdump of a pcap program know well, can produce an unbelievable amount of data) and write to log files or produce alerts. Testing how fast a Snort host's hard drive fills up for a given deployment of this tool is best, but nothing less than 10 to 20GB will normally do. Additionally, a single NIC is not likely to be sufficient. One NIC is necessary for promiscuous capture of network traffic but, another is generally required to allow remote connectivity to each Snort host for maintenance and operational access purposes. The larger the volume of data, the more likely a large amount of memory (such as 1GB of RAM) and a fast processor (such as 1GHz) will be needed. The same is true of the NIC that captures traffic.

Software

Once you obtain the hardware you need, you have to select an OS on which to run Snort. Although, in theory, Snort can run on virtually any Unix or Linux platform, some potential problems exist with certain platforms. Solaris, for example, does not support bpf, something needed in many Snort deployments. Additionally, Snort can run on platforms such as Windows NT and Windows 2000 but, if you choose a Windows OS, then you must deal with the many eccentricities (including a legion of security-related woes) of these systems. You also need current versions of the following software:

- ▼ A pcap implementation
- ■ gcc, automake, and autoconf (only if you compile Snort from source)
- ■ lex and yacc, or flex and bison (depending on the parsing environment needed)
- ▲ libnet 1.0.2a for the latest version of flexrep (if you want automated report generation)

If you want to dump Snort bulk trace dumps to a database, you need a database engine such as Oracle, MySQL, or Postres. If you want to monitor Snort, a convenient way to do this is to set up an Apache or Internet Information Server (IIS) server on the Snort host. (Caution: because of all the security problems that have surfaced in IIS, be sure to configure this web server properly and keep up with hot fixes if you decide to use it in connection with Snort.) Installing SSL and SSH on the web server ensures that all connections to and from the server will be encrypted. Certain Snort plugs-ins also require PHP and Perl. And, if you want to write Snort alerts to Windows hosts using WinPopup, you need to install smbclient.

MORE ABOUT SNORT 2.0

We've already covered some features of Snort 2.0, but many more features and enhancements exist than have been covered so far. This section covers additional features and enhancements of this Snort release.

New and Optimized Features

Snort 2.0 represents an effort both to improve Snort itself and to introduce new functionality. This functionality includes (but is not limited to)

▼ An optimized detection engine (discussed earlier)

■ A Protocol Flow Analyzer (discussed in the section "Protocol Flow Analyzer")

■ Improved protocol decoding (discussed in the section "Improved Protocol Decoding")

■ A new detection engine that includes a rule optimizer (discussed previously), a multirule search engine that deploys algorithms that use optimized rule sets, and an optimized event selector that more efficiently selects the appropriate event from the event queue for each packet Snort receives.

■ New, updated rules

■ Stateful pattern-matching based on knowing whether data sent between clients and servers has been sent by the client or the server

■ New pattern-matching algorithms

■ Keywords based on actual byte content

■ Enhancements to preprocessor plug-ins that reproduce session streams and reassemble packet fragments (named "stream4" and "frag2," respectively)

■ Improved anomaly detection for major protocols

■ An improved flexresp mode that allows special kinds of real-time countermeasures (such as sending RST packets or icmp host unreachable packets in response to packets from attacking hosts) to be deployed

■ An improved tag function that allows someone to log extra traffic that pertains to a matched rule

■ An updated version of snort.conf

■ Capability to create a virtual root (chrooted) directory other than the directory containing the Snort executable

▲ Elimination of numerous bugs from 1.*x* versions of Snort

Protocol Flow Analyzer

One of the most important new features in Snort 2.0 is the Protocol Flow Analyzer. This section describes what this analyzer is, its advantages, and how it performs one specific type of analysis: the analysis of HTTP traffic.

What Is the Protocol Flow Analyzer?

The Snort 2.0 Protocol Flow Analyzer performs a high-level inspection of application-protocol traffic, breaking it into two separate flows: client-to-server and also server-to-client data flows. Instead of analyzing everything in each protocol flow, it looks only for several critical important parts of each, such as the nature of a server response to a client request (as determined by the response header or data) or the type of request a client has sent to a server, and then performs a thorough analysis of the information it uses, looking for content matches within each protocol flow.

Advantages

The main advantages of the Protocol Flow Analyzer are performance and accuracy. This analyzer tries to diminish the volume of network traffic the fusion detection engine needs to evaluate. It does this by knowing how client- and server-based communications occur for each network protocol of which it is aware and weeding out data not related to attacks. This applies both to packet-level analysis and to TCP stream reassembly, resulting in a substantial reduction of the amount of data that must be inspected for content matches. Having to examine only parts of protocol flows helps speed processing considerably. Restricting analysis to only certain parts of client-to-server or server-to-client communications also helps lower the false alarm rate. The analyzer will not erroneously find matches based on data that would have been analyzed in the previous release of Snort, but that now are not analyzed.

CASE STUDY: The HTTP Flow Analyzer

The HTTP Flow Analyzer capitalizes on the fact that client requests generally contain relatively little data (because they generally consist of requests such as GETs and POSTs) compared to server responses. The overwhelming majority of server responses to client requests consist of response data, rather than response headers. Snort has a Fusion TCP State Engine that determines whether a client or server has sent data, allowing the HTTP Flow Analyzer to pick only the data flows of interest. Assuming a typical web server has at least an adequate level of security controls, presuming any data sent by that server are trusted and legitimate is reasonable. Client requests generally contain relatively little data compared to server responses and, as just mentioned, there is no reason to analyze server response data. The only parts of web-related traffic that need to be analyzed by the up to 500 HTTP-specific rules in Snort, therefore, are client packet headers, and data and server headers.

Packet-Based Versus Session-Based Processing

HTTP packets are processed in two ways: one is based on packets and the other is based on sessions. The following explains the differences.

Packet-Based Processing   As implied by its name, *packet-based processing* uses only information contained within each packet. When HTTP requests and responses are being processed packet-by-packet, the only processing information available is what is available in the packet. A variable you can set—HTTP Maximum Response Bytes—determines how many bytes within the packet will be processed. A few upfront checks verify the packet is a TCP packet, and the source port and destination ports appear legitimate and, finally, that the initial four bytes of the payload contain the string "HTTP" (meaning the packet is a response header, so the bytes in the packet will be processed until the byte corresponding to whatever the value of the HTTP Maximum Response Bytes parameter is reached). Otherwise, the packet is not processed, something that results in greatly improved processing efficiency.

Session-Based Processing   The key to understanding session-based processing is that it tracks the state of TCP connections. When client- or server-initiated HTTP data are sent, the HTTP Flow Analyzer determines whether they are part of an ongoing session. If not, the data are not analyzed. If they are part of an ongoing session, the analyzer determines whether the initial four bytes of the payload contain the string "HTTP." If so, the analyzer conducts an analysis of the entire HTTP header. If not, it moves on to the next packet.

Improved Protocol Decoding

Although the preprocessor function in Snort 1.*x* was by no means bad, Snort 2.0 offers a much-improved preprocessor functionality, including enhanced protocol decoding. One of the major problem areas in the Snort 1.*x* preprocessor function was its inability to adequately handle the huge potential range of data with which Snort had to deal. "Weird" data also often escaped analysis. One of the major improvements in the Snort 2.0 preprocessor function is that it converts a wide range of data to a standard format, so the data can be processed. For example, a major type of attack on web servers today is to send specially formatted URLs that the web server cannot properly process, often causing execution of commands embedded in the URLs or DoS. The potential number of URL formats that can be sent to a web server is gargantuan. Accordingly, Snort 2.0 has an http_decode preprocessor that converts URLs to a standard format before the Detection Engine attempts to perform content matching on them.

Another challenge, one by no means unique to Snort, is dealing with packet content in which additional characters were inserted into data sent as part of an attack. Hacking tools, such as Fragroute, can, for example, launch "insertion" attacks, in which malicious commands sent to a server are disguised from IDS recognition by inserting extra, illegitimate data. When the commands reach the IDS, the IDS does not recognize them as attack signatures. The victim host, meanwhile, often discards the bad data, allowing the commands to run on it. The following is an example of this kind of input:

```
GET //cgi-bin//any.cgi
```

This command represents an attempt to get to the ever-dangerous cgi-bin directory, something that could well happen (depending on whether the intended victim host accepts and processes this request anyway). Still another challenge is dealing with fragmented packets. Some of the preprocessors unify all fragments into a single fragment for processing purposes.

You can select preprocessors the preprocessors you want. Simply go to the snort.conf file located in ~(source_root)/etc/snort.conf.

ADDITIONAL TOOLS

Open source software has many advantages, one of which is that additional tools are often developed to expand the functionality of a package. Three tools—Swatch, ACID and SnortSnarf—have, in particular, proven useful in connection with Snort. This next section discusses these tools.

Swatch   Simple log WATCHer and filter (Swatch) is a fairly easy to install and use Perl program developed by Todd Atkins. This tool automates responses to Snort alerts. Swatch is an active log-file monitoring tool. Swatch monitors logs and sends alerts to the appropriate person when designated events occur, and is available at http://swatch.sourceforge.net.

Analysis Console for Intrusion Databases (ACID)   Analysis Console for Intrusion Databases (ACID) is a consolidation and analysis tool. ACID is a PHP-based analysis engine that searches for security events of interest. Two extremely useful features are query-builder and packet-viewer. *Query-builder* finds alerts matching meta information and network details. such as source and destination address, ports, payload, and/or flags. *Packet-viewer* graphically displays layer 3/4 packet information. ACID can be downloaded from http://www.andrew.cmu.edu/~rdanyliw/snort/snortacid.html.

Snortsnarf   *Snortsnarf* takes data and files from SNORT, and produces HTML output that can be used for diagnostic inspection of problems. It can produce information at any desired time interval—hourly or daily, for example—producing output of all alerts. SnortSnarf is available at http://www.silicondefense.com/software/snortsnarf.

EVALUATION

Snort is an open-source tool, lightweight, fairly easy to use, inexpensive to run, and constantly being expanded and improved. Its primary developers care so much about the security of this tool, they paid to have independent security audits of Snort performed, something most IDS and IPS vendors have still not done. At the same time, Snort's simplicity (especially the simplicity of version 1.x) can prove a big limitation. Snort simply cannot identity a number of attacks that more sophisticated (but also financially costly) IDSs can. Snort false-alarm rates have also been a persistent problem over the years but, again, this is true more of version 1.x than of version 2.0, the latter of which has a number

of capabilities designed to minimize the false alarm rate. Additionally, even in version 1.*x*, someone can substantially reduce the false alarm rate by tuning Snort rules, that is, by removing unneeded rules and rules that elevate the false alarm rate unacceptably. Finally, several serious vulnerabilities in Snort have surfaced. Probably the most publicized DoS tool that works against Snort is one named stick (visit http://www.eurocompton.net/stick). *Stick* uses every Snort signature, and then creates and transmits packets containing each signature to Snort, causing massive amounts of alerts and tying up virtually all resources. Upgrading to version 2.0 is the best solution because Snort 1.*x* vulnerabilities (such as a bug in the "stream4" preprocessor that can result in a heap overflow, allowing execution of rogue code) are not found in Snort 2.0. Patches for all these and other Snort bugs can be found at http://snort.sourcefire.org. Given how widely used Snort is, failure to install all of them is extremely unwise.

So, how much good can Snort do? The answer is that Snort can potentially do considerable good for organizations if it is deployed in the proper context for that organization. Consider the following possible deployment contexts:

▼ One context in which deploying Snort almost always makes sense is giving technical staff and students the opportunity to learn about and experiment with an IDS. Snort's simplicity makes it almost ideal in this respect. People can then make a transition to a more complex IDS if this is what is needed.

■ A small start-up company that cannot afford to invest a large amount of money to obtain a commercial IDS (and we are not even talking about monitoring and maintenance expenses here) would be well served by Snort.

■ Snort can be used as a validation tool for other IDSs. Snort output can be compared to the output of the other IDSs to get an impression of the hit and false alarm rates of the others.

■ Another possible context of use is to provide a more complete intrusion-detection capability. Snort can pick up events the other IDSs might miss.

■ Snort can be used to provide supplementary data for subnets and other network zones for which inadequate intrusion-detection data-collection capability is in place.

▲ In some cases, Snort can be used as the only IDS, even possibly in extremely large organizations. After all, Snort keeps getting better and better, and the Snort developers have a reputation of fixing bugs that emerge in this tool faster than some vendors do.

Snort is not *the* answer for intrusion detection and intrusion prevention, but it is certainly is an attractive possibility. The mileage you get from Snort might vary, so to speak, but the longer you use this tool, the more mileage you should get.

SUMMARY

Snort is a rule-based, rather than a signature-based, IDS. Snort runs in one of three modes: sniffer mode (in which Snort gathers packet headers and data and writes them to the screen); packet-logger mode (in which data and/or headers are dumped to the hard drive); and network intrusion-detection mode (which does not record packets but instead analyzes their content in comparison to rules that have been chosen). The Snort intrusion detection mode has four main components: the packet capture engine (which collects traffic using libpcap or WinPcap), the preprocessor plug-ins (which analyze packet data they obtain from pcap, determining what to do with each packet, and also dropping weird input), the detection engine (which systematically compares data in each packet it collects to rules), and the output plug-ins (which generate alerts and perform other functions such as terminating undesirable sessions).

Snort rules have a defined format and are numbered in a systematic manner, so related rules are mostly within the same numerical range. Although Snort offers a large number of rules, not all of them must be used. Snort, in fact, runs more efficiently if a reduced rule set is used. Custom rules can also be created to supplement the existing Snort rules. Snort 2.0 performs selective searches of data within rule sets, resulting in better performance. Snort's alerting function enables alert data to be sent in a variety of ways, including using SNMP, or written to a log file or a database.

The hardware Snort depends on the size of the Snort deployment. Disk space, memory, and processor speed are important considerations. Software used in connection with Snort is also critical. Choosing an appropriate OS to run on the Snort platform is the first step. You also need software, such as pcap, gcc, automake, autoconf, lex and yacc or flex and bison, and flexrep.

Snort 2.0 offers numerous improvements, among which is the Snort 2.0 Protocol Flow Analyzer. This analyzer conducts a high-level analysis of application protocol traffic, breaking it into client-to-server and also server-to-client data flows. For the sake of efficiency, the analyzer inspects only certain portions of the data in data flows. Snort 2.0 also has improved protocol decoding in which the preprocessor function transforms a wide range of data to a single format to facilitate processing the data.

The key to getting value out of Snort is deploying it in the proper context for the organization that uses it. Snort's growing sophistication and a number of other factors make it a very viable choice for intrusion detection.

CHAPTER 11

NFR Security

NFR Security was founded in 1996 by Marcus Ranum, a pioneer in IDS technology called Network Flight Recorder or NFR. As of 2003 NFR has been renamed to NFR Security, Inc., and the procuct line has been renamed to Sentivist Intelligent Intrusion Manager. The NFR software differs from most other products, as it provides analysis of data starting at the packet level as a sniffer would, and then it provides stateful packet inspection (misuse detection) and protocol anomaly detection using a scriptable open source language called N-Code. NFR can operate as a true IDS hybrid solution, inspecting everything in the OSI reference model from layer 2 protocols (Ethernet 802.1-based packets) up to layer 7 applications.

NFR DETECTION METHODOLOGY

The meaning of stateful packet inspection and protocol anomaly detection is highly misunderstood. Most of the confusion arises from the notion that examining TCP header information will provide sufficient information to successfully detect an attack. In fact, it is necessary to buffer the entire connection, including the headers and bodies of the messages transmitted, to truly identify what is happening in a connection, and most IDS products fail in that respect. Solutions that do not guarantee that data is reassembled (defragmented) correctly have an almost impossible time ensuring the correctness of the originating data.

NFR's methodology is focused on achieving data correctness during the capture and decoding of packets. NFR provides a two-layer detection mechanism, shown in Figure 11-1. The lower layer is a high-speed engine with advanced buffering techniques that ensures proper state is maintained in packet transactions, data is correctly defragmented, and entire message bodies are recorded and reassembled in sequence for accurate detection and analysis. The upper layer provides a scriptable detection language. N-Code is a unique detection language that provides a rapid signature-development platform for intrusion detection.

NFR ARCHITECTURE

The Sentivist product operates in a three-tier environment, consisting of the sensors, a Central Management System (CMS), and an Administrative Interface (AI), as shown in Figure 11-2.

Sentivist Sensor

The Sentivist sensors are passive devices that collect data on the wire. The sensors provide detection capabilities from <10 MB/s connection rates through Gig speeds, using multiple network connections per single sensor. NFR's sensors are 1-unit high rack-mountable appliances. The sensor software boots off their CD-ROM, which contains a custom written OS boot code for the sensors' operation.

Sentivist Central Management System CMS

The collection point or Central Management System provides a single collection/aggregation point for data collected by the sensors. The data spooled on the sensors are pushed into a proprietary data file store located on the CMS. The Many to one relationship provides for 20 to 30 sensors push of alerts and forensics data to the CMS.

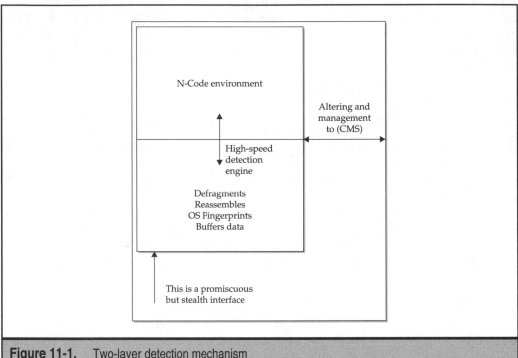

Figure 11-1. Two-layer detection mechanism

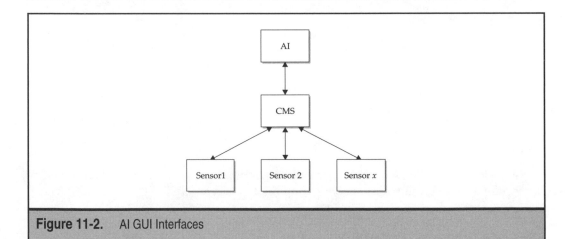

Figure 11-2. AI GUI Interfaces

CMS also provides for a multifaceted Output mechanism. The CMS can provide data via any scriptable data format (such as shell scripts, or perl programs) or via the AI.

Administrative Interface (AI)

The AI is a Windows 32 program that provides a GUI interface to the alerts, forensics, and controls of the Sentivist environment. The AI allows you to select and set up the sensors' detection capabilities, to monitor alerts and events collected by the sensors in real time, and to query supporting data collected by the sensors. All management of the IDS environment can be done via the AI.

SENTIVIST SIGNATURES

One of the most unique characteristics of the Sentivist system is its attack signature model. Unlike other systems that rely on either Snort-based signatures, or closed proprietary signature models, NFR's Sentivist provides an open signature format. The signature library permits true hybrid detection capabilities within the N-Code language. Much like Perl, N-Code provides the flexibility of a true lexical language for exploring traffic streams in real time.

The following function illustrates N-Code's lexicon. In the example, we are looking at an excerpt that will record the time, IP source, source port, IP destination, destination port, and the source's operating system if the real-time datastream being monitored is a returning device (that is, if it has been seen before and is stored in the $same_host[$hostarray] array).

```
<snip>
func detect_os {
    $os_type = (tcp.connSrcOS); # will return a OS id string of the source
#operating system seen in the current connection.
    If ($same_host[$hostarray] = $current_host){ #Let's check and see if we
#have seen this host before? Same host is an array element and current host is
#the host detected this session, the values are defined elsewhere in the code.
        If ("$same_host[$osarray]" eq "$os_type" ){ #Same host, is it the
#same operating system? If it is then let's save the information.
            record attack:CURRENT_TIME, tcp.connsrc, tcp.connsport,
tcp.conndst, tcp.conndport, $os_type, "Returning system";
#we record the information including source and destination IP and port
#information, along with the selected operating system.
        $osarray++;
        }
    $hostarray++;
}
<snip>
```

N-Code provides Sentivist with the capability to analyze data from any OSI layer including the application layer. Here are some samples of data types that N-Code can analyze.

▼ **MAC information**   In N-Code this is an `eth.blob`, which collects any 803 packets and all the payload

- **IP-based traffic**   In N-Code this is an `ip.blob`, which looks at the IP segment of the stack and its payload
- **TCP, UDP, and ICMP traffic**   N-Code calls this `udp.blob`, and this collects the UDP segment and its payload
- ▲ **Established TCP connections**   In N-Code this is a `tcp.connSym`, which collects a complete TCP session

N-Code can also delve into the payload of most protocols, such as HTTP, FTP, POP, SMTP, and so on, and then can look at the payload of the actual application within the session. We will look at some of the signatures offered by NFR's Rapid Response Team (RRT), a group dedicated to and responsible for the creation of the detection signatures in the "Sentivist Deployment Strategy" section of this chapter.

Organization of Signatures

Out of the box, Sentivist's sensors provide a clean detection canvas because no signatures are loaded. Once a sensor is plugged in and configured, a sensor examines all traffic but does not start to analyze the data until the first time N-Code packages or *backends* are uploaded from the CMS. (NFR refers to signatures as *backends*.)

Sentivist provides signatures that are ordered in a hierarchy. Figure 11-3 shows a screen shot of the file hierarchy from the AI. Packages are parent groups that contain similar signatures or backends. A single package can contain multiple backends, such as the web package called "WWW," which contains signatures related to web-based activity. "IIS Attacks" is a backend belonging to the WWW package, since IIS is a web-based application. Frequently the parent package will do some form of logical operation and will pass parameters off to the signature. For the WWW package, all state activity is maintained in the root package, so if a Code Red attack is detected, HTTP state will be established, and maintained by the WWW root package. The WWW backend will recognize that a web session was established, and that the content of the web session meets the criteria IIS based traffic passing parameters to the IIS signature, so that the actual IIS signature can detect the Code Red worm.

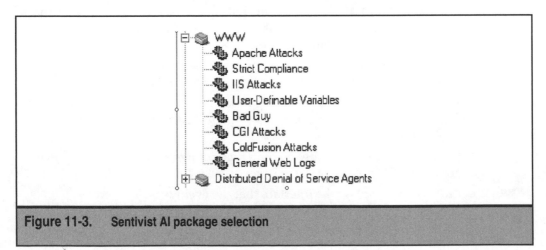

Figure 11-3.   Sentivist AI package selection

A State Model in N-Code

Sentivist can maintain state and execute anomaly-detection N-Code packages. The RRT (Rapid Response Team) has successfully crafted packages that maintain state and anomaly detection for several protocols, such as Web (based on RFCs such as 1945 and 2616 defining HTTP 1.*x*), POP, SMTP, and so on. This means that all ISO-based activity that requires state and anomaly intelligence is done by the package.

Once data has been reassembled and sorted, it is typically passed off to an application-based backend, such as the IIS Attacks backend in the WWW package. The IIS Attacks backend will then parse and alert on attacks that are relevant to the particular server type. Providing a granular means of analyzing data also makes it easier to deal with false positives when they occur. For instance, in a network environment that has no Apache servers serving as web servers, the package can be configured to alert only on IIS-based attacks.

ALERTS AND FORENSICS

N-Code provides two primary forms of data collection: *alerts* and *record statements*. It is important to understand their purpose.

Alerts

As we see in the following, both examples refer to ALERT_ID 27-64, which is the Code Red Worm event. The alert ID is assigned by the RRT as a unique event identifier. Let's look at the alert's details in the AI Figure 11-4 and examine the associated N-Code that generated the event in Figure 11-5.

We can see the components of the N-Code displayed in the AI with all the appropriate fields completed. We can the particulars of the Alert ID 27-64 with a Alert Confidence of 90, Alert Severity High, and Alert Impact as a code execution. Let us look at the components that make up the alert data type in more detail.

▼ **ALERT_CONFIDENCE** Indicates the level of confidence that this is a true attack by using a value ranging from 0 to 100. This value can be changed on the fly by N-Code if correlating evidence mandates that it be lower or higher.

■ **ALERT_SEVERITY** Indicates how severe the attack would be if it succeeds—this can have values of LOW, MEDIUM, or HIGH.

■ **ALERT_IMPACT** Provides a text string describing the impact that the attack would have on a system if successful. For Code Red, success means that code can be arbitrarily executed on the host.

■ **ALERT_EVENT_TYPE** Provides a string that defines the type of attack, such as "informational" for scans, or "attack" for attacks.

■ **PACKET_INTF** Displays the interface that the event was detected on.

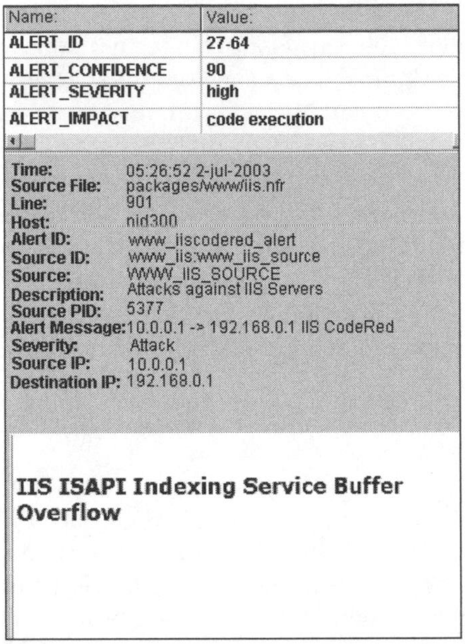

Name:	Value:
ALERT_ID	27-64
ALERT_CONFIDENCE	90
ALERT_SEVERITY	high
ALERT_IMPACT	code execution

Time: 05:26:52 2-jul-2003
Source File: packages/www/iis.nfr
Line: 901
Host: nid300
Alert ID: www_iiscodered_alert
Source ID: www_iis:www_iis_source
Source: WWW_IIS_SOURCE
Description: Attacks against IIS Servers
Source PID: 5377
Alert Message:10.0.0.1 -> 192.168.0.1 IIS CodeRed
Severity: Attack
Source IP: 10.0.0.1
Destination IP: 192.168.0.1

IIS ISAPI Indexing Service Buffer Overflow

Figure 11-4.   Alert Detail from the AI

- **ETH_VLANID** Provides information about the virtual LAN (VLAN), as per the IEEE VLAN ID standard. This information would be available if VLAN ID information was enabled within the network segment.

- **IP_PROT_NUM** Provides the protocol information.

- **IP_ADDR_SRC and IP_ADDR_DST** Displays source and destination IP address information.

▲ **PORT_SRC and PORT_DST** Displays the associated source and destination ports.

```
alert(www_iis_source, codered_alert, tcp.connsrc, tcp.conndst,
substr(CODERED_VARIANTS[www:GLOBAL_RAWURI], 0, 1024), "--AlertDetails",
"ALERT_ID", "27-64", "ALERT_CONFIDENCE", 90 90, "ALERT_SEVERITY", "high",
"ALERT_IMPACT", "code execution", "ALERT_EVENT_TYPE", "attack",
"ALERT_ASSESSMENT", "unknown",
"PACKET_INTF", $pintf, "ETH_VLANID", $vlanid, "IP_PROTO_NUM", 6,
"IP_ADDR_SRC", tcp.connsrc, "IP_ADDR_DST", tcp.conndst,
"PORT_SRC", tcp.connsport, "PORT_DST", tcp.conndport);
```

Figure 11-5.   The alert statement in N-Code

Record Statements (Forensics)

In addition to the alert statements Sentivist provides a means to collect forensics data associated with an alert. This data is called a *query* and is accessible in the AI interface in packages. The data is collected by an N-Code statement called a *record*. The record statement permits Sentivist to extend its ability to analyze data that is provided in an alert. The *query* data is available via the AI. In fact, the content of a query consists of supplemental forensics data that is representative of the particular alert being examined. The supplemental information is available for all of the signatures provided by NFR.

Following the information in the CodeRed alert shown in Figure 11-4 we see the supporting forensics data that was recorded for the Code Red alert event in Figure 11-6. This was a result of running a query in the AI for CodeRed, which executed the following N-Code to generate the results.

```
record www:CURRENT_TIME, tcp.connsrc, tcp.connsport, tcp.conndst, tcp.conndport,…
```

This record statement is not the entire signature for detecting the CodeRed Worm, nor does an operator of the AI require to see or modify the signature during operation. This information is provided to illustrate how N-Code is executed to achieve results.

This record statement is *not* the entire signature for detecting the Code Red worm. In fact, the signature examines the whole HTTP state, both client and server side session is checked for correct state and ensures no hidden content exists in the traffic. The www signature identifies the Code red worm as it assembles the client request to the server during the initial connection and GET request. This is only a short excerpt from a complex signature (state engine) written to maintain web transactions of all kinds.

NOTE   You can read more about N-Code in the resources provided by NFR: https://support.nfr.com/nid-v3/nde/docs/Customizing_NFR_NID_Sensor_Using_N-Code.pdf.

```
Time:              22-Jul-2003 11:23:43
NFR:               nid300
Source Address:    217.88.162.86
Source Port:       3465
Destination Address:207.115.76.186
Destination Port:  80
Reason:            CodeRed II
Content:           /default.


      ida?XXXXXXXXXXXXXXXXXXXXXXXXXXXXXXXXXXXXXXXXXXXXXXXXXXXXXXXXXXXXX
XXXXXXXXXXXXXXXXXXXXXXXXXXXXXXXXXXXXXXXXXXXXXXXXXXXXXXXXXXXXXXXXXXXXXXXXXX
XXXXXXXXXXXXXXXXXXXXXXXXXXXXXXXXXXXXXXXXXXXXXXXXXXXXXXXXXXXXXXXXXXXXXXXXXX
XXXXXXXXXX%u9090%u6858%ucbd3%u7801%u9090%u6858%ucbd3%u7801%u9090%u6858%ucbd3%u7801%u
9090%u9090%u8190%u00c3%u0003%u8b00%u531b%u53ff%u0078%u0000%u00=a
```

Figure 11-6.   Query result

COOL THINGS YOU CAN DO WITH N-CODE

N-Code is a very flexible language. It allows you to explore the realm that traditionally only network sniffers used to address, and it offers you the flexibility of writing your own detection conditions.

For example, NFR could be used to identify all devices that are performing port address translation (PAT) that are present on your network. This could be accomplished by collecting MAC addresses and matching them to IP addresses—when multiple MAC addresses are associated to a single IP, you could then trigger an alert.

NFR could also be used to detect certain protocol behavior. For instance, if you want to see whether a particular port is used during certain times of the day, such as port 31,337 after 6 P.M., you could use N-Code to generate an alert. The possibilities are truly endless, and it only requires short development efforts to explore N-Code's capabilities.

CENTRAL MANAGEMENT SERVER

The Central Management Server provides a central repository for all data collected, and it is a central point for managing the sensors, but it also provides for direct manipulation of events within the CMS environment.

The CMS runs as a client application on either Sun Solaris or Linux. By default, the CMS is installed into the /usr/local/nfr directory, as shown in Figure 11-7, and it is recommended that /usr/local/nfr receive a dedicated partition, or potentially a dedicated drive.

The amount of space required will depend on how much date needs to be stored. Space usage is dependent on the number of sensors, the number of backends loaded, and

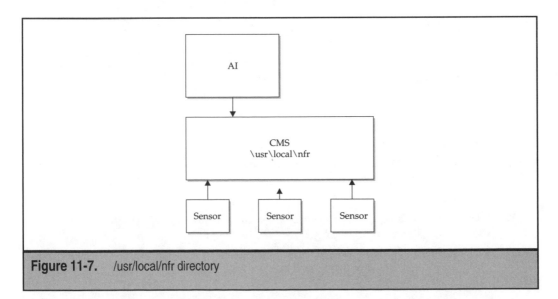

Figure 11-7. /usr/local/nfr directory

the length of time the data is to be saved. A 30GB hard drive is a good starting point. Further information on installation can be found at the NFR web site.

Starting Sentivist

Sentivist runs a collection service on the CMS that will pool information from sensors and distribute backend signatures, variables, and updates to sensors. Once installed, start the Sentivist services by executing `./nfrstart.sh start`. This will start Sentivist on the CMS.

This startup process can be automated by setting up a self-demonizing program:

```
Command -> Chkconfig -add nfr


Result ---
nfr        0:off   1:off   2:on   3:on   4:on   5:on   6:off
```

Sentivist Services

The best way to explore Sentivist CMS is to see it operating, so we will examine some of the key services that Sentivist runs on the CMS. Other processes do exist, but will not be examined in depth.

These CMS services can be observed by running `ps -fu nfr`. On doing so, the first thing we see is that all nfr daemons run as the user that was selected during installation, which in our case is nfr (as listed in the UID column). This is the default.

```
UID         PID  PPID  C STIME TTY          TIME CMD
nfr       21849     1  0 11:45 ?        00:00:00 bin/nfrwatch
nfr       21852 21849  0 11:45 ?        00:00:00 bin/alertd
nfr       21854 21849  0 11:45 ?        00:00:00 bin/getserver
nfr       21856 21849  0 11:45 ?        00:00:00 bin/guisrv
nfr       21857 21849  0 11:45 ?        00:00:00 bin/remotestatd
nfr       21858 21849  0 11:45 ?        00:00:00 bin/spaceman
```

Let's look at the running services:

▼ **bin/nfrwatch** The nfrwatch daemon maintains the operational status of all the Sentivist services that are running. If any of the services get hung up, nfrwatch will terminate them and recover the service.

■ **bin/alertd** The alertd daemon will collect and queue alerts as presented by the sensors. Alertd will also execute the rule that an alert is expected to execute.

■ **bin/guisrv** The guisrv daemon is a listener waiting for AI connections. It is very much like a tty daemon.

■ **bin/remotestatd** This daemon collects statistics from the sensors—when a sensor pushes up stats, the remotestatd daemon will parse and display the information.

▲ **bin/spaceman** This daemon monitors and maintains the space allocation. A space computation is executed when the Sentivist services are first started, running an internalized program called space_compute, its purpose is to allocate the space required for the CMS to operate correctly.

There are other important services that are not listed in the ps excerpt that can be invoked by NFR when needed or invoked manually: bin/run_mirror and bin/get.

bin/run_mirror

This binary provides for the sensors and CMS to be synchronized. The mirror function will synchronize or mirror signatures and variables to all or selected sensors. This can be executed manually by running the binary from a command line.

▼ **bin/run_mirror** This will execute a mirror to all sensors.

▲ **bin/run_mirror -x** [*device_name*] This will mirror only to the host selected

For example, the following script will allow a user to monitor the status of the mirror: Users can execute the following command to see the process of a mirror occur, the purpose of the mirror will give insight into the services running on the Sentivist CMS.

```
do while true; ps -fu nfr; sleep 3; clear; done;
```

While this script is running, you will see the packages and backends copy out to the sensors in the process list. Once the mirror finishes copying files to a sensor, a sensor synchronization stage occurs. During this time, the sensor is compiling the signatures to byte code, and it will start using the newly loaded signatures immediately.

bin/get -n [*nid name*] -s [*filename*]

This binary provides the CMS with the means to collect information and system files from the sensors. The binary can provide an extensive capability to collect information from sensors directly. The following components can be accessed via bin/get from the sensor. From sy/ : sample usage would be sy/ipaddr0 or sy/ntpkey.

▼ sy/ipaddr0

■ sy/license

■ sy/netmask0

■ sy/ntphost1

■ sy/ntphost2

■ sy/ntpkey

■ sy/ntpkeynum

■ sy/admin_pass

■ sy/admin_pass2

- sy/crypto
- sy/crypto2
- sy/defroute
- sy/hostname
- sy/iface0
- sy/ip_central
▲ sy/ip_central2

For example, bin/get –n [*NID name*] –s sy/*hostname* will return the name of the sensor. Here is an example:

```
>bin/get -n nid300 -s sy/hostname
nid300
```

Additionally bin/get provides a means to execute diagnostics on a sensor by executing bin/get –n [*NID name*] –x exec_sys_info.

Here's an example:

```
>bin/get -n nid300 -x exec_sysinfo

/release
--------

NID-315 3.2 CD
Copyright (c) 1996-2003, NFR Security, Inc.
NFR Security, Inc.
http://www.nfr.com


/hostname
-----------
nid300

etc/patch_info
--------------

756 0


Network interfaces (ifconfig)
-----------------------------

fxp0: flags=8843<UP,BROADCAST,RUNNING,SIMPLEX,MULTICAST> mtu 1500
      inet 10.0.0.8 netmask 0xffffff00 broadcast 10.0.0.255
      ether 00:02:b3:87:f9:b4
      media: Ethernet autoselect (100baseTX)
      status: active
```

```
fxp1: flags=9943<UP,BROADCAST,RUNNING,PROMISC,SIMPLEX,LINK0,MULTICAST> mtu 1500
        ether 00:20:ed:11:01:06
        media: Ethernet autoselect (100baseTX)
        status: active
fxp2: flags=9943<UP,BROADCAST,RUNNING,PROMISC,SIMPLEX,LINK0,MULTICAST> mtu 1500
        ether 00:20:ed:11:01:07
        media: Ethernet autoselect (10baseT/UTP)
        status: active
lo0: flags=8049<UP,LOOPBACK,RUNNING,MULTICAST> mtu 16384
        inet 127.0.0.1 netmask 0xff000000

<SNIP>
```

In this example, `exec_sysinfo` returned information from the sensor, including version info and an `ifconfig` equivalent showing the state of the interfaces on the sensor.

SENTIVIST DEPLOYMENT STRATEGY

Deploying Sentivist IDS is relatively simple and designed to be done quickly. However, the second step is tuning and configuring, and this is by far the most important step for successful upkeep of any IDS product.

Sensor deployment for Sentivist follows the same general principal as for all IDSs—covering network elements from the inside out will provide for more thorough protection. Sentivist signature elements can be selected for each sensor based on the sensor's placement.

Sentivist provides several system-wide variables and backends. These enable the sensors to be aware of their surroundings:

- ▼ **my_network** A list of network devices (provided in either dot notation or CIDR (Classless Inter-Domain Routing block) that includes the network segments owned by the internal network and network segments that are behind or are monitored by the sensor. Multiple entries can be made for this variable.

- ▲ **Broadcast_addrs** The broadcast address of the network elements that are watched by the sensor. Multiple entries can be made for this variable.

The following discussions will look at basic placement principals and consider what signatures would be best suited for each sensor's respective environment. The discussion of where to place backends and signatures will also provide some insight into their use. Note that the placement of backends in these particular cases are not to be considered universal solutions—they are simply the best solution for the case.

CASE STUDY: Web Farm

A web farm is a high-speed network segment that is populated by web-based servers. In this case, the firewalls are considered secured as per the manufacturer of the solution, up and provide no access outside of the web-based applications required to run a web server. These servers provide web transactions, such as HTTP (on port 80) and HTTPS (on port 443) services. Additionally, management services such as Simple Network Management Protocol (SNMP) and ICMP are permitted in order to manage the web farm devices.

For this case, see the Web Farm sample illustration, the following core backends would be necessary:

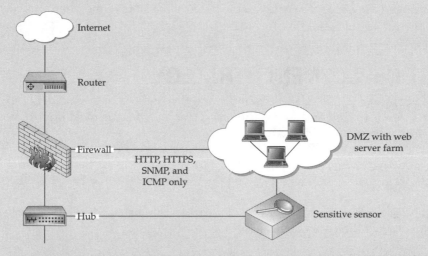

▼ **WWW backend** This backend covers all the key elements of NFR's web-based stateful detection capabilities. It provides for thorough examination of HTTP traffic, as defined by RFCs on HTTP traffic types. Besides detecting web-based attacks, this backend can also be used for logging web traffic. This backend can be tuned by changing its associated variables, such as these:

■ **WWW servers** This variable should be populated with known web servers that are active on the network.

■ **WWW ports** This variable provides for additional ports to be monitored for web-based traffic.

■ **IIS attacks** Setting this variable to 1 will cause the backend to watch specifically for IIS servers listed in the WWW servers list.

■ **Apache attacks** Setting this variable to 1 will cause the backend to watch specifically for Apache attacks against the list in WWW servers.

▲ **SSH monitor package**   SSH is frequently used to manage all non-Microsoft devices. Additionally SSH has been exploited in the past. Monitoring the SSH negotiations and version numbers is valuable for any administrator.

Here are some additional signatures that could be used for this case:

▼ **Authentication backend**   This backend can be useful for network administrators who need to keep an eye on weak passwords and potential breach attempts based on password hacks. This is an excellent policy-control backend that allows for monitoring password strength and whether they are passed in cleartext or are encrypted. This backend relies on other backends, since it does very little password detection itself. It relies on backends such as POP, SMTP, WWW, FTP, and Telnet. These backends actually trigger the Authentication backend when a usernameand password combination is seen in their respective backends. Several policy-driven variables can be set in this backend, such as a dictionary ook-up to check for common usernames and passwords. Here are a couple of other variables that can be set in this backend:

- **RECORD_PASSWORDS** Can be set to record passwords in the clear.

- **MIN_PASSWORD_LENGTH** Can be set to watch for password lengths that are shorter than this value.

■ **SNMP backend**   This backend detects traditional SNMP-based network attacks. It checks for common community names (public, private), and it will also watch for common attacks against SNMP. Several variables can be modified in this backend:

- **SNMP_INT_AND_INT, SNMP_INT_AND_EXT,** and **SNMP_EXT_EXT** These variables provide for tuning of SNMP backend that is internal to internal, internal to external, or external to external. This variable relies on the *my_network* variable to identify the internal segment.

- **BAD_COMMNAMES** This is a list of well-known or bad community names, such as

  - public
  - private
  - system
  - all
  - manager

- default
- password

To shore up the IDS detection capability, the Policy backend is used. The policy backend provides for an ipfilter style or access control list (ACL) style of control. The variables allow for TCP, UDP, and ICMP filtering. The rules are made up of the following elements:

```
command source_ip destination_ip source_port destination_port
```

▼ **Command** This can be either "Alert" or "OK." An alert command will create an alert if the condition is met. OK provides for an exception clause to alerts. OK statements can be used to exclude subsets of a network, hosts, ports, or any other combination of conditions that are permitted network elements. For example, if we use an Alert on any, using OK for a single IP address will prevent the alert from occurring.

■ **Source IP** This can be assigned a single IP address or one of the following values:

- ■ `inside` Refers to the network specified by the `my_network` variable.

- ■ `outside` Refers to all networks not listed in `my_network`. For example, if my_network (or inside) is 10.1.2.1/255.255.255.0, outside refers to everything except 10.1.2.1/255.255.255.0.

- ■ `any` Any IP address

- ■ `CIDR block` A range of IP addresses, denoted by the slash notation. For example, 10.0.0.0/8 would represent 10.0.0.8 255.0.0.0.

■ **Destination IP** Same as the source IP, except it applies to the destination addresses.

■ **Source port** This can be a single port or one of the following:

- ■ `low` For ports 0 through 1,023

- ■ `high` For ports 1,024 and up

- ■ `any` For any ports

▲ **Destination port** Same as the source port, except it applies to destination ports.

For our web farm, the Policy backend variables would reflect the following rules.

CASE STUDY: Web Farm   *(continued)*

▼ RULES_TCP

```
"alert    any         any   any   any"
"ok       any         any   any   80"
"ok       any         any   high  any"
"ok       any         any   any   443"
"ok       inside      any   22    any"
```

UDP and ICMP rules would also be used RULES_UDP and RULES_ICMP would be configured in the following manner.

▼ RULES_UDP

```
"alert    any         any   any   any"
```

■ RULES_UDP will allow only for SNMP management capabilities from a trusted network segment.

■ RULES_ICMP

```
"alert    outside      any   any   any"
```

▲ RULES_ICMP will alert on any activity that is not generated by the trusted network. This allows for inside network devices to use tools such as ping without alerting the IDS.

CASE STUDY 2: Corporate Network Services

In this case we will look at a corporate network segment that much like the web farm segment, but smaller and more diverse. In this case, we will include services that would commonly be used by a corporate network in daily operation, such as mail, DNS services, web services, and potentially an Internet Relay Chat (IRC) type of messaging service. This is a protected network segment, and it includes critically important network elements.

We can use the following backends that were used in the previous case:

▼ WWW backend for web services detection

■ SSH backend for all secure communication detection

■ SNMP backend for management services detection

■ Authentication backend for policy enforcement

▲ Policy backend (changes to the rules will be noted at the end of this section)

CASE STUDY 2: Corporate Network Services *(continued)*

The following backends should also be considered:

▼ **Telnet backend**   This backend allows you to make sure that an unsecured service, such as telnet, cannot be seen on an Internet-exposed segment.

■ **Cisco IOS backend**   This backend watches for potentially damaging events to routers running Cisco IOS, which is vulnerable to brute force attacks and existing exploits.

▲ **SMTP backend**   This backend detects and logs the SMTP mail protocol. The backend provides for alerting on common SMTP attacks, and it also provides logging for all SMTP traffic. It will ensure that the server had received one of the expected "MAIL", "RCPT", or "DATA" commands before mail is forwarded. Otherwise, the backend will investigate the traffic for unusual behavior. This backend can be tuned differently based on whether it will primarily be working behind a Unix-based sendmail servers or Microsoft-based Exchange mail servers. This backend permits tuning with the following variables:

  ■ `SMTP_BAD_SUBJECT` Provides a means to watch for keywords in mail headers. When turned on, this could alert on statements or words that should be restricted to intranet traffic.

  ■ `SMTP_DUPLICATE_COMMANDS` Watches for commands that are frequently duplicated for attack purposes. However, in instances of MS Exchange this may happen normally as a result removing the following may avoid false positives:

    ■ ehlo
    ■ helo

■ **POP backend**   This backend detects common attacks on and logs Post Office Protocol (POP) traffic. This backend contains the same features as the SMTP backend, except they pertain to the POP protocol.

■ **SMB backend**   This backend ensures that no Server Message Block (SMB) activity exists on any web server. Isolated segment damage from SMB attacks can be devastating. The following variables can be changed to prevent false positives:

    ■ `NBT_SESSION_REQUEST_FLOOD_THRESHOLD` Quell excessive (NetBIOS over TCP/IP) NBT flood events. NBT floods often reflect DOS attacks and compromise attempts against Microsoft devices.

CASE STUDY 2: Corporate Network Services *(continued)*

- ■ `PURGEFREQ` Adds additional granular control of the flood threshold in NBT sessions.

- ■ **DNS backend** Provides full coverage of the DNS protocol. This backend provides true anomaly detection on DNS traffic.

  - ■ `MY_DNS_SERVER` Should be supplied to identify the network's DNS servers. This will allow the backend to detect all anomalous behavior against DNS services, especially when the attacks are against the DNS server listed in this variable.

- ■ **FTP backend** Provides full state and anomaly detection within the FTP protocol. The package can be tuned to watch for specific attacks aimed at certain accepted hosts, and it also watches for services that may allow for anonymous FTP. The following variables may require changing:

  - ■ `ALERT_ON_BINARY_REQUEST`, `ALERT_ON_BINARY_RESPONSE` Provides the ability to curtail false positives related to binary data embedded within FTP traffic.

  - ■ `BAD_DIRNAMES` Watches for specific directories that should not be exported by FTP under any circumstances, such as these:

    - ■ .appz
    - ■ .codez
    - ■ .c0dez
    - ■ .sitez
    - ■ .warez

  - ■ `BAD_USRNAMES` Watches for special users who should never be seen on the network connection:

    - ■ adm
    - ■ daemon
    - ■ nobody
    - ■ null
    - ■ root

- ■ **TCP backend** Offers the ability to watch for devices that port-scan network devices.

  - ■ `INTERVAL` This value can be set to limit false positives as it relates to scans. If the interval is set high, it is likely that more false positives will be seen, since regular network behavior will seem like a port

scan. Likewise, a value too low may allow for slow scans to be missed.

■ **IP backend** Provides the ability to watch for host-scanning.

　■ **MAXHOSTS** This value can be changed to prevent scans that may fall below the threshold of maximum hosts. Certain protocols and applications that scan for port access may trigger false positives.

■ **TFTP backend** Provides monitoring for proper operation of batch update devices.

▲ **IRC backend** Provides protocol decoding of IRC traffic. Since this protocol can be especially dangerous when unchecked, this monitoring is extremely important.

With this environment, shoring up the configuration with the policy package may be a bit more difficult, but it is still a viable way to provide a "catch everything else" solution. Let's look at the three policy backends and how they complement the sensor deployment.

▼ RULES_TCP

```
"alert    any             any    any    any"
"ok       any             any    any    80"
"ok       any             any    high   any"
"ok       any             any    any    443"
"ok       inside          any    22     any"
```

NOTE These variables will require a separate entry for all incoming and outgoing protocols, the "ok" entries will prevent alerting on protocols, and port that are expected, and will cause false alert.

RULES_UDP

```
"alert    outside         any    any    any"
```

RULES_ICMP

```
"alert    outside         any    any    any"
```

CASE STUDY 3: Bare Internet Connection

When using an IDS on a bare Internet segment, it can become quite difficult to separate false positives from true positives. More often than not, the purpose of the IDS in this case is to alert people that "a-ha it is an attack." Tuning of this sensor is a bit more complicated, since we are trying to watch everything. As a result, the alerts will provide information about both benign and malicious activity. Even if the events are malicious, attacks may not affect the network the sensor is watching, since the event may have been stopped by the firewall, it may not involve any of the protected hosts, or it may simply have been an automated scan that just happened to sweep the protected network.

For this scenario, we will take a stock system and tune down some elements that will create extensive false positives or that would load the system down so significantly that it might be difficult to read through the alerts.

The following backends have been covered in the last section.

▼ Authentication   ■ POP

■ DNS   ■ SMB

■ FTP   ■ SMTP

■ ICMP   ■ SSH

■ IMAP   ■ Telnet

■ IRC   ■ TFTP

■ MISC   ▲ WWW

Here are some other packages that may provide additional value:

▼ **BADFILES backend**   Provides the ability to watch for certain filenames that should not be seen on a network segment. The variable can be set to specify the filenames:

    ■ `BADFILES_FILES` Specifies certain file types that may be of interest, such as gone.scr.

■ **SCANNERS backend**   Provides a compilation of signatures that watch for scanner-like activity from scanners such as Cybercop, Iss, Nessus, and Retina.

■ **DDoS backend**   Provides a compilation of signatures that are related to DDoS events, this includes backends such as Mstream, Shaft, Stacheldraht, Tfn, and trinoo.

CASE STUDY 3: Bare Internet Connection *(continued)*

▲ **TROJANS backend**   Watches for common Trojan-like behavior. Included this backend are services that may be used for management; however, they are included because of the impact that the particular service can have if compromised, such as by pcAnywhere. A successful compromise of this service on a system permits total system control. The package includes signatures for Back orifice, pcAnywhere, telnetbd, bo2k, net bus legacy, net
cat, vnc, deep throat, net bus pro, and sub7.

Using the Policy package is not advisable outside the default installed state, since a large number of false positives will be seen as a result of the backend being enabled incorrectly. This backend would have to be used with caution and careful observation. By default, the backend is set up to monitor IP ranges inside TCP, ICMP, and UDP that are part of the reserved IP ranges.

CASE STUDY 4: LAN Segment

A LAN segment can be the most interesting case to work with, and NFR can provide useful information for managers when the cost of ownership for security equipment becomes an issue.

Traffic on an internal network segment will consist of data created or altered by staff, people on associated networks (partners or affiliates), and guests, invited or not! The organization's assets are located on the internal segments, and this includes traffic that may or may not follow corporate policy. For this type of case, tuning requires hands-on exposure to the data. Since no two network environments are the same, no two IDS deployment tunings will be the same.

Initially it is best to disable all the backends, and then start adding in backends such as Trojans, DDoS, WWW. Once these are in place, they should be used to watch the network traffic for a period of time to identify trends. These results will dictate what packages and backends will cause a flood of false positives. Normalization will occur once false positives are reduced to almost zero, this can be called a normal traffic pattern. Once the data starts to normalize, additional backends can be loaded. However, after each backend is loaded, you should wait for a while to see the results of the change. If well executed, this can take from several hours to several days. The result of this process is guaranteed to provide a clear definition of the types of data on the network.

NFR REPORTING

Within the AI several reports can be generated for trending and general graphing of alert traffic. All these reports are available via the AI. The reports are simple and functional to produce. Additionally the report data can be exported to .CSV format for use in a spreadsheet application such as MS Excel.

NFR provides several report mechanisms, for detailed usage of the reporting mechanisms refer to the nfr AI users manual https://support.nfr.com/nid-v3/console/ai/docs/NFR_AI_v3_Users_Guide.pdf.

EXTENDING NFR

The extensibility of NFR is a true strength of the product. We have seen how we can extend the product's detection ability with N-Code, and how interacting with the CMS can extend visibility to the sensors. NFR additionally provides generic alerting and command line access. All of these provide a means to extend the alerting and management in an automated fashion.

One such extension uses Perl. The NFR's Perl tools provide access to the data and alerts that NFR stores on the CMS via command line (CLI). There are several Perl tools provided by NFR: `popups.pl`, `isummary.pl`, `query.pl`, all provide a quick means to access the data without starting the AI.

SUMMARY

In this chapter we looked at the NFR Sentivist Intrusion Detection system and examined how it operates and handles data in a unique fashion. We also examined the product three tier architecture and several key services that operate the product and can be used to diagnose the services. The chapter examined four deployment scenarios examining the signatures used in context of each case deployment. We examined Sentivist signatures, as it would relate to Web Farm, Corporate Network Services, Bare Internet connection, and Lan Segment deployments, looking at the best way to approach each of the solutions when deploying Sentivist Intelligent Intrusion Manager.

PART IV

Security and IDS Management

CHAPTER 12

Data Correlation

This chapter covers another very important issue—correlating attack-related data. So far we've covered intrusion detection and intrusion prevention as it is normally performed. Intrusion-detection analysts and intrusion-prevention systems check the output of network- and host-based intrusion-detection tools, they evaluate system audit and firewall logs, they analyze the data from packet-capturing tools, and so on, making decisions concerning not only what has actually occurred, but also about the degree of threat that various attacks pose. Analyzing output in this manner is almost invariably worthwhile, yet many organizations need more—they need to put the data into a larger context. As the saying goes, the whole is greater than the sum of the parts.

Increasingly, data about attacks and potential attacks are being subjected to a greater degree of analysis than simply being summarily inspected. It is, for example, increasingly commonplace to have all such data gleaned from sensors and host-based intrusion-detection or intrusion-prevention tools transferred to a central repository where all these data can be accessed by logging into a single host. This not only results in more convenient access to data, but it also increases the likelihood that relationships between data are discovered. An analyst may find that a particular apparent IP source address has scanned several hundred hosts within a particular network. The analyst may initially not pay much attention to the fact that these hosts have been scanned; after all, unauthorized vulnerability scanning is (lamentably) common. Perhaps automatic mechanisms will also shun the particular IP address in question. But consider the potential implications if the analyst soon afterward discovers that the same IP address has also launched what appears to be a successful attack against a firewall in another network belonging to the same organization. The combination of events, vulnerability scans targeting the organization's IP address space, and a possible compromise of a device designed to provide perimeter security, all from the same apparent IP source address, should now prompt urgent intervention, perhaps in terms of blocking all inbound traffic from that IP address at all external gateways to that organization's networks. And although they are still not widely available, databases that integrate in-band data (data captured by monitoring and intrusion-detection tools) and out-of-band data (data not related to monitoring and intrusion-detection tools, but rather consisting of results of background investigations, arrest histories, and so forth) are starting to be more widely used in intrusion detection, especially by military and law enforcement agencies.

In this chapter, we'll look at how analysts generally correlate the attack data they obtain and then move on to advanced data fusion and correlation methods. Following that, we'll look at statistical correlation, Bayesian inference, and real-time versus after-the-fact correlation. Finally we'll look at a real-life case study.

THE BASICS OF DATA CORRELATION

It is easy to get data correlation confused with other, somewhat similar terms. We'll start by defining and comparing *data correlation*, *data aggregation*, and *event reconstruction*.

Data Correlation Definitions

Data correlation means associating sets of events detected through various means and applying knowledge to determine whether they are related, and if so, in what manner and to what degree. This kind of correlation requires comparing observations based on different types of parameters, such as source and destination IP addresses, an identifiable network route, commands entered by a suspected attacker, and the time when activity began or ended. Data sources can be intrusion-detection sensors, logs, databases (such as threat databases), and so forth, as shown in Table 12-1.

Type of Data Source	Major Advantages	Major Disadvantages
System logging	Indicates what actually happened on targeted system	Can be tampered with or turned off altogether; differences in formats can be confusing
Firewall logging	Generally provides a complete picture of inbound and outbound traffic at the point in the network where the firewall is placed	Overwhelming volume of data; differences in formats can be confusing; limitation in dealing with encrypted traffic; packet fragment reassembly issues
Packet dumps	Provides a detailed analysis of traffic going over the network	Overwhelming volume of data (unless dumps are for short time periods); analysis is tedious
Network-monitoring tool output	Can provide easy-to-comprehend picture of the state of the network; particularly valuable in spotting denial-of-service attacks	Financial expense (because most of these tools are commercial)
Target-monitoring output	Target-monitoring tools run in the background; changes in files and directories are often indications of attacks	False alarms; financial expense of commercial versions of tools

Table 12-1. Possible Sources of Intrusion-Detection Data to Be Correlated

Type of Data Source	Major Advantages	Major Disadvantages
SNMP traps	Easy to set up and administer; provides remote near-real-time alerting; usefulness of certain kinds of traps (failed logins)	Many versions of SNMP are riddled with vulnerabilities; can flood network
IDS output	Usually reasonably convenient to access, and easy to understand	Quality of output (hit rate, false-alarm rate) varies considerably from one IDS to another; limitation in dealing with encrypted traffic; limited throughput rate (in many IDSs)
Databases containing data about attacks	Can provide considerable amount of relevant data; allows data mining	Financial cost of setting up and maintaining database; privacy issues
Web postings	Search engines can make a wide range of information about incidents available; attackers who evade intrusion detection may reveal information about their attacks on the web	The accuracy and validity of information posted on the web, especially information concerning attacks, is at face value dubious—false information abounds

Table 12-1.   Possible Sources of Intrusion-Detection Data to Be Correlated *(continued)*

The knowledge that is needed to correlate the events includes knowledge possessed by analysts as well as information in databases and other data repositories. Data correlation, at least to some degree, occurs implicitly whenever humans are involved in intrusion detection. Those who analyze intrusion-detection data develop new knowledge about types and sources of attacks, and they apply this knowledge as new events occur. For example, an analyst might recognize that an attacker is repeatedly attempting to exploit a vulnerability in the traceroute utility in Linux systems to obtain a root shell. This person might also notice that a large amount of this activity appears to originate from a limited number of Internet addresses, all of which end in .nl. The analyst has, at least to some degree, already correlated intrusion-detection data (although the sophistication of the correlation is fairly crude) and is certain to continue to do so as events unfold in time. The working hypothesis that a group of individuals from the Netherlands is attacking

Linux systems in an attempt to exploit a vulnerability in traceroute is the byproduct of the analyst having correlated several observations.

Data correlation is *not* the same as *data aggregation*. *Data aggregation* refers to the process of acquiring more and more data. Amassing as much data as possible is normally prerequisite to performing effective data correlation. *Data correlation* is, however, for all practical purposes synonymous with the concept of *data fusion*, a term used frequently (but not exclusively) in military circles to describe the correlation of data in time (and space, if necessary) and the assignment of importance weights to the output. The output of IDSs and possibly IPSs designed to fuse data can include identification about one or more individuals believed to have perpetrated attacks, where the attacks originated, the nature of the attacks, the frequency with which the attacks occurred, the degree of impact (including damage), and many other variables.

Data correlation is also not equivalent to event reconstruction. *Event reconstruction* means piecing data together to determine exactly what event or events occurred in what order (or perhaps even at what precise time). The most basic type of event reconstruction in intrusion detection and prevention is reconstruction of session data, in which data from session packets are gleaned to determine all the particular commands entered and data transmitted from the start to the end of the session. Tools such as NetIntercept by Sandstorm (www.sandstorm.com) are built to provide event reconstruction by reassembling packets into streams. Provided that a special ssh client that enables NetIntercept to obtain private keys is running on hosts for which event reconstruction is desired, this tool is even capable of decrypting SSH sessions to allow you to read session content.

The Value of Data Correlation

From a practical point of view, data correlation is potentially valuable in several respects. First, it can validate data. To some degree, all data acquired from intrusion-detection tools and other sources should initially be viewed with a healthy degree of suspicion, anyway. Having an additional source of information about a particular event or parameter in a packet is particularly useful when considerable uncertainty concerning the origin, accuracy, scope, and so forth, of data exists. The validity of all source IP addresses in a conventional IPv4 packet is, for example, always initially questionable, given the widespread availability of tools that launch IP spoofing and similar kinds of masquerading attacks. (Fortunately, the IPSec protocol offers an Authentication Header (AH), providing what amounts to "sealed contents" of IP packet headers. If anyone tampers with any value, such as the source IP address, the computed cryptochecksum or hash value does not agree with the sealed value, causing the receiving host to drop the packet.) Comparing the origin time of a particular packet, however, with entries such as process-accounting log entries in Unix systems, which list commands entered by users, the time, the amount of CPU utilization, and more, can facilitate verifying whether the packet actually originated from the machine in question.

Second, data correlation can aid in determining the origin, magnitude, and degree of threat of an incident or suspected incident. In the same way that a detective pieces together evidence at the scene of a crime, correlation of intrusion-detection data can lead to a thorough understanding of an incident and its impact. This understanding helps in

identifying and deploying optimal response strategies that contain damage and ultimately eradicate the cause of an incident.

A few currently available tools such as TruThreat Risk Correlation (www.arcsight .com) perform not only data aggregation, but also event correlation for risk assessment. TruThreat Risk Correlation, for example, collects security-related events from a variety of sources (including IDSs and firewalls) and then correlates them with other data, such as the results of vulnerability scans. Correlation of all these data produces a risk index figure that helps guide intervention efforts. Using one or more of this class of tools can make the potentially overwhelming task of integrating data from a variety of sources much more manageable.

Unfortunately, tools of this nature are currently not widely used. At a bare minimum, though, it is important to avoid relying on the output of a single sensor or intrusion-detection tool. A combination of public domain and commercial signature-based and anomaly-detection tools, such as Snort (www.snort.org) and Symantec's ManHunt (http:// enterprisesecurity.symantec.com/content/productlink.cfm), with a high-end packet-capture program (such as tcpdump or windump) or device is highly desirable. Note that some intrusion-detection tools (such as NetIntercept from Sandstorm) not only provide output indicating that certain events of interest have occurred, but also allow inspection of individual packet data, thereby precluding the need for a separate packet-capturing program or device. Being able to reconstruct entire events is critical. Something about the output of sensor or audit-log data may suggest a deeper level of analysis is needed, analysis that helps confirm or refute whether incidents have occurred. Sensor output and audit logs thus really provide only an initial glimpse of events that may have transpired.

In intrusion prevention, data correlation deployed at the sensor provides a level of accuracy for prevention decisions that does not exist with signature-based approaches. Correlating sequences of events within the context of an application's behavior greatly reduces the potential for false positives. When an application starts logging keystrokes, for example, a signature-based tool typically generates an alert that keystrokes are being captured. However, Instant Messenger, a debugger, or a pcAnywhere–type of application that captures keystrokes may be running—an event not necessarily indicative of a security breach. (Note, though, that if an unapproved application is logging keystrokes and sending them to other hosts on the Internet, the implications are entirely different.)

Intrusion-prevention correlation within a central server enables security to be more adaptive. By correlating the events on distributed agents, intrusion-prevention policies can be dynamically updated to prevent propagation of malicious code, thus preventing widespread damage to numerous resources as well as allowing deeper insight into the nature of distributed attacks, such as distributed port scans and distributed denial-of-service attacks. An example is an intrusion-prevention tool, Cyber-Defender (www .cyber-defender.com), which runs on individual hosts. If it cannot recognize the behavior of a program that tries to run on a host, it initiates a transfer of this program to the Cyber-Defender Alert Server, which performs analysis and correlation on the program based on changes to files, network activity, and the Registry of Windows systems. If the threat level associated with the suspicious program is high, the Cyber-Defender Alert Server updates a threat pattern file and then sends it to clients.

ADVANCED APPROACHES TO DATA CORRELATION AND FUSION

Although most data correlation performed by analysts is currently rather ad hoc, more advanced ways of dealing with data correlation exist. Identifying features in raw data that match a template is one of the potentially most useful of these ways.

A *template* is nothing more than a particular pattern used in pattern recognition. A template could, for example, be a characteristic pattern of attack by an individual attacker or group, or a set of IP addresses in a certain order, representing the trail or path used by one or more attackers who leapfrog from system to system to make attacks more difficult to trace. Rudimentary forms of templating are, in fact, already being used in leading edge IDSs. Other systems incorporate rule-based knowledge systems or use neural networks to perform data fusion or correlation.

Data Fusion

Tim Bass, a leading thinker in the area of intrusion-detection data correlation and fusion, views data correlation in terms of different levels of abstraction (see Figure 12-1).

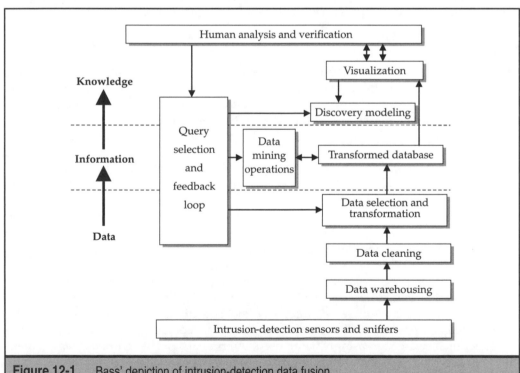

Figure 12-1.   Bass' depiction of intrusion-detection data fusion

The lowest form of abstraction, *level-zero refinement*, is raw data collected from devices such as packet-capture tools. These data include variables such as indicated IP source and destination addresses, timestamps, time-to-live values, and other low-level data. These data are neither validated nor put in a common framework by which they can be compared and analyzed.

The next higher form of abstraction, *level-one object refinement*, is when data are placed in some type of context. Data are cleaned, meaning they are calibrated and filtered. Next-time correlation, determining whether data have been created or sent at the same time, is performed to determine the streams of data that have temporal commonality. For instance, TCP packets coming from a variety of apparent IP source addresses may have all been received by a single host within a period of a few seconds. A level-one object refinement might indicate that the activity is all related. Additionally, different weights can be assigned to various events, such that some will be considered more important than others (for example, because the outcomes they represent constitute a much higher threat to business interests).

The highest level of object refinement is *knowledge fusion*—deriving inferences, explanations, taxonomies, and even threats to critical infrastructures based on events that have occurred. The source of the attack and the motivation for launching the attack are just two of the many important possible by-products of knowledge fusion.

Bass feels that knowledge fusion is still in its infancy. Today's intrusion-detection tools lack this capability, but Bass predicts that future systems will have this ability.

Alert Fusion

Alfonso Valdes and K. Skinner have developed a model of performing intrusion-detection data correlation for the purpose of fusing alerts, which means sending a single alert rather than multiple ones if very similar intrusion-detection-related events occur. Valdes and Skinner's model is based upon the features of events related to incidents, weighted by values based on expectation of similarity. To trigger a fused alert, these features must reach a minimum criterion for similarity, such as a set of specific ports being targeted, in different observations. Other bases of similarity for producing fused rather than separate alerts are dimensions such as similarity of incidents reported by heterogeneous sensors, and correlated attack steps. Although this model is currently of more interest to theoreticians than practitioners, it is potentially useful to organizations that perform intrusion detection, because being overwhelmed with alerts generated by IDSs almost invariably results in operational chaos. Being able to fuse alerts—sending a single alert for a series of highly similar events, for example—is thus advantageous.

By now you may be wondering what all this means. In simple terms, automated intrusion-detection data correlation is becoming increasingly necessary as the diversity and complexity of attacks increases, but for the most part, correlation analysis is currently being done in a rather limited and haphazard manner. Tools that deliver event-correlation functionality are increasingly being used, but perhaps not as frequently as the magnitude of the problem would seem to dictate. Approaches such as template-based data correlation, Bass's approach, and Valdes and Skinner's model give us a picture of just

how systematically data correlation can be performed, but humans cannot really do so without the aid of an appropriate algorithm and considerable computational power. Unfortunately, algorithms of the nature that Bass and Valdes and Skinner have derived are not yet available to the public. Until such algorithms become widely available, those who are involved in intrusion detection should at least become aware of the need for data correlation and also of methods that are currently available. Fortunately, other alternatives are available. Statistical correlation methods, the next topic of this chapter, provide a very promising direction.

UNDERSTANDING AND USING STATISTICAL CORRELATION

The traditional correlation of events in intrusion-detection data is often called *rule-based event correlation* because one or more identifiable conditions (such as repeated sequences of events that can be traced back to a small number of hosts or possibly even a single host) are the basis for event correlation. Not all event correlation is rule-based, however; statistical event correlation is a viable alternative.

Statistics-based event correlation uses statistical methods to discover mathematical relationships between variables that can then be used to identify patterns and origins of events. A major advantage of using the statistical approach is that it is based on metrics—something that is not only conducive to objectivity, but which also lends itself to clarity and precision when intrusion-related events are being analyzed and discussed. Given that statistical packages such as SPSS (Statistical Package for the Social Sciences, www.spss.com) are widely available, statistical approaches provide an excellent approach to correlating intrusion-detection data. Accordingly, we'll cover several topics related to statistical correlation, including what it is, what a correlation coefficient represents, how statistical inference is used in connection with correlation methods, and how to compute a Pearson product-moment correlation.

The Basics of Statistical Correlation

One of the most widely used statistical methods is statistical correlation, which involves taking measurements on two or more variables, then determining the statistical extent of the relationship between the variables.

A *variable* is a symbol for a quantity that may take on different values. For example, the number of vulnerability scans launched by a particular host is a variable. The number of web connections by a host is another. If we counted the number of vulnerability scans on a particular day and also counted the number of web connections by the same host on the same day, and then repeated this process day after day for perhaps 20 days, we would obtain the data necessary to correlate these two variables.

A *correlation* indicates the degree of relationship between the variables. The result of correlation analysis is a value that ranges between –1.00 and +1.00. A negative correlation

means that the value of one variable increases as the value of the other decreases. So if, in the example of correlating the number of vulnerability scans and web connections, we find that on days in which there are more vulnerability scans there are fewer web connections from the host in question, there would be a *negative correlation* between the variables, as shown in Figure 12-2. In this figure, each dot represents an observation or measurement in which a value of both variables (X and Y) is obtained. The value of –1.00 represents a perfect *negative correlation*—one in which the value of the increase in one variable and the decrease in the value of the other is 100 percent accounted for by a linear relationship between the two variables. A perfect correlation is, of course, extremely unlikely—perfect predictability between variables is rare, in part because of measurement error, and also for a number of reasons well beyond the scope of this chapter.

A *positive correlation* means that that the value of one variable increases as the value of the other increases, or conversely that the value of one variable decreases as the value of the other decreases). For example, it is reasonable to expect a positive correlation between the number of log entries in a given system and the number of attacks launched against that system (see Figure 12-3). The value of +1.00 represents a perfect positive correlation, one in which the size of the increase (or decrease) in the value of one variable in a relationship to the change in value of the other is 100 percent predictable.

A value of 0 represents a complete lack of relationship between variables. Another way of saying this is that the variables are randomly related to each other. It would, for example, be reasonable to expect a zero correlation between the memory size of a host and the number of attacks launched against this host (see Figure 12-4).

Correlation Coefficient

The number that is calculated in a correlation analysis is called the *correlation coefficient* (r), and it represents the degree to which the relationship between variables is linear or predictable. Squaring this value produces r^2, the *coefficient of determination*, which

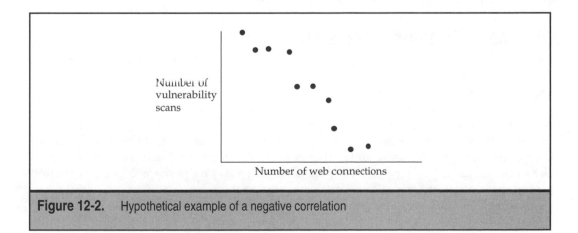

Figure 12-2. Hypothetical example of a negative correlation

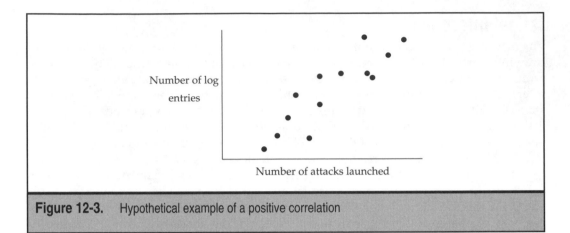

Figure 12-3.   Hypothetical example of a positive correlation

measures the proportion of common variation in the variables in question. The higher the coefficient of determination, the more of the variation that can be accounted for.

In order to analyze the correlation between variables, it is essential to determine the magnitude of the correlation. If a correlation coefficient is +0.5, the coefficient of determination is +0.5 * +0.5, or +0.25, meaning that 25 percent of the variance can be accounted for. If a correlation coefficient is –0.7, the coefficient of determination is –0.7 * –0.7, or 49 percent. This value means that we can account for slightly less than half of the variance in the data. So for intrusion-detection-related events, the higher the coefficient of determination, the more basis an intrusion-detection analyst would have for concluding that the variables in question are related.

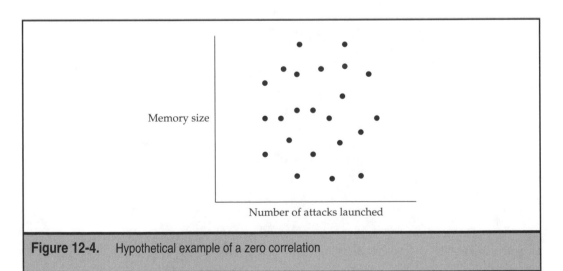

Figure 12-4.   Hypothetical example of a zero correlation

Statistical Inference

The magnitude of the coefficient of determination alone is not really enough to warrant drawing conclusions, however. *Statistical inference*, applying statistical methods to test which of two hypotheses is correct, is necessary if systematic methods are to govern the interpretation of computed correlation coefficients. One hypothesis, the *null hypothesis*, states that the results are simply the product of chance, a random occurrence. The second is that the results are trustworthy—that the same pattern of results would be obtained if another set of measurements of the variables in question were performed.

The likelihood that one's results are due to chance alone greatly diminishes as the size (positive or negative) of the correlation coefficient increases and as the number of observations (measurements) increases. Correlation coefficients produced by chance alone for any given number of measurements are computed, and obtained correlation coefficients are then compared to the "chance alone" values. If the obtained values deviate sufficiently from the "chance alone" values, the null hypothesis is rejected, and the results are said to be *statistically significant*. In most cases, a likelihood of 5 percent or less that obtained results are due to chance alone is considered sufficient for results to be statistically significant.

Pearson Product-Moment Correlation

The most commonly used type of correlation method is the *Pearson product-moment correlation* (often abbreviated as the Pearson *r*). Pearson correlation requires that two variables have been measured on at least *interval scales* of measurement, meaning that each unit on the scale represents the same magnitude for the characteristic being measured across the entire range of variables. The value of *r* indicates the degree to which values of the two variables are "proportional" or "linear" to each other.

The formula for computing *r* is as follows:

$$r = \frac{\Sigma(x-\bar{x})(y-\bar{y})}{\sqrt{SS_x \times SS_y}}$$

X stands for each value of one variable, X, and Y stands for each value of the other variable. $\bar{X}$ is the statistical mean (average) of the X values; $\bar{Y}$ is the statistical mean of the Y values. The formula indicates that the sum of each value of X minus $\bar{X}$ times each value of Y minus $\bar{Y}$ be divided by the square root of SSx (which is computed by taking each value of X minus the mean and then squaring the difference, and finally summing each squared difference) multiplied by SSy. Consider the following set of values for variables X and Y:

X	Y
2	3
4	6
6	7
12	12

Given these values, we can calculate the following results:

$\overline{X}$ is 24 / 4 = 6; $\overline{Y}$ is 28/4 = 7

The sum of:
$(X - \overline{X})(Y - \overline{Y}) = (2-6)(3-7) + (4-6)(6-7) + (6-6)(7-7) + (12-6)(12-7) = 16 + 2 + 0 + 30 = 48$

$SSx = 2^2 + 4^2 + 6^2 + 12^2 = 200$

$SSy = 3^2 + 6^2 + 7^2 \ 12^2 = 238$

$SS_x \times SS_y = 200 \times 238 = 47600$

The square root of 47600 = 218
$r = 48 / 218 = +0.22$

Statistical Correlation

Statistical correlation is potentially a very powerful method of analyzing the relationship between variables. From an intrusion-detection and intrusion-prevention analysis perspective, one of the greatest advantages is that statistical correlation allows investigators to summarize a great deal of data that might otherwise seem overwhelming. Statistical correlation is, in fact, ideally suited for dealing with large amounts of data. Additionally, this method enables those who use it to discover relationships that can be singled out for further statistical analysis using methods such as cluster analysis (see http://obelia.jde.aca.mmu.ac.uk/ and then click on M.Sc. Multivariate Statistics and then CA). Furthermore, statistical correlation is conducive to prediction, provided that obtained correlation coefficients are not equal to 0 or close to 0. If you know the correlation between the number of vulnerability scans and number of FTP-related attacks and are given a known number of vulnerability scans for a given unit of time, you could predict the number of FTP-related attacks. The higher the absolute value of the correlation coefficient, the stronger the prediction.

Like anything else, however, statistical correlation has several distinct downsides. The first and most important is that statistical correlation does not indicate whether or not one variable is *causally related* to another variable. That is, it does not tell you whether or not one variable directly affects the value of another. A common mistake of novice statisticians is inferring causation from correlation. Even variables that have a correlation of +1.00 or –1.00 may not be causally related.

Additionally, statistical correlation does not work very well when the range of one or more of the variables to be correlated is limited. If every value of variable X is either 4 or 5, for example, the range of X is so limited that it will be difficult to obtain a value of a correlation coefficient that is much different from 0. A meaningful correlation minimally requires that a fairly wide range of values for one variable be compared to a fairly wide range of values for another variable.

INFERENCE

Another powerful statistical method that can be applied to data correlation in intrusion detection is Baysian inference. This type of inference is based on Bayes' theorem, a theorem that allows computation of the probability of one event, given that another has occurred. This is the formula:

$$P(A \mid B) = \frac{P(B \mid A)\,P(A)}{P(B \mid A)\,P(A) + P(B \mid \overline{A})\,P(\overline{A})}$$

$P(A \mid B)$ is the probability of event A, given that event B has occurred.

$P(B \mid A)$ is the probability of event B, given that event A has occurred.

$P(A)$ is the probability of event A.

$P(B \mid \overline{A})$ is the probability of event B, given that event A has not occurred

$P(\overline{A})$ is the probability that event A has not occurred.

Among other things, Baysian inference provides a nice way to calculate the probability that a given host is compromised given that a host to which it connects is or is not compromised, something that most IDSs do not do very well. To start this kind of analysis, one must know of at least one "bad" node—a host that is compromised and is used for making connections to other hosts. The probability of any other host being compromised is much higher if it has one or more connections to and from the bad node than if it does not.

Using Bayes' theorem, A is the event in which a host has been compromised, and B represents "symptoms" (remote connections with a bad node). Only 1 percent of all hosts in this hypothetical situation are known to be compromised. The probability that a host is compromised, given that it has one or more connections with a compromised host is .60. So if $P(A) = .01$ and $P(\overline{A}) = .99$, and if $P(B \mid A) = .60$ and $P(B \mid \overline{A}) = .40$, then:

$$P(A \mid B) = \frac{(.60)(.01)}{(.60)(.01) + (.40)(.99)}$$

or a fairly low probability that the host with connections to and from the bad node has been compromised.

Variations of Bayes' theorem can also be applied sequentially to a series of events. Thus, if another connection from a bad node is observed, the recently computed probability of compromise can be used in computing the new conditional probability, which will now increase over the previous value.

The popularity of Bayes' theorem within computer science, operations research, the social sciences, and other arenas very much attests to its usefulness. Although Bayes' theorem is currently not used too frequently in correlating intrusion-detection data, this is likely to change in the future, especially considering that network encryption is growing in popularity, to the point where many network-based IDSs are having a difficult time

analyzing the traffic that goes over the network. Bayes' theorem allows intrusion-detection analysts to predict and correlate events and conditions without having information from the data portion of packets. All one needs is current known or estimated probabilities, such as the probability that a given host is compromised, as well as identification of connections between hosts.

The major limitation of Bayes' theorem is that those who use it often do not really know much about the initial probability that one event will occur given that another occurs. Critics point out that the determination of an initial probability often deteriorates to pure or partial guessing, which can render the meaning of the output of Bayes' theorem dubious.

REAL-TIME VERSUS AFTER-THE-FACT CORRELATION

Real-time correlation means that the output of sensors, packet-capture devices, and other sources of data are correlated as the data are being captured. The term *real-time* is really a misnomer, as machine cycles are required to process whatever information is to be correlated. Real-time correlation requires the availability of a data-correlation program that has a low turnaround time between data acquisition and output, as well as sufficiently high-end hardware to support the required processing speed. As mentioned previously, few intrusion-detection data-correlation programs are currently available. Imagine, therefore, how few near-real-time programs with this functionality are available.

The alternative is *after-the-fact correlation*, meaning that a noticeable time delay occurs before the results of data correlation are available. After-the-fact correlation is in many ways better than real-time correlation in that it can allow a more systematic and thorough evaluation of a broader range of information. The main limitation of after-the-fact correlation is that it is inadequate in urgent situations, where having some information, no matter how crude, is better than having none. But it generally takes time to perform a thorough data correlation, giving the overall edge to after-the-fact correlation if thoroughness is what is most important.

In intrusion prevention, however, the meaning of real-time versus after-the-fact correlation changes considerably. The data required to determine whether or not each pending system call, function within an application, file or Registry access attempt, attempted system modification, and so on, is potentially detrimental need to be continuously available in real time. If such data are not available in real time, systems with intrusion-prevention capabilities could be compromised before an intrusion-prevention engine is finished its analysis. Suppose that someone enters a command in a Unix or Linux system that results in a recursive deletion of the file system without a prompt that gives the user an opportunity to halt the execution of this command:

```
rm -rf *
```

In this case, the intrusion-prevention engine must be able to nearly instantaneously determine that the results of executing this command would be catastrophic and stop the command from being executed. Time is of the essence. But because currently available commercial intrusion-prevention tools are so often host-based, they are neither designed

nor equipped to also instantaneously collect data from sources throughout the network and correlate whatever system event is about to occur with the data gleaned in real time. This is a truly impossible feat for an individual host intended to serve other functions, such file- and application-serving.

Instead hosts usually receive periodic, non-real-time (but nevertheless timely) updates about adverse events—vulnerability scans, attacks, worms, and so forth—often from a master server that performs data correlation and then passes intrusion-prevention policy changes on to each host. The particular policy on each host determines what kinds of operations and functions are and are not allowed. The Cisco Security Agent (formerly Okena StormWatch) intrusion-prevention tool (http://www.cisco.com/univercd/cc/td/doc/product/vpn/ciscosec/csa/21/),works almost exactly in this manner, providing a good case in point. At the same time, however, policy management, particularly tailoring policies to meet the particular security needs of individual hosts, can be a major downside with intrusion-detection technology.

Case Study

Several years ago, an organization was alerted by Snort that a probe directed at the portmapper of a particular Solaris host had been launched. The entry looked like this:

```
[**] [1:1959:1] RPC portmap request NFS UDP [**]
[Classification: Decode of an RPC Query] [Priority: 2]
08/14-04:12:43.991442 192.168.0.0:46637 -> 10.0.0.1:111
UDP TTL:250 TOS:0x0 ID:38580 IpLen:20 DgmLen:84 DF
Len: 56
```

As you will discover in greater detail in Chapter 10, Snort is not a bad intrusion-detection tool (especially considering that it is so lightweight and also is in the public domain), but unfortunately this tool is somewhat prone to producing false alarms (as also discussed in Chapter 10). The intrusion-detection analysts looked for other sources of data to determine what had occurred and when.

Combing through the logs of their Firewall-1 firewall, they found something similar to the following entry (although the source and destination IP addresses here have been changed to private addresses—real addresses have not been used because of the possibility that someone who learns of such addresses attacking these hosts or making false conclusions about what has transpired with them):

```
Aug 14 04:12:43 2003 f_kern_tcp a_nil_area t_netprobe p_major scrip: 192.168.0.1 dstip:
10.0.0.1 protocolname: udp srcburb: 1 srcport: 46637 dstport: 111
```

As they examined the firewall logs more closely, they realized that contrary to their expectations, NFS-related traffic was getting through from the outside to hosts within their internal network. Knowing that NFS (Network File System) is one of the most vulnerability-prone services, they became concerned that one of the main

Case Study *(continued)*

Unix servers within their internal network may have been compromised. Fortunately, after talking to the primary system administrator for the host in question, they found that this host was running a logging tool, NFSwatch (available from http://ftp.cerias.purdue.edu/ pub/tools/unix/netutils/nfswatch/). The system administrator retrieved the NFSwatch output for the host by entering this command:

```
# ./nfswatch -server <hostname> -all
```

The output looked like this:

```
all hosts       Thus Aug 14 20:27:40 2003 Elapsed time: 00:04:01
Interval packets:   898 (network)   766 (to host)    0 (dropped)
Total packets:    21228 (network)  13450 (to host)    0 (dropped)
    Monitoring packets from interface eth0
       int  pct  total          int   pct  total
ND Read          0    0%     0 TCP Packets     450 56% 13678
ND Write         0    0%     0 UDP Packets     448 43%  1051
NFS Read       172   20%   271 ICMP Packets      0   0%    0
NFS Write        1    0%     2 Routing Control    0   0%   36
NFS Mount        0    0%     5 Address Resolution 2   0%   76
YP/NIS/NIS+      0    0%     0 Reverse Addr Resol 0   0%    0
RPCAuthorization 166 20%306 Ethernet/FDDI Bdcst 4   0%  179
Other RPC Packets 25  3%  74 Other Packets       2   0%  131
        2 file systems
 File Sys  int pct total  File Sys  int pct total
waccess(32,17) 0 0%  14
host(32,26)  161 100% 250
```

After looking over the results of this host-based monitoring tool carefully, they realized that the host about which they were concerned was probably not compromised. The overwhelming preponderance of the packets this machine had received were RPC authorization packets, none of which were associated with any known attacks that were occurring at that time. No NFS write packets had been detected, meaning that it was unlikely that someone had mounted a file system and then changed critical files (especially system files).

In this situation, no source of intrusion-detection data was sufficient. The analysts' interest in the event in question was triggered by a Snort alert, confirmed by a log entry in a firewall, and analyzed more fully using data available from a host-based monitoring tool.

SUMMARY

Data correlation is potentially an extremely important issue for many organizations. Simply amassing intrusion-detection data and accepting it at face value is in many cases insufficient, in that it does not go far enough in helping those involved in an incident understand exactly what is occurring, the associated level of threat, and the appropriate intervening action or actions needed. Correlating data, on the other hand, adds meaning and significance to intrusion detection, to the point that if data correlation is done correctly, it leads to deeper levels of understanding and also facilitates the process of responding to incidents that occur.

Currently in most operational settings, data correlation occurs (usually in the form of individuals using knowledge that they have gained when they evaluate new intrusion-detection data), but it is usually rather primitive. Some individuals rise far above the norm, but these individuals are few and far between. And even the most skillful analyst faces massive memory and other cognitive limitations that do not apply to today's computing systems. Automated data correlation provides a much better alternative, but as discussed previously, too few organizations deploy tools that deliver such a capability. Statistical correlation and Baysian methods, in addition to other statistical and mathematical techniques, are also available, but they, too, are underutilized.

What the intrusion-detection and intrusion-prevention arena sorely needs is a next generation of systems capable not only of identifying incidents, but also of correlating events through analysis engines that tie in not only with sensors, but more importantly with large databases of known and suspected incidents. Experts such as Waltz and Llinas have prescribed functionality for systems that will perform advanced data correlation and fusion (see Chapter 17), but except in the military and a few other arenas, too little progress in developing such systems has been evident. As is said throughout this book, intrusion detection is making great headway, but in many respects it is still in its infancy—and intrusion prevention is an even newer technology than intrusion detection. Truly, we have a long way to go.

CHAPTER 13

Incident Response

The number of attacks that an organization faces is growing quickly. To put an IDS or IPS in place with no goals or plan for how to respond is just as risky as not having the systems in place at all. Tracking and responding to intruders on your network is a very complex task that needs to be planned. You need to know when the attack occurred, how it occurred, what the attacker did, and how you can respond to the situation. It is crucial that an incident-response process be set up. There are two ways to deploy IDSs to detect incidents: attack detection and intrusion detection.

Attack detection involves placing a sensor outside the firewall to record attack attempts (see Figure 13-1). This can be useful for tracking the number and types of attacks against your network. The assumption is that the network perimeter is secure, and attack detection will record the attack for use in determining security needs and analyzing attack types. The disadvantage of this type of setup is that it produces a lot of log files that are often ignored and are not used for the intended purpose.

Intrusion detection, on the other hand, involves a sensor placed inside the network. Any detected attacks are possible attacks within the protected perimeter.

This chapter will focus on what needs to be done when these attacks occur and the proper steps for responding to them.

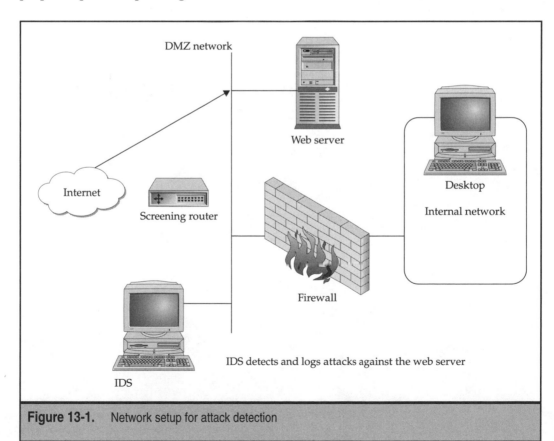

Figure 13-1. Network setup for attack detection

RESPONSE TYPES

The term *response* is used to refer to any action taken to deal with a suspected attack. In general, there are three types of responses that are made: automated responses, manual responses, and hybrid responses.

Automated Responses

Automated responses are responses that happen automatically upon the detection of a specific event. For example, a rule could be set up so that if someone connects to an active port and sends a specific attack string, that connection would be dropped. Automated responses allow the attack to be stopped immediately, and the system returns to a safe state. This is the idea behind an IPS—preventing the attack by blocking the attack as soon as it starts. Automated responses do have their drawbacks, such as when they respond to false positives—activity that appears to be malicious but is not—causing legitimate processes to stop running.

There are several possible automated responses that can be used:

▼ **Dropping the connection**   This response involves stopping all communications on a port, typically at the firewall. The IDS/IPS instructs the firewall to stop the connection. This is typically done if the attack matches a specific string of a known attack. It is important to make sure that the communication is not legitimate, because this response will stop the traffic. Also, it will only affect that single host, and an attacker may just use another host to attack from. Depending on the type of attack, this response will at least buy you a bit of time before the attacker tries again.

■ **Throttling**   This is a technique used against port scans. Throttling adds a delay in responding to a scan, and as the activity increases so does the increase in delay. Since many scanners rely on timing, the added delay can interrupt most script-driven scans.

■ **Shunning**   This is the process of identifying an attacker and denying the attacking system any network access or services. This can be done on the attacked host or at any network chokepoint, such as a router or firewall. The disadvantage of such a response is that if the attacker knows that shunning is being used, they can purposely cause this response to block legitimate services and IP addresses by spoofing the IP address of the attack.

▲ **Session sniping or RESETs**   This technique is used when an attack signature is detected. The IPS sends a forged RESET bit to both ends of the connection to cause the connection to stop. This will cause the buffers to be flushed and the connection to be terminated, averting the attack. Session sniping can be overcome by the attacker by setting the PUSH flag on the TCP packet, which will allow each packet to be pushed to the application as it arrives, which is not normally what happens. Session sniping is not foolproof, but it can achieve moderate success.

There are several ongoing efforts to explore ways not only to automate responses but also to automate tracing methods. While this is still in its infancy, there are two tools worth mentioning. The first is the Intrusion Detection and Isolation Protocol (IDIP), the development of which is funded by DARPA (the Defense Advanced Research Projects Agency), which is the central research and development organization for the U.S. Department of Defense. IDIP sets up components in a virtual security network that allows them to communicate with each other. Upon an attack, the security components alert each other of the attack, and one of the "elected" components will initiate an automated response. IDIP is being tested and used, but it is still in development. The other tool available is DoSTrack developed by MCI, which will run on routers and does automated tracing of packets back to their original source.

Manual Responses

Automated responses are great when they work, but the fact is that humans are still needed to verify and analyze the information. Each attack is different, and humans will consider variables that an automated response cannot. IPS and IDS are still immature technologies, and the need for human reaction is always crucial, but it may be lessened to some degree in the future.

In order to respond manually to an incident, a methodology and team need to be in place, and the plans must be followed. Incident-response methodology and teams will be discussed in the "The Incident-Response Process" section of this chapter.

Hybrid Responses

Hybrid responses are the most common type of response, as no IPS or IDS will be able to respond effectively without the combined efforts of technological and human intervention. A hybrid response is simply a combination of both of the response types already discussed.

For example, suppose you detect a connection to active port 21 on your network that is coming from an unauthorized IP address. Your firewall drops this connection as an automated response. In addition, the security staff looks through logs for this same IP address and similar attacks. You investigate the situation and make adjustments to your network security as needed.

THE INCIDENT-RESPONSE PROCESS

The incident-response process consists of several steps. The first is to do a proper risk analysis, design a proper methodology, and create a response team that will follow the methodology. The following sections discuss these issues in more detail.

Performing a Risk Analysis

The first step in developing and understanding the incident-response process is to do a risk analysis. Risk analysis involves identifying risks within your organization and the

potential loss resulting from those risks. It is imperative that this is done so that a proper response can be put in place, based on the amount of risk. For example, information that is critical for the organization may be protected with all means necessary, while less important resources will not be protected in the same manner.

Risk can be looked at from either a quantitative or qualitative point of view. While it is beyond the scope of this book to get into the details of how to analyze and compute risk, it is important to understand the basic concepts. *Quantitative risk analysis* attempts to assign an objective numeric value, usually monetary, to components of the risk assessment and to potential loss. Quantitative risk will typically use *annual loss expectancy* (ALE) to determine the amount of loss that is associated with a particular risk. ALE can be calculated by multiplying the probability of the loss by the value of the loss itself—this produces the risk loss (Probability × Loss = Risk). For example, if the probability of a virus attack is 4 percent, and the average loss for this type of event is $150,000, the risk would be $6,000.

Qualitative risk analysis does not assign numeric values to components of the analysis but uses a more intuitive approach. For example, you can look at how likely an attack is to succeed and how critical the target of the attack is, and then rank them on a scale, such as from 1 to 10. Then you can also rank the countermeasures you have in place from 1 to 10. The formula would look like this:

(Attack Success + Criticality) – (Countermeasures) = Risk

The problem with this sort of approach is that it is very subjective. Who is to say how likely an attack is to succeed or what collateral damage you should base the criticality on? There are too many variables to consider for this to produce an accurate assessment of risk.

Designing an Incident-Response Methodology

When responding to an incident, it is very important that there be a sound methodology to follow. A *methodology* is a set of working methods for a discipline, in this case incident response. A good methodology gives the incident-response team a set process to follow when responding to an incident. In addition, the use of a sound methodology helps demonstrate an organization's due diligence, especially when legal repercussions are possible.

There are several methodologies that are used, and many organizations use variations on different models, but the model presented here is the most thorough. The model (see Figure 13-2) consists of six stages:

1. Preparation
2. Detection
3. Containment
4. Eradication
5. Recovery
6. Follow-up

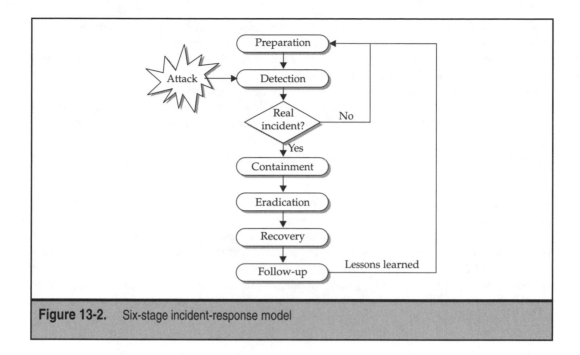

Figure 13-2.   Six-stage incident-response model

The *preparation* stage is when information is gathered on how you would respond to various incidents. The first thing you need to do is gather as much information as possible about the network and the constituent hosts as possible. This includes network diagrams, a list of populated IP space, previous vulnerability scanning records, and if possible, a list of individual hosts' operating systems and arpwatch or DHCP (Dynamic Host Configuration Protocol) data. You then must gather tools for creating procedures and policies, set up predetermined roles and a list of contacts (such as staff from Legal, Human Resources, and Management) for an emergency situation. In addition, you will want technology deployed that will enable a better response to possible attacks—this includes an IDS or IPS, backups, and enhanced logging. This preparation stage is relied upon throughout all the following stages.

The *detection* stage happens when a possible incident has occurred—it is the first reactive stage in the process. Typically the incident will have been detected through logs, IDS alerts, or other similar methods. Once the detection has occurred, it is imperative that the incident be recorded. This includes the date and time, who is involved, any direction from management, the nature of the attack, and what is being attacked. In addition, the scope of the incident needs to be determined, because this will be important in deciding how the incident can be contained and who should be involved. The scope of the incident will determine the overall impact of the attack on the organization.

In the *containment* stage, decisions and actions need to be made about how the incident can be prevented from causing more damage, and how it can eventually be eradicated. For example, if your web server is being attacked by a ping flood, the containment measure could be to turn off ICMP echo requests on your network. Containment may in-

clude shutting down ports on a firewall, disconnecting from the Internet, disabling services or accounts, or shutting a system down. It is important to remember that each of these steps is only a temporary solution to help stop the spread of the attack. It is also important to weigh the impact of taking or not taking these steps against the impact on the business or organization.

Once the event has been contained, it must be eradicated. *Eradication* is the process of eliminating the root cause of the incident, whether it was a back door, virus, or operating system vulnerability. Processes and procedures should have been put in place during the preparation stage to enable the incident team to handle this process.

The *recovery* stage is when you get all systems back up and online as they would normally be. This process assumes that the eradication has taken place and that processes and procedures are followed to bring the systems back up. This often involves using known good media dating from before the incident, and this is why proper backups are important.

The *follow-up* stage is very important, as it reviews the previous steps and analyzes what was done correctly and what could be improved upon. Any improvements can be made a part of the preparation stage for the next incident. Follow-up also includes making sure that steps are put into place to mitigate this type of event in the case of it happening again. For example, a better OS patch-management system could be implemented to prevent known vulnerabilities from being exploited.

Once a methodology, such as the one previously discussed, is put into place, there are other things that should be developed:

▼ **Guidelines on system outages**   Be sure to log how long a system can be disconnected from the network without disrupting critical business function.

■ **Backup and restoration plans**   Identify tools that are likely to be needed in an incident. It is recommended that you have a tool kit with the software and utilities needed to respond appropriately to attacks.

▲ **Incident-reporting and contact forms**   Create forms on which you can record the people contacted, the systems and networks targeted by the attack, purpose of the attack, and evidence of the attack. Figure 13-3 shows a sample incident-reporting form.

 NOTE   It is important to remember that all the information needs to be stored on more than one server, in case that machine is attacked or becomes unusable.

Creating an Incident-Response Team

The incident-response methodology assumes that there is a team that is dedicated to understanding the incident-response process and is ready for action when needed. The reason for having an incident-response team is to ensure that the coordination of the effort goes smoothly. With a team, you have the properly trained experts on hand when needed—the organization identifies with these individuals, and they have a distinct role in the organization during incidents. Depending on the size of the organization you may or may not need to have a full-time dedicated team.

XYZ– Incident Handling Form   PAGE __ OF __

DATE UPDATED: _____
General Information

Incident Handler:
Name: _____ Date and Time Detected: _____
Title: _____
Phone: _____ Alt. Phone: _____ Location Incident Detected From: _____
Mobile: _____ Pager: _____ _____
Fax: _____ Additional Information: _____
E-mail: _____
Address: _____
_____

Signature: _____ Date Signed: _____

Location:
Site: _____
Site Point of Contact: _____
Phone: _____ Phone #2: _____
Mobile: _____ Pager: _____
Fax: _____ E-mail: _____
Address: _____
_____

Additional Information: _____
_____
_____

Incident Summary

Type of Incident Detected:
Please describe incident type and details:
_____
_____
_____
_____
_____
_____
_____
_____
_____
_____

—

Figure 13-3. Incident identification form

It is best if there are specific roles laid out for individuals. Each organization will define the roles differently, but these are some common roles:

▼ **Incident Coordinator (IC)** The role of the incident coordinator is to be a liaison between the different groups that are affected by the incident, such as Legal, Human Resources, different business areas, and management. The IC can help play an important role coordinating between the security teams and

networking groups—during an attack is not the appropriate time to be dealing with who should configure what. The IC will help with the communication process and keeping everyone updated as needed. The IC should have solid communication skills, as well as a good technical and business understanding of the organization.

- **Incident Manager (IM)**   The role of the incident manager is to focus on the incident itself and on how it is being handled from both a management and a technical point of view. The IM is responsible for the actions of the incident analysts and for reporting that information to the IC for further communication. The IM should be a technical expert with a broad understanding of both security and incident management.

- **Incident Analyst (IA)**   The incident analysts are the technical experts in their particular area. They are responsible for direct interaction with the technology and for trying to contain, eradicate, and recover from the incident. These individuals are technical experts in many technologies, as well as technical incident response and security.

▲ **Constituency**   The constituency is not a part of the incident-response team itself, but is a stakeholder in the incident. This group may include various business areas, as well as technical and management teams.

Responding to an IDS or IPS Incident

One of the most important aspects of incident response and intrusion detection and prevention is being able to handle the alerts that are generated. An IDS can generate large numbers of alerts. Being able to identify which ones are legitimate and which are false is crucial. The most common attacks detected by both IDSs and IPSs are scanning attacks, penetration attacks, and denial-of-service attacks, which were covered in Chapters 2 and 3.

Scanning attacks are very common—hackers can download scanning tools from the Internet and can start scanning IP ranges trying to find vulnerable targets. Scanners will help identify open ports and applications that are vulnerable to attack. Nmap is one such tool, and it even has some IDS-evasion capabilities (see Figure 13-4). As discussed previously, throttling is one method that can help against script scans.

Penetration attacks are attacks that try to exploit known vulnerabilities to break into a system. This can include any exploit that has been discovered in an OS that makes the system vulnerable. Attackers can either launch large untargeted attacks, hoping to find a vulnerable system, or they can do OS-fingerprinting for a specific system to find out what it is vulnerable to and then attack.

Denial of service (DoS) attacks violate a system or network by diminishing the system's ability to function as expected under normal circumstances, hence the name *denial of service*. Several forms of DoS attacks were discussed in Chapters 2 and 3. Both IPSs and IDSs look at many different signatures and behaviors to detect DoS attacks.

  It is a good practice to filter outbound IP packets to avoid having them be used in a spoofing attack on someone else.

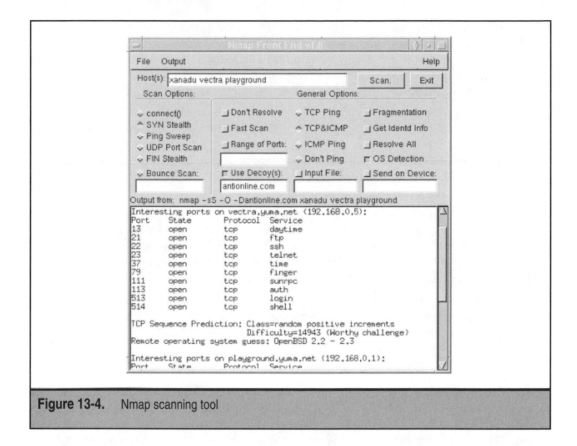

Figure 13-4. Nmap scanning tool

IDS AND IPS INCIDENT-RESPONSE PHASES

There are five phases to dealing with a possible attack:

1. Confirmation
2. Applicability
3. Source
4. Scope
5. Response

Each phase builds off the previous ones, and they should all be a part of your response methodology for IDS and IPS events. As Figure 13-5 demonstrates, the confirmation, applicability, and source phases are all a part of the detection stage of the incident-response methodology (described earlier in the "Designing an Incident-Response Methodology" section of the chapter). Determining the scope will typically be done during the containment stage, though it does cross into the detection stage as well.

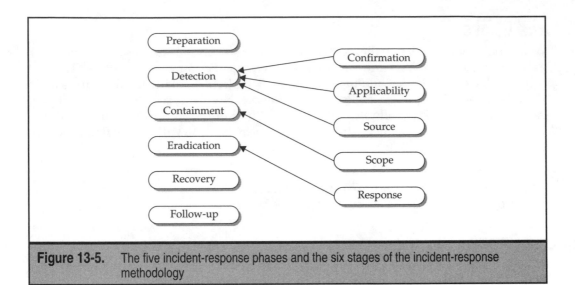

Figure 13-5.   The five incident-response phases and the six stages of the incident-response methodology

Finally, the response phase will happen during the eradication stage of the incident-response methodology.

The incident handler should have a solid knowledge of TCP/IP and the signatures for the particular IDS they will be investigating. If the organization has multiple IDS or IPS systems, it is important to have people with the appropriate expertise for each one.

Confirmation Phase

The first phase is to confirm that an attack is actually happening. The majority of alerts will be false positives, but this can be lessened to some degree by tuning the IDS. Understanding the network you are working on is crucial, as it will help you identify what may or may not be a legitimate attack. You can start by looking at the alert message itself and determining the type of attack that it might be.

Applicability Phase

Once you have determined that the attack is legitimate, you can determine whether it is applicable to your network. Many attackers launch attacks in the hope that they will work, but they do not actually know what your network is comprised of. An attack may have no effect on your particular type of network. For example, if you only run Linux, and an IIS Unicode exploit is launched, it will not hurt your network, but if it is a Linux attack, you will need to take a look at the alert.

Suppose you get the following alert on your Snort IDS:

```
alert tcp $EXTERNAL_NET any -> $TELNET_SERVERS 23 (msg:"BACKDOOR MISC linux rootkit
attempt";flags: A+; content:"wh00t!"; classtype:attempted-admin; sid:213; rev:4;)
```

Because you are running Linux and have telnet enabled, you determine that the attack is applicable to your network.

Source Phase

At this point, you know that the alert is not a false positive and it applies to your network as a legitimate attack. You now must try to determine the source of the attack. The first step is to look at the packet and find the source IP address. Looking the IP address up in the Whois and ARIN (American Registry for Internet Numbers) registries on the Internet can do this. The lookup will reveal the owner of the address and their contact information. Many ISPs give dynamic addresses, which mean that you will need to find the entire address assigned to the ISP to locate the attacker.

 IP addresses can and are spoofed easily, so the source IP address may not identify the actual attacker. However, it is a starting point and can lead to further information to be investigated.

Scope Phase

Now that you have determined the source of the attack, you can look at the scope of the attack. You need to determine what may have been done to the network. This can be accomplished by trying to get an understanding of the attack and the possible effects it could have on your network. You then can look for these possible effects.

You should look through logs from the attacker's IP source and look for other alerts that may relate to the event. The idea is to uncover as much as possible about the attack and other possible attacks that may be occurring. You want to see the big picture to determine what the attacker may be trying to do.

This is easier said than done, as it may take considerable time to piece everything together. This does not mean you have to wait until everything is figured out to respond, but you do need enough evidence to warrant your responses.

Response Phase

Finally, you need to determine the appropriate response for the attack. This may involve disconnecting a system from the network and isolating the specific machine, or you may just need to block the source IP address from your network. Responses can be automated or manual, as discussed earlier in the chapter. The point is to respond quickly to the situation.

This is also the point at which the source IP address's administrator should be contacted and the event should be reported to the CERTCC or law enforcement. Your legal rights and obligations will be discussed in more depth in Chapter 16.

 The CERT® Coordination Center is a federally funded research and development center to which you can report Internet security incidents and vulnerabilities and learn about them in turn. CERT publishes security alerts and researches long-term changes in networked systems. You can send incident reports to cert@cert.org. They have incident reports that can be filled out on their web site at www.cert.org.

Incident-Response Wake-Up Call

The following example incident shows how the five incident-response phases can be applied in an attack situation. Real life does not usually provide such clear-cut situations, but it does help illustrate the topic.

You are the security expert for Company X, and you are awakened at 3:00 A.M. on January 13 by a page from one of your junior security analysts, Bob. As you rub the sleep from your eyes, Bob states, in the page's long text message, that he believes there has been a potential attack. Bob also states that he is unsure of what to do and needs your expertise. You call Bob on the phone, and he is noticing what he thinks may be a host trying to exploit the remote procedure call (RPC) service. He needs your help. You unhappily get dressed and head to work to help figure out the problem.

When you query your Snort IDS logs, you see the following:

```
Jan 13 2:34:05 ids snort[1260]: RPC Info Query: 221.26.52.18:962 ->
172.16.1.101:111
Jan 13 2:34:06 ids snort[1260]: RPC Info Query: 221.26.52.18:963 ->
221.26.52.21:111
Jan 13 2:34:31 ids snort[1260]: spp_portscan: portscan status from 221.26.52.18: 2
connections across 1 hosts: TCP(2), UDP(0)
Jan 13 2:34:31 ids snort[1260]: IDS08 - TELNET - daemon-active: 172.16.1.101:23 ->
221.26.52.18:1209
Jan 13 2:34:34 ids snort[1260]: IDS08 - TELNET - daemon-active: 172.16.1.101:23 ->
221.26.52.18:1210
Jan 13 2:34:47 ids snort[1260]: spp_portscan: portscan status from 221.26.52.18: 2
connections across 2 hosts: TCP(2), UDP(0)
Jan 13 2:34:51 ids snort[1260]: IDS15 - RPC - portmap-request-status:
221.26.52.18:709 -> 221.26.52.21:111
Jan 13 2:34:51 ids snort[1260]: IDS362 - MISC - Shellcode X86 NOPS-UDP:
221.26.52.18:710 -> 221.26.52.21:871
Jan 13 2:34:03 ids snort[1260]: spp_portscan: portscan status from 221.26.52.18: 2
connections across 1 hosts: TCP(0), UDP(2)
Jan 13 2:34:23 ids snort[1260]: spp_portscan: portscan status from 221.26.52.18: 1
connections across 1 hosts: TCP(1), UDP(0)
```

You confirm that the information is accurate and that this is a viable attack that could affect your network.

At this point, you want to find the source of the attack, so you look at the source IP address, 221.26.52.18, and do a whois lookup and find that it is coming from a local ISP in your town.

You now know the source of the attack and want to see if it correlates with any other data. You notice several port scans from the previous few days that came from IP addresses that are assigned to the same ISP that this attack is coming from.

You now need to decide what response needs to be taken. In this case, you simply block the IP range from that ISP and contact the ISP's administrator about the event.

FORENSICS

Though this is a brief overview of the forensic process, it is an important topic. *Computer forensics* is the process of collecting and analyzing information to establish facts in a computer-related investigation. *Forensics gathering* is the search for evidence.

Evidence typically comes from two main sources: Common business records, such as logs, and evidence from investigations, not a part of normal business records. It is important to note that business records are much easier to introduce into court as evidence; investigative evidence can be more challenging, as it is not a part of normal business records. Your IDS and IPS are logging all the time, and that makes those logs a part of normal business records (and thus evidence).

There are two main stages in the forensic process: acquiring the evidence and analyzing the evidence.

Evidence acquisition is critical for a successful forensic evaluation. The decision as to whether you want to prosecute or not will dictate how evidence can be handled, but in general, it is best to collect evidence as if you were going to prosecute. There are several steps that need to be taken to ensure that evidence is preserved correctly—generally, the systems need to be made secure, the surroundings should be examined thoroughly, and the media should be copied and then secured. The entire process needs to record in detail what has taken place and the chain of custody of the evidence.

Once the evidence is collected, copied, and secured, you can analyze it. There are many software packages that perform forensic analysis. The most important step is to determine what evidence you are looking for—it should be unique and unlikely to occur unless nefarious activity is taking place. You can search for evidence in files that have been deleted, as they leave traces and you can search in the slack space. In addition, you can look in the OS files, such as registry settings, for evidence.

NOTE When files are deleted, they typically are not truly erased, but are just tagged as deleted so that the disk space can be written to when it is next needed. Therefore, when searching for evidence, you may find files that were "deleted." In addition, certain file systems use fixed cluster sizes for data to be stored. If the file is smaller than the cluster size, the fixed size is still all reserved for that data, and some of the space will not have been overwritten and will contain old data. This extra space in the cluster is referred to as *slack space*.

Forensic Analysis on IDS Logs

Forensic analysis on IDS logs can be helpful in piecing together the events of an attack. There are some IDSs that capture all packets as well as send alerts, such as Snort. This is valuable when an attack occurs, because you can go back with a protocol analyzer and do packet analysis to find out more details about what was happening. One such network protocol analyzer is Ethereal, which is a freeware tool for Unix and Windows. It will allow the examination of data from a live network or from a capture file on disk.

Packet analysis works great if you have little traffic, as in a small network, but for a medium to large network it is just not feasible to capture and store all the packets. It is also important to note that there can be a "happy medium," where you might record

"interesting" traffic, like incoming interactive traffic, RPC traffic, mail and web traffic, but leave out known encrypted connections.

Many of the mainstream commercial IDSs do not capture packets, but just send an alert. This, coupled with the fact that it is not likely that a medium to large network would want to capture all the packets, somewhat limits packet-capturing and analysis. This does not limit the value of the logs and alerts you have from these IDSs, though, as they are still admissible in court as evidence. Capturing packets is ideal, but simply doing so does not a forensic investigation make. Vendor signatures can and are very useful in investigations. In addition, if an attack is detected, a sniffer can be used to capture packets for that specific attack, and these packets can be analyzed.

CORPORATE ISSUES

When you are a law enforcement agent and you are investigating a computer incident, your goal is simply to get evidence and prosecute. This is not always the case with corporate investigators. They are reluctant to prosecute, and they have more issues to contend with than just prosecution, such as loss of corporate reputation if the information gets out. Many companies would rather let an attacker go than suffer a loss of reputation.

This does not mean that corporations are not concerned about attackers and stopping them. In addition to attacks and loss of reputation, they need to deal with the fact that if they do not have the proper security controls in place, they can be considered negligent. Negligence needs to be considered, because the corporation can be sued for not having proper security controls in place or proper procedures to handle attacks.

There are four things that any organization, private or public, can do to help reduce loss of reputation and negligence litigation. These are following a standard of due care, ensuring accountability, having proper procedures for handling public relations, and following the rules of evidence.

Standard of Due Care

An organization demonstrates that it has met a *standard of due care* when it has followed at least the minimum and customary practices for responsible protection of assets in that particular industry or society. Failure to follow these standards would be considered negligence on the part of the organization. This is why standards of good practice are followed, so that the organization can demonstrate that sufficient due care was taken, based on standards that have been developed by experts in the field. Due care not only helps avoid negligence litigation—it ensures that controls are being used in the most cost-effective manner and that the controls are deployed appropriately for the system that is being managed.

Due care does not mean that a control will not have problems, but that it is being used to the best of its ability. When due care is managed and executed properly, it is called *due diligence*. If an organization fails to show *due diligence*, it can be liable for negligence which can lead to financial loss and loss of reputation.

Accountability

Accountability needs to be associated with exercising a standard of due care. This means that organizations and their management have an obligation to make sure that proper controls are put into place to provide information security. Management may not know technically what needs to be done, but they are responsible for making sure that someone with that knowledge does. Failing to meet this obligation shows negligence on the part of the organization and its management.

Accountability also comes in the form of legislation. As described earlier in this chapter, there are numerous laws that hold organizations and individuals accountable. This includes regulatory bodies for specific industries, as well. An example is the Health Insurance Portability and Accountability Act of 1996 (HIPAA). Any organization that deals with individuals' health information is required to show due care by following the HIPAA requirements, and they will be held accountable for failing to comply.

Public Relations

Having the proper procedures in place to handle an incident is very important. However, it is also important to understand that the way in which an incident is handled can affect the reputation of the company. This is especially true when it comes to how the media is dealt with.

The media are always interested in a good story, so the incident-handling team needs to have procedures for dealing with the media during a disaster to keep the company's message under control. The Public Relations department or a chief security officer can handle the task of relating the news.

The following steps are recommended when dealing with the media:

▼ Have an established unified response for the organization.

■ Maintain a mailing list for larger audiences.

■ Relate the story quickly, easily, and honestly.

■ Determine in advance the appropriate approvals required and clearance processes needed to convey information.

■ Ensure that a spokesperson is accessible to the media.

■ Identify emergency press conference sites in advance.

■ Record events as the crisis evolves.

■ Review and update crisis communications plans and documents on a regular basis. This ensures that information, as well as tactics, are relevant to the time frame and situation.

▲ Consider follow-up communications to allow for fair and impartial reporting of an event.

In addition, proper forensic procedures for handling intrusion-detection data are essential, in case the company needs to press charges against someone. Civil lawsuits can

also result from the use of or mishaps in intrusion detection. If, for example, an organization deploys an IDS that captures information about individuals, but did not warn people that it was monitoring in this manner, the organization is open to a civil lawsuit for breach of privacy. Host-based intrusion detection introduces special risks in this regard, since such an IDS can sometimes single out individuals, especially when there is only one user on a particular machine where the intrusion-detection software runs. Contractors and consultants who set up and operate IDSs can also be sued if some catastrophic incident occurs unbeknownst to them and their IDS. And if IPSs keep critical systems from operating because of false alarms or other reasons, an organization can sue for business losses incurred.

Rules of Evidence

U.S. federal rules of evidence state that for evidence to be admissible in court, it must be gathered, properly acknowledged, and marked so that it can later be identified as being found at the scene of the crime. There are four main sources of evidence:

▼ Oral evidence

■ Written evidence

■ Computer-generated evidence

▲ Visual or audio evidence

The evidence life cycle has seven stages:

1. **Collection and identification** The collection of evidence should be recorded in a logbook detailing each particular piece of evidence. This log should include the initials of the person who found it, the date, the case number, and when and where it was collected.

2. **Analysis** For electronic data a bit-by-bit copy of the evidence should be made, and a forensics examination on the copy of the evidence should be conducted. This can be done by utilizing forensic software. Written evidence can be evaluated for written content.

3. **Storage** Evidence needs to be properly handled and prepared for storage to protect it from damage during transportation, during storage prior to court, and upon its return to the owner.

4. **Prevention** Once evidence has been properly preserved, it should be transported to a storage facility and guarded until it is needed for a trial or is returned to its owner.

5. **Transportation** During transportation of evidence from storage to court, the same care should be taken as when it was initially collected.

6. **Presented in court** Evidence is presented to the court.

7. **Returned to the owner** Evidence is returned to its owner, if applicable.

Hearsay evidence is information that was not personally observed by the witness, but that was learned through another source, such as something they heard another person say. Computer-generated evidence is regarded as hearsay. Business records are also considered hearsay, because there is no way to prove that they are accurate, reliable, and trustworthy. However, should business documents be an integral part of the business activity and be presented by an individual who is competent in their creation and use, it may be possible to submit business documents as evidence.

To do so, three things must be true:

▼ The witness must have regular custody of the records in question.

■ The records must be relied on in the regular course of business.

▲ The records should be gathered in the regular conduct of business.

The following are the characteristics of admissible evidence:

▼ The relevancy of evidence must prove or disprove a material fact.

▲ The reliability of evidence must be proven.

The admissibility of evidence establishes trustworthy evidence through

▼ Witnesses

■ The identification of the owner of the information

■ How evidence is collected

■ How errors are prevented and corrected

▲ Legal means of collection

SUMMARY

This chapter examined responses pertaining to intrusion detection, in which an attack is detected within the protected perimeter. An incident is any malicious activity that would cause harm to data communications, computer systems, or the network. There are three response types that can be made: automated, manual, and hybrid. Hybrid responses are the most common, as they combine the automated responses with human (manual) responses.

In order to respond successfully to an attack, a proper methodology needs to be in place. The most common incident model consists of six stages: preparation, detection, containment, eradication, recovery, and follow-up. Each stage builds upon the previous ones. In addition, a dedicated incident-response team needs to be established with predefined roles within the organization. Responses to incidents that pertain specifically to IDSs and IPSs can follow the five stages of confirmation, applicability, source, scope, and response.

We finally looked at the forensic process and the importance of collecting evidence in a secure manner.

CHAPTER 14

Policy and Procedures

The key to any successful intrusion detection and prevention program is based on sound policies, standards, guidelines, procedures, and baselines. This chapter attempts to define the differences among these as they're often referred to in the same context. Then, the focus will be on the creation of policies and procedures that can help your organization achieve optimal success.

POLICIES, STANDARDS, GUIDELINES, PROCEDURES, AND BASELINES

First, let's define the terms. A *policy* is a high-level statement of beliefs, goals, and objectives, and the general means by which they can be achieved. Policies help to determine strategies for standards, guidelines, procedures, and baselines. A *standard* is a mandatory activity, action, rule, or regulation designed to support policy structure and lend specific direction. Standards are often expensive to administer and, therefore, should be used judiciously.

A guideline is similar to a standard, but it's a more general statement of how to achieve policy objectives. *Guidelines* provide the framework needed to implement procedures. Where standards are mandatory, guidelines are recommendations and more flexible. Guidelines are "recommended actions" only.

A *procedure* outlines the specific steps of how the policy, supporting standards, and guidelines will be implemented. A procedure is a description of tasks that must be executed in a specific order. Procedures are sometimes referred to as "practices."

A *baseline* is a method of implementing security mechanisms and products. Baselines are platform unique and should be employed throughout an organization. They detect differences between various operating systems (OSs) to ensure uniform security implementation.

IDS/IPS Policy

When creating a strong defense-in-depth policy, a good deal of time must be spent on researching the tools that will be used. Creating an IDS policy can be a daunting task, but one that can reap many benefits when done correctly. An IDS policy is a stand-alone policy, but it integrates with other policies, such as the firewall, routers, and incident response. When creating a policy, it's important to include enough detail to be able to determine the strategies for standards, guidelines, procedures, and baselines. The policy needs to include why it's important to the organization, and it must be prepared for signs of intrusion and lead to procedure development. Once the policy is written, it needs to undergo legal review. Once reviewed, the procedure can be drawn from the policy and implemented in the organization. Finally, it's critical that the policy remain current with up-to-date procedures and information.

Creating an IDS/IPS Policy

Earlier in this book, the importance of risk analysis was discussed. The relationship between risk analysis and the security policy is important for an effective security program. When defining your organizational needs, a risk analysis can and should help to determine what will go into your policies.

When you create a policy, having input from the organization as to what they want to achieve is critical. The policy wants to cover the why and the how. One effective way to do this is to cover the following seven steps:

▼ Introduction

■ Purpose

■ Scope

■ Policy

■ Enforcement

■ Definitions

▲ Revisions

The introduction and the purpose help set the stage for the rest of the document. Having the correct policy language in place can help prepare your organization to detect signs of intrusion in a timely, controlled manner. The *introduction* should give a general statement about what the document will cover. The *purpose* shows why this technology is important and why it's necessary to have a policy. These could seem like simplistic topics that might not be needed but, for the nontechnical management, it helps to clarify the reasoning and gives a high-level definition of the technology. The scope is important because it helps define who this policy affects. This can be an entire department, all users, or a group of individuals. The scope must be defined for legal reasons to make certain it's clear for whom the policy is intended and for clear understanding of the perspective on which the policy should be taken.

The policy itself is the section that states what's expected. This section helps give general guidance and could include or refer to procedures that need to be taken. The policy section should be more clear and concise about what must occur in given situations. This is the how and why of the document.

Enforcement defines what the consequences are to those defined in the scope. This section can define specific consequences or point to other documents, such as an HR manual or a code of conduct.

Finally, there are the definitions and revisions sections. The *definitions* section helps put forth specific meaning for your organization and helps eliminate any assumptions. The *revisions* section reflects the current policy and indicates when it was last updated. This is important for keeping current and usable policies.

The following is an example policy using this seven-step process:

Section*x*	*<Your Organization Here>*	mm/dd/yy: Effective
		mm/dd/yy: Revised
Policy *x.xx*	**Intrusion Detection Policy**	Security Analyst Author

Step 1: Introduction

Intrusion detection is a critical piece of the organization's security policy. Effective security systems must evolve to handle the vast amount of vulnerabilities introduced by the use of distributed systems. Having some type of reassurance that the systems and network are secure is important, and intrusion detection systems can help provide part of that assurance.

Step 2: Purpose

The purpose of this policy is to provide guidance for the use of intrusion detection at *<Your Organization Here>*. This document is to be followed for intrusion-detection monitoring using intrusion detection tools and system audit logs for the system servers, software, database, networks, and firewalls under its control.

Step 3: Scope

This policy applies to all constituents at *<Your Organization Here>*. More specifically, this policy applies to all individuals who are responsible for the installation of new information resources, the operations of existing information resources, and individuals charged with information resource security.

Step 4: Policy

24×7 intrusion-detection monitoring will be conducted by using intrusion-detection tools and system audit logs for the system servers, software, database, networks, and firewalls under its control. Reports will be submitted daily for assessment and possible corrective action. Immediate corrective action will be taken to help eliminate system vulnerabilities or to prevent future intrusion attempts. This can also be seen as a contract with the rest of the organization regarding the expected quality of service (that is, 24×7 or maximum response time).

Procedures for system break-ins:

▼   Immediately notify management via a predefined emergency notification list and notify the affected network manager.

■   Follow up with a system security report to management in the System Security Template, as shown in the following example. The report will include an assessment on compromised systems or information, system risks, and corrective actions.

▲   Security management will determine the appropriate corrective action and direct the corrective action based on priority.

System Security Template
Date:
Time:
Security Incident Report—Number _____
Incident Details:
Information Resource Effect:
Incident Identified By:
Source of Attempt:
Analyses and Recommendation(s):
Reporting Manager:

Other procedures include the following:

▼   Operating system, user accounting, and application software audit logging processes must be enabled on all host and server systems.

■   Alarm and alert functions of any firewalls and other network perimeter access control systems must be enabled.

■   Audit logging of any firewalls and other network perimeter access control system must be enabled.

■   Audit logs from the perimeter access control systems must be monitored/reviewed daily by the system administrator.

■   System integrity checks of the firewalls and other network perimeter-access control systems must be performed on a routine basis.

■   Audit logs for servers and hosts on the internal, protected network must be reviewed on a weekly basis. The system administrator will furnish any audit logs as requested by the ISO.

■   Host-based intrusion tools will be checked on a routine basis.

- All trouble reports should be reviewed for symptoms that might indicate intrusive activity.

▲ All suspected and/or confirmed instances of successful and/or attempted intrusions must be immediately reported according to the Incident Management Policy. Users will be trained to report any anomalies in system performance and signs of wrongdoing to the IS Help Desk.

Step 5: Enforcement

Any employee found to have violated this policy could be subject to disciplinary action, up to and including termination of employment. Additionally, individuals are subject to loss of information resources, access privileges, and the possibility of civil and criminal prosecution.

Step 6: Definitions

▼ **Constituent**   Any employee, contracted employee, or affiliate of the company.

- **Information Resources**   Any computer-related or computer-generated material. Including, but not limited to, printouts, online display devices, magnetic storage media, and any computer-related activities involving any device with e-mail receiving capabilities, browsing web sites, or otherwise capable of receiving, storing, managing, or transmitting electronic data including, but not limited to, mainframes, servers, personal computers, notebook computers, hand-held computers, personal digital assistants (PDA), and pagers.

▲ **Security Incident**   Any attempt or action of unauthorized access to a information resource.

Step 7: Revision History

▼ Policy: Version 1.0 April 2000

- Revised: Version 1.1 June 2002

▲ Revised: Version 1.2 May 2003

Legal Review

Creation of any security policy needs to be reviewed by your organization's legal representation, so the policy can be legally reinforced and defensible. Your legal department can help determine if the policy reflects best practices and due care on the part of your organization. When investigations of an incident occur, it's critical that your organization does everything in its power to protect the information and preserve evidence for legal proceedings. In addition, making sure that your organization adheres to all local, state, and federal regulations can help.

Another key issue is to make sure the policy is in touch with legislation that affects your organization. Your policy should include a clause regarding compliance with any legislation. Because much legislation is required, it's wise to incorporate your policies with this legislation. Your legal department is in the best position to do this.

Procedure for Implementation of Your Policy

Just having a policy written isn't nearly enough. Proper implementation of the policy is key. At this stage, the staff needs to be educated on the policy and what needs to be done for the policy to succeed. Therefore, all staff who have access to, or are responsible for, the IDS or the IPS program must have the policy made available to them. The policy should be easily accessible, but also secured. This can be done via an intranet site or on a server on the internal network.

Keeping Your Policy Current

Keeping your policy current is critical for a successful policy. If your policy is outdated, it won't do anyone any good when it's needed. Make certain you review your policy at least annually. Things that might need to be updated include the following:

▼ Any new software added

■ New legislation

■ Changes in procedures

■ Changes in critical assets

■ Roles and responsibilities

■ Contact information

▲ New detection methods

Also important is to look at what happened during an incident and revise your policy to reflect these issues. You might find your policy lacks certain steps or actions that should have been addressed.

SUMMARY

This chapter examined the need for a good intrusion policy. We looked at the creation and implementation of an intrusion detection policy. A seven-step methodology including Introduction, Purpose, Scope, Policy, Enforcement, Definitions, and Revisions was discussed. Once a policy is created, it is important to make sure that it is legally compliant and kept up-to-date, at least on an annual basis.

CHAPTER 15

Laws, Standards, and Organizations

There are several laws, standards, and organizations that affect intrusion prevention and detection. The beauty and danger of the cyberworld is that it respects no jurisdictional boundaries between states and countries. We can exchange information freely across borders. From a legal perspective, this offers unique challenges. For example, in the U.S. the Fourth Amendment allows only for limited search and seizures to target a specific piece of evidence, but this is usually not what is done in computer investigations. Investigators typically do not know what exactly they are looking for when they start searching. The U.S. constitution gives the United States government the right to regulate interstate and foreign commerce, and it is because of this regulation that many of the laws pertaining to the protection of networks are federal statutes.

Internationally the same is true. For example, the European Union Privacy Directive (EUPD), also known as the EU Data Protection Directive, took effect on October 25, 1998. This directive set forth privacy and data protection policies that have set the stage for international laws. The EUPD will be discussed in more detail later in this chapter.

UNDERSTANDING LEGAL SYSTEMS

It is important that we start off with a basic discussion of the primary legal systems that exist today. These are common law, civil law, and Islamic law. Both common and civil law characterize the majority of the legal systems used in the world today; the other 20% are based on Islamic law.

Common Law

Common law started in the traditions of the English. Later these laws were written down and refined over hundreds of years. Common law is based on the historical precedents set by society over a period of time. Judgments are arrived at by looking over the facts and applying the legal precedents.

Common law is in force in England, Canada, and the United States. When settlers came from England to the United States, their common laws were adopted by most states as basic laws. Presently, most common law has been enacted into statutes with some modern variations by all the states with the exception of Louisiana, which is still influenced by the Napoleonic code.

Civil Law

The basic document of all civil law, *Corpus Juris Civilis*, came from the Byzantine Emperor Justinian I. Civil laws are codified laws, which mean they are an orderly arrangement of laws into understandable, compact volumes. The Romans prepared codes and revised obsolete laws from time to time. Civil laws work on the legal principles of free introduction and evaluation of evidence. The United States, countries on the continent of Europe, Latin American countries and many countries that have adopted Western legal systems, like Japan, follow civil law.

Islamic Law

Islamic law controls the family and property interests of Muslims in countries where personal law is determined by religion. The church and state are not separated. This type of law is based on punishment. Crimes are considered "taazir" which means that one has the personality of a criminal. Under Islamic law, the religion of Islam and the government are one. Islamic law is controlled, ruled, and regulated by the Islamic religion.

U.S. COMPUTER-RELATED LAWS

There are several U.S. computer-related laws that are relevant to intrusion detection and prevention. This is by no means a comprehensive discussion of law affecting computer-related crimes, but simply a general look at how the law may affect the use of IDSs and IPSs.

Computer Fraud and Abuse Act, 18 U.S.C. § 1030

In the United States, statutes are written by the government to help define criminal activity. The primary statute pertaining to computer-related crimes is 18 US Code 1030, the Computer Fraud and Abuse Act (CFAA).

The CFAA was enacted to protect any computer that is used in interstate or foreign communication. This essentially brings all computers in the United States that have Internet access into the scope of the statute. The statute criminalizes unauthorized access to computer systems, theft of information in computer systems, and unauthorized modification of data in computer systems.

Electronic Communications Protection Act, 18 U.S.C. §§ 2510–22 and § 2701

The U.S. Congress, in response to the changing nature of technology, enacted Public Law 99-508 or the Electronic Communications Protection Act (ECPA) of 1986. The act is divided into two parts: 18 U.S.C. Title I (section 2500), Interception of Communications and Related Matters, and 18 U.S.C. Title II (section 2700), Stored Wire and Electronic Communications and Transactional Records Access. Title I restricting people from listening in on private communications, including computer communications. This key word here is *private*, as there are public communications, such as bulletin boards, that are freely accessible. Title II deals with accessing systems in which one is not authorized or even in which one has been authorized access but has exceeded the authorized level access on a system, such as gaining superuser privileges on a system in which only regular user privileges are authorized. This Act makes these kinds of access a federal offense and prescribes punishment for violations.

If you are using an IDS or IPS on your network, how do you justify looking at packets of private communications without breaking the law? An IDS or IPS will invariably

capture personal data, such as social security numbers, drivers license numbers, credit card numbers, and so on. When you run an IDS/IPS on a network, it is typically a private network of the organization, not the individual using it. Therefore it is important that you make it clear to your organization's users that all communications within the network are the property of your organization and not to be used for private/personal communications (except possibly for allowed "incidental use"). Advising users that anything they do when they are using a computer or network owned by your organization is subject to inspection and/or search is also critical. Warning banners on computer systems generally provide the best avenue for advising users of these policy provisions.

Title I 18 U.S.C. section 2703 allows law enforcement agencies to seize data, such as intrusion-detection data, and all hardware associated with those data. The ramifications for an ongoing intrusion detection effort are potentially huge—an ongoing IDS/IPS capability could conceivably be dismantled by a law enforcement agency acting in accordance with this lawThis is another good reason to have a second line of intrusion detection/prevention capabilities in place.

The Sarbanes-Oxley Act

Corporate governance was changed in the wake of recent financial scandals. Congress enacted the Sarbanes-Oxley Act of 2002, which requires that organizations follow rigorous guidelines to validate the accuracy of their financial data and management due diligence. CEOs and CFOs must personally certify that their companies' statements are complete and accurate. Large penalties, including imprisonment, are specified for violation of this act.

This act affects organizations using IDS and IPS because it requires that *all* evidence, including evidence stored on computers used in connection with intrusion detection and intrusion prevention, be properly preserved and cared for if that evidence is needed in a federal investigation. Taken literally, Sarbanes-Oxley might even require that bulk packet dumps gleaned by an IDS or IPS be preserved, something that would require massive archiving and storage capabilities. The "bottom line" here is that every organization that engages in intrusion detection and/or intrusion prevention needs to determine how the need to comply with the Sarbanes-Oxley Act affects the procedures used in connection with these activities are affected and then modify them accordingly.

Health Insurance Portability and Accountability Act (HIPAA)

For the improvement, privacy, and efficiency of the current health care system, the Health Insurance Portability and Accountability Act of 1996 (HIPAA), Public Law 104-191, was passed. HIPAA establishes a foundation of federal protections for the privacy of protected health information. HIPPA sets the foundation, but in no way replaces more in-depth and specific federal or state laws. Specifically, HIPAA requires thorough analysis of risk and of information-handling processes for information systems to help ensure the integrity of patient health information. Full compliance requires that health care companies to which this law applies comprehend the threats and liabilities to health-related data and that they put a range of safeguards and best practices in place. In addition

Interpreting HIPAA

Few pieces of legislation have caused as much confusion in the health care and information security arenas as has HIPAA. HIPAA compliance requires five phased steps—specification of privacy rules for larger health providers, system testing, compliance with transactions and code sets, specification of privacy rules for small health providers, and final security compliance. Although HIPAA specifies what must be accomplished to meet the requirements of this law, how to do this is a matter of interpretation. Vendors have developed compliance methodologies and products such as the SES HIPAA Compliance Product (visit http://www.sesecure.com/main.asp) to make compliance easier. But no one really knows how the U.S. government will actually evaluate the degree to which each organization has complied with the requirements of this act.

HIPAA requires a clear way to detect and report security violations and specifies penalties for failure to comply.

HIPAA affects organizations IDS/IPS efforts in a similar manner to Sarbanes-Oxley, as the need for preserving logs and evidence is needed. "Due care" in the process and reporting of information is crucial to compliance to organizations dealing with health information such as hospitals, insurance companies and clinics.

Gramm-Leach-Bliley Act

The Gramm-Leach-Bliley Act (GLBA), also known as the Financial Services Modernization Act of 1999, provides privacy protection against the sale of private financial information. GLBA includes three requirements to protect the personal data of individuals: First, banks, brokerage companies, and insurance companies must securely store personal financial information. Second, they must advise consumers of their policies on the sharing of personal financial information. Third, they must give consumers the option to opt out of some sharing of personal financial information. There are fewer potential implications for intrusion detection and intrusion prevention than with the Sarbones-Oxley and HIPAA Acts. Nevertheless, organizations would be well-advised to examine the implications of the Gramm-Leach-Bliley Act if they sell or exchange intrusion detection data that may contain private financial information.

STATE LAWS

An entire book could be written about the different state laws that are in effect. Table 15-1 provides a partial list, by state, of computer-related laws in effect. California's SB1386 statute has wide implications to other states but also other countries as well. A good source with which to research state laws can be found at http://nsi.org/Library/Compsec/computerlaw/statelaws.html.

State	Computer Crime Laws
AL	Computer Crime Act, Code of Alabama, Sections 13A-8-100 to 13A-8-103
AK	Statutes, Sections 11.46.200(a)(3), 11.46.484(a)(5), 11.46.740, 11.46.985, 11.46.990
AZ	Revised Statues Annotated, Sections 13-2301(E), 13-2316
CA	Penal Code, Section 502, California Statute SB1386
CO	Revised Statutes, Sections 18-5.5-101, 18-5.5-102
CT	General Statutes, Sections 53a-250 to 53a-261, 52-570b
DE	Code Annotated, Title 11, Sections 931-938
FL	Computer Crimes Act, Florida Statutes Annotated, Sections 815.01 to 815.07
GA	Computer Systems Protection Act, Georgia Codes Annotated, Sections 16-9-90 to 16-9-95
HI	Revised Statutes, Sections 708-890 to 780-896
ID	Code, Title 18, Chapter 22, Sections 18-2201, 18-2202
IL	Annotated Statutes (Criminal Code), Sections 15-1, 16-9
IN	Code, Sections 35-43-1-4, 35-43-2-3
IO	Statutes, Sections 716A.1 to 716A.16
KS	Statutes Annotated, Section 21-3755
KY	Revised Statutes, Sections 434.840 to 434.860
LA	Revised Statutes, Title 14, Subpart D. Computer Related Crimes, Sections 73.1 to 73.5
ME	Revised Statutes Annotated, Chapter 15, Title 17-A, Section 357
MD	Annotated Code, Article 27, Sections 45A and 146
MA	General Laws, Chapter 266, Section 30
MI	Statutes Annotated, Section 28.529(1)-(7)
MN	Statutes (Criminal Code), Sections 609.87 to 609.89
MI	Code Annotated, Sections 97-45-1 to 97-45-13
MS	Revised Statutes, Sections 569.093 to 569.099
MT	Code Annotated, Sections 45-2-101, 45-6-310, 45-6-311
NE	Revised Statutes, Article 13(p) Computers, Sections 28-1343 to 28-1348
NV	Revised Statutes, Sections 205.473 to 205.477

Table 15-1. Computer-Related Crime Laws by State

State	Computer Crime Laws
NH	Revised Statutes Annotated, Sections 638:16 to 638:19
NJ	Statutes, Title 2C, Chapter 20, Sections 2C:20-1, 2C:20-23 to 2C:20-34, and Title 2A, Sections 2A:38A-1 to 2A:38A-3
NM	Statutes Annotated, Criminal Offenses, Computer Crimes Act, Sections 30-16A-1 to 30-16A-4
NY	Penal Law, Sections 155.00, 156.00 to 156.50, 165.15 subdiv. 10, 170.00, 175.00
NC	General Statutes, Sections 14-453 to 14-457
ND	Century Code, Sections 12.1-06.1-01 subsection 3, 12.1-06.1-08
OH	Revised Code Annotated, Sections 2901.01, 2913.01, 2913.04, 2913.81
OK	Computer Crimes Act, Oklahoma Session Laws, Title 21, Sections 1951-1956
OR	Revised Statutes, Sections 164.125, 164.377
PA	Consolidated Statutes Annotated, Section 3933
RI	General Laws (Criminal Offenses), Sections 11-52-1 to 11-52-5
SC	Code of Laws, Sections 16-16-10 to 16-16-40
SD	Codified Laws, Sections 43-43B-1 to 43-43B-8
TN	Code Annotated, Computer Crimes Act, Sections 39-3-1401 to 39-3-1406
TX	Codes Annotated, Title 7, Chapter 33, Sections 33.01 to 33.05
UT	Computer Fraud Act, Utah Code Annotated, Sections 76-6-701 to 76-6-704
VA	Computer Crime Act, Code of Virginia, Sections 18.2-152.1 to 18.2-152.14
WA	Revised Code Annotated, Sections 9A.48.100, 9A.52.010, 9A.52.110 to 9A.52.130
WI	Statutes Annotated, Section 943.70
WY	Statutes, Sections 6-3-501 to 6-3-505

Table 15-1.   Computer-Related Crime Laws by State *(continued)*

California Statute SB1386

California's Notice of Privacy Breech statute, usually referred to as SB1386, was passed on September 26, 2002, and took effect on July 1, 2003. This statute is broad in reach and intends to affect any organization anywhere in the world that does business in California and/or maintains personal data on California residents. If that information is acquired by

an individual without authorization, or is reasonably believed to be acquired by an unauthorized person, the organization that has stored this information is subject to the statute and is required to notify every California customer of the breech in a timely manner. What "timely" means is a matter of interpretation; the punishment for violation is also not specified (although the law states that offenders can face civil lawsuits). Although how or even if this law can be enforced outside the United States is uncertain, SB1386 does set a potential precedent for international law.

Applying SB1386 to intrusion detection and intrusion prevention will be interesting to watch. As stated earlier, it is inevitable that data on individuals will be collected wherever IDS/IPSs are in place. There has been no court precedence set for SB1386 at the time this chapter was being written.

INTERNATIONAL CYBER SECURITY-RELATED LAWS

There are many laws that have been enacted internationally that affect computer crime and privacy, specifically relating to intrusion detection and prevention. This section covers some of the more notable ones.

The § 28 EC European Union Privacy Directive

The European Union Privacy Directive, also known as the EU Data Protection Directive, took effect on October 25, 1998. It requires that organizations set forth policies that will keep personal data private. The directive requires a host of policies to be followed, including these:

▼ **Purpose limitation**   All data that is collected needs to be collected for a specified purpose and kept only for enough time to fulfill the stated purpose.

■ **Data transfers**   Transferring authorized data to a third party is restricted without permission of the party providing the data, or the data's subject. In addition, if the data transfers across national boundaries, the Directive prohibits data transfers to any country that lacks adequate protection, as defined by the EU.

▲ **Individual redress**   Data subjects have the right to access information about themselves, make corrections to any inaccurate statements or information, and deny the use of their personal information.

United Kingdom Computer Misuse Act, 1990

The United Kingdom Computer Misuse Act was created in 1990 and states that any attempted or actual computer access, without the proper authority, may be regarded as a breach of security. The act covers any incident where one or more components (for example, the user, telecommunications, or computer) are located within the United Kingdom.

Germany's Datenschutz Law

The Federal Data Protection Commission (Bundesbeauftragte für den Datenschutz) is responsible for supervision of the Data Protection Act or the Datenschutz law in Germany. The Datenschutz law prescribes jail time for those who fail to protect data adequately.

Republic of China Laws

The Republic of China has two computer-related regulations that have an impact on computer crime: the Revised Provisional Regulations Governing the Management of Chinese Computer Information Networks Connected to International Networks and the Computer Information Network and Internet Security, Protection, and Management Regulations. These regulations set out specific guidelines that need to be followed for communications within the Republic of China.

The Problems with International Law

Computer laws have come a long way in the past decade and are continuing to improve. The biggest problems are in applying them between international boundaries, because many countries still do not have substantive laws that specifically criminalize computer crimes. This can hinder the investigation and prosecution of computer crimes. An example is the U.S.-Philippine investigation of the suspected perpetrator of the ILOVEYOU virus, which bought down many e-mail systems worldwide. This investigation was restricted by the lack of specific computer-crime statutes.

The other problem is that there is a lack of case law and legal precedents in most countries for handling computer-related crimes. While there has been an effort to establish legislation to deal with computer-related issues, there is a lack of case law to create new legislation, which is how most legislation is produced. Because computer technology has grown very quickly, there hasn't been enough time to get the legal precedents needed for jurisprudence. This will take time.

There are also issues of jurisdiction. It is very difficult to investigate and prosecute computer-related crimes. Who has jurisdiction if a crime is committed from one country and the victim is in another country? An attack may also be committed from multiple locations around the globe. Attackers may look to attack from a country with less or no legislation in effect, enabling them to elude prosecution.

STANDARDS

In addition to the many laws that are in place to help guide you, there also many, sometimes competing, standards that have been developed in the IDS and IPS field. Standards help to set a common ground for interoperability between solutions, and they help to develop a more mature technology.

The result of these standards is that security professionals can communicate with each other using the same terminology and with an expectation of interoperability, even though they may have different IDSs or IPSs implemented.

This section provides a partial list of the main IDS- and IPS-related standards.

The Common Intrusion Detection Framework (CIDF)

The Common Intrusion Detection Framework (CIDF) was the joint effort of a number of companies and organizations and the Defense Advanced Research Projects Agency (DARPA). The project was started in 1997 and is now dormant. The purpose of the group was to develop protocols and application programming interfaces (APIs) so that there could be a sharing of information between intrusion-detection research projects. Most of the contributions came from the United States, but there was growing international participation in the group. For more information about CIDF, go to http://www.isi.edu/~brian/cidf/.

Intrusion Detection Working Group (IDWG)

Many of the ideas put forth by CIDF were picked up by an Internet Engineering Task Force (IETF) working group, named the Intrusion Detection Working Group (IDWG). The IDWG helped to develop a common format for IDS alerts and exchange procedures for sharing information with systems that need to interact with them.

Two interesting works that have come from the IDWG:

▼ **Intrusion Detection Message Exchange Requirements** This document defines requirements for the Intrusion Detection Message Exchange Format (IDMEF), which is planned to be a standard format that automated IDSs can use for reporting events they have deemed to be suspicious or of interest. In addition, the document entitled *Intrusion Detection Message Exchange Format Data Model and Extensible Markup Language (XML) Document Type Definition* expands on this concept.

▲ **The Intrusion Detection Exchange Protocol (IDXP)** This document describes an application-level protocol for exchanging data between intrusion-detection entities.

Common Vulnerabilities and Exposures (CVE)

The MITRE Corporation maintains the Common Vulnerabilities and Exposures (CVE). CVE is a list of standardized names for vulnerabilities and other information-security exposures, developed in a collaborative effort. The goal is to standardize the names for all publicly known vulnerabilities and security exposures. This will help when sharing data across separate vulnerability databases. CVE is considered a dictionary of known vulnerabilities, not a database. It can be found at www.cve.mitre.org.

Following is an example of CVE vulnerability for Windows Media Player 7. You can see how it cross-references the vulnerability with other sources—in this case, BUGTRAQ (a posting to Bugtraq mailing list), MS (Microsoft), XF (X-Force Vulnerability Database), and BID (Security Focus Bugtraq ID database entry).

```
CVE-2001-0137
Windows Media Player 7 allows remote attackers to execute malicious Java
applets in Internet Explorer clients by enclosing the applet in a skin file
named skin.wmz, then referencing that skin in the codebase parameter to an
applet tag, a.k.a. the Windows Media Player Skins File Download
vulnerability.
Reference: BUGTRAQ:20010115 Windows Media Player 7 and IE java vulnerability
- executing arbitrary programs
Reference: MS:MS01-010
Reference: XF:win-mediaplayer-arbitrary-code(5937)
Reference: BID:2203
```

ARACHNIDS

Whitehats.com has developed an online community resource called the "advanced reference archive of current heuristics for network intrusion detection systems," or arachNIDS. The focus is to support open source security software.

The arachNIDS database has a comprehensive list of attack signatures, and lists of these signatures can be dynamically generated to be exported to IDS software such as Dragon, Snort, and Shoki. The database is a great resource if you are using the supported IDS software, or even if you want to do research into different security vulnerabilities. The database, shown in Figure 15-1, is fully searchable and it correlates to other security databases and listings, such as CVE and Bugtraq.

International Symposium on Recent Advances in Intrusion Detection (RAID)

The International Symposium on Recent Advances in Intrusion Detection (RAID) workshop series is an annual event dedicated to the sharing of information related to intrusion detection. RAID has been active since 1998, and it consists of experts from government, industry, and academia who gather to discuss state-of-the-art intrusion-detection technologies. The symposium is held in a different location every year, and it is intended to further progress in intrusion detection by promoting the exchange of ideas in a broad range of topics among researchers, system developers, and users, the symposium is held in a different location every year. Information about the past symposia is available at www.raid-symposium.org.

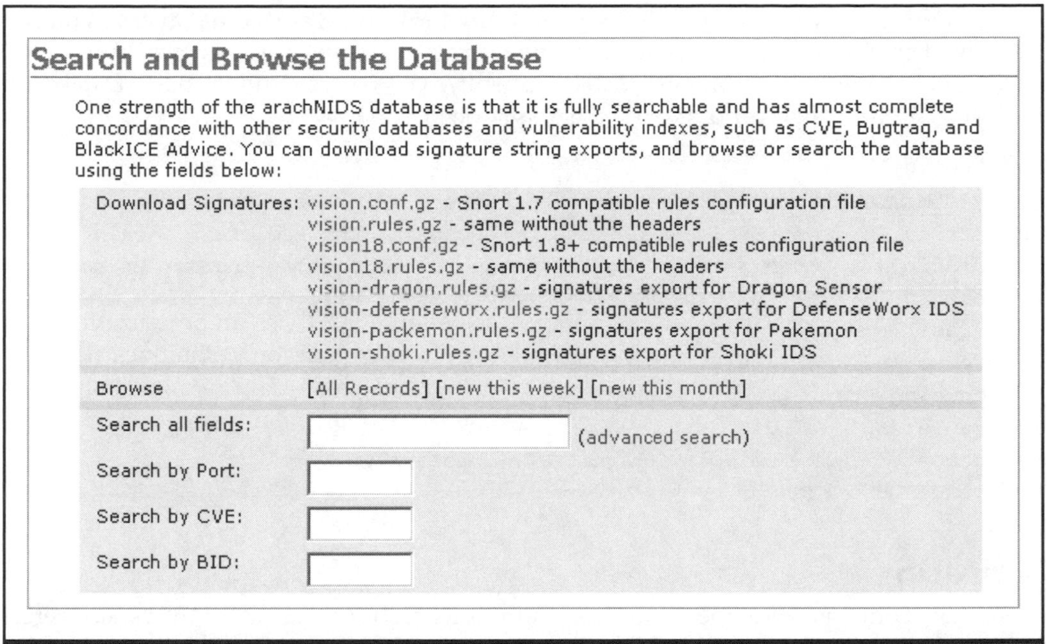

Search and Browse the Database

One strength of the arachNIDS database is that it is fully searchable and has almost complete concordance with other security databases and vulnerability indexes, such as CVE, Bugtraq, and BlackICE Advice. You can download signature string exports, and browse or search the database using the fields below:

Download Signatures:	vision.conf.gz - Snort 1.7 compatible rules configuration file
	vision.rules.gz - same without the headers
	vision18.conf.gz - Snort 1.8+ compatible rules configuration file
	vision18.rules.gz - same without the headers
	vision-dragon.rules.gz - signatures export for Dragon Sensor
	vision-defenseworx.rules.gz - signatures export for DefenseWorx IDS
	vision-packemon.rules.gz - signatures export for Pakemon
	vision-shoki.rules.gz - signatures export for Shoki IDS
Browse	[All Records] [new this week] [new this month]
Search all fields:	_____ (advanced search)
Search by Port:	_____
Search by CVE:	_____
Search by BID:	_____

Figure 15-1.   The arachNIDS search screen

ORGANIZATIONS

There are several organizations that deal with computer crimes. While they may not focus directly on intrusion detection and prevention, they are an invaluable resource for research, and they help to advance the information security field.

National White Collar Crime Center (NW3C)

The National White Collar Crime Center (NW3C) is a federally-funded, non-profit corporation (www.nw3c.org). (The organization started in 1972 and worked under the name The Leviticus Project until 1992 when they changed the name.) The purpose of the organization is to train and research cybercrime issues, including economic crime and investigations, in an effort to support law enforcement agencies. In addition, the NW3C educates the general public on their research and explains how to avoid being victimized by cybercrimes. This is done through an effort to help individuals register Internet crime complaints and contact the appropriate authorities to deal with the situation.

The NW3C has computer databases that contain information on suspected criminal organizations and individuals. It also provides help in areas of financial crimes, such as check fraud, money laundering, and credit card fraud, as well as cyberstalking, identity theft, copyright law, and Internet gambling.

National Cybercrime Training Partnership (NCTP)

The National Cybercrime Training Partnership (NCTP) is a partnership that helps law enforcement agencies on a state and international level (www.nctp.org). The group has helped to set up guidelines, jurisdictional cooperation, and public education. At the time of writing, the NTCP's activities have been in hiatus, pending the formation and initial meeting of the NW3C Cybercrime Advisory Board.

High Technology Crime Investigation Association (HTCIA)

The High Technology Crime Investigation Association (HTCIA) is an organization that helps to train and research information relating to investigation techniques (http://htcia.org). To participate in the HTCIA as a member, one needs to be involved in investigations, whether from a legal, law enforcement, or corporate position. The HTCIA has individual local chapters that hold regular meetings to promote and educate individuals on different investigative or technological issues.

LEGAL RESOURCES ON THE WEB

There are a number of web sites dedicated to the legalities of intrusion detection. Here are a few popular resources.

www.lawguru.com   Lawguru.com has a vast resource of information relating to law of all types. It includes an extensive law library that is searchable on the web.

www.findlaw.com   Findlaw provides a comprehensive set of legal resources on the Internet for legal professionals, businesses, and individuals. These resources include Web search utilities, cases and codes, legal news, and message boards.

LACC (Legal Aspects of Computer Crime mailing list)   THe LACC list discusses legal aspects of computer crime. It tends to have an English Common Law focus. This list was created in an attempt to mitigate the lack of tangible resources people involved with computer crime have at their disposal. To subscribe: mail lacc-request@suburbia.net, put "subscribe lacc" in text of message.

SUMMARY

This chapter takes a look at the laws, standards, and organizations that affect computer-related crime and issues, in the U.S. and internationally. It also examines different standards that affect intrusion detection and prevention. Finally, it looks at the organizations that have an effect on the security industry as a whole.

CHAPTER 16

Security Business Issues

Your organization has worked hard to ensure that the correct security measures are in place. Intrusion detection and prevention is a method of identifying and mitigating the impact of attacks that can breach existing security measures. Therefore, it can be used by an organization to ensure that it is showing due care.

A successful intrusion detection and prevention program hinges critically on many business issues. An organization may have the technically best intrusion prevention technology in place, but if the cost, planning, processes, and operations are not dealt with properly, the entire initiative can result in failure. Management support of the initiative is vital, and a clear and concise business case needs to be clearly demonstrated. Implementation should be accomplished in a phased manner to help manage the risks of the initiative.

This chapter sets out to explain why you need intrusion detection, how to justify the cost of such a program, and how to determine the return on investment (ROI) of implementation and the acquisition process. If you are prepared to determine and deal with these issues, your chances of implementing a successful intrusion detection and prevention program will improve significantly. We will also discuss managing a successful intrusion detection and prevention program with deployment issues.

THE BUSINESS CASE FOR INTRUSION DETECTION AND PREVENTION

The first place to start is by understanding the need for intrusion detection and prevention for your organization. Establishing the need is critical for management buy-in and for the program to be effective. An intrusion detection and prevention program needs to be implemented for the following reasons:

▼ It is an important part of an overall security strategy.

■ It lets you obtain measurable metrics of actual attacks against your organization's network.

▲ It lets you better manage risk in your organization's environment without impacting the day-to-day business processes.

Overall Security Strategy

Can implementing an intrusion detection and prevention program help better manage risk in your organization's environment without impacting business processes? Is an intrusion detection and prevention program a part of your overall business strategy? These are important questions that need to be addressed. The organization's business goals need to be examined and discussed with executive management. In addition, it is important to determine what type of compliance the organization may be subject to. For example, if the company deals with personal health information, it may need to comply with HIPAA privacy requirements; if it's a financial institution, it will need to deal with the

Office of Thrift Supervision (OTS). These regulatory bodies are likely to be a part of the organization's strategy and will have an impact on your intrusion detection and prevention strategy. Many of these regulatory issues are discussed in Chapter 15.

After gaining a solid understanding of business strategy, the organization must determine whether this strategy fits with its security strategy. Typically, some sort of risk assessment sets the strategy for an organization and allows it to determine what security controls can be put in place to mitigate defined risks. IDS/IPS can be used to help manage an organization's risk in environments where insecure services are needed to allow the business to operate. The following questions need to be asked: Are sufficient security controls currently in place? What are the risks? How are the risks being measured? After answering these questions, the organization can determined whether intrusion detection and prevention fits into the plan.

Cost is also an issue. What has the organization budgeted for the security strategy, and will the cost of implementing an intrusion detection and prevention program fit this budget? Later in this chapter, we will deal with determining the ROI of an intrusion detection system (IDS) and the value to the organization, but at this point it is important to understand the initial outlay in cost, including not only the hardware and software, but also the staff, training, and time involved.

Finally, as discussed in Chapter 1, an organization needs to have defense-in-depth. Multiple layers of security must be present. An intrusion detection and prevention program can be a successful part of this program; it will allow detection and automated prevention capability that other technologies may not have. Network intrusion-prevention systems (IPSs) allow an organization to enforce the security policy.

NOTE   An important, and often overlooked, use for an intrusion detection and prevention system is to monitor continuously the effectiveness of the current security infrastructure. The system can be set up to monitor and notify you when, for example, unexpected traffic is found on the "wrong" side of the firewall.

Attack Metrics

One of the most powerful aspects of implementing an intrusion detection and prevention program is that you can obtain measurable metrics of actual attacks against your organization's network. You have quantitative data to measure what your network is dealing with, which will help you put other compensating security controls in place to mitigate these threats. Following are examples of some quantitative data that can be useful:

  Attack type   It is important that you are able to collect data on the amount and type of attacks that threaten your organization. While this is a dynamic number, at any time it can be helpful to determine what areas of your security program can be bolstered and what areas have sufficient controls in place.

■ **Probability of detection**   This will allow an organization to create a metric that identifies the amount of correctly detected attacks during a specific time

frame. This is an effective measurement of your IDS capabilities and the fine tuning that may be needed.

▲ **Correlation abilities**   This will help you determine your ability to correlate information from other systems, such as firewalls, with the current IDS and IPS data to detect attacks. This can be very effective, especially when detecting "low-and-slow" attacks.

Proactive vs. Reactive Technology

Much of the technology deployed on a network is *reactive* in nature. For example, firewalls will react and block a port after an unauthorized attempt, but with intrusion prevention and some intrusion detection capabilities, you are able to be *proactive* in attack situations. Being proactive means you actively look for anomalies of what may be the start of an attack *before* it happens. Proactive response methods are still in their infancy, but technology is progressing. By being proactive, you can better manage risk in your organization's environment without impacting the business processes.

IDS DEPLOYMENT COSTS

When considering costs, it is important that you evaluate three areas: the infrastructure cost, the residual costs, and the support costs (see Table 16-1). This section will look at each of these in more details to help you determine the cost of implementing a successful IDS/IPS system.

Infrastructure costs are the costs in setting up the actual IDS/IPS system. You will need to determine what hardware and software you will need, what consulting services you may need, and the number of hours needed to install the hardware and software and deal with network connectivity issues. Another important factor to consider is the cost of educating the technical staff on the proper use of the product. Even if staff members educate themselves, a non-trivial cost can affect the company because some other project is not getting done while the staff is learning to use the product.

Residual costs include extra cabling, more bandwidth, and new networking hardware. Finally, you must consider the support costs related to keeping the IDS/IPS up and running. This will include hardware and software upgrades and time spent on analysis and responding to events, upgrading and tuning the systems, and basic administration. In determining these costs, you may find it helpful to talk with organizations of similar size and with similar security needs.

Justifying the Cost

Once you have determined a solid need to implement an intrusion detection and prevention program, you will need to justify the cost. This is typically accomplished in one of two ways:

▼ **Soft return on investment (SROI)**   Bases the decision on fear, uncertainty, and doubt (FUD); unfortunately, a surprising amount of security decisions are made this way.

Infrastructure Expenses	Item		Cost	Units	Total
Hardware	Sensors		$250	10	$2500
	Taps		$100	10	$1000
	Software		$7500	1	$7500
	Server		$2000	1	$2500
Service Hours	Internal		$35	1000	$35,000
	External		$125	100	$12,500
Subtotal					$61,000
Residual Expenses					
Hardware	Bandwidth		$5000	1	$5000
	Cabling		$1250	1	$1250
	Switches		$900	3	$1800
	Other				
Service Hours	Internal		$35	200	$7000
	External		—	—	—
Subtotal					$15,050
Support Expenses					
Hardware	Upgrades		—	—	—
Service Hours	Internal (yearly)	Analysis	$35	1000	$35,000
		Response	$35	500	$17,500
		Admin	$35	3000	$105,000
	External	Consult	$125	200	$25,000
Subtotal					$182,000
Total					**$258,550**

Table 16-1.   IDS Deployment Cost Estimates

▲ **Hard return on investment (HROI)**   Bases the decision on quantifiable data that will help determine the real business value of the product.

Determination of the HROI can be accomplished by finding the annual loss expectancy (ALE), which can be figured by first looking at the single loss expectancy (SLE)—the expected impact of a specific one-time event in some terms, usually monetary, on the organization. An SLE is usually derived from formal documentation on business impact or a business

impact analysis (BIA). The SLE is not a precise number but and estimate. Once the SLE has been determined, the annual rate of occurrence (ARO) of an event should be determined. The ARO is done on an annualized basis in which the frequency of an event is to occur. This data can be derived from industry research or your own attack metrics. For example, if a threat occurs once every three years, it has an ARO of 1/3 or 0.33, while a threat happening five times in a year has an ARO of 5/1 or 5.0. To arrive at the ALE, use the following formula: Single Loss Expectancy (SLE) X Annual Rate of Occurrence (ARO) = ALE

The ALE can be used to justify the need for intrusion detection and prevention. For example, let's say you want to protect a mission-critical server that holds customer data. If damaged or destroyed, the server itself is valued at $5000, but the loss of information and reputation could be valued at $10,000,000. You have determined that the SLE for this asset is 70 percent and the ARO is once in every three years or 0.33. Using the formula, we would determine the ALE to be $2,310,000. From this information, management can determine whether it is justifiable to implement a $500,000 IDS or IPS system for protection of this asset.

NOTE The determination of the ALE can be accomplished for the entire IT infrastructure or for specific mission-critical technologies, such as proprietary systems or payroll servers. The determination of how this should be done lies within the practicality of obtaining the data. In a smaller organization, determining the ALE for the entire enterprise can be effective, but as the organization grows, this can become an insurmountable task, and it may be more practical to determine the ALE only for mission-critical technologies or areas. This format becomes less and less useful as resources become less and less centralized.

ACQUISITION

After you have determined the need for the technology and the ROI, you can start the acquisition process. Most organizations have their own process in place to acquire new products. Thus, discussing the detailed acquisition processes of writing a request for information (RFI), request for proposal (RFP), and request for quotes (RFQ) won't add value to this book. But because providing specific information relating to the acquisition of intrusion detection and prevention will prove valuable, we will look at the basic acquisition steps and then examine what to look for that's specifically related to IDS or IPS. The steps are

1. Define your organization's requirements.
2. Research the IDS/IPS products.
3. Select a vendor's product to test.
4. Test the product.
5. Select the product.

Requirements

When defining the requirements for your organization, consider the cost and purpose. In a perfect world, money would not be an issue and you would just implement the "best of

breed"—but this is not a perfect world. Therefore, you need to consider what an IDS or IPS costs. Cost is one of the many advantages to open-source (free) applications such as SNORT. But there are also some financial advantages to going with a commercial product, such as liability for the product and better support. You also need to determine what it is you are trying to accomplish by implementing this technology. Do you want to be more reactive to intrusions? Maybe you want to be more proactive because you are aware of intrusions that exist on your network? Or maybe it is both of these. You also want to identify specific objectives, including the ability to

▼ Detect denial-of-service (DoS) attacks

■ Detect attacks against your web server

■ Detecting attacks against routers or firewalls

■ Increase forensic capabilities

▲ Be able to handle evasion techniques

You may find it useful to put all of your requirements, monetary considerations, goals, and objectives into a matrix for each product. The matrix can be created based on the requirements you define and then filled in with your research and testing results, as exemplified in Table 16-2. (Rate each product 1–5; 1 being the lowest rating and 5 the highest.)

Research

When researching an IDS/IPS product, you can collect data from three main sources: peer-reviews, third-party analysis, and testing materials. Testing will be covered in detail a little later in the chapter. Peer review would entail gathering information from other companies about the product and getting their input on what has and has not worked for them. This can be done at industry conferences, via message boards, and at other security-related events where security administrators can share their experiences. Third-party analysis is done by groups that test IDS capabilities. One such group is Open Security Evaluation Criteria (OSEC), a trademark of Neohapsis, which provides a framework for evaluating the security functionality of networked products. OSEC is currently testing various IDS systems for the following:

▼ High sensor stability and integrity

■ Counteract attack evasion

■ Attack recognition with maximum real traffic stress

■ Comprehensive detection without discarding traffic or missing attacks

▲ Inline mode detection

Results for OSEC's most recent finding can be found at http://osec.neohapsis.com/results/.

Requirement	Product A	Product B	Product C
Cost	4	5	3
Host Log analysis	5	3	4
Detect DoS attacks	3	4	2
Detect attacks against your web server	3	3	4
Detecting attacks against firewalls	3	3	5
Detecting attacks against routers	2	2	3
Forensic capabilities	3	3	4
Ability to handle evasion techniques	5	4	5
Scalability	4	4	4
Log analysis	2	3	3
Reporting	5	4	5
Attack detection	4	5	5
False alert handling	5	4	5
OS support			
Windows	5	5	5
Linux	4		
HPUX	4		4
AIX			5
Solaris	5	5	5
Target monitoring	3	4	3
Total	68	61	73

Table 16-2. Example of a Requirements Matrix

Vendor Selection

Vendor selection is the evaluation of the vendor after you have decided that the vendor's product is worthy of testing. It is important that you take a look at the following qualities in a company:

▼ **Financial stability** If a company is not financially secure enough to be around for the next few years, you may want to look somewhere else.

■ **Service** What services does the vendor offer? How is the service you have received so far? How willing are they to help you with your unique needs?

▲ **Reputation** A company's reputation is important. Ask colleagues in the industry about how they have been treated by the company.

In addition, the questions that you ask are important, such as the following:

▼ What do signature updates and maintenance cost?

■ What is the turn-around time for a new signature on a hot vulnerability?

■ At what real-world traffic levels does the product become unable to handle traffic, in packets/second? What is the size of the packets? What about fragmentation?

■ How scaleable is the IDS as a whole?

■ How many signatures does the system support?

■ What intrusion response features does the product have?

▲ How usable is the management console/interface?

Testing

Testing allows you to evaluate the product's performance on your network. This process can help you to

▼ Verify vendor's claims

■ Provide insight into the implementation

▲ Test performance

Generally, testing can be done quantitatively or comparatively. In quantitative testing, multiple IDS/IPS applications are tested against the same exact traffic or a baseline. In comparative testing, the IDS/IPS applications are tested against each other. While quantitative tests are scientifically valid, they can be more complex to implement. Comparative tests will allow you to see which IDS/IPS performs best against the others.

At the beginning of this process, you should determine what you want to measure. The following is a common list of measurable attributes, which may vary depending on your organization's circumstances:

▼ The number of false positives

■ The number of positive detections

■ Packets per second

■ Attack variety

■ Attack diagnosis

▲ Network impact

It is important that you have someone with expertise with IDS/IPS evaluate the results for these tests. This may mean you will need to hire a consultant. Measuring the differences between Network Intrusion Detection Systems (NIDS) and host-based intrusion-detection system (HIDS) can be difficult and beyond the basics of attacks detected versus attacks launched. Also important to note is that it is best if real network traffic is used for the tests, because synthetic load generators are designed more for testing routers than IDS/IPS. Most synthetic load generators will provide pseudo-random traffic, which is rarely seen on a production network unless it's under attack. Another important issue to consider is the presence or absence of network devices such as routers and firewalls, as in a production environment you are likely to see them both.

Selection

The final step is to make a selection based on the requirements, research, and testing that has occurred. This information can be put into a matrix similar to the requirements matrix discussed earlier.

MANAGING INTRUSION DETECTION

This section will cover some other important issues in managing a successful intrusion detection and prevention program: deployment and managing in a distributed environment.

Deployment

Once an intrusion detection or prevention technology has been selected, it is time for implementation of the technology. The basic steps to a successful implementation are

1. Having a well-planned policy
2. Installing the software
3. Planning for and hiring staff resources

We will briefly provide a high-level overview of what policy planning needs to occur. Each IDS or IPS will have its own specific issues that will need to be dealt with on an individual basis. In Chapter 15, we discussed policies and procedures; during the implementation process, you need to use your organization's policies as a guide to what needs to be considered at this stage. You must also consider how IDS will fit into your organization's incident response plan.

Once the policy is determined, the next logical step is to install the software, which usually involves an installation of the IDS manager. Once the manager is installed, you will be able to install agents. This step is often the point at which problems arise as you may deal with trust relationships between agents and managers and communication issues. If you do not have experienced staff, it is highly suggested that you obtain outside assistance from the vendor.

NOTE   Most successful implementations have taken place in small steps rather than by trying to get everything working correctly on the first try with the whole complex rule set.

Once a successful implementation plan is in place, it is important that you plan for resources. The first resource to plan for is staffing. It is important to have trained individuals who understand your unique network. While some organizations have monitoring done by a third party, resident experts are still necessary to help with issues that arise. In some cases, if you do not have the experienced staff, you will need to provide training, and staff will need ongoing training to keep them abreast of new threats and issues.

Managing in a Distributed Environment

Managing IDS in a distributed environment offers many challenges. This section will discuss some of the issues that occur in dealing with a distributed environment. You can handle your setup in two ways: use a decentralized setup where each location manages its own agents (sensors), or use a decentralized environment that is managed from one location.

Managing a decentralized environment has the advantage of a less complicated setup that can be managed locally, and information can be communicated with the other locations as needed. However, in a decentralized environment, the cost of more equipment, difficulties in data correlation, inconsistent management across the enterprise, and operational inefficiencies may prove to be disadvantages. Managing on a centralized basis, in most cases, is a better solution in a distributed environment.

Another issue to consider is the communication across a distributed environment. With one location in Lisbon, Spain, and another in Chicago, how do you send large amounts of highly sensitive data, such as agent activity with IP addresses and server names, across securely and efficiently? One way to do this is to use the native communications built into the IDS. It may be possible to transmit this information over a private line, such as a T1 line, depending on your company's capabilities. When a private line is not available, you can use a virtual private network (VPN).

SUMMARY

This chapter examines the various business cases for implementing an intrusion detection and prevention program. These include the being proactive, building to one's security strategy and having measurable metrics to validate your security measures. In addition, it discusses justification of an IDS/IPS program and being able to determine the ROI of the implementation. The chapter also reviews issues dealing with selecting and implementing the correct product for your particular organization.

CHAPTER 17

The Future of Intrusion Detection and Prevention

As mentioned in previous chapters, many changes are in store for intrusion detection and intrusion prevention. Some of these changes could actually be negative—at least from the perspective of intrusion detection. For example, the Gartner Group, a technology research and consulting organization, asserts that IDSs will soon be relics of the past. Gartner says that IDSs have not established themselves in the IT marketplace, that they produce too low a return on investment (ROI) for all the resources expended, and that excessive false alarms and misses have greatly impaired their usefulness. Gartner predicts that intrusion prevention technology will prevail in the belief that shutting off intrusions altogether is better than allowing intrusions to occur and just monitoring them. Accordingly, Gartner recommends that IT organizations turn to firewalls, not IDSs. Many IT security experts denounced Gartner's prediction, though, saying that Gartner does not really understand how intrusion detection fits in with a layered defense approach (of which many believe that intrusion detection is a critical part) and that intrusion detection technology is still growing and improving.

Regardless of whatever sliver of truth there may or may not be in Gartner's prediction, two things are certain—intrusion detection is still a long way from being mature, and intrusion prevention technology is in its infancy. Massive changes are in store for both areas. This chapter focuses on some of the areas within intrusion detection and intrusion prevention in which substantial and beneficial progress is likely to occur. These areas include the following:

▼ The continued reduction in reliance on signatures in intrusion detection

■ The growth of intrusion prevention

■ Advances in data correlation and alert correlation methods

■ Advances in source determination

■ Inclusion of integrated forensics functionality in IDSs and IPSs

▲ Greater use of honeypots

We'll begin by considering why signature-based intrusion detection will become less mainstream in the future.

LOWER RELIANCE ON SIGNATURE-BASED INTRUSION DETECTION

The signature approach to intrusion detection, which traces back to the early 1990s, represents a major advance over the previous statistical-based approaches of the 1980s. Signatures are not only a relatively straightforward and intuitive approach to intrusion detection, but they are also efficient—often a set of only a few hundred signatures can result in reasonably high detection rates (albeit often at the cost of false alarm rates, as discussed earlier). Signature-based IDSs have proven popular and useful, so much so that you can count of some of these tools being available for a long time.

Signature-based intrusion detection is beset with numerous limitations, however, including the following:

▼   Because attacks have to occur before their signatures can be identified, signatures cannot be used in discovering new attacks. The "white hat" community is thus always one step behind the "black hat" community when it comes to new attack signatures.

■   Many signatures in IDSs are badly outdated. One commercial IDS for many years contained the signature for a Unix exploit in which an attacker could enter the `rlogin` command with the `-froot` switch to obtain a root shell on a victim system. This exploit was for early versions of the AIX operating system, versions almost never used anymore. You can always "weed out" obsolete signatures, but doing so requires a reasonable amount of unnecessary effort; good IDS vendors do not include such signatures in their products' signature sets in the first place.

■   Some attacks do not have single distinguishing signatures, but rather a wide range of possible variations. Each variation could conceivably be incorporated into a signature set, but doing so inflates the number of signatures, potentially hurting IDS performance. Additionally, keeping up with each possible variation is for all practical purposes an impossible task.

■   Signatures are almost useless in network-based IDSs when network traffic is encrypted.

▲   The black hat community is becoming increasingly better in evading signature-based IDSs, as discussed in the sidebar "IDS Evasion Tools."

IDS Evasion Tools

The number of methods for evading signature-based IDSs has been increasing dramatically over the last few years. For example, powerful tools that can defeat signature-based IDSs are available. One class of tools (such as Fragroute) launches "insertion attacks," in which malicious commands sent to a server are disguised by inserting extra, bogus data. When the IDS processes the traffic in which these commands are embedded, the IDS does not recognize anything as an attack signature, but when the destination server processes the input it receives, it discards the extra data, allowing the commands to execute.

For example, an attacker can send the following command to a web server:

```
GET //cgi-bin//some.cgi.
```

The web server cannot recognize some.cgi, so it may discard this part of the input, connecting the attacker to cgi-bin instead. Unfortunately, cgi-bin is the

IDS Evasion Tools *(continued)*

directory for common gateway interface scripts, one of the places just about every web hacker wants to be.

Another trick is to insert a premature null character:

```
GET%00 /cgi-bin/some.cgi HTTP/1.0
```

Alternatively, an attacker can send ASCII-coded input that invokes a malicious command to an interpreter:

```
perpetrator@host$ perl -e
'$bad=pack("C11",47,101,116,99,47,112,97,115,115,119,100);
@hack='/bin/cat/ $bad'; print"@hack\n";'
```

Another evasion method is rexmit inconsistency. An attacker sends a TCP stream in which some of the data within the stream is garbled. The receiving host (intended victim) sends a message to the sending host (the attacking host) asking it to retransmit. The sending host then sends malicious commands. The IDS analyzes the first stream and determines that it does not match any attack signatures. However, for efficiency's sake, the IDS may not analyze the second stream (which in theory should be identical to the original one), resulting in a missed attack. Many other evasion techniques work against signature-based IDSs, too. IDS evasion techniques do not exclusively target signature-based IDSs, however. There are evasion techniques for rule-based IDSs, too, for example.

If reliance on signatures in intrusion detection will dwindle in the future, what intrusion detection methods are likely to become increasing important? Several alternatives discussed in the next section appear probable.

Protocol Analysis

Protocol analysis means analyzing the behavior of protocols to determine whether one host is communicating normally with another. For example, the TCP handshake (discussed in Chapter 2) is initiated by sending a TCP SYN packet to another host. The other host responds with a SYN ACK packet, to which the originating host responds with an ACK packet. Suppose that a host sends nothing but SYN packets to another host—an indication of a "SYN flood" attack designed to deplete memory and other resources in the receiving host. In another kind of protocol attack, a host might send malformed IP packets, perhaps IP packets in which one or more values in the IP header is out of range. In still another, a malicious code may send malformed "chunks," parcels in which data are transferred from a browser to a web server to provide an orderly way for the web server to encode the input.

Although these are simple examples, protocol analysis is by no means any kind of "lightweight" way of performing intrusion detection. A wide range of attacks (particularly DoS attacks) can be detected in terms of anomalous protocol behavior. Identifiable signatures may exist for many of the same attacks, but identifying these attacks at a lower level of networking (such as the network or transport layer by looking at the behavior of protocols such as IP, TCP, UDP, and ICMP) is more efficient than having to go to a higher layer. The rules of normal protocol behavior are well defined in RFCs (see www.ietf.com/rfc.html), so deviation is usually (but by no means always, given that a certain percentage of network traffic does not behave in accordance with any RFC) rather straightforward to determine. Additionally, many attacks that would require literally scores of signatures to detect can often be identified in terms of only a very few protocol behavior irregularities. Many of today's IDSs perform protocol analysis; IDSs of the future are likely to do more and also do it better.

Target Detection

We're also likely to see more widespread use of target detection in the future. As mentioned previously, target detection has proven to be one of the most robust and reliable methods of intrusion detection. Attackers almost invariably make changes in systems, often to create back doors, but sometimes (especially in the case of novice attackers) changes occur simply by accident. Attackers may be able to evade signature-based IDSs, and they may also be able to delete system logs to hide evidence of their activity, but they are less likely to escape the notice of a target detection tool that uses a variety of strong cryptographic algorithms and requires strong authentication for access to the target detection functions.

Although commercial target detection tools such as Tripwire (http://www .tripwiresecurity.com/) and Intruder Alert (http://enterprisesecurity.symantec.com/ products/products.cfm?ProductID=171) are widely used within Fortune 500 companies, the price of deploying these tools on many systems often serves as a deterrent to their use in smaller organizations. Freeware versions of Tripwire (http://ftp.cerias.purdue.edu/ pub/tools/unix/ids/ tripwire/) and Windows-based integrity checking tools such as ForixNT (http://www.incident-response.org/forix-nt.htm) are available, but hurdles such as worries over software support have at least to some degree inhibited their widespread use.

Commercial target detection tools have established themselves in the marketplace; they will not disappear any time in the near future. What is likely to happen, however, is that operating system and application vendors will build powerful integrity checking capabilities into their products. To at least some degree, vendors already do this. Unix vendors, for example, have for a long time included the sum command for computing simple cryptochecksums and the diff command for detecting changes in file contents. Microsoft also includes the System File Checker and Windows File Protection in many of its operating system products. But these capabilities are relatively crude compared to the capabilities of many commercial tools.

Vendors are likely in time to expand the scope of integrity checking programs to include more than simply device driver or system file checking capabilities and also to pro-

vide real-time alerting capabilities. It would not be surprising, for example, to learn sometime in the near future that one or more vendors had incorporated the commercial Tripwire tool into an operating system. Doing this would make target detection easier to manage and possibly also more secure, given that operating system defenses could also be used to protect target detection executables and data files.

NOTE In the past generation (and in all likelihood, the future) of kernel-based Unix exploits, the existence of changes to the file system has almost always been well hidden from system administrators and users. An example is the sk Linux rootkit, which initially was found in systems only because of numerous implementation bugs. Ultimately, kernel-based exploits are the greatest threat to target-based IDSs, in which detection depends on subtle changes in the behavior of the system.

Rule-Based Intrusion Detection

Rule-based intrusion detection is more of an eclectic approach than the other alternatives to signature-based intrusion detection covered in this section. In this approach, logic conditions based on possible incident-related observations are defined. Observations could be signatures, irregularities in protocol behavior, unusual system events, changes in files and/or directories, and so on. Rule-based intrusion detection analyzes elements derived from these observations and then uses logic to identify attacks. For example, suppose that element A is defined as a probe from a certain IP address, that B is defined as attempted access via anonymous FTP, and that C is defined as an attempt to obtain the password file. If A or the combination of B and C occur, this could be defined as an attack pattern.

Rule-based intrusion detection is used in a number of IDSs today, especially prototype systems used in connection with intrusion-detection research. The rule-based approach is potentially more powerful than signature-based intrusion detection because it relies on multiple variables/indicators—events based on signatures, protocol analysis, target detection indicators, and so on. Because this approach seldom equates a single event with a rule, it is likely to produce a higher hit and lower false alarm rate than signature-based intrusion detection. The higher hit rate is particularly significant. An attack may manifest itself in multiple but nondeterministic ways; rule-based intrusion detection can define long strings of "or" rules, one of which might apply to a particular set of observations, enabling it to detect attacks that simple signature-based IDSs might very well miss.

The main limitation of rule-based intrusion detection is the potential complexity associated with all the rules that are normally created. Only those with advanced technical skills and knowledge are likely to be able to understand the rules in the first place. It generally is difficult to create rules (which can often involve many steps of logic) and also to maintain rules (for example, weeding out obsolete rules). Processing the rules themselves can also cause massive CPU and memory utilization in the host that houses a rule-based intrusion detection system. Still, rule-based intrusion detection represents a significant advance over simple signature-based intrusion detection; it is likely to be used increasingly over time.

Rule-Based Intrusion Detection

Rule-based intrusion detection can involve long sets of complex rules, something that may make this approach seem nebulous and impractical. Rules can, however, be as simple as needed. The tcpdump tool discussed in Chapter 5 provides an almost ideal example how rules can be created at the protocol level. Consider, for example, the following tcpdump expression:

```
(tcp src port 27374 ) and ( tcp[2] > 3 )) or ((tcp dst port 27374)
and (tcp[0] > 3))
```

This expression represents a rather simple rule—the source port must be TCP 27374 and the 2nd byte of the TCP header (destination port) must be at least 4×256 or 1024 OR the destination port must be TCP 27374 and the 0th byte of the TCP header (source port) must be at least 4×256 or 1024. A rule-based intrusion detection system could include and use this type of rule to detect the presence of the deadly SubSeven Trojan horse remote control program in Windows systems. If there is a connection from port 27374, the most used port in connection with this particular Trojan, to an ephemeral port or a connection to port 27374 from an ephemeral port, the IDS would in this example report an attack.

Neural Networks

Neural networks are systems that perform pattern recognition on inputs they receive based on models of how neurons in mammals process information. Neurons are nerve cells; they are densely interconnected and interface with each other at *synapses*, small gaps between individual neurons. They also work in parallel to other neurons at any given level of brain structure. Neural networks are sets of mathematical models that imitate how neurons learn, assigning different weights to connections between elements within the neural network similarly to how electrical potentials for neurons are built up at synaptic junctions based on their frequency of firing. The more frequently a neighboring neuron fires, the more electrical potential there is at the synapses of the neurons that react to this pattern. In neural networks, elements that receive inputs from neighboring elements receive higher weights.

Although complicated and still somewhat mysterious, the neural networks approach can be applied to a wide range of pattern recognition problems, intrusion detection included. The beauty of neural networks in intrusion detection is that no signatures or even rules are needed. You simply start feeding input—data concerning network- or host-based events—to a neural network, and it does the rest. Neural networks are, therefore, well suited to picking up new patterns of attacks readily, although some learning time is required. The neural networks approach has been around for a long time, and if

anything it is likely to become more widely used and relied on in intrusion detection in the future as reliance on signatures diminishes.

INTRUSION PREVENTION

Intrusion prevention is another area that will grow dramatically in the future. Intrusion prevention is in its infancy. Anyone who thinks that IPSs and IDSs are diametrically opposed or that IPSs will eventually supplant IDSs is badly mistaken, however. An IDS is like a burglar alarm, something that provides information about past and ongoing activity that facilitates risk and threat assessment as well as investigations of suspicious and possibly wrongful activity. IPSs are designed to be defensive measures that stop or at least limit the negative consequences of attacks on systems and networks, not to yield the wealth of information that IDSs typically deliver.

The number of potential, useful variations in "intrusion prevention" is mind-boggling. Consider, for example, the first type of intrusion prevention used in connection with intrusion detection—*shunning*. Shunning is a mainstay feature in today's IDSs, yet shunning is, all things considered, a rather crude way of performing intrusion prevention. In all likelihood, malicious packets will already have arrived at the intended victim host by the time any firewall or router ACLs are changed to block future packets from the apparent attacking host—not exactly the desired results if shutting off the attack in the first place is the goal.

IPSs such as Cisco's Okena StormSystem product (see https://www.okena.com/pdf/stormwatch_datasheet.pdf) represent another extreme in the intrusion prevention continuum in that a number of hosts can be spared from having to suffer the malicious consequences of an attack because they have received a policy change based on detected malicious activity on the network. Others view intrusion prevention in terms of a set of interrelated (and very possibly cooperating) devices and capabilities that work together to diagnose system and network events and shut off incidents at any point where they can be shut off.

One of the major, new offshoots of the last permutation of intrusion prevention discussed here is called "active defense" (as opposed to "passive defense," such as passively monitoring systems and networks and deploying static access control lists [ACLs] in routers and firewalls). Active defense means analyzing the condition of systems and networks and doing what is appropriate to deal with whatever is wrong. According to Dave Dittrich of the University of Washington, there are four levels of active defense:

▼   Local data collection, analysis, and blocking

■   Remote collection of external data

■   Remote collection of internal data

▲   Remote data alteration, attack suppression, and "interdiction"

Figure 17-1 portrays one possible active defense architecture. Numerous hosts within a hypothetical network collect intrusion detection data and send them to a central analyzer that, whenever appropriate, sends policy changes to individual hosts to keep them from executing certain instructions in memory, changing the content of certain files, and so forth. The external firewall, the outermost layer in the active defense infrastructure, detects relatively straightforward attacks such as SYN flooding attacks and shuns offending IP addresses immediately. A network-based IDS within this network gathers information from sensors at the external gateway and at entrances to several subsets; it sends ACLs changes to the firewall and data to the central analyzer on the basis of attack patterns that it deciphers.

One of the most important (and controversial) facets of the active defense approach to intrusion prevention is determining the appropriate response. The notion of appropriate response includes a consideration called " proportionality of response," which ensures that the response is proportional to the threat. In the case of a host that is flooding a network with fragmented packets, blocking traffic sent from that host is almost certainly the

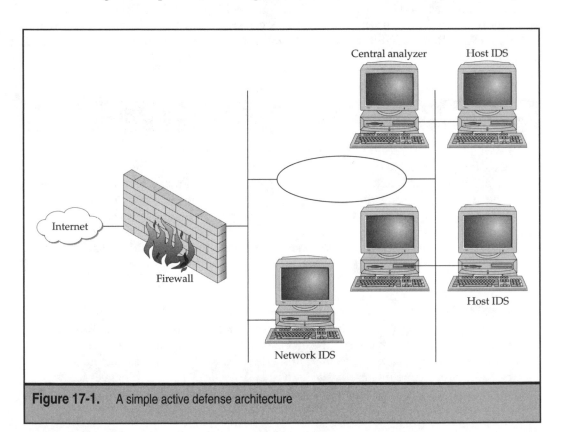

Figure 17-1.   A simple active defense architecture

most appropriate response. If several dozen hosts known to be operated by an ISP repeatedly attack an organization's network, blocking all the traffic from the range of IP addresses owned by that ISP might be the most appropriate response. Some advocates of the active defense approach even believe that if a remote host is repeatedly attacking an organization's network, counterattacking that host, perhaps by flooding it with fragmented packets, thereby causing it to crash, is the appropriate course of action. Many, the authors of this book included, strongly disagree with the notion of counterattacking, however, as discussed in the "Striking Back" sidebar.

Although intrusion prevention appears promising, (as mentioned) it is very much in its infancy. Attack stave-off rates for intrusion prevention systems are nowhere as high as they need to pose a major deterrent to attacks. Additionally, false alarms can easily cause what effectively amounts to DoS within individual systems. Intrusion prevention systems of the future are likely to be able to prevent a wider range of attacks, not only at the level of the individual host, but also within organizations' networks and possibly even within the Internet itself. The last possibility is particularly intriguing. Perhaps some organization such as the U.S. government's federal incident response team, FedCIRT, will continuously monitor all traffic bound for U.S. government sites and stop selectively malicious packets long before they reach the gateways of the government sites for which they are destined.

Striking Back

"Striking back" has recently been a hot topic within information security and other discussion groups. Some advocate doing whatever is necessary to prevent attacks from a known source of trouble. In some cases this would mean causing DoS in the offending host; in other cases, it might mean destroying the offending host altogether by breaking into the host and then erasing critical system files. The lack of sufficiently strong cybercrime legislation throughout the world makes this approach more attractive to its advocates; some individuals even think that it is important to teach attackers a lesson by letting them "have a taste of their own medicine."

Striking back has raised a plethora of ethical controversies, so many that at this point in time, the information security community as a whole is firmly opposed to it. Striking back is also illegal in numerous countries around the world. But in the military arena, striking back could well be the appropriate course of action—an important countermeasure in information warfare. If, for example, an opposing military force were causing DoS in systems used for military intelligence analysis, shutting out the source of the attacks would make perfect sense. The striking back issue is likely to grow in connection with the active defense approach to intrusion prevention over time.

> ### Striking Back *(continued)*
>
> But striking back is dangerous, especially from a legal aspect. Anyone who considers deploying strike-back methods should at a minimum obtain management's approval and also (if management approves striking back) consult one's legal department before proceeding. Remember at the same time that you may end up getting sued by the individual or organization whose host you attacked, even if you have management approval.

DATA AND ALERT CORRELATION

As mentioned in Chapter 12, data correlation is becoming increasingly important. IDSs, IPSs, firewalls, personal firewalls, and TCP wrappers are each capable of generating large amounts of data; collectively, they are capable of overwhelming intrusion detection analysts with data. Data aggregation helps ensure that data are available in a single location; data correlation enables analysts to recognize patterns in these data. Although current data correlation methods are for the most part not very sophisticated, future data correlation is likely to become much better. How will data correlation algorithms need to change? Waltz and Llinas (in *Multisensor Data Fusion*, Boston: Artech House, 1990) have developed criteria for systems designed to fuse data must be able to, saying that these systems must be able to do the following:

▼ Distinguish parameters of interest (hit rate, range of events detected, and so on) from noise

■ Distinguish among different objects in space and time

■ Adequately track and capture each desired type of event and data

■ Sample the data and events of interest with sufficient frequency

■ Provide accurate measurements

■ Ensure that each variable that is measured adequately represents the desired types of categories

■ Provide access to both raw and correlated data

▲ Preserve the temporal characteristics of data and events

It is unlikely that all systems designed to fuse data will meet every one of these requirements. The more of these requirements that a system meets, however, the more useful in data fusion/correlation it is likely to be. Currently, one of the greatest barriers to automated data fusion has been the lack of a common format for data from intrusion detection systems. Although common formats have been proposed, little agreement has resulted. Agreement upon a single data format would thus constitute a giant step forward.

Additionally, user interfaces of applications that perform data correlation are likely to improve dramatically in the future. Deficits in the usability of software used in data correlation are by no means unique; usability problems plague the information security arena as a whole. Human-computer interaction methods for controlling what is displayed tend to be nonintuitive and excessively complex. Data displays are often cluttered to the point of being overwhelming to view; few options for data reduction or displaying a patterns and profiles typically are available. Fortunately, vendors are addressing these problems in their products and are already incorporating substantially improved user interfaces into these products.

The user interface of ArcSight, a current commercial product used for correlating intrusion detection data, allows flexibility in what is displayed, color codes different conditions appropriately, and offers a variety of pattern displays such as pie charts.

Alert fusion (also covered in Chapter 12) is a closely related area that is likely to become increasingly important over time. Improved algorithms for alert fusion are likely to be developed; as they are, alerting will become more efficient in that fewer alerts will be necessary to warn analysts and operators about a series of events, some of which may be related, others of which may not.

SOURCE DETERMINATION

Source determination means determining the origin of network traffic. Given how easy it is to spoof IP addresses, any source IP address in conventional IP packets must be viewed with suspicion. Tools that fabricate packets, inserting any desired IP address into the IP headers, are freely available on the Internet. Many countermeasures, most notably strong authentication methods (such as the use of Smart Cards) and digital signatures, can remove doubt concerning the identity of individuals who initiate transactions, but they are not designed to identify the source IP addresses from which transactions originate. IPsec, the secure IP protocol, effectively removes any doubt concerning the validity of IP source addresses, but IPsec has, unfortunately, not grown in popularity in proportion to its many merits.

New source determination methods that are potentially valuable in intrusion detection and intrusion prevention efforts are emerging. Some are rather crude (but nevertheless potentially useful), such as measuring the latency between the time a packet arrives at a network node and the time it moves on to the next destination. The longer the latency, the further away the origin of the connection is (at least in theory—in reality, latency can fluctuate based on traffic conditions or routing table changes.) Another intriguing source determination method measures the difference in the packet sequence numbers of packets within TCP streams over time. Packets with little deviation in the packet sequence number over time can be assumed to be part of the same stream. In still another method, packets are marked at each hop over which they travel. Each intermediate switching point on the network adds its signature or identifier to each packet, enabling investigators to determine exactly which route a packet took as it traveled from the source to the destination host.

Source determination is, unfortunately, yet another area in its relative infancy. Advances in this area are particularly important. Knowing exactly where an attack has originated is critical in determining the appropriate course of action. As someone who is involved with intrusion detection virtually every day, I often wonder how many IP addresses that are shunned are addresses of hosts that have actually launched attacks and how many are completely innocent of any wrongdoing, unrelated to anything that an intrusion detection system has reported. Readily determining the source of attacks is also extremely important for the sake of law enforcement; it can eliminate much of the work that is normally involved in investigating exactly where each attack has originated.

INTEGRATED FORENSICS CAPABILITIES

Forensics means using special procedures that preserve evidence for legal purposes. When people think of forensics, they normally envision investigators archiving the contents of hard drives to a machine that runs forensics software, making hard copies of audit logs, and labeling and bagging peripherals such as keyboards and mice. Many people fail to realize that IDSs are potentially one of the best sources of forensics data, especially if the IDSs capture and store keystrokes. A few IDS vendors are starting to build forensics capabilities into their products, capabilities that enable those who use the systems to make copies of IDS output, create a hash value of the output (to ensure its integrity), search it for special keywords or graphic content, and so on.

Having an integrated forensics capability is potentially advantageous in that everything that is needed for forensics purposes resides on a single machine (or possibly in some circumstances, a few machines) with a single user interface, greatly simplifying the process of obtaining and preserving evidence. Sophisticated forensics capabilities are likely to routinely be built into IDSs (or at least high-end IDSs) and possibly also IPSs in the future.

USE OF HONEYPOTS IN INTRUSION DETECTION AND PREVENTION

A *honeypot* is a decoy server that looks and acts like a normal server, but that does not run or support normal server functions. The main purpose of deploying honeypots is to observe the behavior of attackers in a safe environment, one in which there is (at least in theory) no threat to normal, operational systems. Having proven especially useful as a reconnaissance tool that yields information concerning what kinds of attacks are occurring and how often, honeypots have gained a great deal of acceptance within the information security arena.

Honeypots are not, however, usually used in connection with intrusion detection and prevention efforts. This is unfortunate, because honeypots often glean information that conventional IDSs and IPSs miss. A honeypot server can, for example, be given an

especially interesting name such as "peoplesoft6.abc.corp," attracting connection attempts that conventional servers and workstations would not normally receive. Provided a honeypot is set up and deployed properly, there is also little risk to the rest of the network, something that is not necessarily true for a host that runs intrusion detection software.

More effective honeypots create "virtual environments" that appear to be real but that in fact do not support a normal interactive environment. The result is that attackers cannot gain control over the honeypot and then use it to launch attacks against other machines within the network in additional to external hosts. Honeypots will almost certainly be used increasingly as a source of information for analyzers and ultimately as a basis for intrusion prevention policies that are sent to hosts.

FINAL CAVEAT

This chapter has presented a glimpse of how intrusion detection and intrusion prevention are likely to change in the future. These glimpses are, of course, nothing more than predictions, some of which will come true and others of which will not. Although certain predictions have been covered this chapter, other potential predictions have for brevity's sake been omitted. For example, it is reasonable to expect that IDSs of the future are likely to improve in their ability to deal with encrypted network traffic. Although it does not provide a general encryption solution, Sandstorm's NetIntercept IDS will (if each client has a backdoor SSH client and if NetIntercept is provided the correct encryption keys) allow replay of encrypted network sessions (see http://www.sandstorm.net/products/netintercept). This represents an advance for network IDSs that is likely to be followed by similar but improved functionality (such as ability to crack SSH encryption in clients not under the control of an organization that deploys such a tool) in future IDSs.

A considerable amount of research on data visualization methods for intrusion detection data is also currently being conducted. At some point, the major breakthroughs from this research will be incorporated into IDSs of the future, resulting in output that will be much more useful in terms of identifying threat magnitudes, patterns of elements within incidents, and so forth.

The intrusion detection and intrusion prevention arenas are extremely dynamic, with new findings, functions, and models being created all the time. At the same time, it is important to be wary of the claims of some vendors who add a few "bells and whistles" to their IDS or IPS products and then claim that their competitors' products are obsolete. Watch for the many changes that are currently occurring or are about to occur with great anticipation, but be sure to carefully evaluate each in terms of its genuine value to your organization's business and operational goals.

SUMMARY

This chapter has considered the future of intrusion detection and intrusion prevention. Great change is in store for both of these areas. First, given the significant pitfalls in the signature-based approach, there will continue to be less reliance on signatures in intrusion detection and intrusion prevention. Protocol analysis, target detection (using the output of cryptographic algorithms to detect unauthorized changes in files and directories), rule-based intrusion detection (using logic based on observations combinations of elements), and neural networks (systems that process inputs to recognize patterns based on models of how nerve cells process information) are viable alternatives to signature-based intrusion detection that are likely to grow in importance.

Intrusion prevention will continue to grow rapidly because of its capability to shut off attacks, potentially preventing damage and disruption altogether. The active defense approach, evaluating the condition of systems and networks and responding appropriately to remedy whatever is wrong, is new but already gaining rapidly in popularity. Advances in data correlation and alert fusion methods are also likely to occur. Correlation and fusion methods will meet a larger number of requirements and user interfaces for access to correlated data and are likely to improve substantially. Advances in the determination of the origin of network connections are also extremely probable. Finally, it is reasonable to expect that improved forensics functionality will be built into IDSs and IPSs in the future and that honeypots will be used much more in connection with intrusion detection and intrusion prevention.

APPENDIX

Intrusion Detection and Prevention Systems

The following is an alphabetical list of available commercial and open source intrusion detection and prevention systems. The list is not to be seen as recommendation for any particular system, but rather as a resource that shows you what is available.

AAFID (Autonomous Agents for Intrusion Detection)

http://www.cs.purdue.edu/coast/projects/autonomous-agents.html
Purdue University, West Lafayette, Indiana

AppShield

http://www.sanctuminc.com/solutions/appshield/index.html
Sanctum Inc, Santa Clara, CA 95054

ARMD (Adaptable Real-Time Misuse Detection)

http://www.isse.gmu.edu/~jllin/system
George Mason University, Fairfax, Virginia

ArcSight

http://www.arcsight.com/product.htm
ArcSight, Sunnyvale, California

BlackICE

http://www.networkice.com/html/products.html
Network ICE Corp., San Mateo, California

Bro

Lawrence Berkeley National Laboratory, Berkeley, California
http://www.icir.org/vern/bro-info.html
The ICSI Center for Internet Research, Berkeley, California, and
Lawrence Berkeley National Laboratory, Berkeley, California

Cisco Secure IDS

http://www.cisco.com/warp/public/cc/pd/sqsw/sqidsz/prodlit/netra_ds.htm
Cisco Systems, Inc., San Jose, California

Cyber-Defender

http://www.unionway.com
UnionWay, Palos Verdes, California

CyberTrace

http://www.cybertrace.com/ctids.html
Ryan Net Works, LLC Fairfax, Virginia

EMERALD (Event Monitoring Enabling Responses to Anomalous Live Disturbances)

http://www2.csl.sri.com/emerald/index.html
SRI International, Menlo Park, California
Enterasys Dragon Intrusion Defense System
http://www.enterasys.com/products/ids
Enterasys Networks, Andover, Massachusetts

eTrust Intrusion Detection

http://www.cai.com/solutions/enterprise/etrust/intrusion_detection
Computer Associates International, Inc., Islandia, New York

GFI LANguard

http://www.gfi.com/lanselm
Kingston upon Thames, Surrey, United Kingdom

Hummer

www.cs.uidaho.edu/~hummer
University of Idaho, Moscow, Idaho

IDA(3) (Intrusion Detection Agents Systems)

http://www.ipa.go.jp/STC/IDA/index.html
Information Technology Promotion Agency, Tokyo, Japan

ManHunt

http://enterprisesecurity.symantec.com/products/products.cfm?ProductID=156&
EID=0
Symantec Corporation, Sunnyvale, California

Net Intercept

http://www.sandstorm.com/products/netintercept/
Sandstorm Enterprises, Cambridge, Massachusetts

NFR (Network Flight Recorder)

http://www.nfr.net
NFR Security, Inc., Rockville, Maryland

NIDES (Next-generation Intrusion Detection Expert System)

http://www2.csl.sri.com/nides/index.html
SRI International, Menlo Park, California

RealSecure

http://www.iss.net
Internet Security Systems, Inc., Atlanta, Georgia

SecureNet
http://www.intrusion.com
Richardson, Texas

SHADOW (Secondary Heuristic Analysis for Defensive Online Warfare)
http://www.nswc.navy.mil/ISSEC/CID
Naval Surface Warfare Center, Dahlgren Division, Dahlgren, Virginia

Snort
http://www.snort.org
Martin Roesch

TCP-Dump
http://www.tcpdump.org

T-sight
http://www.EnGarde.com/software/t-sight/index.html
En Garde Systems, Inc., Albuquerque, New Mexico

UnityOne Network-Based Intrusion Prevention
http://www.tippingpoint.com
TippingPoint Technologies, Austin, Texas

WatchGuard
http://www.watchguard.com/products
Seattle, Washington

INDEX

▼ E

K

 L

T

X

 Y

 Z

Sound Off!

Visit us at **www.osborne.com/bookregistration** and let us know what you thought of this book. While you're online you'll have the opportunity to register for newsletters and special offers from McGraw-Hill/Osborne.

We want to hear from you!

Sneak Peek

Visit us today at **www.betabooks.com** and see what's coming from McGraw-Hill/Osborne tomorrow!

Based on the successful software paradigm, Bet@Books™ allows computing professionals to view partial and sometimes complete text versions of selected titles online. Bet@Books™ viewing is free, invites comments and feedback, and allows you to "test drive" books in progress on the subjects that interest you the most.

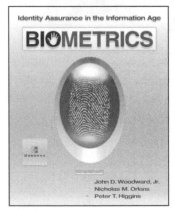

Check Out All of Osborne's Hacking Books

INTRUSION DETECTION & PREVENTION